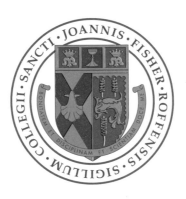

POWERFUL AND BRUTAL WEAPONS

POWERFUL AND BRUTAL WEAPONS

Nixon, Kissinger, and the Easter Offensive

STEPHEN P. RANDOLPH

Harvard University Press

Cambridge, Massachusetts

London, England

2007

Library of Congress Cataloging-in-Publication Data

Randolph, Stephen P., 1952–
Powerful and brutal weapons: Nixon, Kissinger, and the
Easter offensive / Stephen P. Randolph
p.   cm.
Includes bibliographical references (p.   )
ISBN-13: 978-0-674-02491-5 (alk. paper)
ISBN-10: 0-674-02491-5 (alk. paper)
1. Nixon, Richard M. (Richard Milhouse), 1913–1994.
2. Kissinger, Henry, 1923–   3. Easter Offensive, 1972.
4. Vietnam War, 1961–1975—Aerial operations, American.

DS557.8.E23 R23 2007
959.704/348 22   2006049899

CONTENTS

MAPS

ABBREVIATIONS USED IN THE TEXT

AAA	Antiaircraft artillery
ARVN	Army of the Republic of Vietnam
CINCPAC	Commander in Chief, Pacific
CJCS	Chairman, Joint Chiefs of Staff
CNO	Chief of Naval Operations
COSVN	Central Office for South Vietnam
CTF	Carrier Task Force
DMZ	Demilitarized Zone
DRV	Democratic Republic of Vietnam (North Vietnam)
FAC	Forward air controller
GVN	Government of Vietnam (South Vietnam)
JCS	Joint Chiefs of Staff
LGB	Laser-guided bomb
MACV	Military Assistance Command Vietnam
MR	Military Region
NSC	National Security Council
NVA	North Vietnamese Army
PACAF	Pacific Air Forces
PACOM	Pacific Command

POL	Petroleum, oil, lubricants
RVN	Republic of Vietnam (South Vietnam)
RVNAF	Republic of Vietnam Armed Forces
SAM	Surface-to-air missile
SAR	Search and rescue
TACAIR	Tactical aircraft: fighters or fighter-bombers
USA	United States Army
USAF	United States Air Force
USMC	United States Marine Corps
USN	United States Navy
VC	Viet Cong
VNAF	Vietnam Air Force (South Vietnam)
WSAG	Washington Special Actions Group

We are determined and will throw everything we have into this effort to accomplish our strategic intentions, no matter what it takes. However, the enemy also knows that this offensive will be decisive in determining the outcome of the war on the battlefields of all three nations of Indochina. For that reason, he will take ferocious countermeasures. We need to be on guard against the possibility that the enemy might employ even more powerful and brutal weapons in response to our attacks, because Nixon is a very daring individual who might take that risk, no matter what the consequences. We should not underestimate him.

—*Politburo Guidance Cable 119, March 27, 1972*

We're playing a much bigger game—we're playing a Russia game, a China game, and an election game, and we're not gonna have [South Vietnam] collapse.

—*President Richard Nixon, April 3, 1972*

INTRODUCTION

Richard Nixon was a war president from the moment he swore the oath of office on January 20, 1969. Upon his inauguration, he inherited a conflict engaging over half a million American servicemen, a conflict that had split the nation and that showed no signs of ending. From that day on, the war in Indochina defined his presidency. It shaped his foreign policy goals. It poisoned his relations with Congress and the domestic political environment. It created deep and rancorous divides in his circle of advisors. Daily it absorbed his attention, as he sought a strategy that would extricate the nation from Indochina while sustaining its credibility and cohesion. Ultimately, the war destroyed his presidency.

Yet for all this close, even obsessive attention, there was no other period of the war during which Nixon so closely directed events as during North Vietnam's 1972 spring-summer offensive. Circumstances demanded this. The North Vietnamese attacked at the outset of the 1972 presidential campaign, and at a time of historic shifts in the alignment of the Cold War: during the delicate and momentous opening of relations with Communist China, and on the eve of the Moscow Summit that would usher in the era of détente, forever recasting the forms of the Cold War. The situation demanded subtle and sure coordination of political, diplomatic, and military measures—not just in defining strategies in the Oval Office, but in ensuring that a military leadership that had forfeited the trust of the commander in chief would implement these strategies.

However sure the president's strategic touch, in the end his success would rest on the ability of military forces in Indochina to carry out the missions defined in the White House. There the prospects were mixed. The American withdrawal from ground combat was nearly complete, but potent air and naval forces still stood ready to support the South Vietnamese and to punish North Vietnam at the president's direction. U.S. forces in Indochina had the advantage of a galaxy of weapons developed through nearly a decade of war—precision weaponry, satellite communications and imagery, computer-based mission planning, magnetic and acoustic sensors, digital fire-control systems, night and infrared imagery, to name but a few. But these systems had been developed at different times and by different communities, and many had lain largely dormant through the years of relative quiet preceding this offensive. The Americans had a wealth of technology—but they lacked the command systems, doctrine, and training programs to exploit the capabilities of the new systems. Nixon's political future would depend on the ability of the U.S. military to adjust to the new circumstances of high-intensity combat over North Vietnam, and to reverse the long, slow atrophy of capabilities that had accompanied the withdrawal of forces from the South.

That success would also have to come at the expense of a resourceful enemy: the North Vietnamese. There would always be a vast gulf in technology between the United States and its adversaries, one that seemed to foreclose any chance of victory for the Communist forces. But they had advantages of their own: endless persistence, fed by a total national commitment to the war; careful organization of combat and support forces; and an ability to study their enemy and patiently take advantage of any weakness in technology or tactics. It was a classic asymmetrical struggle, and its outcome would decide the fate of South Vietnam and Nixon's presidency.

Three conceptual threads run through this account. The first addresses presidential leadership in wartime, and the implementation of strategic guidance. The White House taping system that Nixon ordered installed early in 1971, supported by declassified NSC, Pentagon, and military archives, offers the opportunity to trace the president's thought processes at all points—from the growing awareness of North Vietnam's military buildup, through the breaking attack, the crisis in theater, and the dramatic restructuring of American military strategy in response, as Nixon ordered the sustained bombing campaign against North Vietnam known as Linebacker.

The dynamics of military effectiveness form the second thread. American forces had gradually assimilated a new generation of technology in the years preceding this campaign, incrementally and without any central plan governing its employment. The North Vietnamese Army (NVA) had undergone a similarly extensive transformation, but it had been centrally directed by the Politburo, aimed specifically at this offensive, and conducted in deep secrecy and against tight time constraints. This account traces the interaction of equipment, training, command capabilities, and doctrine in defining combat effectiveness on both sides.

The action-reaction cycle between the Americans and the North Vietnamese forms the third major theme. All strategy represents the interplay of reactive adversaries—defining objectives and adjusting operations to defeat an intelligent foe. Declassified sources on both sides now enable us to see how these enemies viewed each other, and how they responded to events to achieve their strategic and military goals.

Perhaps most important, this account places the blood and carnage of this battle into a broader context of American and North Vietnamese strategic objectives. In the absence of strategy, warfare is just an effusion of blood and treasure. Or as Nixon phrased it, in shaping American military strategy he was not just looking toward success on the battlefield; he was "playing a much bigger game—we're playing a Russia game, a China game, and an election game." The demands of combat would play a role in his strategic calculus, but only alongside a wide range of other considerations. This account will trace that balance of motives, and the results of Nixon's calculations as they played out on the battlefield, in the skies over North Vietnam, and at the negotiating table.

1

NIXON'S WAR

On May 14, 1971, the North Vietnamese Politburo issued guidance for the 1972 campaigning season, directing the high command to plan an offensive that would transcend, in scope and effect, the Tet Offensive that had convulsed Indochina three years before. The Politburo ordered an all-out attack, one that would hurl the entire North Vietnamese Army (NVA) against South Vietnam. It would be an immense gamble, justifiable only by the prize: this offensive, they expected, would finally bring the decisive moment in their decades-long war for independence and unification, ending the bloodshed and sacrifice that had persisted for thirty years.

The Politburo assigned the Central Military Party Committee and the General Staff the task of devising a specific military strategy to achieve these goals. A month later, in June, the plan was ready. The offensive would open with main force action in three theaters. One arm, the main axis of attack, would extend out of the Cambodian base camps north of Saigon, directly threatening the capital. Another would slice into the central highlands from base camps to the west; this attack would complement action in the coastal lowlands, a long-standing communist stronghold. A third theater would open south of the Demilitarized Zone (DMZ) that divided the two Vietnams along the 17th parallel. These attacks would strike simultaneously in the spring, spreading and confusing the South Vietnamese forces.

The plan committed fourteen of the NVA's fifteen army divisions to the attack. Beyond this mass, the offensive would feature combined-arms operations including armored forces and heavy artillery, complementing the infantry that had long been the mainstay of NVA forces. With the Republic of Vietnam Armed Forces (RVNAF) called to counter these main-force attacks, the Politburo expected the Viet Cong and other NVA units to seize the countryside that the communists had lost in the years since the Tet Offensive. As the wave of violence swept the country, urban uprisings would seal the doom of the Thieu regime.

This offensive would disrupt the prevailing rhythm of the war, bringing a violent and dramatic end to three years of relative quiet. That relative calm extended back to the Tet Offensive and its aftermath, and reflected the trauma and casualties that had fundamentally altered the shape and course of the war. On the communist side, the fighting during Tet and the lesser offensives that followed had devastated the Viet Cong, the South Vietnamese communists who had conducted the bulk of the fighting to that point. After Tet, North Vietnamese soldiers had played an increasingly large role in the fighting, both as integral units and as "fillers" in nominally Viet Cong units.[1] By the early 1970s a large majority of the communist combatants were NVA soldiers. With their forces weakened by the fighting at Tet and in the subsequent counteroffensives, the North Vietnamese adopted a "protracted war" strategy, seeking to maintain their positions on the ground while they rebuilt their strength.

The effects of the Tet Offensive on the U.S. war effort were even more vivid. It shattered Lyndon B. Johnson's hold on political power, ultimately leading to the presidency of Richard M. Nixon. Even before Nixon's arrival, however, the fighting in early 1968 forced a recalculation of American strategy in the war, and an end to the escalation of U.S. troop strength in Southeast Asia. It also triggered, over time, the hesitant and initially sterile negotiations among the warring parties in Paris. These sessions evolved from frustrating stalemate, to farce, and finally to propaganda theater. At no point did they offer any real prospects of breakthrough.

The North Vietnamese had exacted a high price for these generally futile negotiations. In his pursuit of a diplomatic settlement, Johnson had first restricted the ongoing Rolling Thunder air campaign to attacks over the DRV's panhandle, then ended it entirely in the days before the 1968 presidential election. Rolling Thunder had opened in 1965, and it remains a model for mismanaged military operations: hesitantly begun, micromanaged from Washington, subject to frequent halts in search of negotiations, hamstrung by command and control issues and by the American forces' unreadiness to fight a conventional war. It never succeeded in its military purpose of restricting the flow of forces and matériel to battlefields in South Vietnam. Nonetheless, by 1968 it had gained momentum and was punishing North Vietnam. Its suspension, in return for unwritten understandings that the DRV would respect the DMZ, negotiate in good faith, and cease bombardment of South Vietnamese cities, represented a major victory for North Vietnamese diplomacy.

As president-elect, Nixon inherited a war in which more than half a million Americans struggled in Asian jungles, with no pathway toward victory and dwindling domestic support. Facing the responsibilities of office, he had no real formula for winning or ending the war, only a general plan to leverage the Soviet Union into pressuring its North Vietnamese clients into serious peace negotiations. Based as it was on a series of miscalculations—on America's influence over the USSR, and on the Soviets' ability to move the North Vietnamese—the plan inevitably failed, leaving Nixon and his advisors seeking a more effective strategy.

The search for a coherent strategy was hamstrung by incessant, rancorous bureaucratic warfare among Nixon's foreign policy advisors. Their intrigues reflected in part the normal interplay of personalities and the challenges of waging war in a democracy. Most of all, however, they reflected the "internal contradictions," to use the North Vietnamese phrase, in the American strategic position. It was impossible, given the strategic setting and U.S. politics, to meet the nation's declared goals in Indochina. The war seemed beyond winning at any cost that the public was willing to pay. It was gradually eroding the U.S. economy and enabling the Soviet Union to build toward equality in strategic forces in the Cold War. Unable to win the war, Nixon was also unable to quit. He believed that any rapid withdrawal would trigger further communist adventures around the world, planting the seed for future conflicts.

Nixon reached into his rival Nelson Rockefeller's camp for his national security advisor, selecting Henry A. Kissinger for that key position. Kissinger came with a solid reputation as a creative foreign policy theorist and historian. He also possessed a deep-seated personal insecurity, ferocious bureaucratic skills, and boundless energy. These attributes played an important role in shaping the administration, especially since the president-elect would come to rely heavily on his inner circle of advisors. After an initial shakedown period, Nixon and Kissinger settled into a remarkably close, though often fractious, partnership. Kissinger was an extraordinarily high-maintenance advisor, and at times the cost of keeping him on the team led Nixon to contemplate his replacement. In every case, however, the mutual reliance that the president and his national security advisor had formed led Nixon to work through the challenges to maintain the relationship.[2] Beyond his talent and his access to the president, Kissinger's influence rested on the restructuring of the interagency policy apparatus that he and Nixon engineered immediately on coming into office. This restructuring centralized power in the White House and the National Security Council (NSC), largely at the expense of the state department. Crisis response and operational oversight rested in the Washington Special Actions Group (WSAG), which over time also assumed a major role in political-military planning.[3]

The president-elect was forced to accept a rebound choice as his secretary of defense. Disappointed by Senator Henry "Scoop" Jackson's refusal, Nixon turned to Melvin R. Laird, who had been helping him staff his administration. Laird was a veteran of fourteen years in Congress with strong and healthy ties across the legislative branch. More closely attuned than either Nixon or Kissinger to the domestic political climate, Laird incessantly pressured the administration toward a rapid withdrawal from the war. He went to the Pentagon hoping to have a role in the president's domestic policy as well, but was quickly consumed by the details of managing the war and the enormous bureaucracy of the department of defense. A skilled and persistent bureaucratic combatant, Laird proved a worthy rival for Kissinger in the struggle over the course of U.S. policy in Vietnam.

Leadership of the state department also went to a second choice, William A. Rogers. An old friend and law partner of Nixon's, Rogers had little background in foreign affairs and displayed little flair for them once in office. His efforts to sustain the traditional role of the state department in foreign relations triggered fierce battles with Kissinger, who viewed his own policies and position as threatened by these forays. Normally Nixon directed his chief of staff, H. R. "Bob" Haldeman, to referee these skirmishes. Invariably these tussles were resolved to Kissinger's short-term advantage, but at great cost in tension to the president and in the working environment of the administration. Aside from offering formal advice in his role on the NSC, Rogers would have little effect on the unfolding drama in Southeast Asia.

Nixon's willingness to settle for second-choice candidates for leadership of his critical executive departments reflected his concept of governance. He had scant interest and no agenda in domestic policy. He was endlessly fascinated with the world of international security, however, and focused on the exertion of America's power to meet its national interests. He expected to play the lead role in defining policy in that area, and he valued execution of his directives much more than advice from the men statutorily charged with responsibilities on the NSC.

Kissinger selected Colonel Alexander M. Haig as his military assistant, bringing him onto the NSC staff from a tour at the Military Academy at West Point. Haig had served a command tour in Vietnam and had high-level staff experience in the Pentagon. In time, Haig earned Nixon's trust as an advisor and emissary; the president considered him complementary to Kissinger, a man of action who would complement Kissinger's academic perspective. Beyond his policy contributions, Haig proved to be an effective organizer and a stabilizing influence in the NSC system.

During the late 1960s and early 1970s, the American military leaders who had led U.S. forces through the Johnson years retired or moved to other assignments. William Westmoreland left Vietnam in July 1968, replaced by his deputy General Creighton Abrams as commander of Military Assistance Command Vietnam (MACV). Abrams, a 1936 West Point graduate, had built a brilliant reputation as an armor commander under George Patton during World War II. In the intervening years he had served at all levels up to an Army corps, then had spent four years as the Army's vice chief of staff from 1963 to 1967. He moved to Southeast Asia as Westmoreland's deputy for an uncomfortable fifteen months before assuming command.

As commander of U.S. forces in Vietnam (COMUSMACV), Abrams reported to the commander of the Pacific Command (PACOM), Admiral John S. McCain, whose headquarters were in Hawaii. Abrams never felt much in need of McCain's guidance, and their relationship was distant at the best of times. The bombing halt had removed one possible irritant, however. Decisions made early in the war had designated PACOM as the command responsible for air operations over North Vietnam. MACV, however, retained responsibility for operations over South Vietnam, Laos, and Cambodia. In the quiet years after Tet, this arrangement remained satisfactory. Clearly, though, there remained the potential for a struggle over priority, with two commands calling on a single pool of air assets for different purposes.

From PACOM the reporting chain extended to the Joint Chiefs of Staff (JCS) in the Pentagon, where the chairman of the JCS (CJCS) served as the link between the military and civil authorities in the Pentagon, the NSC, and the White House.

In July 1970 General Earle "Bus" Wheeler retired, turning over his duties as CJCS to Admiral Tom Moorer. A naval aviator, Moorer had long experience in the Pacific, extending back to World War II. During the 1960s he had served as commander of the Seventh Fleet and then as commander in chief of the Pacific Fleet (CINCPAC) and of the Atlantic Fleet before returning to Washington as chief of naval operations in 1967. Forced to navigate the complicated currents among Laird, Nixon, Kissinger, and Abrams, Moorer rarely fulfilled his statutory role as primary military advisor to the president. However, he played an important role in translating the directions coming from the White House into executable military guidance as action passed from the policy sphere into the operational chain of command.

After an initial series of policy reviews, Nixon's new administration moved to withdraw U.S. troops from the war, seeking to compensate for the loss of American combat power by strengthening the South Vietnamese armed forces. In principle, the pace of withdrawal was tied to the progress of the upgrades to the South Vietnamese military and to the progress of negotiations in Paris. In practice, the rate reflected a combination of domestic political pressures and the internecine struggles between Kissinger and Laird. On the whole, the administration adopted a pace of withdrawal that would end the American combat role in late 1972, with the overall aim of maintaining a stable situation in South Vietnam for the U.S. elections that year while defusing the war as a campaign issue.[4]

There were two other components to Nixon's overall strategy. First, convinced that the four-party negotiations taking place in Paris would never yield a peace treaty, he authorized Kissinger to conduct secret talks with the North Vietnamese. Kissinger and his primary interlocutor, Politburo member Le Duc Tho, met intermittently in 1970 and 1971. By late 1970 the United States had dropped its demand for a mutual troop withdrawal, and had given up any prospect of leaving a residual force in South Vietnam after the withdrawal of U.S. combat forces. Those concessions left only one major issue to be decided: the preservation of the Thieu regime. Negotiations foundered on that fundamental difference.

Meanwhile, Nixon and Kissinger worked to isolate North Vietnam dip-

Indochina and U.S. Airbases

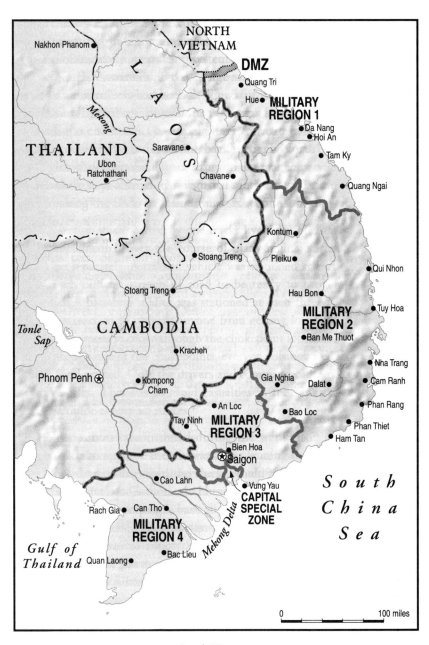

NAKHON PHANOM ●

NORTH
VIETNAM

L A O S

DMZ

● Quang Tri

Hue ● **MILITARY
REGION 1**

THAILAND

● Da Nang
● Hoi An

Saravane ●

● Tam Ky

Ubon
Ratchathani

Mekong

Chavane ●

● Quang Ngai

Kontum ●

● Stoang Treng

Pleiku ●

● Qui Nhon

Stoang Treng ●

Hau Bon ●

● Tuy Hoa

CAMBODIA

**MILITARY
REGION 2**

Tonle
Sap

● Ban Me Thuot

Kracheh ●

● Nha Trang

Phnom Penh ⊗

● Kompong
Cham

Gia Nghia ●

Dalat ●

● Cam Ranh

● An Loc

● Phan Rang

Tay Ninh ●

**MILITARY
REGION 3**

● Bao Loc

● Phan Thiet
● Ham Tan

Bien Hoa ●
⊛Saigon

● Cao Lahn

● Vung Yau

**CAPITAL
SPECIAL
ZONE**

S o u t h

C h i n a

Rach Gia ● Can Tho ●

**MILITARY
REGION 4**

S e a

*Gulf of
Thailand* Quan Laong ●

● Bac Lieu

Mekong Delta

0   100 miles

South Vietnam

lomatically from its allies in Moscow and Beijing. The American maneuvers were assisted by the ever-deepening enmity between the communist superpowers, which led them to reassess their national interests and their relations with the leader of the Western bloc. The U.S. movements toward détente with the Soviet Union and a diplomatic relationship with the People's Republic of China (PRC) fundamentally altered the geostrategic landscape, establishing a complex series of relationships among the Soviets, the Chinese, the North Vietnamese, and the Americans, with the South Vietnamese sometimes figuring in the equation as well. The North Vietnamese watched this shift with suspicion and unease. As time went on, they were forced to the bitter conclusion that "Vietnam had become a bargaining card for the balance of forces between the great powers in Southeast Asia."[5]

Ultimately the American strategy rested on the ability of South Vietnam to build its own security forces, governance, and economy. Of these, the most pressing and visible requirement was to strengthen the South Vietnamese military. During the early 1970s the South Vietnamese rapidly upgraded their forces, both quantitatively and qualitatively. By 1971 this nation of 17 million citizens had 1.1 million men under arms. The relatively rapid upgrade in military capabilities, especially within the local forces, lay at the heart of the Republic of Vietnam's pacification program, the campaign to extend and maintain the government's control over the countryside.

The South Vietnamese military establishment consisted of a hierarchy of forces allocated across four army corps, each responsible for securing a military region (MR). I Corps covered the northernmost five provinces, immediately south of the DMZ. South of MR I lay the central highlands and the central coastline, designated MR II and defended by II Corps. III Corps operated north and east of Saigon, and IV Corps secured the Mekong Delta. Army of the Republic of Vietnam (ARVN) divisions provided the foundation of the national military establishment, complemented by militia organized as the Regional Forces and the Popular Forces (RF/PF). At the apex of the hierarchy rested the strategic reserve units, the Airborne and the Marines, operating as fire brigades to meet crises across the length of the country. These elite groups would be special targets of the North Vietnamese offensive.

The South Vietnamese military's improvement was rapid and impressive, as it grew, assimilated new equipment, and gained new capabilities

and confidence. All knew, however, that until the ARVN faced major combat with its North Vietnamese enemies, its true capabilities would remain
untested.

General Abrams, for his part, worked ceaselessly to reorient MACV's
theater strategy to a "one war" approach, attempting to balance and integrate pacification, withdrawal, combat operations, and improvements to
the South Vietnamese forces. His larger task was to manage this complicated series of processes while holding the U.S. Army together during its
withdrawal.[6] As combat troops left the theater in the early 1970s, and as it
became clear that this was a war to be survived and not won, the discipline
of American forces gradually declined.

Clearly the withdrawal entailed significant military risk, as U.S. combat
strength waned in Indochina. The sequence of withdrawal, with combat
troops the first to depart, multiplied the long-term risk while minimizing
casualties in the short term. The Americans conducted a fierce bombing
campaign against the infiltration routes feeding NVA forces from North
Vietnam into base areas in Laos and Cambodia, but this rear-guard action
could not be relied upon to prevent a communist offensive. Nixon therefore ordered a series of escalations in the war to throw the NVA off balance in its base areas—with these strikes filling a diplomatic purpose as
well, demonstrating Nixon's willingness to use force in ways that Johnson
had always considered too risky. The first of these was the secret bombing
of Cambodia, which began in 1969. The following year Nixon sent a
mixed force of Americans and South Vietnamese into Cambodia, triggering a wave of antiwar protests that eventually led to a congressional prohibition of the use of U.S. ground forces outside South Vietnam.

In early December 1970 the Nixon administration decided to direct a
South Vietnamese offensive against the NVA logistics network in Laos.
The offensive, code-named Lam Son 719, would commit the three best
South Vietnamese divisions—the Airborne, the Marines, and the 1st
ARVN—to a rapid, slashing attack along Route 9 west of Khe Sanh. The
attack would culminate at the logistics node at Tchepone, where the South
Vietnamese units would remain for ninety days, blocking the infiltration
routes and destroying supplies stored in the area. The plan then called for
the invading force to withdraw to the southeast, destroying another North
Vietnamese base area on the way back to South Vietnam.

It was a bold plan, well calculated to gain Nixon's approval, especially
since an attack of this kind had been debated and rejected under his prede-

cessor's leadership. Its aggressiveness, he thought, would contrast well with the timidity of the Johnson administration. The plan's greatest shortcoming, as Kissinger later recalled, was that it "in no way accorded with Vietnamese realities."[7] The South Vietnamese force would have to attack along a single dirt track, in terrain favoring the defenders, with weather that would inevitably limit air support. The RVNAF units would operate without the American advisors who had solidified their operations in the preceding years. The RVNAF forces had very little experience operating as full divisions, and none in operating together. Nor did they have an opportunity to train for this major offensive operation. The Americans and South Vietnamese expected the NVA to withdraw westward in the face of the offensive, as they had done in Cambodia the year before. This projection, however, misread the importance of the Ho Chi Minh Trail to the communist war effort. While the NVA had not fought to defend bases in Cambodia, it had little choice but to defend its bases around Tchepone.

The operation opened on January 30 with a preparatory American operation, Dewey Canyon II, to open Route 9 as far as the Laotian border. On February 8 the South Vietnamese launched their attack. All went roughly as planned for a few days. Then on February 11 the attack stalled, for no reason discernible to the American command structure. Operating on his own counsel, President Nguyen Van Thieu had ordered the South Vietnamese force to halt when its casualty count reached 3,000. The speed and momentum of the attack, its only chance of success, disappeared as the North Vietnamese deployed reinforcements. Thieu's decision caught Abrams unawares. Confusion and frustration extended from MACV up the chain of command to the White House.

The NVA high command always placed a premium on weakening South Vietnam's elite forces. Now Thieu had delivered them into the NVA's hands. The North Vietnamese sent elements of four divisions into the fight, supported by armor and heavy artillery. On February 28 Thieu again changed the operational concept, directing a rapid heliborne raid on Tchepone followed by a brief stay and a rapid withdrawal back along Route 9. On March 7 ARVN forces entered Tchepone, and a day later they began the most difficult and risky part of the operation: withdrawal in the face of a prepared enemy. Abrams tried to persuade the South Vietnamese to reinforce the operation in order to bring it closer to its original intent. Thieu agreed to send the 2nd ARVN division into the battle, but only if the Americans would insert a mechanized brigade and two brigades of the

101st Airborne into Laos.[8] Everyone involved in the conversation knew this was impossible, and the ARVN withdrawal continued.

The withdrawal turned into a rout, with televised views of soldiers clinging to helicopter skids, fleeing the combat zone. However unfairly, this snapshot froze the historical image of the operation. More significantly, it froze the American public's perception of their South Vietnamese allies. Vietnamization had faced its first major test, and to all appearances it had proven an abject failure.

The operation was significant both for what it revealed about the South Vietnamese military and for its direct effects, which echoed through the remaining years of the war. Despite the evident improvement in the RVNAF over past years, Lam Son 719 showed that it still had severe, systemic weaknesses at the strategic, operational, and tactical levels. Moreover, these shortcomings had largely been features of South Vietnamese operations from the first days of the war, and their persistence called into question the prospects for improvement. Lam Son 719 had also demonstrated serious problems in American support for the South Vietnamese and in the internal coordination of the U.S. forces remaining in theater.

The trauma of the retreat triggered an after-action review in the White House, to complement those routinely conducted by units in Southeast Asia. Conducted half a world apart, both reviews focused on the same grievous problems. The first was that the various South Vietnamese units committed to the operation, though nominally under the command of I Corps Commander Lieutenant General Hoang Xuan Lam, refused to follow his orders until they had cleared them with their own chains of command—or sometimes not even then. The assessment by the XXIV Corps, the U.S. headquarters directly supporting the operation, noted that the South Vietnamese Marine and Airborne units, though nominally subordinate to Lam, "seemed sure enough of their position in the Vietnamese political/military hierarchy to act quite independently. In consequence, many orders given by the I Corps Commander were ignored or were violated with impunity."[9] The NSC analysis added, "Commanders of the major units disagreed openly with General Lam with the consequence that the command relationship was dangerously strained."[10] As a result, Lam never was able to gain a firm grip on the operation or create any real unity among the American and various South Vietnamese forces.

More seriously still, security measures both before and during the operation were a complete failure. Through a combination of strategic projection and intelligence, the North Vietnamese learned of the attack months in advance. The NVA general staff began drawing up plans for a battle in southern Laos, deploying forces, and preparing the battlefield long before the opening of the campaign. In October 1970, over four months before the offensive, they established the 70th Corps-Sized Group to exercise command over the forces that would be committed to defensive operations in southern Laos. Through the dry season, NVA engineers constructed a road network to support the reinforcement and mobility of forces engaged in the battle along Route 9.[11] By early January communist agents infiltrating the RVNAF's Joint General Staff had smuggled the plan out of Saigon and into the hands of the Viet Cong; a month later, radio intercepts provided the NVA commanders with a full picture of the South Vietnamese force that would be entering Laos.[12] The NVA projected likely helicopter flight paths and landing zones for the operation, preparing their defenses to exact a heavy toll on the invading RVNAF forces. The wonder is not that the operation failed, but that so many South Vietnamese troops returned home alive once they had crossed into Laos.

Security lapses continued throughout the operation and extended to the highest levels of command. RVNAF units relied on the radio net for command and coordination, and as the American assessment commented, "communications security was virtually ignored by the Vietnamese . . . This is a major problem area that must be addressed in planning any future operations." The South Vietnamese adopted the practice of planning for operations only one day in advance, hoping to minimize security breaches. The delay in planning disrupted coordination across units, especially air-ground coordination, while doing little to conceal intentions from the enemy.[13]

The tactics employed by the South Vietnamese generally reflected the experience of a decade-long war against a low-technology threat. They were ill-suited to the new circumstances, facing a prepared enemy with armor and artillery of its own. The artillery firebases long used to protect ARVN forces now proved to be terribly vulnerable, with North Vietnamese artillery able to target these fixed locations. Losses of helicopters, primarily American, were prohibitive, as the North Vietnamese placed heavy antiaircraft artillery along approach routes and landing zones. Finally, air-ground coordination in this intense battle was difficult. To some extent this was inevitable, with American forward air controllers (FACs) attempting to work with South Vietnamese forces in a high-intensity conventional battle. Those technical issues, however, proved secondary to the broader failures within the American command structure. Army General Phillip Davidson later summarized a situation in which "the Americans embarked on their support mission with inadequate planning, deficient cooperation with ARVN, and major service differences over the concept and execution of the operation."[14] These flaws would cripple American efforts to support the South Vietnamese.

Lam Son 719 changed the trajectory of the war in several critical respects, with effects that would linger until the final North Vietnamese victory in 1975. The operation displayed, and widened, the gap between the American and South Vietnamese leadership. It had been conceived by Americans, and although Thieu seems to have eagerly accepted the plan, the fact that only ARVN soldiers were placed at risk drove a wedge between the partners. Moreover, the U.S. leadership had completely failed to project Thieu's reaction to South Vietnam's casualties. As a politician, Thieu, facing an election in the autumn, could ill afford a serious defeat; as a military leader, he could not afford to see his strategic reserve destroyed in the jungles of Laos. The U.S. leaders, so acutely sensitive to their own domestic opinion, failed to consider Thieu's parallel concerns.

The confusion and frustration evident in the planning stage continued through the precipitous South Vietnamese withdrawal. On March 26 Kissinger dispatched a cable to the American ambassador in Saigon, Ellsworth Bunker, spelling out the view from Washington: "It would be hard to exaggerate the mystification and confusion caused here by the ARVN's latest scheme of maneuver which envisages a rapid pull-out from Laos."[15] Kissinger continued, "it is intolerable to have the President vulnerable to constant changes of plans which are unilaterally implemented," and closed with a stern warning: "I hope Thieu understands that the President's confidence is an asset he should not lightly dissipate and that this may be his last crack at massive U.S. support." Given the fact that Thieu and General Lam routinely communicated over open lines, it is very possible that Hanoi knew more about ARVN planning than Washington did.[16] Kissinger later wrote of Lam Son 719: "The operation, conceived in doubt and assailed by skepticism, proceeded in confusion."[17]

On the basis of this experience, and their ability to throw the South Vietnamese force out of Laos in the teeth of American air support, the leadership in Hanoi concluded that the ARVN could not stand up to the NVA, even under the best of circumstances. This conclusion opened a range of strategic possibilities for the future and was a major element in the decision to conduct a major offensive the following year. It stood in stark contrast to the South Vietnamese view, summarized in one soldier's bitter comment that the Americans were using South Vietnamese troops "as training aids for the senior staff."[18]

Lam Son 719's impact in Washington was almost entirely negative. The operation deepened the animosities among Nixon's advisors and shattered Nixon's confidence in his theater commander. As the South Vietnamese entered Laos, Nixon considered Abrams a fine combat officer, a real no-nonsense leader. Two weeks into the incursion, Nixon and Kissinger were wrangling with Laird over their desire to send Haig to review the operation. On March 23, as the operation neared its close, the president and Kissinger rehearsed a litany of problems in the command and with Abrams: that he was stale, that he hadn't gotten enough "push" into the operation, that he had stayed too long with his initial plan, that American support for the South Vietnamese had set them up for failure, that he was drinking now in the middle of the day, that MACV had become too inbred, that "our people let us down."[19]

At one point Nixon's frustration led him to direct Haig to fly out to Saigon and take command of U.S. forces there.[20] He reversed the decision as his anger faded, but he never regained his confidence in Abrams. Nixon did not expect any more major combat for American forces, and so was unwilling to pay the political price of relieving a respected commander. Nonetheless, he remained uncomfortable with Abrams, especially as he never could be quite sure what direction the general was receiving from Laird—and how this direction might upset the president's own plans. The painful experience of Lam Son 719 was to leave permanent scars on the relationship between the commander in chief and his theater commander.

But of all these effects, none was so powerful as the operation's impact on the American people and their elected representatives. Lam Son 719, and the images of South Vietnamese fleeing the fighting by hanging onto helicopter skids, finally broke the American public's long-standing patience with the war. For seven years of combat, a majority of Americans had supported the war effort—a remarkable testimony to the nation's perseverance, trust in its leadership, and willingness to sacrifice. But the Laotian incursion convinced the majority of Americans that the war was unwinnable, and that sacrifices on behalf of the South Vietnamese were no longer warranted. A Harris poll taken in early May 1971 opened its summary: "The tide of American public opinion has now turned decisively against the war in Indo-China. This latest shift of public opinion against the war was triggered by the feeling, 45 to 24 percent, that the recent South Vietnamese move into Laos was a 'failure.'"[21] Johnson's war had become Nixon's war, and the American people were dissatisfied with his management of the conflict. Domestic political pressure was building, as the president sought to disengage from the war without destroying America's strategic position in the Cold War. Congress reflected the shift in public opinion, and for the first time, a legislated withdrawal from the war became a serious prospect.

Overall the operation marked a breakdown in the civil-military planning process, within the United States and across the alliance with the South Vietnamese. The operation was conceived in the basement of the White House and developed in deep secrecy by a small cell in the Pentagon. From there it was exported to MACV for sale to the South Vietnamese. The operational development of the plan left rifts between the Americans and the South Vietnamese, and between the Air Force and Army planners within MACV. The South Vietnamese forces executed the invasion and faced the bulk of the risk, but they were critically reliant on U.S. support. Nobody knew who was finally in charge or who was accountable for results on the battlefield. It was a very poor way to fight a war.

Remarkably, a year that began so badly nonetheless got worse and worse. The war largely receded from the view of the U.S. public, as the drawdown of troops accelerated and American casualties declined. The stories that did reach the public all seemed to reinforce the general willingness to end America's role in the war. Shortly after the end of Lam Son 719, on March 29, an Army court-martial found Lieutenant William L. Calley guilty of twenty-two counts of premeditated murder in the My Lai massacre. A few months later the *New York Times* published the *Pentagon Papers*, opening to public view the hesitant and discordant process that had led the country into the war. In the autumn Thieu engineered an unopposed re-election to South Vietnam's presidency, thus seeming to validate the antiwar movement's contention that his was not a regime worth shedding American blood to preserve. Thieu's re-election ended any hope the North Vietnamese might have had that Nixon might engineer Thieu's removal from power. With Thieu ready for another term in office, the die was cast: the offensive would go forward once North Vietnamese forces were ready.

That winter, Nixon's stance in the Indian-Pakistani war exposed his administration to bitter, sustained criticism in the press and on Capitol Hill. The White House's policy of favoring Pakistan over India placed the administration in direct opposition to "the bureaucracy," particularly the state department. The White House found its innermost workings exposed in the press when the *Washington Post* published a series of columns by Jack Anderson revealing the extent of the American tilt toward Pakistan. An internal investigation quickly revealed that Charles Radford, a Navy yeoman assigned to the Joint Staff liaison office within the NSC, had been stealing documents and providing them through his supervisors to the JCS.[22] The investigators believed he had given the documents to Anderson as well, though this was never confirmed.

Nixon decided to dispose of the matter quietly, without pursuing it publicly or confronting the JCS. In doing so, he avoided what might well have become a political firestorm and strengthened his hold over the Pentagon; Nixon's aide John Ehrlichman described the JCS chairman, Admiral Moorer, as "preshrunk" after this sequence of events, more willing to serve the White House's ends in the internal struggle with Laird.[23] Although the affair passed quietly, the incident heightened the mistrust and animosities among the executive departments, the military, and the White House by late 1971.

Through that dismal year, however, the fragile relationship between the United States and Communist China continued to prosper. In early April, directly after the South Vietnamese withdrawal from Laos, the Chinese invited an American Ping-Pong team to play exhibition matches in China. On April 14 Nixon announced the end of the twenty-year-old trade embargo between the two countries. On April 27 Ambassador Hilaly of Pakistan delivered an invitation from the Chinese for Kissinger, and perhaps later Nixon, to travel to China for direct discussions.

Nixon and Kissinger conducted their contacts with the PRC in the greatest secrecy, to avoid conflict with the China lobby. Consequently, Nixon's announcement on July 15 that Kissinger had just returned from China, and that the president himself would visit Beijing the following year, shocked people around the world. Kissinger made a second visit to China in mid-October, just after the announcement that Nixon would travel to Moscow for a summit the following May.

Triangular diplomacy among the United States, the USSR, and the PRC had taken hold. Approaching an election year, Nixon could look forward to summits with both communist superpowers, with the Moscow meeting expected to yield the first significant arms-control treaty of the Cold War. These meetings would reshape the geostrategic landscape. Given their combination of spectacle, drama, and substantive achievement, they would also nearly ensure Nixon's re-election. With these fundamental changes in the international order, the war in Southeast Asia assumed a whole new complexion.

2

THE POLITBURO'S STRATEGIC CALCULUS

The North Vietnamese Politburo's process and objectives in ordering an all-out offensive in 1972 puzzled Western observers at the time, and remained a mystery even after all the events had played out. The scale and drama of the attack seemed beyond explanation, as did the decision to unleash the offensive only months before the United States planned to end its combat role in South Vietnam.

In the absence of definitive accounts, speculation reigned. At the end of 1972 the distinguished Vietnam scholar Douglas Pike counted no fewer than fifteen different published explanations of the decision, "all from respected observers, each in itself reasonably persuasive." Pike noted: "The major sources of strategic intention—captured documents and prisoner interrogations—soon reached flood proportions but did not yield the clarification that might be expected. The reports were consistently contradictory and as the volume of data increased so did the number of proffered theories on [North Vietnam's] grand strategy."[1] Articles in the North Vietnamese press offered hints of a contentious debate over the strategy to be pursued, but nothing specific enough for outsiders to trace the lines of contention or the alignment of the North Vietnamese leadership. Only recently, with the publication of the Politburo's guidance cables to its southern headquarters, has a full picture emerged of North Vietnam's strategic calculus, the relationships among the components of its strategy, and its national and military objectives.

Pike's explanation turned on his analysis of the Politburo's composition and the processes by which it reached decisions. In 1971 the Political Bureau of the Central Committee, or Politburo, consisted of ten members, each of whom represented a major institution—the Party, the armed forces officer corps, the government bureaucracy, and so on. Pike characterized the Politburo as "the field of last resort" where the members "struggle and ultimately determine the most important of state policies. Each Politburo member has a constituency which he runs, but which also runs him." All had worked toward independence and unification for decades; none had any deep experience overseas. They were parochial, xenophobic, and unswervingly committed to their mission of unifying Vietnam. As Pike put it, they had never "deviated from this objective as far as we know, nor have they ever lost confidence in their abilities ultimately to achieve it. Unification for them long ago passed from mere state policy to Holy Cause."[2]

The members of the Politburo were expected to manipulate their constituencies, but they were not free agents, and their positions in policy debates reflected the internal situations in the institutions they represented. Party First Secretary Le Duan was by a wide margin the first among equals, followed in influence by Truong Chinh, Pham Van Dong, and General Vo Nguyen Giap. However imbalanced their authority, the members held to the consensus decisionmaking code they had followed since Ho Chi Minh's death in 1969. Any decision taken had to be acceptable to all. According to a contemporary CIA study: "The rule of 'democratic centralism' is strongly applied. Once decisions are reached, everyone falls into line and further debate ceases, particularly outside the Politburo meeting room. Also, no policy is ever avowedly scrubbed or reversed."[3]

The North Vietnamese leaders shared a strategic perspective that was foreign to the West but extremely effective, especially when coupled with their endless persistence and their organizational talents. They viewed the war for unification as a single entity, indivisible but taking different forms depending on the strategic requirements of the moment. This entity they termed *dau tranh*, generally translated as "struggle," though with connotations of a vast effort toward a noble end.[4] This struggle played out in two forms, either as armed *dau tranh* or as political *dau tranh*, both within Vietnam and on the international scene. The two were philosophically equivalent. There was no fundamental difference between negotiations, urban struggle, and armored warfare; they were all means toward the single agreed end, with only the emphasis shifting as the circumstances demanded. Action in any sphere would, in principle, be taken with regard to its effects in the other realms of struggle.

This conceptual framework offered a sound basis for national planning, creating an integrated strategic perspective unifying the diplomatic, political, and military aspects of the battle for unification. As with all strategic affairs, however, the difficulties arose with the need to apply these concepts in the specific context of the existing situation—the balance on the battlefield, the political and economic situations in America and South Vietnam, and the shifts in the international alignments among the great powers. The complexities of the situation in the early 1970s fed lengthy, contentious debates within the Politburo, leading in the end to a bitterly contested majority decision to conduct the 1972 offensive.

The full details of these debates have never been publicly disclosed. However, a declassified summary of a conversation between Le Duc Tho and members of the French Communist Party provides a broad sketch of the process and the lines of argument. Tho maintained close ties with the French Party during his stops in Paris and had frequent conversations with its members in various forums. In May 1972 he was asked about the planning and the objectives of the offensive, by then in progress for over a month.[5] In his reply he noted that the 1971 South Vietnamese invasion of Laos had "showed us that, contrary to what was being published, Vietnamization could not pose any obstacle to our operations even if they took place far from our bases in the North." With this basic military issue settled, the Politburo conducted an extended debate, finally deciding to order the full-scale offensive only by a majority vote. Tho also noted the role of North Vietnam's socialist allies: "The Soviets, who had been informed (this was in 1971), told us that they would provide all necessary assistance but they did not want to advise us one way or the other. This was, above all, because they knew Peking was very much in favor of such a plan. So in a manner of speaking, we acted alone." He represented the final decision as a reflection of Chinese pressure, telling the French: "We are obliged to take into account the desires of our nearest neighbors, and if the bombings continue we will need their help in transporting material. We cannot always reject their suggestions or advice, even if we discuss it with our Soviet friends, who understand us better."

Tho admitted that the Politburo had miscalculated the American response: "One unknown for us at the time of launching the offensive turned out to be a surprise: the position taken by Nixon. We had considered it, but had eliminated the eventuality as impossible during the year of the Peking and Moscow visits and during a presidential election year in the USA." The Politburo members had expected, in other words, that both international and domestic politics would restrict Nixon's options for responding to the invasion. In Tho's view, this assumption had been "a mistake, but not a catastrophic one. The only disadvantage is that military action will be slowed down and in order to win a political victory we will have to step up our diplomatic activities."

Tho's account offers some useful insights into the Politburo's thinking, but it cannot be taken entirely at face value. In particular, his description of China's role conflicts with a great mass of evidence indicating that the PRC was more concerned about Soviet than U.S. influence in Indochina and preferred a gradual, negotiated end to America's presence in the region. The rapid warming in US-PRC relations that began in 1971 further operated to restrain any Chinese enthusiasm for an offensive. In November 1971, in fact, tensions between Hanoi and Beijing increased, as Mao advised Pham Van Dong to accept a negotiated settlement leaving Thieu in power.[6] In short, there is no evidence elsewhere to confirm Tho's depiction of strong, sustained Chinese pressure to launch an offensive. It is likely that Tho, well aware of the French Communists' close ties to Moscow and of the Soviets' annoyance with the offensive, offered this account in the expectation that his comments would reach Moscow quickly. His explanation served to shift the blame, for the miscalculations that had by then become evident, from the Politburo to Vietnam's great neighbor to the north.

Tho's description of Moscow's role, in contrast, tracks well with the evidence made available by the partial opening of Soviet archives. The relationship between Moscow and Hanoi was difficult from the outset of the war, with the Democratic Republic of Vietnam (DRV) demanding ever-increasing aid while nevertheless "trying to preserve to itself the exclusive right to a solution of the Vietnamese and Indochinese problems."[7] Determined to maintain their freedom of action, the North Vietnamese provided the Soviets with little information on their strategy or military planning—a matter of continuing frustration for the Soviet leadership.

The Politburo ordered planning and preparation for the offensive in May 1971, then reconfirmed its strategic objectives in a resolution issued shortly before the attack:

> 1972 is an extremely important year in our struggle against the enemy on all three fronts: military, political, and diplomatic. The urgent military task is to intensify military and political attacks, to strengthen the work on the enemy, to enhance the strategic offensive position on the whole SVN front, and at the same time, to step up the diplomatic offensive, closely coordinating with the people and armies of Laos and Cambodia, to push forward the offensive on all the Indochinese fronts, to defeat the US policy of Vietnamization, thereby creating a fundamental change in the battlefield situation of SVN [South Vietnam] and the Indochinese peninsula as a whole, so as to win a significant victory obliging the US to end the war in a losing position through a political solution that the US must and can accept, but advantageous to us.[8]

The offensive was intended to create a fundamental change on the battlefield, thereby transforming the negotiating environment. While the negotiators in Paris worked across a wide gulf of mistrust and misperception, Kissinger and Le Duc Tho shared one conviction: that neither side would gain anything at the conference table that it had not first won on the battlefield. The offensive was an essential component of the endgame negotiations, a huge investment in improving the DRV's negotiating position. The specification that a diplomatic settlement would have to be something that the United States "must and can accept, but advantageous to us" outlined a rather narrow window for action. The North Vietnamese did not contemplate a full-scale rout of the United States, which would not be "acceptable" to American leaders, but they sought a victory sufficient to induce a negotiated final withdrawal of U.S. forces.

The offensive would also strike at the two pillars of U.S. strategy in Indochina: it would confirm the failure of Vietnamization by exposing the ARVN's weakness; and it would reverse the tide of pacification by reestablishing the NVA's control over the countryside. The attack on pacification was especially important in the area commanded by Hanoi's southern headquarters, the Central Office for South Vietnam (COSVN). During the offensive, COSVN Directive Six asserted: "Our key mission is to attack pacification; seize the bulk of the country-side, and expand the liberated areas, particularly those in the Mekong Delta." The directive focused on the role of main-force units in drawing enemy troops to peripheral areas—along the DMZ, in the central highlands, and north of Saigon—"so that pacification in the Mekong Delta and the provinces around Saigon can be attacked more carefully." As the main forces executed these attacks, however, it was equally important for the Viet Cong local forces to "seize every opportunity to attack the enemies, expand our control, destroy enemy outposts, and raise our flag. Can this be done without in-place armed forces? Can we have main-force troops, northerners who know nothing about the area's people and religious groups, quarter around the area and claim to be the people's liberation armed forces?" It was essential that the strategy, and its execution, include all the elements of the North Vietnamese army and the South Vietnamese communist infrastructure, acting in concert.[9]

That would be possible only if communist leaders in the South shared the Politburo's vision for the offensive, and so, as the attack neared, Le Duc Tho sent a cable to COSVN outlining the course and objectives that Hanoi envisioned for the operation. He emphasized that the Politburo intended the 1972 offensive to be "even more massive than the Tet Offensive," greater in its "targets, goals, content, and even its scale."[10] This would be a coordinated military, diplomatic, and political effort to bring a decisive end to the war. It would differ from the 1968 Tet Offensive in integrating the use of main-force units, local forces, and guerrillas. Further, where earlier attacks had lasted only weeks or months, in this case the Politburo expected to "fight continuously for a long time, till the end of the spring-summer season and into the fall." A sustained campaign would deny the South Vietnamese the opportunity to rest, regroup, and regain strength after the opening blows were struck. The combination of massive blows and continuous attacks would bring about the enemy's disintegration.

Formidable as it was, the main-force attack to open the offensive would be only the first phase. The planned second wave of violence would build on the momentum established in that phase, expanding the rural liberated zone and extending the conflict into the cities. It was as much apocalyptic vision as military strategy: a vision of a crescendo of violence moving from front to front, integrating every form of conflict, isolating and confusing the Thieu regime, ultimately triggering its collapse. Tho was keenly aware that the precise course of the offensive could not be accurately predicted: "The situation will develop in an extremely complex manner and there will be changes that we cannot fully anticipate. For that reason, we must continue to closely monitor developments in the situation in order to hone our assessments of the situation further and to make timely decisions in response to developments."[11]

In the best case envisioned by the North Vietnamese leadership, a collapse of the South Vietnamese military would lead to Thieu's ouster and the creation of a coalition government. If the NVA forces failed to achieve the Politburo's objectives, its members would "review the pluses and minuses to decide whether to continue to fight or whether to enter into a peace settlement." In any case, they expected the offensive to lead to U.S. withdrawal from the war. The key point was that "the battlefield is where victory will be decided. On the foundation of the victories we win on the battlefield, we will reach a successful resolution at the negotiating table."[12]

It is noteworthy that already, before the offensive began, the Politburo members were looking toward the struggle that would continue after the negotiated settlement with the Americans. They expected a later phase to follow the offensive and the peace settlement, one that would end only with the unification of Vietnam. The nature and duration of this phase would depend on the outcome of the 1972 offensive, which would define the degree of political and territorial control wielded by each side. If the offensive accomplished the goals set by the Politburo, it would end with a coalition government dominated by communists and a quick and easy transition to full communist control. If the offensive fell short of its military objectives, ultimate victory would be more difficult and would take longer. Given the Americans' withdrawal from South Vietnam, however, the Politburo considered final victory to be certain.

The North Vietnamese strategists expected the offensive to have decisive political effects as well, triggered by the military and diplomatic action. The bloodshed and trauma of renewed fighting would widen the split between the United States and the Thieu regime and revitalize the American antiwar movement. In the best case, this would lead to Nixon's defeat in the fall elections; at worst, it would minimize the possibility of U.S. reengagement in the war and ease the eventual overthrow of the Thieu regime.[13]

The North Vietnamese carefully projected Nixon's likely military response, both to shape their operational planning and to determine what preparations were necessary. As noted by Tho, they assumed that the upcoming elections in America and summits in Moscow and Beijing would constrain the U.S. response. They expected Nixon to direct a sustained air campaign against the North Vietnamese panhandle, possibly with intermittent raids farther north.[14] But they thought that the possibility of recommitting American ground forces would pose an awkward dilemma for Nixon. To send in small numbers would be to risk seeing them overwhelmed in the attack, but any deployment large enough to be decisive would be unacceptable to the U.S. public and Congress. At most, they expected the Americans to commit a Marine division to the fighting "to lift the morale of the puppet army and stabilize the situation until the storm passes, at which time these forces would be withdrawn."[15]

The North Vietnamese leaders could make their best estimate of America's response to the offensive, but they also clearly understood the greatest unknown involved in this undertaking: Nixon's reaction. As the Politburo summarized:

> We are determined and will throw everything we have into this effort to accomplish our strategic intentions, whatever it takes. However, the enemy also knows that this offensive will be decisive in determining the outcome of the war on the battlefields of all three nations of Indochina. For that reason, he will take ferocious countermeasures. We need to be on guard against the possibility that the enemy might employ even more powerful and brutal weapons in response to our attacks, because Nixon is a very daring individual who might take that risk, no matter what the consequences. We should not underestimate him.[16]

The risks accepted by the Politburo were remarkable. The decision to attack the following spring allowed only a short time to build the new capabilities needed to succeed. Defense Minister Giap warned about the dangers to the logistics pipeline that would have to support the buildup and the offensive.[17] The use of mechanized forces would multiply logistical requirements, with demands for fuel, munitions, and equipment all increasing to support the armor and massed artillery that would lead the offensive. More broadly, the movement to a comparatively high-technology force, away from the traditional "people's army" strategy, would move the NVA into exactly the sort of confrontation at which the U.S. military was most effective—one in which it could use its massive firepower to best advantage.

While no available documents directly compare the chosen strategy with its alternative, an extension of the strategy conducted after Tet, undoubtedly these two approaches framed the Politburo's debates. The projection of existing trends led to no good outcome from the DRV's perspective. The Americans would continue to withdraw, but in the absence of a negotiated peace settlement, a residual force of advisors and logistics units would remain. These remnants of the U.S. presence would funnel American aid and advice to the South Vietnamese, and perhaps more important, would serve as a sensitive tripwire in the case of subsequent DRV offensive action. It would be much easier to bring large numbers of American forces back with a logistics base already in place, and with the mission of protecting the remaining U.S. troops. Further, a delay past 1972 would cost the DRV the benefits of the domestic constraints on Nixon, and of the summits. An offensive would be costly and risky, but its alternative offered few attractions. It is a measure of the burden that the offensive would pose that only a narrow majority supported it in the Politburo.

Military planners defined operational objectives to achieve the political goals set by the Politburo. For each of the primary axes of attack, planners defined both geographical objectives and goals in terms of South Vietnamese forces to be destroyed. In the north, for example, the political leadership outlined a series of missions for the Quang Tri Offensive Campaign. The first, and most important, was to "destroy the majority of enemy forces in Tri Thien, essentially destroy two enemy divisions, and inflict heavy casualties on one additional enemy division." The second mission was to "coordinate the military offensive with mass uprisings in the rural lowlands; intensify our urban struggle movement and our military proselytizing operations." Geographically, the NVA forces were to "liberate the majority of the territory of Tri Thien, and if conditions are right take determined action to totally liberate both provinces in the area, Quang Tri and Thua Thien." The northern axis of attack was also directed to "destroy and disperse (tie down) enemy forces to support our other battlefields throughout South Vietnam in order to contribute to the overall success of the 1972 strategic offensive."[18]

These missions are of interest for several reasons. First, they called for a near-total annihilation of the South Vietnamese forces in the north. Two of the three RVNAF divisions there were to be destroyed, with the third suffering heavy casualties. The plan's expectation of rural uprisings and a renewal of the urban struggle movement would prove unrealistic, and the 1972 campaign would unfold as a purely conventional attack. This was not by intent. It is clear that the campaign planners were aware of the weakness of the local forces, but they still expected these units to play a major role in the campaign.[19]

On the basis of the guidance from Hanoi, "the Campaign Headquarters and Party Committee agreed on the following overall goal: in a period of approximately 20–25 days, we will destroy four or five enemy regiments, launch uprisings to liberate Quang Tri Province, and then continue our advance." It is noteworthy, in light of later events, that "the Campaign confirmed that the initial mission was to liberate Quang Tri, and only after that was done could we develop a follow-up plan."[20] This may have been an unavoidable aspect of the plan's structure, but it imposed an almost inevitable delay in the development of the attack.

The Politburo issued its direction to execute the attack in May 1971, less than a year before its projected opening. For the offensive to work as envisioned, the North Vietnamese army would have to field systems never before seen in Indochina and adopt tactics and operational doctrine foreign to its tradition. It was a massive undertaking, but essential to any prospect of success for this ambitious and risky strategy.

3

THE NVA PREPARES

The Politburo's decision in May 1971 to conduct a strategic offensive the following spring required that the NVA accelerate a process of transformation it had begun the previous year. In the wake of the 1968 Tet Offensive and its progressively weaker successors, the Politburo had decided in June 1970 to "focus our efforts on building a powerful main force army strong enough to fight major battles of annihilation and to serve as a strategic mobile force for all battlefields." It was understood that this would require mobilization of "the entire Party, the entire armed forces, and the entire population of both North and South Vietnam."[1]

Certainly anything short of national mobilization would have proved inadequate. The Politburo's decisions in 1970 and 1971 required that the army conduct a near-total revision of its strategy, tactics, and command relations; develop whole new sorts of combat skills and spread them through the force in a very limited time; multiply its technical base several-fold; and send this transformed force into battle down a contested resupply corridor, under steady air attack, while revealing as little as possible of its new nature. Many NVA units would have to develop an entirely new style of warfare while intensely engaged in combat. In two years the NVA would turn away from the skills and traditions of its thirty-year history and adopt a new generation of combat technology. In scale, scope, and time, this was a remarkably ambitious undertaking.

Before taking any of these steps, however, the North Vietnamese had to secure essential supplies and equipment from their allies. By the early 1970s the DRV could manufacture small arms and ammunition, but the vast bulk of its military and economic matériel flowed from the USSR and China.[2] Through the preceding years, the two communist superpowers had provided generally complementary assistance, with the Soviets contributing equipment for air defense and relatively high-technology ground warfare, and the Chinese sending masses of lower-technology gear such as uniforms, radios and other communications equipment, and small arms.[3]

Party First Secretary Le Duan made an extended visit to Moscow in the spring of 1971, and he probably negotiated the flow of arms, petroleum, and supplies needed by his military planners.[4] The Soviets signed formal aid agreements with the DRV in August, October, and December 1971, and according to a CIA estimate, increased their military aid to North Vietnam from $70 million in 1970 to $100 million in 1971. Even the 1971 figure, however, was less than one-fifth of the Soviet aid provided in 1967, at the height of American combat action in Indochina.[5]

The CIA analysts noted the strategic context of Soviet aid patterns. The Soviets felt a special obligation to assist with the air defense of their socialist ally, which was under the threat of bombing attack. The requests for other equipment had by 1971 become routine, and there was no avenue in the aid program for the Soviets to offer the North Vietnamese advice or assistance in either strategic or operational planning. Their advisors were strictly limited to technical assistance and advice on use and maintenance of the equipment. The North Vietnamese, for their part, gave the Soviets a minimum of explanation with their requests and were wary of entering into any forms of negotiation that might have given the USSR real influence over their strategic planning. While the Soviets should theoretically have had great leverage over their smaller ally, the CIA noted: "In this concrete situation theoretical leverage does not have much practical effect. The North Vietnamese themselves are immensely jealous of their independence, and they assiduously work their relations with their two big supporters not only to maximize the aid but also to minimize the influence of the donors." Conversely: "There is no indication that Moscow at any time has withheld aid from North Vietnam in an attempt to influence Hanoi's military policies."[6] It was a remarkably distant relationship between allies, especially compared with the intricate and intrusive relationship of the United States and the South Vietnamese.

The Soviet assistance would be used in part to replace the matériel destroyed during Lam Son 719, in part as original issue to the troops, and in part to replace equipment issued from North Vietnamese stockpiles. By doctrine and long practice, the North Vietnamese emphasized the importance of maintaining stockpiles at the strategic, campaign, and combat levels, ideally totaling twenty-one months' worth of supplies. In practice, the CIA estimated, stores did not meet that level, but were "substantial."[7] In many cases, equipment issued to the units for the 1972 offensive would come out of the stockpiled matériel, which would then be replenished by the newly arriving gear.

During 1971 the Soviets provided the North Vietnamese with ten battalions of SA-2 missile systems, nearly a tenfold increase over the air defense aid given in 1970. These new systems enabled the North Vietnamese to extend an air defense umbrella over their logistics network while sustaining coverage over their national heartland. In addition, the CIA discovered at least 100 tanks being shipped to North Vietnam, as confirmed by photos taken at a Chinese rail terminal just north of the border with North Vietnam. American intelligence also detected eight M-46 130-mm artillery pieces in 1971 and another six in the first three months of 1972. These Soviet systems outranged anything in the RVNAF arsenal, and would be a formidable component of the NVA offensive. Even with their truck inventory at over 20,000, a record level, the North Vietnamese had ordered another 5,000 for delivery in 1972.[8] The Soviets, who supplied 90 percent of the DRV's petroleum, sent 390,000 tons in 1971 and another 145,000 tons in the first quarter of 1972. These shipments amounted to a significant reserve for the North Vietnamese military. They were equally essential in enabling the DRV's economy to function, as only 5 percent of all the imported petroleum went to NVA forces outside North Vietnam.[9]

The Chinese, too, accelerated the flow of aid in every category. In 1970 they sent the North Vietnamese 2,212 artillery pieces and 1,899,000 shells; in 1971 the corresponding figures were 7,898 and 2,210,000. Ammunition supplies nearly doubled, from 29,010,000 rounds to 57,190,000. In 1972 the PRC provided 2,464 radio transmitters, 4,424 telephone sets, 80 tanks, and 4,011 vehicles, mostly trucks. Their contributions, though less spectacular than those of the Soviets, were indispensable to the conduct of NVA operations.[10]

While the diplomats secured access to the necessary equipment, military planners analyzed the operational tasks that would be required in this new phase of the war. By August 1970 the Central Military Party Committee and the ministry of defense staged a month-long training course on "a number of problems regarding the military policies of the Party; new fighting methods for campaign- and tactical-level combat; staff operations; party and political operations; and campaign- and tactical-level rear service operations." Returning to their units, the participants began to build expertise in the use of "campaign-level large-scale concentrated combined-arms tactics to annihilate enemy units."[11]

The nation's minuscule industrial base contributed what it could to the expansion and transformation of the army. A decade earlier, men marching down the Ho Chi Minh Trail had been armed and outfitted entirely with Communist Chinese equipment, every stitch of clothing and piece of gear originating outside North Vietnam. By the early 1970s the DRV had developed some ability to manufacture uniforms, small weapons, ammunition, and personal gear. The North Vietnamese followed the Soviet model in organizing their industrial sector. In 1971 the slowly growing military-industrial base included "seventy-seven national defense enterprises, 86 large and medium-level repair stations, and hundreds of small repair stations subordinate to divisions and regiments" working to fabricate, service, or repair some portion of the army's equipment.[12] The scientific-industrial base also worked to adapt the largely Soviet equipment to meet the requirements of warfare in Southeast Asia. Successful projects included modifying rockets to extend their range, lightening the steering rods of T-54 tanks, and developing more effective explosive devices for obstacle clearance. The North Vietnamese cast a wide net in their search for counters to American air attacks, going so far as to modify captured American 2.75 inch rockets for use as unguided antiaircraft projectiles, and to mount shoulder-fired SA-7 surface-to-air missiles on L-29 trainer aircraft. These steps had some nuisance value but offered little real hope of protecting forces under air bombardment.[13]

In spite of the contributions of the national technical base, the movement to a Soviet-style mechanized force inevitably increased the DRV's reliance on its allies. Stockpiled equipment provided some degree of strategic autonomy and enabled the NVA to begin the expansion and upgrade of its armored forces before the arrival of new supplies from the Soviet Union and China. From documents captured in destroyed tanks, it appears that most of the T-54 medium tanks employed in the offensive had arrived in Southeast Asia in the mid-1960s and had been in storage for years.[14] They were run only for maintenance, a few minutes per year, until they were pulled out of depots and issued to tank units in late 1971.[15]

The training given NVA tank crews seems incredibly meager by Western standards. The demands of secrecy and speed forced the Armored Command to accept minimal levels of training even in basic skills—driving and repairing the tanks, firing the weapons—let alone in the vastly more complex tasks of integrating armored, artillery, and infantry forces on the field of battle. The 397th Battalion of the 203d Armored Regiment, for example, served in the Lower Laos Campaign in early 1971, operating PT-76 light amphibious tanks. Stationed northwest of Tchepone, the battalion planted sweet potatoes and manioc and raised pigs and dogs through the summer. In October the unit was told its missions for the upcoming campaign. Over the following month it received reinforcements from other tank units and added specialized elements such as signal, engineer, and antiaircraft personnel.

Before dawn on January 9, 1972, the 6th Company set out for North Vietnam to pick up its new T-54 medium tanks. Having left its equipment behind in Laos, the unit marched back up the Ho Chi Minh Trail, plagued by malaria, taking two weeks to work its way through the jungles and mountain passes. The unit had been deployed on its "international mission" for over a year, and was returning for the first time to its homeland. Nonetheless, "cadre and personnel were to keep absolute secrecy and avoid contacting unconcerned personnel. They were forbidden to write about their missions to their families and friends. During the move, if they were asked about their missions they had to answer that they were transporting goods."[16]

Carefully confined, the company embarked on a rapid and haphazard process of learning to employ the new tanks, practicing driving and repairing the vehicles for ten days before setting out on the march to battle on February 11. The unit's tactics during its return to combat were shaped by the ever-present threat of American air attacks. The unit moved in column formation, with intervals of 30–40 meters between tanks and 100–150 meters between platoons. It traveled at night to avoid detection. If attacked while on the move, the drivers were to turn off their lights and drive at full speed to a bush area for shelter, while maintaining radio silence.

Given the limitations of their training, it is not surprising that the soldiers of the 6th Company had problems during their return march from North Vietnam. As summarized in captured documents:

> The majority of cadre and soldiers of this company were new soldiers, who possessed poor technical skill and feared the fierceness of war and

death. Most of their weapons and equipment are modern, therefore, they did not thoroughly understand all their technical characteristics. Since the K1 (T54 tanks) were quite new to the majority of cadre and soldiers in the company, they could not promptly detect and repair all mechanical failures. Because there were many passes, hills, streams, and bomb craters along both sides of the infiltration route, and the drivers were not familiar with the K1 tanks, many of them were accidentally turned over or bogged down. There were some drivers who drove the tank in a zigzag way or did not know how to properly operate the gun turret.[17]

It was a risky way to go to war, but necessary to meet the demands of timing and security levied by the Politburo's decisions. The experience of this battalion was not universal, but it was representative enough to explain the erratic performance of NVA armored forces in the 1972 campaign.

Combat operations during 1971 had mixed effects on the NVA's effort to create combined-arms forces. On the one hand, the fighting slowed the training programs in the new skills and level of coordination required by the new operational concepts. On the other hand, and probably more significantly, large-scale operations in lower Laos and north of Saigon provided an opportunity for the NVA to create and exercise corps-level commands in these areas. In lower Laos, the NVA created the B-70 Corps-Sized Group in October 1970, consisting of the 304th, 308th, and 320th divisions plus a number of specialty-branch regiments and battalions. Similarly, the following spring the Central Office for South Vietnam (COSVN) created a forward command center, Group 301, to exercise direct command over the three divisions and specialty forces operating north of Saigon.[18] It was a remarkable achievement for an army that had begun with mere platoons, then gradually built its forces and command organization, and now finally achieved the ability to coordinate multidivisional operations.

With the decision finally taken in May 1971 to execute the combined-arms offensive, the North Vietnamese could construct specific plans for the flow of the attack and designate the roles to be assumed by the units that would participate. In the area north of Saigon, for example, "the 7th Infantry Division trained in mobile offensive attacks combined with blocking operations, the 9th Infantry Division trained in combat operations in cities and towns, and the 5th Infantry Division trained in envelopment and siege operations and in destroying enemy forces holding solid defensive positions."[19] Given the limited opportunities for training available to combat units, it was necessary and appropriate to offer sharply focused training programs, but clearly this would come at the expense of operational flexibility in the upcoming campaign. Along with the specific training for their missions, the troops received ideological education, as commanders and party leaders took care that their forces understood the scale and the stakes of the offensive that was soon to come.[20]

In November 1971, as final preparations for the offensive began, the military training department of the General Staff sponsored a four-day field exercise with the 308th Infantry Division. The troops practiced the techniques used to overrun an enemy base camp, and so "the training area included a mock-up of an enemy regiment-sized base camp, including a system of blockhouses, trenches, bunkers, obstacles, fallback positions, etc." Afterward, "live firings were conducted with a number of Soviet-made weapons, including anti-tank missiles and shoulder-fired anti-aircraft missiles, which had just been issued to our units."[21] With the weapons arriving just months before the offensive, it was a major task to develop the individual skills and tactics for these unfamiliar weapons systems, implement training programs, and deploy them in time to take effect on the battlefield.

Ultimately, the new armored and technical capabilities rested on the foundation of manpower, masses of infantry exceeding anything seen since the Tet Offensive in 1968. MACV intelligence reported that to prepare for this all-out offensive, the North Vietnamese extended the draft age at both ends, changing it from 17–30 to 16–35. Moreover, the basic training period was compressed from six months to five, enabling a higher throughput for the training establishment, at the cost of individual effectiveness among the soldiers. Through the months of preparation, the North Vietnamese high command carefully planned its manpower allocations across the requirements of the three campaigns to be fought in South Vietnam, with the demands of this campaign competing against the needs for men to fight in Cambodia, in northern Laos, and along the Ho Chi Minh Trail. American intelligence estimated that the North Vietnamese inducted 150,000 men into their military forces to prepare for the 1972 campaign, with 127,000 committed to combat in South Vietnam.[22] Clearly the Politburo was ready to pay a very high price for its campaign.

Meanwhile, preparations continued throughout the communist infrastructure and among the deployed forces in South Vietnam. Devastated by the Tet Offensive and the subsequent counteroffensive, and further weakened by the pacification programs of the South Vietnamese, the once formidable Viet Cong structure struggled to meet its mission requirements. The most basic need was for food, whether grown, shipped in, or bought. By one estimate, about 90–95 percent of the rice consumed by NVA and Viet Cong forces was purchased in areas under South Vietnamese control.[23] The South Vietnamese imposed a "rice blockade" on the communist-occupied areas, creating severe difficulties for cadres working to build stockpiles for the coming offensive. By early January, VC purchasing agents had bought only 10 percent of the rice that would be needed through March. These purchases were made with RVN currency, often converted from U.S. dollars. The agents conducted their missions at night, whenever possible on moonless nights, not patronizing particular vendors exclusively, but spreading their business as widely as they could. One agent commented that the prices they paid seemed excessive, but that "the cell was under strict instructions not to extort any foodstuffs from local merchants, and not to refuse to pay the prices asked."[24] Given that an army runs on its stomach, the struggle to find food boded ill for the health and success of NVA soldiers in the campaign that loomed ahead.

Inevitably, there were holes in the pattern of NVA preparation for the offensive. The two-year effort to prepare yielded a transformation of the North Vietnamese military, a very distinctive remaking of a light infantry force into a Soviet-style mechanized army. Yet the pace and scale of the effort forced the NVA leadership to reduce training cycles to a dangerous degree, and prevented any thorough exploration of the complexities of the new style of combat contemplated for the upcoming campaign. Moreover, the NVA's dependence on external sources of supply restricted its ability to structure its forces uniformly. As 1971 closed, the NVA history records: "Our armed forces still had many weaknesses, such as the fact that our technical equipment was not standardized, reserve levels and replacement capabilities were still low, and our level of mobility was not high enough."[25] Nonetheless the army had taken a new form, and soon it would go to battle.

The massive rearmament and training programs of the previous eighteen months would do no good if the men and machines could not be deployed into the theater of conflict. The first battle of the campaign would thus be a battle for access, with the North Vietnamese forces fighting their way toward the staging areas for the offensive. That battle opened in early November 1971, as the dry season began in Laos and men and matériel began to move down the Ho Chi Minh Trail.

4

COMMANDO HUNT VII

The first battle of this campaign was fought in and over the jungles and the mountain passes of Laos, as the North Vietnamese army moved men and supplies toward the staging areas for the offensive. In this battle there were no dramatic scenes of mass casualties, no single moments that marked victory or defeat, but rather a series of small, deadly skirmishes, as the Americans sought to cut off the flow of forces southward. It pitted American technology and firepower against the persistence and organization of the NVA; the result would shape all the battles to follow, and eventually the outcome of the war.

In the most basic sense, the Ho Chi Minh Trail was a logistics network, funneling soldiers and supplies from North Vietnam, across Laos and Cambodia, to the battle sites in South Vietnam. In the context of this war, however, the trail was far more than a simple pathway toward the South. For the North Vietnamese, it was the backbone of their war effort, the lifeline extending from their fighting forces in the South to the "great rear area" in the North and to their communist allies beyond. Their victory would rest on their ability to maintain the flow of traffic, regardless of weather, terrain, and illness—and despite the most ferocious, sustained interdiction campaign that U.S. technology and weaponry could generate.

The Americans recognized the importance of the trail as clearly as did the North Vietnamese, and with the prohibition on air strikes on the North in 1968, turned the full might of their aerial firepower against the trail. In time, as U.S. ground forces withdrew from the theater, the battle over Laos became a strategic rear-guard action for the United States, reducing the risk to the remaining Americans and buying time for Vietnamization to take effect. From 1968 through 1972 the Americans conducted a continuous series of interdiction campaigns, code-named Commando Hunt, attacking the network's infrastructure, the troops, and the trucks moving along the system. The campaign in the winter of 1971–1972, called Commando Hunt VII, can be seen as the first battle of the Easter Offensive, determining where and how the later battles would be fought.

Weather cycles ruled this battle as they did every aspect of the war. The rainy season in Laos extends from April through October, with the southwest monsoon sweeping across Indochina, flooding roads and taking a heavy toll of both personnel and equipment. During that period each year the North Vietnamese upgraded the road network, readying it for the dry season to follow. In early November, as the monsoon passed, the trucks began to roll through the passes from North Vietnam into Laos, and troops started their march southward. The journey was a difficult one for the North Vietnamese soldiers. From the first day of the war to the last, the greatest threat facing infiltrating troops was malaria, which struck down as much as 50 percent of some units; fatigue and hunger were also constant companions for the forces marching south.

Aware of the stakes in this battle, both sides lavished their most valued resources on its prosecution. The North Vietnamese relied on their strengths in manpower, organization, and persistence. Since the Ho Chi Minh Trail's humble origins in 1959, as a series of footpaths along the eastern side of the Truong Son Mountains, the North Vietnamese year by year had extended and strengthened it—adding motorable roads, then bypasses and alternate routes, oil pipelines and waterways. By 1971 the trail was almost impervious to complete interdiction. The North Vietnamese organized the trail under the command of Transportation Group 559, which operated a series of *binh tram*, or way stations, each responsible for maintaining the flow of troops and supplies through its assigned area. Each *binh tram* commanded its own engineers, communications, trucks, antiaircraft forces, and infantry units, and maintained its own facilities for vehicle maintenance and storage. This mode of command gave the system a great degree of flexibility and integration, as each *binh tram* reacted to attack by rerouting convoys within its area. It also created a distinctive mode of movement for the matériel en route to the battle. During the rainy season the North Vietnamese built up their supplies in southern North Vietnam, awaiting the opening of the infiltration campaign. Once the roads dried, they first deployed the forces and equipment necessary to operate the network, and finally dispatched the supplies, moving from station to station, being unloaded, stored, and reloaded for further movement.[1] All in all, there were about fifty thousand North Vietnamese troops assigned to the network, and they were supplemented by civilian "assault youth" employed as laborers.

The trail extended about three hundred miles, from the passes leading out of North Vietnam, into Laos, down to the base camps in southeastern Cambodia. By 1971 the North Vietnamese had built a 2,710-mile route structure characterized by single-lane roads with multiple parallel routes, bypasses, and spur roads. Nevertheless, the North Vietnamese, from Defense Minister Giap on down, feared that the American interdiction campaign would threaten the logistics essential to the coming campaign. And so, during the 1971 wet season, the NVA built or upgraded six north-south roads through western Laos. Still more remarkably, a number of *binh trams* constructed a secret road along dry streambeds through the western route structure. This "green road" ran under jungle canopy, camouflage nets, and trellises, maintaining the green of the forests through its 1,000-kilometer length. Group 559 added to the deception by building fake vehicles, storage areas, and gun positions along the older network. These would dilute the American air attacks, leaving the new system free to operate day and night.[2] Through that wet season the North Vietnamese also prepared to extend an air defense envelope over the trail, both with MiG-21 fighter-interceptors based in the North Vietnamese panhandle and by deploying the 377th Air Defense Division into Laos.

The division was built around the SA-75 "Dvina" surface-to-air missile operated by the 275th Missile Regiment. Known in the West as the SA-2 Guideline, this missile was fielded in the late 1950s as a strategic defense system for use in prepared installations against bomber attacks. The Soviets first delivered the system to North Vietnam in 1965, and it had seen extensive use in the air battles of Rolling Thunder from 1965 to 1968. The missile could be outmaneuvered by fighters, and the radar guidance-and-control system was susceptible to various jamming techniques. Nonetheless, the missile formed the cornerstone of the North Vietnamese defenses, operating in tandem with antiaircraft cannon to form "air defense clusters" of mutually supporting systems.[3]

The North Vietnamese faced a huge array of technical problems in deploying this missile. It had been designed for use in fixed sites, against medium-altitude bombers. Instead the NVA was forced to use it in the jungle against fighter aircraft. The supply lines for maintaining the missiles extended up the Ho Chi Minh Trail, back through North Vietnam, and into the Soviet Union, inevitably creating maintenance problems. The NVA addressed these problems with its usual meticulous planning and preparation, breaking the SAM battalions into six sections for movement:

> Each section was escorted by one tracked vehicle. The movement plan was implemented over the course of many nights, with each section moving separately. A tracked vehicle was stationed at each chokepoint and each difficult stretch of road to be ready to provide support if needed. A battalion soldier was stationed at each three-way and four-way intersection to prevent anyone from getting lost and to select the proper moment to move through the chokepoint locations. When passing through one of the chokepoints, everyone dismounted from the vehicles and walked. Only the drivers and command cadre remained with the vehicles. This was to avoid casualties in the event of unexpected high-altitude enemy air strikes.[4]

The Americans concentrated during the wet season on impeding the NVA's efforts to upgrade the trail, and on planning their operations for the impending dry season, when the trucks would roll and the hunt would resume. Their plan for Commando Hunt VII, controlling operations for the 1971–1972 winter campaign, basically repeated the concepts used for the previous dry season. The campaign would follow three phases, shifting as the North Vietnamese supply effort surged southward toward the battlefields. The first phase would focus on closing the passes from North Vietnam into Laos and destroying the trucks passing into the Laotian route structure. The second phase would focus on the central road network leading through Laos. In this phase Seventh Air Force planned to create "blocking belts" along the infiltration corridor—using precision weapons to cut the roads, then dropping antipersonnel and antivehicle mines to keep them closed, and finally attacking the traffic backed up at the cuts. In the third phase, as the season progressed, the focus would shift to the exit points from the Ho Chi Minh Trail into the operational and storage areas along the border of South Vietnam.[5]

American planners hoped to compensate for their declining force structure through advanced technology and firepower, employing three generally complementary capabilities: B-52 bombers, fighter aircraft, and gunships developed from cargo aircraft, now modified for night detection and attack of trucks. The B-52 heavy bombers would be used primarily against area targets like NVA base camps or troop concentrations, guided by ground-control radar to drop their bombs into a "box," normally three kilometers by one kilometer. Almost always the bombers operated in three-aircraft cells, delivering 198 bombs into that confined area, about 66 tons of high explosive. The results were devastating, with effects as much psychological as physical. North Vietnamese intelligence worked hard to gain tactical warning of the B-52 drop zones. Generating and executing an attack required so many different players and actions, and so many radio transmissions, that some warning was often available. When warned, troops in the target area could withdraw in a near-panic, moving perpendicular to the drop zone. But when their tactical intelligence failed and the bombs cascaded out of the sky without any advance warning, the impact and shock were terrible. Truong Nhu Tang, who survived a series of B-52 attacks, later recalled the effects: "The concussive *whump-whump-whump* came closer and closer, moving in a direct line toward our positions. Then, as the cataclysm walked in on us, everyone hugged the earth—some screaming quietly, others struggling to suppress attacks of violent, involuntary trembling. Around us the ground began to heave spasmodically, and we were engulfed in a monstrous roar."[6]

This account was of a strike a kilometer away from Tang's shelter. Of a later strike that hit the camp, he wrote: "There was nothing left. It was as if an enormous scythe had swept through the jungle, felling the giant teak and go trees like grass in its way, shredding them into billions of scattered splinters. On these occasions—when the B-52s had found their mark—the complex would be utterly destroyed: food, clothes, supplies, documents, everything. It was not just that things were destroyed; in some awesome way they had ceased to exist."[7]

The chronic problem for the Americans planning these strikes was to locate and target the mobile, dispersed enemy. Nixon, Kissinger, and Laird all understood this problem, and they took some comfort in the thought that with so many bombs falling, some of them had to be hitting something useful. However, this was not an efficient approach to warfare, and theater commanders worked to increase the bombers' flexibility by improving targeting procedures and generating the ability to divert airborne bombers to high-priority missions.

By the early 1970s American tactical air forces had moved beyond the generation of fighters that had conducted the Rolling Thunder campaign. The Air Force relied on the two-seat F-4 Phantom as its all-purpose fighter, employing it for both air-to-air and ground attack missions. This versatility gave mission planners a great deal of flexibility, at the expense of some operational capability, since neither the aircraft nor its crews were optimized for any particular role. The Navy normally used the A-7 and the A-6 for ground attack missions; both aircraft incorporated avionics that provided significantly better bombing accuracy than the F-4, which was generally regarded as the least accurate fighter-bomber in the U.S. inventory. Neither of these aircraft could match the F-4's aerodynamic performance, but both had better endurance than the notoriously fuel-thirsty Phantom.

Just as the bombing halt was imposed in 1968, new precision weapons appeared that promised to revolutionize air-to-ground capabilities and tactics. The laser-guided bomb (LGB) was the most important of these new weapons. This system used laser technology to illuminate the target, and the bomb was fitted with a receiver and a flight-control system enabling it to home in on the designated point.[8]

The multiplication in accuracy was dramatic, and it had a series of reinforcing effects. A flight of four bombers could now routinely achieve results better than had been available from larger strike forces dropping unguided bombs. Delivery accuracy was no longer affected by the altitude at which bombers released their weapons, and so the fighters could stay above the antiaircraft artillery's range, operating with near-impunity, so long as there were no SAMs or MiGs around. Finally, the laser-guided bomb had something of the effect of the Colt 45, the "great equalizer," in making every fighter crew effective bombers. The task of the delivery aircraft was just to get the bomb into a "basket" with enough airspeed so that it could maneuver to the target. Pinpoint accuracy was now up to the bomb, not to the bomber.

The fighter-bombers normally worked under the control of forward air controllers (FACs), observers flying small, slow aircraft to spot and direct attacks. This mission lacked the panache of the attack role, but it was critical to the entire American air effort, right from the beginning in the early 1960s. The fighter planes generally flew too fast and too high for their crews to find the targets. The FACs performed that role, finding targets and then directing attacks by the fighter aircraft. It was an essential role, very hazardous, and quite unsung. The FACs normally returned to the same operating area day after day, each pilot becoming intimately familiar with a small sector and able to detect any slight change in movement patterns or infrastructure.

The FAC-fighter combination largely managed to deny the NVA the ability to move by day, but they were unable to suppress traffic by night. The third major component of the interdiction effort, the gunships, filled that role. These aircraft were probably the most remarkable technical innovation of the war—converted cargo planes, outfitted with advanced avionics and armed with cannon. By 1971 the most advanced type, the Lockheed AC-130, had been fitted with an integrated fire-control system incorporating low-light television, an infrared detector, an electronic-emissions sensor, and a digital fire-control computer. Crews used these sensors to cue and direct an array of weapons, by 1971 including 105-mm cannons on the most advanced models. Developed to defend fixed installations against attack, these aircraft proved supremely useful when turned to the interdiction effort.[9] They quickly gained the respect of their North Vietnamese opponents, who attributed about 60 percent of the trucks destroyed in 1970–1971 to them.[10] Unique among the weaponry fielded by the Americans and the South Vietnamese, the AC-130 gunship received NVA praise for its "modern equipment and its logical and intelligent tactics."[11] These aircraft were a special concern for the North Vietnamese as they planned their infiltration campaign for the 1971–1972 dry season.

The air forces in theater could wield incredible amounts of firepower; the hard part was to find the enemy precisely enough and quickly enough to permit attack. The NVA forces' proficiency at deception and camouflage had been honed by decades of fighting opponents with superior systems. They were abetted by the weather, and by the extent and the terrain of their operating arena. The Americans' task of finding and targeting the NVA infiltrators grew more difficult as the U.S. withdrawal continued and reconnaissance elements, both Air Force and Army, left the theater.

The Americans attempted to solve this problem through the lavish use of advanced technology, creating history's first electronic battlefield in the jungles and mountains of Laos. To achieve that end, they deployed a sensor field extending through the passes and the Laotian route structure. By 1971 the system employed two types of sensors, acoustic and seismic. These relayed their signals through aircraft orbiting Laos to the heart of the system, an IBM 360/65 computer at the Infiltration Surveillance Center at Nakhon Phanom Royal Thai Air Force Base (RTAFB). The computer generated real-time tracking of the truck traffic.[12]

The whole system, consisting of the sensors, the relay aircraft, and the computer, carried the code name Igloo White.[13] Igloo White fell under the command of Task Force Alpha (TFA), a 13th Air Force organization that operated the system and integrated its intelligence with that gained from other sources—visual sightings, human intelligence, communications intercepts, signals intelligence, and so on.[14] The structure was aimed at bringing together every source of intelligence available to permit rapid and accurate attack.

The interdiction program as a whole fell under the command of Seventh Air Force, the Air Force command under MACV. Its headquarters were at Tan Son Nhut Air Base, outside Saigon; from there the command ran the theater air-control system, integrating the Navy fighters flown off the carriers under Carrier Task Force 77 with Air Force operations, now predominantly launched from airfields in Thailand.

In early November the monsoonal rains ended, and the enemies joined in battle over Laos. The first movement through the passes triggered massive B-52 and fighter strikes aimed at destroying the road structure and the trucks in transit. Over the first twenty-two days of the season, American air forces dropped more than 14,500 500-pound bombs, 17,100 750-pound bombs, and a range of other weapons—laser-guided bombs, bombs fused by magnetic sensors, and cluster bombs designed to disperse bomblets over large areas. The NVA worked ceaselessly to keep the passes open and the trucks moving, and attempted to counter the bombers in late November by sending SAMs and fighters against the B-52s.

These attacks failed to bring down any bombers, but their indirect effects were powerful. By demonstrating some ability to threaten the B-52s, the North Vietnamese imposed a high cost on the American air operations. During the five months of this air campaign, American intelligence tracked 72 MiG-21 incursions into Laos. To counter these, U.S. fighters flew 3,664 air defense missions. Even more seriously, SAC, profoundly reluctant to risk its prize assets in areas defended by SA-2s, unilaterally suspended B-52 operations in these areas. Abrams issued a formal protest, noting both the primary and secondary effects of this decision. If allowed to stand, it would materially weaken the interdiction campaign. Perhaps more seriously, it would change the operating philosophy for U.S. forces throughout the region: "If too great a reluctance to risk losses becomes the dominant psychology in SEA, it should be a matter of highest concern. Such a psychology is infectious and could have widespread impact."[15]

But this was no longer a war to be won, but a war to be managed, and the decision stood. The psychology of the war effort had changed. The overriding emphasis was now on limiting American casualties of all types, and especially avoiding the loss of highly visible assets like the B-52. The United States was winding down its involvement in the war, the elections loomed not far in the future, and the risk-gain calculus for military operations in theater shifted as a result. SAMs fired in the Mu Gia Pass on December 10 induced SAC to end B-52 operations along the three northern passes for the remainder of the dry season.[16]

By this point, the leading edge of the NVA supply operations had reached the central route structure, and Commando Hunt VII moved into its second phase. Seventh Air Force began the laborious and complex task of establishing the blocking belts, with their elaborate combination of weapons and sensors. The first belt went in near Tchepone on December 7, and was repeatedly reinforced until late December, when it finally became clear that the North Vietnamese had converted the area into a "flak trap," an ambush site for attacking aircraft. Over the weeks that followed, Seventh Air Force orchestrated three other blocking belts, progressively farther south along the infiltration corridor. The last expired on March 1, as the command turned to attacking the exit routes into South Vietnam.[17]

As the flow of traffic moved away from the entry passes, the trucks came within the operating envelope of the AC-130 gunships, their most effective predators. As NVA losses mounted, the task of engaging and destroying the AC-130 became an urgent requirement for the NVA's 377th Air Defense Division.[18] The division's operational staff conducted a study of gunship tactics and countermeasures that might counter this threat. The staff went so far as to draft a training curriculum and conduct classes for missile and antiaircraft artillery troops, specifically in tactics against AC-130s. Unable to match the gunships' level of technology, the NVA commanders sought to counter them through careful study and tactical adjustments.[19]

In mid-January the air campaign's focus moved to the exit routes from the Ho Chi Minh Trail into South Vietnam. American intelligence defined seven exit routes and established target boxes around each. Seventh Air Force also extended the blocking belt concept into this phase of the campaign. Meanwhile the opposing North Vietnamese air defense forces struggled to rebuild their strength after a wave of American attacks. The 377th Air Defense Division launched a concentrated effort to reconstitute its units, digging out guns that had been buried or destroyed and repairing or cannibalizing them for parts. The division once again reviewed its tactics, identifying the adjustments required for the last phase of the campaign: more mobility and more concentration of firepower. The division also continued to deploy its forces toward the South, providing some protection for the convoys now reaching the exit routes.

As American operators fought to stem the flow of NVA units, U.S. and South Vietnamese intelligence gradually reassessed projections for the upcoming campaign season. At the outset of this infiltration campaign, the prevailing view of U.S. intelligence was that the North Vietnamese would continue the "protracted warfare" strategy of the previous few years—generally a low level of activity, punctuated by intermittent "high points" designed to affect world opinion more than the situation on the battlefield. In part, this view reflected the normal tendency of intelligence agencies to predict for tomorrow what they have seen today. But there was also strategic logic behind this conservative estimate. It seemed foolhardy for the North Vietnamese to attack in 1972, when another year would bring a near-total American withdrawal of U.S. forces. There seemed no reason for them to accept the risk and the cost of an unnecessary confrontation with a departing power. Beyond this deductive approach, analysis of deployment patterns indicated that there was no possibility that the North Vietnamese could stage a major offensive. They had neither the troops nor the supplies that would be required.

However, it quickly became clear to intelligence analysts both in Saigon and in Washington that this dry season infiltration campaign was breaking the patterns of the previous few years. By this point in the war, the Americans had penetrated Transportation Group 559's communications network, beginning with the northernmost outpost of the Ho Chi Minh Trail. MACV and the CIA had a very accurate view of the number of troops marching down the trail and their destinations, though their grip on the volume of supplies moving down the trail was much less certain. By November 20, MACV had identified a fourfold increase over previous years in troops destined for the central highlands front. By early January, four NVA divisions stationed in North Vietnam were preparing for a deployment southward to the battlefields. By late January, Abrams signaled Washington that "there is no doubt that this is to be a major campaign," requesting a series of broadened operating authorities that would enable his forces to attack the air defenses and the supply buildup visible in southern North Vietnam and in Laos.[20]

Nixon and Kissinger watched the buildup as well, factoring in the risk to South Vietnam, the relationship of this campaign to their diplomatic efforts in Moscow and Beijing, and the domestic political climate as they weighed their options. In late December the president directed a five-day air operation in southern North Vietnam, deciding that it was time to give the North Vietnamese a "pop." Intended as a signal to the North Vietnamese that the United States expected serious negotiations to resume, the operation was equally effective in demonstrating the "internal contradictions" of the American war at that point.[21] The White House directed that the attacks continue for no more than five days, entirely during the Christmas holidays—ensuring that neither Congress nor colleges and universities would be in session, but also nearly guaranteeing bad weather for the strike forces. The first attack wave set out in bright clear weather, only to find the targets socked in by the time they arrived. The crews attempted to transition to an instrument attack. Limited by the technology of the day, the attack was further hamstrung by the lack of proficiency of the crews, who had been operating almost exclusively over the Ho Chi Minh Trail for the previous months. The results that first day were disappointing and set a tone that would continue for the duration of the brief operation.[22]

As expectations of an NVA offensive grew, Nixon directed a policy review in early February, with Ambassador Bunker flying back from Saigon to discuss the situation. With the summit in Beijing just two weeks away, Nixon and Kissinger were unwilling to permit a general air attack on North Vietnam; an air offensive might have forced the Chinese to visibly side with their clients, jeopardizing the administration's diplomatic coup. Instead Nixon directed a limited reinforcement for the theater, with the deployment of an aircraft carrier, B-52s, and fighter planes.

Nixon also directed a novel series of attacks on the North Vietnamese buildups in base areas in Laos and in the DMZ. Seeking concentration and shock effect, he directed that all theater air forces would be used in intensive 48-hour strikes, first against the bases in the tri-border area at the intersection of Laos, Cambodia, and South Vietnam, and then in the DMZ. These attacks were to occur before the president's departure for China on February 17, at which point they would cease. This was the first case of Nixon's triangular diplomacy directly affecting military operations.

The military command structure was generally skeptical about this tactic, concerned that the command and control system could not efficiently use this massive influx of airpower. Nonetheless, on receiving the tasking order from the Joint Chiefs on February 6, MACV and Seventh Air Force worked to build a target base and a scheduling flow to execute the plan. The strikes on the communist bases in the tri-border area took place on February 12–13, and those around the DMZ on February 16–17.

In early March, on opposite sides of the world, the North Vietnamese Politburo and the American strategic leadership gathered to assess the situation. In Hanoi, military leaders outlined the state of their preparations to the national leaders, noting the problems that continued to afflict their operations. Main-force units had built up only limited capabilities in combined-arms operations, and had not improved their ability to attack large, fortified positions. Slowed by weather and air attack, logistical preparations had been slower than planned, as had road construction in the campaign areas. The local forces and infrastructure that had been expected to support and participate in the offensive "had not grown rapidly enough to enable them to carry out their duties in this campaign."[23]

This was a sobering assessment. The entire operational approach for the campaign rested on the mutually supporting capabilities of the armor, infantry, and artillery that would provide the offensive punch. The enemies' large fortified positions were precisely the most important targets of the operation. The offensive finally would have only the success that its logistical foundation provided, and preparations lagged in this area. Finally, the inability of the North Vietnamese to rebuild local forces created the risk that the offensive might be an entirely conventional attack, with little element of insurgency and little reinforcement between the two most important elements of the NVA strategy—main-force action and rural uprisings.

The scale of these problems was reflected in a remarkable last-minute change in the fundamental strategy of the campaign. The North Vietnamese shifted the primary attack axis from the COSVN area, north of Saigon, to the front immediately south of the DMZ. The high command justified this major reorientation because in this area, bordering North Vietnam, "we could mass our forces, centralize command, and provide adequate logistics for a massive, extended operation."[24]

Indochina's geography had not significantly changed since the original concept for the operation had been approved the previous May. All of these factors—the location of the theater, the access to central command guidance, the logistical ties between the DMZ area and the north—remained unchanged. It seems clear that the American interdiction campaign, coupled with the abnormally long wet season in Laos, had seriously disrupted the NVA logistical buildup and its readiness to take the offensive. The change in the basic strategy of the campaign was an extraordinary decision, less than three weeks before the opening of an all-out offensive, and it was especially remarkable given the painstaking North Vietnamese planning cycle. The internal dynamics shaping this decision have not been made public, but given the division in the Politburo about undertaking the offensive, it is likely to have been a contentious time. This all-out offensive had always been a high-risk venture, certain to cost heavily. Now there were problems evident in operations, logistics, and political preparations. The Politburo's willingness to continue indicates the importance they assigned to this effort.

Unaware of the debate in Hanoi, the American strategic leadership grappled with the same set of issues: how to proceed in preparation for the upcoming campaign season. Abrams submitted a comprehensive survey of the theater's military status on March 8.[25] In it he detailed the buildup occurring in all three theaters in South Vietnam, as well as in Cambodia and Laos. The danger, as he saw it, was that a communist offensive across these far-flung areas would overstretch the air forces that would be the primary weapon of the defenders. He requested authority to conduct a large-scale air offensive in North Vietnam throughout the DRV panhandle, to blunt the imminent offensive. His assessment went to McCain at PACOM, who forwarded it to Moorer for transmittal to the secretary of defense.[26]

Abrams's request then entered the tangled web of personalities, domestic policy concerns, and international diplomacy that complicated all national-level considerations of the war in Vietnam. Laird forwarded Abrams's assessment to the White House, but his recommended response to the buildup was a pale shadow of Abrams's. He proposed that the air offensive be reduced to three 24-hour attacks on North Vietnamese forces. These would be confined to the immediate area of the DMZ and along the southern DRV-Laos frontier.[27] As always, Laird was mostly concerned with the domestic reaction to any strikes that might be made. Kissinger then received his proposals and reduced the action yet again, this time in consideration of international political problems that the attacks might create. He especially feared damage to the new and fragile relationship with China. In the end, the memorandum he forwarded for Nixon's signature authorized only the use of wide-area munitions in the DMZ.[28] The decision offered little prospect of countering the buildup that was very visible and very troubling in Saigon.

And so the NVA campaign wound on largely as before. In mid-March the forces committed to the offensive reached their assembly positions; the flow of supplies continued into the NVA base camps along the border. The air defense forces committed to protecting the Group 559 corridor were stretched and dispersed as their area of responsibility grew. The 377th Air Defense Division also had begun to show the effects of protracted combat. Many of its experienced personnel were transferred to provide initial cadres in new units. On the material side, "after a rather extended period of combat under adverse living conditions the health of our division's personnel had deteriorated, as had the condition of the weapons and equipment."[29]

By this point the NVA's careful study of the AC-130 had yielded a clear understanding of its tactics, its strengths, and its vulnerabilities. The gunships wielded magnificent technology, but that same technology forced a pattern on their operations that the NVA air defenders would seek to exploit. The aircraft's weaponry was mounted on its left side, and the standard tactic was to fly a left-hand orbit around the target. Once the aircraft had located a truck, it would establish the orbit and gradually whittle away its aiming errors, wind corrections, and so on, until it achieved a hit. That sequence normally took about eight minutes.

Lieutenant Colonel Stephen Opitz served as a fire control operator with the gunships, flying out of Ubon RTAFB during the interdiction campaign and the conventional operations that were to follow. He later recalled that at the outset of Commando Hunt VII the gunship crews felt inviolable, with AC-130s not having taken a serious hit since 1969. In November one of the Spectres took a 57-mm round in the belly; Opitz saw the aircraft after it landed and noted: "I looked at the hole—oh, you could stand four people in it." That ended the crews' sense of invulnerability, and as the campaign proceeded the sense of threat intensified. Opitz recalled that through the months of the interdiction campaign the antiaircraft threat grew in density and in capability, with the NVA deploying more and better systems into the operating area. Finally by March it became clear that the NVA gunners had gained a clear picture of the gunship operating patterns and how to counter them. Opitz commented: "They were clever. They knew how long it took to make a circle. They would coordinate their fire . . . what Charlie would do, he'd wait until about the 7th or 8th minute on orbit hitting the truck and then just unload on us."[30] Eight or ten gun positions would suddenly open fire, bracketing the AC-130. It is a difficult ballistics problem to hit an aircraft at two miles' range, but with the weight of fire from the ground, and the nightly exposure of the aircraft, the gunners on the ground had time and chance on their side.

On March 29 the bill finally came due. Spectre 13 was just beginning its mission when a missile struck it directly. Lieutenant Colonel Opitz was flying in an adjacent sector, and he heard the radar-warning signal as the SAM acquired its target. His copilot said, "Holy Christ, look at that." Opitz ran to the gunner's port and saw the aircraft as it began its fall toward the earth. "It was big orange flames," he recalled. "I guess it looked like the size of a football field just arching down the sky . . . They took a direct. They were loaded with fuel and it turned into a big orange ball."[31] None of the fifteen men aboard survived. Seventh Air Force imposed a restricted area, pulling the gunships out of the heart of the infiltration system.[32] This constituted a tremendous operational advantage for the NVA logisticians, opening the core route structure to almost unimpeded night movement. The NVA 377th Air Defense Division history commented: "Just one hour when AC-130s did not operate over our choke-points was both precious and rare. This time we got 15 days, or 360 hours. During this time a great many truck convoys were able to transit the entry points to carry their supplies to the front lines."[33] The next night the NVA antiaircraft gunners registered their own success, downing another AC-130 with a 57-mm cannon round.

On March 30, promptly at 1100, the North Vietnamese artillery opened fire on the ring of ARVN firebases south of the DMZ. The Spring-Summer Offensive was finally under way, and Commando Hunt VII came to a close.

Like any battle, the five-month struggle in the skies over Laos had winners and losers. There was never a question of terrain changing hands, and so the conventional means of judging victory did not apply. The battle was never one in which some single stunning blow would decide victory; it can be likened to the Battle of the Atlantic during World War II, a crucial yet shadowy conflict in which victory would be determined through statistical indicators and fractions of a percentage of supplies moving through the system.

Both sides kept meticulous statistics, and while in some cases they diverge wildly, they do permit some conclusions to be drawn. First, the American forces flew 43,860 sorties in the interdiction campaign, exclusive of the B-52s. The pilots reported antiaircraft fire on 8,535 of these, about one reaction for every five sorties. Fifty aircraft were damaged by antiaircraft fire and thirteen were lost; small arms destroyed another eight. The NVA 275th Missile Regiment fired 163 missiles in 84 engagements, downing seven aircraft. Two more aircraft ran out of fuel during missile engagements. Another went out of control while maneuvering against an SA-2, and the crew ejected. Overall, despite the deployment of the 377th Air Defense Division, the hit and loss rate for U.S. fighters in this infiltration season was comparable to that in previous campaigns.[34] The value of the NVA's deployed air defense forces lay more in harassment and denial than in the losses they imposed.

American intelligence reckoned that Commando Hunt VII destroyed 4,727 trucks and damaged another 5,882, with the AC-130s accounting for over 70 percent of this total. And, much more important: "Of the 30,947 tons of supplies the NVA brought into Steel Tiger from NVN, only 5,024, or 16 percent, reached SVN or Cambodia . . . This figure is probably the best overall indicator of the success of the Commando Hunt VII interdiction campaign."[35]

North Vietnamese figures tell a roughly congruent tale about the destruction of trucks. For the 1971–1972 dry season, an NVA history of the Ho Chi Minh Trail records a total of 1,970 trucks on hand assigned to the transportation forces to open the season. The various units assigned to Group 559 possessed another 1,571. The transportation units received another 3,768 trucks during the infiltration campaign, and the supporting units another 1,007. The number of trucks employed in the infiltration system, then, totaled 8,316. During that dry season, the Americans destroyed 4,228 trucks. Losses among the transportation units were a staggering 58.54 percent of the trucks committed to the campaign, with the supporting units losing 33.16 percent. It is a reflection of the intensity of this battle that these truck losses were about 50 percent higher than any other dry season in the ten-year history of the war. Air attacks also killed 2,450 troops assigned to Group 559 and wounded another 4,565.[36]

While their estimates of trucks destroyed roughly matched, American and NVA statistics differed widely in their estimates of supplies delivered to the South. NVA statistics indicate that the system delivered 132,518 tons of supplies in 1972—a figure nearly 50 percent higher than any campaign to that date. Although the figure is for the entire calendar year, it does reflect a significantly different view of the supply system's effectiveness from the American analysis. Further, the NVA history reflects only a 10.12 percent loss rate among the supplies entering the transportation system, the lowest of the four dry-season Commando Hunt campaigns.[37]

The divergence between these U.S. and North Vietnamese figures had strategic significance. The low estimates of NVA logistical levels reinforced the Americans' expectation that the dry-season campaign to follow would basically follow the pattern of other "high point" offensives since Tet—a brief, largely political offensive designed to capture outposts and inflict casualties but not to hold onto captured territory. The American estimate of about 5,000 tons of supplies entering South Vietnam during a five-month dry season supported that conviction. Moreover, it seemed to eliminate the possibility of a broader, lasting and intensive NVA offensive. There would be strict limitations on any campaign fought with such limited supplies.

Beyond its implications for the upcoming campaign, the course of this logistics offensive offers some very powerful lessons in what is termed, in current parlance, asymmetrical conflict, in which the adversaries have entirely different strengths. The outcome would seem to have been preordained. The Americans had at their disposal all the fruits of the world's most advanced military-technical complex, with all the tools developed in eight years of war. Sensors, computers, satellites, advanced weapons and aircraft, all contributed to a network of capabilities that was unified by operational concepts refined through three previous interdiction campaigns. Yet somehow the North Vietnamese countered all this power.

The first factor enabling them to succeed was the nature of the battle, which operated entirely to their advantage. The predominant U.S. weapon was air power, which is most effective when its users have the initiative and can inflict the sudden shock of overwhelming force. In this campaign, however, the Americans were forced to find and engage a multitude of point targets in a gradual battle of attrition, and to react to NVA moves. The nature of the environment, too, favored the North Vietnamese. The campaign took place across vast stretches of jungle and mountainous terrain, which enabled the North Vietnamese to conceal and enlarge their infrastructure and forces.

The North Vietnamese themselves constituted the third major factor in their success. Other observers have commented on their "ant tactics": their lavish use of manpower and their willingness to absorb prohibitive losses. These tactics helped, but they would have done little good without the NVA's extraordinary organizational effectiveness. The tightly knit operation of the *binh tram* system stands in stark contrast to the array of seams visible in the American command structure. The NVA histories illuminate the careful analysis—both of their enemies and of their own shortcomings—that was also characteristic of North Vietnamese operations. They worked to understand American technology and tactics, and they missed no opportunity to complicate their adversaries' task.

For example, the blocking belt strategy lay at the heart of the American interdiction campaign in 1971–1972. Conceptually elegant, theoretically formidable, it nonetheless demanded a degree of operational integration that was beyond American capabilities at the time. Effective belts required the use of a series of weapons in a carefully timed sequence. Each belt consisted of a series of road cuts, usually created by fighter planes using laser-guided weaponry. Follow-on sorties then dropped antipersonnel mines to protect the cuts in the road. Once these were in place, the mix of weapons progressed to magnetic-fused antivehicle systems delivered by the Navy. The sequence concluded with the delivery of sensors that would alert the U.S. command system to NVA breaches or bypasses of the belts.

In practice, it proved very difficult to deliver this specific blend of weapons at the time intervals necessary for the system to work. It was especially difficult to coordinate the efforts of the Air Force and the Navy so as to have the antivehicle munitions delivered at the right place and time. The constant rotation of personnel, in both Air Force and Navy units, made it necessary to continually reeducate both command systems on the sequence and the contributions of the different service forces.[38] The director of Task Force Alpha through this period, Colonel D. L. Evans, noted that during his year in Southeast Asia, TFA had had four commanders, with nine different colonels occupying the top three positions in the organization. Their tenure averaged four months.[39] This constant turnover of the senior leadership inevitably imposed a cost in the effectiveness of planning and operations, with the cost increasing with the complexity of the operation.

By 1971–1972 the flood of new munitions entering the American inventory had slowed, and the Americans fought Commando Hunt VII with the same weapons used in the previous campaign. The North Vietnamese were able to use the expertise developed in earlier campaigns once again, without going through the expensive process of devising and disseminating new techniques through their forces. The Seventh Air Force history of the campaign noted that in places where the NVA had repair teams deployed, they were "able to clear packages delivered in the middle of the day in time to have traffic moving through the minefield by dusk."[40]

The NVA minefield-breaching operations could be rapid, but they used some harrowing methods. The North Vietnamese military journals disseminated information on U.S. systems and their counters. The articles published there provide a vivid record of the techniques used to defuse American weapons in the field. The process began with observers maintaining a lookout for air raids and sounding the alarm. During attacks, the lookouts' task was to "count the number of bombs and rockets which have poured down on the road, and to record how many of them exploded, how many had not exploded, and where they were located."[41]

Once the attack was over, the process of finding, identifying, and disposing of the ordnance began. *Quan Doi Nhan Dan* provided a visual description of each type of bomblet in use at the time and the best means available of responding to each type of attack. For magnetic mines, for example, it advised: "Use a megaphone and warn the people not to run pell-mell, but to remain calm, to leave behind all metallic objects (knives, watches, pens . . .) in their shelters, and one person at a time leave the area of danger and await the technical squad's dismantling of the bomb." For antipersonnel bomblets the advice was: "In case a bomb lands right in a shelter where we are hiding and fails to explode, we must calmly pick it up and throw it out. We must absolutely not jump outside because at that time there may be other bombs falling." Duds were to be collected and moved in exactly the same orientation in which they fell, "without turning them over, which could be very dangerous."[42] Once the bombs were collected, disposal followed: "Just wrap the bomb in strips of cloth soaked with fuel oil, put it in a hole and set it afire; the bomb will automatically break into two parts . . . These bombs can also be destroyed by explosives or burning firewood."[43]

The NVA countermeasures provided no dramatic breakdown in the American system, nor did they overwhelm any single element of the interdiction campaign. They did, however, build enough stress across the system to deny the interdiction campaign much of its theoretical effectiveness. Every step they took added to the friction within the U.S. military machine, reducing MACV's ability to marshal its power rapidly to counter NVA moves. On the whole, the North Vietnamese earned a Pyrrhic victory in this campaign—successfully moving their supplies into position in the face of determined resistance, but paying a high price to do so.

There is one last element to this story. During this campaign Seventh Air Force operated under the command of General John D. "Jack" Lavelle. Never a confidant of the Air Force chief of staff, General John D. Ryan, Lavelle had gained his position through his work on the early development and deployment of the Igloo White system. In the months of the Commando Hunt VII campaign, Seventh Air Force conducted reconnaissance missions in southern North Vietnam. These sorties were flown under very restrictive rules of engagement, permitting ordnance delivery only in response to fire from NVA units. Early in Lavelle's tenure, Abrams sent him a message outlining his interpretation of the rules: "Interlocking and mutually supporting NVN air defenses constitute unacceptable hazard to air crews attempting to identify a particular SAM/AAA firing site. Accordingly, on occurrence of any SAM or AAA firing or activation against our aircraft, it is considered appropriate for escort forces to direct immediate protective reaction strikes against any identifiable element of the firing/activated air defense complex."[44]

Lavelle decided to operate under the assumption that the NVA air defense system was "activated" every time American aircraft flew into the country, and that this activation constituted grounds for lethal response against any element of the NVA defenses. He and his predecessors had been encouraged to interpret the rules of engagement liberally, and he believed that his decision was implicitly approved by his supervisors right up the chain of command: Abrams, McCain, Moorer, and Laird had all urged him to use the most aggressive possible interpretation of the rules. However, his decision required Seventh Air Force to falsify routine mission reports summarizing the defenses' reaction to sorties. An enlisted intelligence debriefer at Udorn RTAFB detected the falsification and wrote to Senator Harold E. Hughes about it. The letter triggered an Air Force investigation of the events and eventually led to Ryan's decision to relieve Lavelle. Ryan recalled Lavelle to Washington on March 23, right at the

conclusion of the Commando Hunt VII campaign and only a few days before the North Vietnamese would open their offensive.[45]

Much remains obscure about this episode, especially with regard to the
responsibility of those above and below Lavelle in the chain of command.
Certainly he felt that he had been "hung out to dry" by his superiors; he
had expected their support, but when the criticism arrived, they were nowhere to be found.[46] Two aspects of this story are of interest here. First,
the Lavelle episode could only have happened in a cancerous political-military climate, in which the relationship between civilian policymakers and
their military commanders had become dangerously distant. Obscure rules
of engagement, with creeping implicit reinterpretation over time, are a
recipe for disaster. Nixon was happy enough to strike against the North
Vietnamese, but he feared the domestic price he would have to pay for an
all-out attack. Kissinger was concerned that Lavelle's strikes would disrupt
his complicated web of negotiations, international diplomacy, and calculated military action. Unaware of these overriding considerations, Lavelle
found himself shorn of allies when called to account for the attacks.

Of more direct interest, his removal left Seventh Air Force without
a commander during the critical first days of the Easter Offensive. His
deputy, Lieutenant General Marvin McNickle, was an experienced commander and very familiar with operations in South Vietnam. With
Lavelle's recall, Ryan planned to place McNickle in command of Seventh
Air Force. However, the emergency of early April was to task the command to its utmost. Events might have proceeded differently had Lavelle
still been on the scene, able to draw on the experience of a year in
command.

5

THE INITIAL SURGES

Within days of the March 30 opening of the offensive, the North Vietnamese had committed their full strength of armor, artillery, and masses of infantry, first along the DMZ, then on a second front north of Saigon, directly threatening the capital. In both sectors the initial attacks swept away the South Vietnamese defenders, unable to withstand the shock and mass of a combined-arms assault. The success of the offensive would rest on the North Vietnamese ability to sustain its momentum, generating the whirlwind of effects envisioned in the Politburo's strategy, to culminate in the overthrow of the Thieu regime. Conversely, the fate of South Vietnam would rest on the RVNAF's ability to regain its balance under attack, and on the ability of American forces to support the South Vietnamese with the full weight of air and naval firepower.

The initial attacks in military region (MR) I, just south of the DMZ, struck a ring of firebases situated in an arc extending westward from the coast, then swinging south at the pivot point of Camp Carroll, in the foothills east of the Truong Son mountains. In that area the defenses were manned by the newly created 3rd ARVN Division, commanded by General Vu Van Giai. Giai faced a series of challenges as he sought to mount an effective defense. Within his own division he had the normal challenges of building an effective and cohesive unit from scratch while conducting combat operations. The fact that South Vietnam was nearing the bottom of its manpower pool magnified the difficulty of his task. Among the American advisors in the region, it was generally accepted that the 56th and 57th Regiments of the new division were largely formed from enlisted men who had deserted from other commands, and who were now stationed near the DMZ to deter further attempts at desertion.[1]

Giai also exercised operational control of two Vietnamese Marine Corps (VNMC) brigades, the 147th and 258th. This arrangement provided Giai with well-trained and -equipped forces, which he positioned along the western approaches to the coastal plain. However, the decisions to station marine units in this sector and to place them under the command of an ARVN general also created a significant rift in the command structure. Interservice issues were not unique to the South Vietnamese, but the ARVN did seem to raise them to new heights of complication. The command issues that had crippled the Lam Son 719 operation persisted, as VNMC officers maintained the practice of checking back through their own chain of command before executing orders coming from their nominal commanders in the ARVN.[2]

Giai had built his defensive strategy around the firebases arcing westward and south, protecting the coastal plain and the logistical backbone of the area, National Route 1. The firebases offered interlocking fields of fire commanding the avenues of attack. However, they also offered fixed targets for any attacker able to concentrate enough artillery forces to overwhelm South Vietnamese counterbattery fire. Through most of the war, as the Americans faced a light guerrilla force, these bases were often effective in supporting troops in contact with the enemy. The experience of Lam Son 719 more than a year earlier, however, had demonstrated that this operational concept was outdated. During their incursion into Laos, the South Vietnamese had used firebases to secure the flanks of the westward movement of their attacking columns. In that operation, the bases had proved to be highly vulnerable to indirect fire and direct attack. These developments were noted both in the theater and in Washington, but the gap between observations by the Americans and decisive action by the ARVN grew wider and wider as the U.S. combat role diminished.[3]

The NVA artillery barrage struck as the 3rd Division conducted a major rotation of its regiments, swapping their defensive positions along the northern arc of the ring. The opening salvos caught one of the 56th Regi-

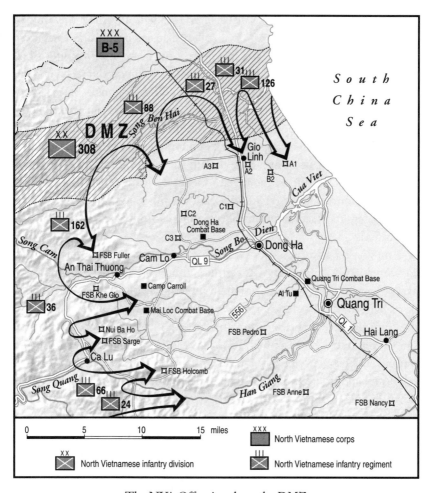

The NVA Offensive along the DMZ

ment's three battalions en route to its new position in the northwest quadrant of the ring of fortifications. The effect was devastating. Losing contact with its regimental headquarters, the battalion simply dissolved before ever facing North Vietnamese ground forces. With the first salvos the North Vietnamese artillery also established its dominance over its South

Vietnamese counterpart. As Turley later recalled, all along the ring of firebases, "back within the ARVN artillery battery positions, crews were abandoning their guns and seeking protection from the incoming steel. South Vietnamese gun crews, unaccustomed to being on the receiving end of an artillery attack, were hesitant to remain on their guns."

At this moment of crisis, Giai could have profited from strong command at the corps level helping him coordinate his forces and ensuring that he had all available support. This support was not forthcoming, however, nor would it be at any time during the fighting that would follow. The I Corps commander, Lieutenant General Hoang Xuan Lam, had always been more highly regarded as an administrator than as a combat commander, and his limitations became increasingly clear as the fighting intensified.

Lam's senior advisor, Major General "Fritz" Kroesen, did what he could to keep MACV informed of the situation and to marshal the firepower available from U.S. forces. At frequent intervals he dispatched situation reports back to MACV, describing events and anticipating the next moves by the NVA. For the first two days of the onslaught, with only probing attacks by NVA infantry, he described the intense and persistent artillery fire and outlined the problems he faced in obtaining American fire support. He had requested additional B-52 and fighter strikes but was frustrated by a combination of dismal weather, which restricted his air support, and poor targeting information from the ARVN.

By the afternoon of March 31, with the attack a day old, Kroesen was able to send in a more comprehensive survey of the situation. It had become clear that this was a major effort by the NVA—not harassment and not a diversion, as previously suspected, but the opening of the long-awaited major offensive. Kroesen identified three axes of attack: south from the demilitarized zone, southeast from the road network in the western DMZ, and eastward from Laos along Route 9. By this time NVA tanks had appeared in the northwest, and ARVN firebases had begun to fall under the onslaught.[4]

He reported that the South Vietnamese performance seemed to be mixed, with some units conducting orderly withdrawals even under heavy pressure, others fleeing in disorder, still others holding their positions. Clearly the situation would demand maximum use of American air forces.

Kroesen declared a tactical emergency to gain priority on air support. Bad weather, however, continued to restrict air activity. The high-performance U.S. aircraft could not work beneath the low ceilings that were plaguing air operations; only the South Vietnamese, still using their old propeller-driven A-1 Skyraiders, were able to work in the marginal weather conditions.

The situation deteriorated rapidly over the first few days of April. Kroesen's report of April 1 featured the same discouraging themes as those of the previous days. "Enemy forces in Quang Tri retain the initiative," he stated. In this they were taking full advantage of their extremely accurate heavy artillery, which Kroesen considered responsible for their achievements thus far. Bad as the situation was at this point, however, Kroesen expected worse to follow, since "the enemy does not appear to have committed the bulk of his infantry. Heavier ground attacks are anticipated against the DMZ and crescent strongpoints." Finally, the North Vietnamese artillery continued to target American command centers, and had severely damaged communications capabilities for the 3rd ARVN Division. As before, Kroesen noted the problems in his air support, which continued to be hampered seriously by low ceilings and bad weather.[5] To some extent, however, the naval forces assembling offshore were beginning to compensate for the problems in air support. On April 2 Kroesen reported that three destroyers had conducted 37 firing missions, despite North Vietnamese counterfire that had driven the ships 10,000 meters offshore.

On Saturday, April 1, as the NVA pressure grew more intense, Abrams reported back to Washington that "the situation in Quang Tri is bad and it is going to get worse."[6] He could now identify the strength and primary axes of the offensive. The NVA 270th and 31st Regiments were attacking southward from the eastern DMZ. The 308th NVA Division was operating on their west. The 304th NVA Division was attacking eastward from its base areas in the northwestern and western sectors of Quang Tri Province. And, southwest of Hue, along the traditional invasion corridor from the A Shau Valley, the 6th Regiment and the 324Bth Division were beginning to pressure the ARVN defenses. The infantry was supported by elements of two armored regiments, an artillery regiment, and an air defense division. It was an overwhelming force to wield against an untried ARVN division, particularly given the surprise of the attack.

The crescendo of violence reached a climax on April 2. On that Easter Sunday, the North Vietnamese finally committed their infantry and armored forces in strength, and the ARVN's ring of firebases collapsed under the pressure. This was perhaps the most chaotic and discouraging day of the war to this point, the day in which the fears of a South Vietnamese collapse seemed closest to reality. The NVA pressure buckled the defensive system in MR I, sending defenders and refugees streaming toward the south along Route 1.

The most dramatic and damaging attacks fell on Camp Carroll. These began in the late morning, and wave after wave followed into the afternoon. At 1520 the senior advisor at the post, Lieutenant Colonel William Camper, radioed the 3rd ARVN Division's forward command post, notifying them that the garrison was surrendering and that he was evacuating. It was a devastating blow to the defenses. The camp was the most powerful position along the ring of firebases, commanding twenty-two artillery pieces and masses of ammunition. This equipment would now fall to the NVA, requiring a costly diversion of B-52 sorties to prevent its use in the next series of attacks.

The loss undermined the I Corps defensive strategy, leaving the remnants of the defensive perimeter untenable. The psychological effects were equally damaging. It was clear that the 56th Regiment had surrendered well before the NVA attack had made capitulation necessary. When the American advisors reached friendly lines, the full outline of the story came clear: some members of the regimental leadership had been defeatist at best, communist agents at worst, and they had engineered the camp's surrender. This betrayal raised the specter of North Vietnamese penetration of the ARVN command structure. The next day, less than twenty-four hours after surrendering Camp Carroll, 56th Regiment commander LTC Pham Van Dinh broadcast an appeal to ARVN soldiers, calling on them to refuse their orders and go over to the National Liberation Front.[7]

A second drama played out that afternoon a few miles east of Camp Carroll, along the Cua Viet River. The first appearance of NVA tanks panicked the ARVN forces, raising the prospect of the NVA conducting a lightning thrust down the coastal plain and into Hue. In fact, to the deep surprise of the ARVN leadership, the major weight of the NVA assault flowed along this route, directly south from the DMZ. This armored spearhead threatened to overrun the garrison at Dong Ha, sweep through the weak defenses holding Ai Tu, and take Quang Tri during this first disorganized rout of the ARVN defenses. With the defense forces in disarray, terrain features became the best prospect of halting the attack. The Cua Viet lay immediately in the path of the armored column, with the bridge at Dong Ha offering the NVA an opportunity to avoid the delay and disruption that the river barrier would otherwise impose. For the Americans and the ARVN it was imperative to delay the advance. Destroying the bridge would prevent the NVA armored units from crossing the river.

And yet the decision to destroy the bridge was slow in coming. There were substantive reasons for the delay. Refugees streamed across the structure, fleeing the battle. There were still South Vietnamese units and troops north of the river that would be cut off if it were blown. The bridge would be essential to any future ARVN counterattack. However, the delay was more a product of indecision and confusion than of any rational calculation. It took time for the South Vietnamese leadership to decide to blow the bridge, and then more time to find a unit able to do so. By the late afternoon, with NVA tanks on the northern bank of the river, Marine advisor Captain John Ripley took matters into his own hands. In an astonishing display of courage, he worked his way along the underside of the bridge, within sight of the NVA forces, placing explosives and preparing the bridge for destruction. At 1630, after six hours of delay and frustration, the charges detonated, destroying the Dong Ha bridge. The North Vietnamese tanks, unable to cross, hesitated and then turned west toward the next bridge at Cam Lo.

Still another drama opened later that afternoon, four miles above the DMZ, as a B-52 strike force neared its targets north of Camp Carroll. At 1702, five batteries of the NVA 365th Air Defense Division loosed a salvo of thirteen missiles at the force, one detonating directly underneath an EB-66 electronic intelligence aircraft escorting the bombers. Struck at an altitude of 24,000 feet, the aircraft nosed over into a 70-degree dive, flames trailing from both wings. At 18,000 feet the left wing broke off and the aircraft disintegrated. Five men died. The sixth crew member parachuted safely to earth, seven hundred yards northeast of the Cam Lo bridge, in the midst of the North Vietnamese invasion force. Thus began the eleven-day saga of the rescue of Lieutenant Colonel Iceal Hambleton, the sole survivor from the downed EB-66.

As he descended under his parachute, Hambleton radioed an O-2 FAC aircraft, Bilk 34, orbiting directly below him, and the FAC watched as Hambleton landed in a rice paddy north of the Cua Viet River. Bilk 34's pilot, Lieutenant Bill Jankowski, immediately took up the search and rescue (SAR) mission, calling on the emergency frequency to gather up any forces in the area able to help in a "quick snatch." He pulled together a rescue force of helicopters and A-1 Skyraiders, and they made a valiant but unsuccessful attempt to pull Hambleton out of an area dominated by NVA forces. One of the helicopters was destroyed, and the others turned away. In the dusk, the Skyraiders continued to attack the North Vietnamese guns, guided by Hambleton as he coolly called in air strikes around his position. Later the flight of Skyraiders recovered at Danang, where Capt. Don Morse, the leader, coordinated the next day's effort. After his long day he turned in for the night but found little rest: "We set up for a first light effort . . . As this was Easter and Lent was over I had a beer and tried to go to bed. Sleep did not come, as I lay awake shaking from fear most of the night."[8]

Through those hours of darkness, word of the rescue effort reached the Joint Search and Rescue Center in Saigon, triggering the most controversial decision of this lengthy operation. On learning of the rescue attempt, the duty controller imposed a no-fire zone with a radius of 27 kilometers around the downed pilot. This was a reflexive imposition of procedures established long before this crisis. No one in the rescue center had any idea that there was a major invasion in progress, and it seemed natural to clear out the airspace to protect the downed airman and give rescue forces freedom of action.

This pattern had generally worked well in previous years, as most American losses occurred over remote areas of Laos. Under the circumstances existing on April 2, with the chaotic decay of the South Vietnamese defenses, the decision had a series of disastrous effects. Some were direct, enabling North Vietnamese units to maneuver free of counterfire from ARVN and U.S. units. There were also indirect effects that were probably just as significant. The no-fire restrictions imposed another layer of confusion on the coordination among the various allied units involved in the defenses. This came at a time when the confusion was already ample. The restrictions, and their arbitrary imposition by higher headquarters, fed the feelings of frustration and betrayal that already infected both the command elements of the 3rd ARVN and the division's American advisors. It fed the pervasive feeling that those in the chain of command above the division had no idea of the ferocity of the battle or the tenuousness of the situation. Most of all, the decision exemplified the gap in commitment between the allies fighting to hold off the NVA attackers. It seemed incredible to the South Vietnamese that the U.S. command structure could jeopardize the entire ARVN force in order to facilitate its rescue of a single American pilot.[9]

This dislocation in command would continue. The rescue effort would reach epic proportions, with the sustained courage of the air crews in stark contrast to the atrophied and ineffective command system controlling their operations. Day after day the SAR forces returned to Cam Lo, suppressing the defenses and committing helicopters to rescue attempts, only to fail as the NVA gunners exacted a prohibitive price. The crews were unaware that they were facing a full NVA division, with an integrated command system, in the midst of an invasion corridor. The Seventh Air Force intelligence system, ponderous at the best of times, failed to get the word out that the situation along the DMZ had fundamentally changed. The command chain, similarly, failed to support the rescuers as they continued their effort.

Over the years the NVA had grown intimately familiar with American rescue operations. They understood exactly the tactics and formations that the SAR forces would employ, and they viewed this as a great opportunity to punish the U.S. forces. The NVA established a "flak trap" in the area, thickening their antiaircraft defenses to take advantage of the situation. One American pilot reported: "The first day and night of the SAR . . . the ground fire was heavy but undisciplined. On the following days, the first line troops were in the field. They had excellent communications. Sam calls were driving us into the small arms threat. Ground fire was accurate and well disciplined. (ie they waited for the best opportunity. It would be quiet for hours then the whole world would erupt.) The NVA were very definitely monitoring and jamming our communications."[10] The Americans continued to send forces into the grinding battle of attrition until, on April 6, the inevitable occurred: Jolly Green 66, an HH-53 rescue helicopter, went down with the loss of six men. The Americans finally turned to a ground-based rescue operation, miraculously recovering Hambleton and another downed pilot on April 9. For this feat, Lieutenant Colonel Mike Norris of the Marines received the Medal of Honor.

By the time of Hambleton's rescue, the NVA offensive along the DMZ had settled into an uneasy lull. The attack stalled on April 3, undone by the NVA's inability to feed supplies forward to its advancing troops. This was the first occurrence of a pattern that would be frequently repeated in the weeks ahead: the NVA paying a steep price to achieve a breakthrough, then failing to maintain operational momentum as its logistics and its command structure proved inadequate to the demands of conventional combined-arms warfare.

As the attack along the DMZ stalled, however, the NVA shocked the U.S. and ARVN defenders with a second combined-arms offensive, this one aimed directly at South Vietnam's capital. Seizing the initiative, the North Vietnamese opened their operations north of Saigon with a well-orchestrated series of attacks under the leadership of the Central Office for South Vietnam (COSVN), the communist headquarters controlling military operations in an area roughly corresponding to South Vietnam's Military Regions III and IV. The opening moves resembled a chess match, with the North Vietnamese playing the white pieces and able to force the action as they desired. Within days they crushed the outer ring of Saigon's defenses and appeared to pose a threat to the capital itself.

The major axis of operations lay along Route 13, the highway extending northward from Saigon toward the Cambodian border, passing through Binh Long Province en route to the frontier. Sixty miles north of Saigon the road ran through the provincial capital of An Loc, with a peacetime population of 25,000 people. Still farther north along Route 13 was the district capital of Loc Ninh, ten kilometers south of the border with Cambodia. West of Binh Long lay Tay Ninh Province, about five times as populous as Binh Long.

This region, which the North Vietnamese called Eastern Cochin China, was pivotal to their plans for victory. As the Politburo and the high command first planned the 1972 campaign, they designated this region as the primary axis of attack, with the two other attacks, along the DMZ and in the central highlands, as supporting efforts. Pham Hung, a Politburo member and COSVN's director, would orchestrate the offensive under the Politburo's direct and detailed guidance. Military command of this assault, which COSVN code-named the Nguyen Hue Offensive, would be exercised through the B2 front, the communist military headquarters controlling operations in the COSVN area. General Tran Van Tra would command the COSVN offensive.

It was clear from simple geography that the decision to make this the primary theater entailed a huge risk. The logistics pipeline for forces in this region extended along the Ho Chi Minh Trail all the way across Cambodia and Laos to North Vietnam, and it was under attack through most of that distance. During earlier portions of the war, this theater had been supplied by seaborne infiltration through Cambodia; the closing of that route in 1970 had vastly complicated the task of the NVA logisticians. Given the invariable preoccupation of the North Vietnamese with issues of supply, the political-military advantages of an attack here had to be overwhelming. Certainly an attack southward toward Saigon offered the quickest, most vital threat to the Thieu regime. It was a threat that could not be ignored. The South Vietnamese military could be counted upon to respond with whatever means were necessary, leaving openings for exploitation elsewhere. If properly prepared, too, the offensive would have the advantage of strategic surprise. U.S. and ARVN intelligence projections for a North Vietnamese offensive sometimes focused on an attack in the Highlands, sometimes along the DMZ, but never on a major assault in this region. As late as March 30, an intelligence estimate for Kissinger and the NSC projected nothing more than intensified terrorism and rocket attacks around Saigon.

The area lay within South Vietnam's MR III, which extended from the southwestern edge of the central highlands to the eastern edge of the Mekong Delta. The ten provinces of MR III fell under the command of Lieutenant General Nguyen Van Minh, who had at his disposal three ARVN divisions and three South Vietnamese Ranger groups. The Rangers constituted his corps reserve, with the three ARVN divisions securing well-defined sectors within the region. The 25th ARVN worked along the western three provinces, including Tay Ninh; the 5th ARVN secured the central and northern provinces, including Binh Long; and the 18th ARVN's area of responsibility extended through the eastern and southeastern areas of the region.[11]

MR III bordered Saigon, so President Thieu was concerned more with Minh's loyalty than with his aggressiveness; as an American assessment noted: "It is apparent that MR-III is the most political of corps."[12] Minh had assumed command in February 1971 upon the death of his predecessor, Lieutenant General Do Cao Tri, in a helicopter crash. Tri had been notably aggressive, though also notably corrupt; his death brought into command an officer much more notable for political skill than for capability on the battlefield.

Upon taking command Minh quickly reversed the aggressive strategy pursued by Tri, who had attempted to keep communist forces in the border area off balance through actions against the NVA base areas. Minh instead executed a strategy of standoff defense at the border, forfeiting the initiative to the communist forces operating in Cambodia.[13] Minh's passivity contrasted sharply with the flamboyant energy of his senior American advisor, Major General James F. Hollingsworth. An armor expert and an old friend of Abrams, Hollingsworth was in his second tour in Southeast Asia. He was profane, tireless, and aggressive, a prototypical combat commander, but less well-suited to his role as senior advisor. Beneath the bluster and profanity, however, lay a thoughtful, analytical mind with the benefit of a previous tour in theater and combat experience extending back to World War II, when he had served under Abrams.[14]

The NVA plan would be revealed only with the opening of the offensive. As noted earlier, COSVN was able to capitalize on its possession of the initiative to shape the opening days of the campaign and gain the advantage in the early fighting. The campaign plan had been designed to reinforce the South Vietnamese commanders' belief that Tay Ninh would be the primary target of the NVA offensive. Two independent regiments, the 271st and the 24th, would open the campaign with attacks in Tay Ninh Province. These attacks were to shield the movement of the primary forces into position, and to divert South Vietnamese attention from the primary attack axis along Route 13.

The NVA plan began to unfold on April 1, as the 24th Regiment attacked Fire Support Base Lac Long, a small outpost near the Cambodian border northwest of Tay Ninh. The attack, supported by tanks, overwhelmed the base within hours. Minh responded by withdrawing his forces from all the advanced outposts along the Cambodian frontier in order to consolidate these units in defensible positions. However, his decision also enabled the North Vietnamese to trigger a series of ambushes as the ARVN forces withdrew. The most successful of these ambushes was conducted by the 271st Regiment north of Tay Ninh.

As these diversionary attacks unfolded in Tay Ninh Province, three divisions moved forward into their attack positions to the east, in Binh Long Province. The first blow fell north of Loc Ninh on April 4, as the VC 5th Division ambushed an ARVN force retreating from its border outpost into the city. The VC division mauled the ARVN force, with very few survivors reaching the town. By nightfall on April 4, the NVA forces reached Loc Ninh. They opened their assault early the next day. As Hollingsworth later recalled: "Enemy activity included ground attacks of long duration (three to four hours) supported by a large volume of rockets (107's and

122's)."[15] Late that afternoon, 105-mm and 155-mm artillery, probably ARVN equipment captured in Cambodia, supported ground assaults on three sides of the city.

As had occurred at Camp Carroll only a few days before, the NVA attack on Loc Ninh aimed directly at a systemic weakness of the ARVN: its leadership. The garrison commander, Colonel Nguyen Cong Vinh, had no confidence that his troops could withstand an attack, and he aligned his units to improve his own chances of surviving an assault, at the expense

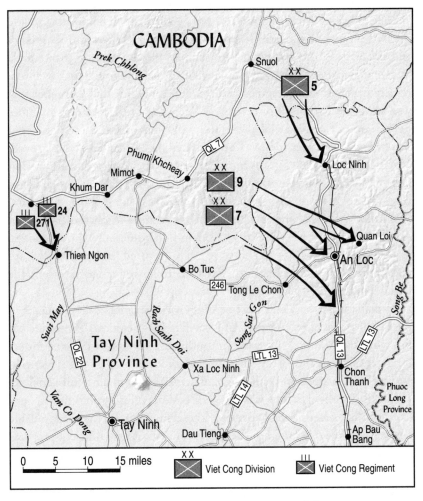

COSVN's Offensive in Military Region III

of scattering and weakening the garrison's defenses. As the NVA attack approached and finally began, American advisor Captain Mark "Zippo" Smith assumed a leading role in the defense, coordinating air support and attempting to inject a fighting spirit into Vinh and his staff.

Waves of NVA attacks overwhelmed the garrison, with massive artillery bombardments followed by tank-infantry assaults, and with the defenses relying on air support to withstand the pressure. As night fell, Vinh's leadership, weak at the best of times, continued to fade as he planned his surrender with his staff and subordinates. The attacks intensified during the night of April 6–7, despite the punishing losses inflicted by American aircraft. That morning there was a brief lull in the U.S. air attacks, and the NVA took advantage of it, swarming into the compounds with tanks and infantry. In the absence of air support there was little to be done; in Hollingsworth's words: "I was unable to do anything about it except remain overhead encouraging the defenders and duck the .51 caliber that was being fired from all directions."[16] After the break in coverage, more fighter aircraft arrived and drove the tanks out of the compounds, but the damage had been done. The defenses had been largely destroyed. Hollingsworth decided it was time to evacuate the American advisors, but helicopters were unable to fight their way through the antiaircraft guns ringing the compounds, even with air strikes suppressing their fire. Hollingsworth lost contact with the advisors at 1846 on the evening of April 7. Of the seven American advisors in Loc Ninh, only one evaded the NVA to make his way to An Loc; the NVA captured four, including Captain Smith, who miraculously survived multiple wounds to return to the United States in February 1973.

In many ways the attack on Loc Ninh was a smaller-scale precursor of the fate that was soon to befall An Loc. The NVA tactics, defined and refined through the preceding winter, outlined a very precise recipe for attacks on fortified towns. The first step was to establish a tight siege ring, cutting land routes and deploying antiaircraft units to close off aerial resupply. Once the garrison was isolated, NVA artillery would destroy enemy supplies, defenses, and artillery. A blocking force on the roads outside the city would cut off the flow of reinforcements. After sufficient preparation, a massive artillery preparation would then lead to a tank-infantry assault. When well executed, this was a formidable sequence; it was especially effective against defenders who were unprepared both materially and psychologically for the new elements of the NVA offensive strategy. At Loc Ninh the defenders were subjected to an artillery barrage exceeding

2,000 rounds per day, a bombardment completely beyond anything experienced before by ARVN units in that region. The recipe provided a high degree of tactical and technological surprise, which operated to the great advantage of the attackers in the opening days of the campaign.

The American response at Loc Ninh likewise established patterns that would again be evident in An Loc. Masses of Air Force and Navy fighters responded to the attack, providing critical firepower. The area offered a great opportunity for Navy crews to refine their tactics before proceeding into higher-threat areas to the north. AC-130 gunships, able to operate in the relatively low-threat environment of MR III, cruised over the battlefield, providing their unique combination of endurance, high-technology sensors, and firepower.

In fact, there was so much airpower engaged in this battle that the command and control system proved incapable of taking full advantage of all the available capabilities. Gunship pilots reported bitterly on the priority given fighter aircraft by forward air controllers. Neither the FACs nor the regional Direct Air Support Center had any real idea of what gunships could do or how they were equipped. The gunships arriving on station were frequently sent away to orbit while fighters conducted attacks, on occasion spending a whole sortie orbiting in frustration, their firepower unused. As one observer put it, the air control system was "saturated by airpower."[17] The tactical aircraft, too, were present in such numbers that often the FACs on station were unable to work them into the attack sequence, or control them during their attacks. One Navy report commented that through these early weeks of the offensive, in fully 40 percent of all fighter strikes the fighters released their ordnance without the guidance of a FAC to spot and prioritize targets.[18] It was a wasteful, inefficient, and ineffective way to employ air forces. There was nothing new about wasteful employment of air power in Southeast Asia, but the ineffectiveness at this point was very costly. With the NVA on the attack, with defenders desperately pressed to hold on, every wasted sortie mattered.

As the 5th VC Division overwhelmed Loc Ninh, the 9th VC and 7th NVA divisions moved into their staging areas farther south. Meanwhile the South Vietnamese, too, prepared for the next phase of the offensive, at all levels: strategic, operational, and tactical. The attack on Loc Ninh convinced General Minh that An Loc would be the major focus of the offensive, and on April 5 he deployed the 5th ARVN Division headquarters and two Ranger battalions into the city.

The following day, with the offensive already breaking on two fronts and the central highlands still at risk, President Thieu convened a meeting of his national security council. He summoned his corps commanders to assess the military situation and to decide on commitment of the national reserves. There were not many reserves left. Most had gone to I Corps in the first days of the offensive, as the northern firebases fell and the threat to Hue became evident. Thieu decided to reinforce MR III with the remaining airborne brigade and with an ARVN division from MR IV. Initially, he decided to send this division to MR I; his concern that the communists would establish a provisional capital in An Loc led him to reverse the decision and commit the division to MR III.[19]

This was an almost unprecedented move. ARVN divisions normally operated exclusively within their own areas of responsibility. They were almost wholly focused on territorial defense. Just as important, their families were from their operating areas, and their whole social and military construct was founded on operations in their usual area. After some deliberation, the IV Corps commander, Lieutenant General Ngo Quang Truong, decided to send the 21st ARVN north to MR III, expecting territorial forces, along with American air power, to compensate for their absence from MR IV.

Meanwhile, in An Loc itself, the 5th ARVN Division, Ranger, and regional forces worked feverishly to strengthen the defenses. The North Vietnamese noted that, after these upgrades, "barbed wire perimeter fences encircled the town and each of the individual defensive areas inside the city. Each position also had a network of earthen berm walls 1.2–1.4 meters high and 0.6–0.8 meters wide, into which were built blockhouses and fighting positions."[20] They considered An Loc "a relatively large, solid, and powerful military strongpoint," but noted the problems facing its defenders. The city was "totally isolated. The roads, and most importantly Route 13 leading up from the south, had all been cut, our antiaircraft firepower dominated the skies."[21] Hollingsworth permitted inessential American advisors to leave the city, but he left key personnel, including the senior advisor to the 5th ARVN Division, Colonel William Miller, in place.

Miller's relationship with his advisee, General Le Van Hung, exemplified the complexity of interactions between the Americans and their allies as U.S. involvement waned. A veteran of World War II and Korea and now on his third tour in Vietnam, Miller had developed a deep-seated skepticism about the ARVN that was matched by Hung's skepticism about U.S. advisors. One of Miller's subordinates later recalled that early in their association Hung had told Miller that he had already had many advisors, and that he himself had known more about war than any of them. A relationship that started on that note, and then underwent deep and continuous stress, could hardly be expected to grow stronger over time, and in fact the two men remained on rocky terms throughout Miller's tour. Hung rarely asked Miller's advice, and often did not keep his advisor informed of his tactical decisions as the battle matured.[22]

With the preliminary phases of the campaign complete, COSVN tightened the noose around An Loc. On April 7 Minh ordered the 1st Airborne Brigade to move northward up Route 13 to An Loc, but the brigade was quickly halted in its tracks by a blocking position established by the 7th NVA Division. The blocking position was only 15 kilometers from An Loc, but those 15 kilometers were to become a terribly long and expensive stretch of road for the South Vietnamese. That same day the 9th VC Division began its operations in the An Loc area, driving two ARVN companies away from the Quan Loi airstrip east of the city. With these attacks the NVA and the VC had cut off both road and air traffic. They had set the stage for a classic siege operation, and had gained high ground dominating the city from the east.

All that remained to be done before the attack was for the NVA to move its supplies into position around the city. But here the offensive followed the unvarying pattern of NVA operations in this campaign. The COSVN planners expected the fall of the border outposts to take a week, during which time they could deploy supplies forward.[23] The unexpected rapidity of their advance threw them off balance and turned to the advantage of the ARVN defenders. The NVA hesitation outside An Loc gave the ARVN time to reinforce and to strengthen the city's defenses. The ARVN took advantage of this brief lull to deploy another regiment into the city by helicopter on April 11 and 12. Gradually, though, the ring around An Loc tightened as the NVA built its forces in the area. Beginning on April 7, the ARVN resupplied the garrison using CH-47 helicopters. That ended on April 12 with the loss of a CH-47. For the next week, C-123s air-dropped supplies, until on the fortieth sortie the NVA shot down one of the aircraft on its low-level delivery run. The city was now isolated by air and by road.

Over the next few days the NVA launched probing attacks, testing the ARVN defenses, in preparation for the major assault. Finally, during the night of 12–13 April, the 9th VC Division launched the attack with an artillery barrage shortly after midnight. As dawn approached, Colonel Miller reported tanks west of town. Over the next hours the attack developed on all sides. By 0700 Miller reported that the attackers had broken through on the northeast side of town, with tanks, armored personnel carriers, and infantry hitting the ARVN defenders' base camp. Gunships and fighters roared overhead, supporting the defenders, until about 0945, when Miller reported that the attacking columns appeared to be withdrawing. As they pulled back, Hollingsworth called on B-52s to pound the attackers.

The North Vietnamese attack had failed, undone by the inexperience of the armored forces and by the NVA's inability to coordinate the movements of the tanks and infantry. The appearance of the tanks had dissolved the defenses, but this initial advantage slipped away as the errors of the armored forces began to add up. Separated from their supporting infantry, the tanks drove straight into the city in two parallel columns, presenting an ideal target. Soon the hunters became the hunted, as the ARVN defenders tracked down and destroyed the tanks, one after another. Eight tanks entered An Loc; one returned. By the late morning, ARVN soldiers were competing for opportunities to destroy the tanks that had filled them with fear before dawn.

Despite the tactical failures and the loss of the armored force, the NVA had gained control of the northern half of the city, and still threatened to overwhelm the defenders. As night fell, with no move to evacuate the population or the American advisors, Seventh Air Force coordinated the air cover for the city: gunships on station continuously, 36 fighter sorties with more available on request, and B-52 strikes throughout the night.

Meanwhile the North Vietnamese Politburo, assessing the situation in the relative security of Hanoi, directed COSVN to resume the attack quickly. A cable to Pham Hung provided very specific guidance to COSVN and its military commanders: "No matter what difficulties you face, you must strive to concentrate your forces to make a resolute and determined effort to capture the Binh Long Province capital, no matter what it takes. The capture of the Binh Long capital will not only have a great impact in Cochin China, it will have a tremendous impact on our entire endeavor."[24] Given this direction, General Tra scheduled the climactic attack for April 15, only two days after the first all-out assault, with little time to reconstitute his forces or prepare for the complexities of this combined-arms operation. On April 14, as artillery pounded the city, eight more T-54 tanks moved into position for another attack. This was the 8th

Tank Company of the 20th Armored Battalion, a unit that had never before seen combat. It was now to be thrown into an attack on a prepared enemy in an urban setting. This was a tough way to start. Meanwhile the ARVN inserted an airborne brigade onto Windy Hill, three kilometers from An Loc. From there the troops worked their way into the city to reinforce the hard-pressed garrison.

The NVA attack followed a script almost identical to that used two days before: once again an artillery barrage followed by an attack at dawn, with the tanks driving from the north in two columns. The NVA committed a tank company with nine T-54s to the operation, but two broke down on the way—one throwing a track, the other running out of oil. The seven remaining tanks attacked at 0600 and within an hour had penetrated the ARVN defenses on the north side of town.[25] By 0913 the NVA had worked to within 200 meters of Miller's command post. At 1330 he radioed that the situation remained "very critical . . . Need help—this situation is big!"[26] Through the day, however, air forces continued to flow into the area, controlled by FACs operating in each sector of the attack and pummeling the North Vietnamese. By midafternoon all but one of the tanks had been destroyed, but the attack continued. Finally, in the late afternoon, the last surviving tank retreated from the city.

The defenders of An Loc had withstood a terrible test, turning back two massed assaults on their positions. The immediate crisis was at an end, but the situation remained grim. With the opening moves of the campaign having been made, the NVA forces settled into a siege, awaiting reinforcements and relying on their artillery to wear down the garrison's strength. The defenders dug in under the constant barrage of NVA fire. With the garrison isolated and NVA artillery dominating the surrounding terrain, the defenders' survival would rest almost entirely on air forces, both for firepower and for resupply. The besieging North Vietnamese deployed an antiaircraft ring of unprecedented density around the city in an attempt to deny this support. The fate of An Loc in the weeks ahead would depend on the ability of the air forces to accomplish their missions in a new, severely hostile environment.

6

NIXON TAKES CHARGE

The first word of the invasion to reach the White House arrived in Haig's office on the morning of March 30, when the Pentagon forwarded a message from MACV. Kissinger was in the Oval Office with Nixon, and Haig sent in a note summarizing events along the DMZ as understood at that point. Three ARVN bases in I Corps were under ground attack, with another eight under artillery fire. Abrams had characterized the situation as "not critical but is developing." Haig noted: "The usual complication exists. Weather is bad . . . a further complication is that the North Vietnamese SAM belt has been extended well into Northern I Corps, making helicopter gunship and C-130 gunship support very risky."[1]

Scanning the note quickly, Kissinger murmured to Nixon: "It looks like they are attacking now, in Vietnam—right at the DMZ. Those goddamned sons of bitches, I made them check whether we—of course, the weather is too bad for us to bomb—we must have the world's worst air force."[2]

Over the next few minutes, the two explored the implications of the invasion for the diplomatic and political landscape. The themes they sounded within a very few minutes of the arrival of the news were to recur repeatedly in the next few weeks. On the role of the Soviets and the fate of the Moscow summit, Nixon directed Kissinger to work through his well-worn back channel to the Soviet leadership, Ambassador Anatoly Dobrynin, to warn the USSR that this offensive could derail the May summit. The president went so far as to give Kissinger the lines he was to use with Dobrynin, emphasizing Nixon's determination and his unpredictability: "I can't vouch for what he won't do . . . if these guys continue, I think I can boldly say, don't assume that it will be limited to the type of bombing we've done before." Kissinger promised the president that he would call the Chinese ambassador to the United Nations and "really lay it into them about Vietnam."

The most consistent theme, then and in the coming weeks, was the White House's frustration with the military in general, and with the Air Force in particular. Kissinger, who had opened the conversation with the remarks about the "world's worst air force," ended it this way: "We tried to get them to attack in March, February, in December the weather was bad—in October, November the weather was bad—I don't know when they can attack, maybe July?"

With this brief conversation Nixon moved into his role as commander in chief, a role he would play with greater intensity over the following months than at any time earlier in his presidency. Although he had been a wartime president since his first day in office, for the most part he had remained relatively distant from military operations. He had carefully avoided taking too direct a role, even in the dramatic circumstances of the incursions into Cambodia and Laos. That would change now. The stakes in this campaign were far higher than any he had faced earlier. If South Vietnam collapsed, as Nixon viewed it, he would have neither a credible foreign policy nor any realistic hope of re-election. As the stakes rose, so did Nixon's need for effective support—but the invasion of Laos had left Nixon deeply disillusioned with the leadership of the department of defense, both in the Pentagon and in the theater of operations. He felt that he had given the members of the military too much leeway in Laos, and they had let him down. He was determined to leave them little latitude this time.

Moreover, this operation occurred in a far more complex international setting than had Lam Son 719. In the intervening months, Nixon had visited China, and triangular diplomacy had grown its first roots. The Moscow summit was imminent as well, offering tremendous potential rewards for Nixon—political, diplomatic, and strategic. Just beyond the summit was the Democratic Convention, and then the presidential campaign. He had every incentive to exert careful control over this operation, and he was determined to do so.

As Nixon tightened his grip on the reins, however, he faced the same delicate balances that confront every commander in chief. His first task was to ensure that the military strategy supported the political ends sought, and that all the instruments and institutions of government acted in unison toward achieving his aims. In more directly military terms, Nixon and his advisors bore the responsibility of providing sufficient direction to enable the military to plan and execute operations. That direction had to be clear and specific, while also permitting military commanders enough latitude to exercise their expertise in support of the strategy. Similarly, the civilian leadership would have to maintain an informed awareness of the state of military activity, but without intruding too deeply into the details of operations and management of the armed forces. These issues are intrinsic to the civil-military relationship, present in every use of armed force, and every president has had to find his own balance among them.[3]

Nixon had conflicting impulses in this regard. In principle, he thought it necessary to let the military execute its operations without close direction. Beyond that, he was determined to avoid anything similar to his predecessor's detailed direction of the earlier years of the air war. Few things agitated Nixon more than any suggestion that his conduct of the war had any common elements with Lyndon Johnson's. But there were powerful forces now impelling him toward detailed and constant oversight of operations. He profoundly mistrusted the federal bureaucracy, and was never confident that he could exercise adequate control over its actions. One of Nixon's senior staffers described the span of presidential control as follows: "We were a film of dust on top of the table; underneath was the bureaucracy . . . Democratic appointees are through the woodwork of this government."[4] Nixon and his staff had no confidence that the executive departments would execute the strategy as they designed it, or that they would keep information flowing to the White House.

Beyond that general perception, Nixon responded very directly to the painful experience of Lam Son 719. That campaign permanently impaired his trust in the theater commander and the secretary of defense, convincing him that Abrams was stale and unimaginative, and that he was in any case under Laird's direction to operate with excessive caution. Further, Nixon and Kissinger believed that the Pentagon had withheld vital information on operations from them. Kissinger recalled as the Easter Offensive opened: "In the Lam Son operation we were getting a lot of optimistic reports. For three days we had no reason to suppose this was more than a major probe. Then Saigon put out the situation was critical. The newsmen were 12 hours ahead of us."[5] In this crisis situation, with his re-election and his foreign policy at stake, Nixon embarked on a series of very specific operational directives, in the process overriding both his theater commander and his secretary of defense.

Nixon had come to rely heavily on his national security advisor to orchestrate the diplomatic and military actions supporting his strategy, and through the early days of the Easter Offensive, Kissinger worked tirelessly to do so. It was exactly the sort of situation Kissinger was made for. It offered nearly limitless access to the president and the opportunity to work with all the pieces of an immensely complex political-military puzzle. The situation enabled him to reach deep into his bureaucratic playbook, and it called on his remarkable energy and stamina. But these events also brought Kissinger's shortcomings into sharp relief. Kissinger had an academic's understanding of the military, demanding that it respond instantly to strategic direction anywhere along a spectrum, from subtle signaling to overwhelming force, with little comprehension of the effects of weather, technology, or enemy countermeasures. Where these factors affected military performance, Kissinger saw ineptitude, cowardice, or passivity. Moreover, he worked hard to extend this perception to the president, in order to strengthen his position in the White House. Kissinger, always aware that he served at the pleasure of the president, spared no effort to create a world in which he and Nixon stood alone against the plots of their enemies and the incompetence and disloyalty of their subordinates. In doing so, he exploited and exacerbated Nixon's two greatest weaknesses as a policymaker: his reclusiveness, and his universal suspicion, verging on paranoia.

As the situation on the ground worsened, organizational skills and emotional steadiness were more and more needed. Neither was among Kissinger's strong points, so in this crisis Haig assumed an increasingly major role, both as a staff officer complementing Kissinger and as an independent advisor to the president. He and Kissinger served as Nixon's window into the world of foreign affairs, as did Bob Haldeman into domestic affairs.

Over the first few days after the NVA launched its offensive, Nixon and his close aides worked to shape the war to meet the president's designs. The process began slowly, as news from the front gradually trickled into the White House. After the first report on March 30, Kissinger made the diplomatic moves he and Nixon had discussed, reporting later that he had taken a tough line with Dobrynin as directed, telling him: "The President feels he has the war won—if we can last until November, and I am sure we can, then we will have four years to settle accounts."[6] That settling could take many forms, against both North Vietnam and those who supported its attack. It was a first step in a strategy of pressuring the Soviets to choose between their support for North Vietnam and their larger strategic interests, thus working to isolate the North Vietnamese from their primary sponsor.[7]

March 31 was Good Friday, and little more news had arrived from the front when Nixon and Kissinger gathered to discuss events. The president approved Kissinger's suggestion to "go after the SAMs in the belt within 25 miles of the frontiers." Nixon commented that he was reluctant to "have a whole lot of war news on Easter Sunday, it's just not a good thing for me—frankly, the way these bastards [the Air Force] are, we could go three years from now and it wouldn't make any difference." Willing to delay the attack at least until after Easter, Nixon nonetheless directed Kissinger to have Moorer prepare a plan to attack the air defenses along the DMZ. "What I have in mind," he said, "I particularly want to take out the SAMs that took out the gunships."[8] This meeting yielded the first visible sign of the vigorous response to the invasion that Nixon planned: on Easter Sunday, April 2, the Joint Staff sent authority to theater forces to execute air, artillery, and naval gunfire strikes within 25 miles of the DMZ, with B-52 strikes authorized throughout the DMZ.[9] The air war against the North, nicknamed Operation Freedom Train, was back on after a three-year pause.

Easter Weekend passed quietly for the president, as he relaxed at Camp David and attended Easter service with his family at the Gettysburg Presbyterian Church. Activity at the Pentagon reflected none of the peace of southern Pennsylvania. The change in tempo and strategy in Southeast Asia triggered a series of meetings on that Easter Sunday, as Laird, Moorer, and Kissinger worked through the military actions necessary to execute the president's direction. The direction had seemed clear enough, but Laird was reluctant to sign the order for the attacks north of the DMZ, angering Kissinger and forcing Moorer, not for the first or the last time, into an awkward role as intermediary between the White House and the secretary of defense. The bureaucratic struggles continued through the day, culminating in a late-night meeting at the Pentagon and a still later series of phone calls among Moorer, McCain, and Kissinger.

Monday, April 3, marked a major turning point in the campaign. It became clear to the White House that this was indeed the long-awaited invasion—and worse yet, that the initial response was going far worse than they had known. Early that morning Kissinger entered the Oval Office and announced: "I have now heard that Laird would not let the reports go forward until he had edited them—and that was why we were twelve hours behind the news—we can't afford—it is clear there's a massive attack—they have fifty tanks near Dong Ha."[10] Nixon responded: "The military can't cop out on this one, Henry . . . they've had the order to do the bombing since we got back from China." Kissinger reinforced Nixon's accusation, charging that Laird and Abrams had suppressed the information about the buildup near the DMZ and had been unwilling to order a preemptive attack.

After this initial flurry, the two men settled into a more serious discussion of the issues and what they needed to do to take charge of the situation. They determined that their immediate imperative was to gain control over the flow of information. Kissinger suggested that he bring in Moorer and Kenneth Rush, the deputy secretary of defense, after his 10 A.M. meeting of the Washington Special Actions Group (WSAG).[11] He recommended that Nixon outline his views on how operations should be conducted and how information should be routed to the White House.

Kissinger then offered an anecdote that reveals how alienated he and Nixon were from the Air Force: "I talked to John Ehrlichman this morning and he asked what the situation was, and I told him and he asked, why won't they fly? I said because of the weather and he said they flew all over the Battle of the Bulge dropping bombs during blizzards, and he's right." Nixon replied: "Yep, something wrong, there's something wrong here." That Kissinger would relay this chance anecdote, and that the president would take it seriously, reflects the extent of their frustration with the service. It also indicates their limited grasp of the situation facing the forces operating along the DMZ.

Moving again to a more strategic plane, Nixon and Kissinger discussed the Moscow summit, agreeing that the Soviet Union had too much at stake in the summit to jeopardize it all by supporting North Vietnam.

They thought that, if handled properly, their leverage on the Soviets could be used to force them to forsake their North Vietnamese allies to protect their new relationship with the Americans. And then Kissinger raised his real hopes for the outcome: "I think we could play this into an end of the war." Nixon returned to the problem at hand, that of getting effective military action: "I think you're right, but I'll tell you, it will providing this bombing attack we put on is the finest damn thing that's ever been done." Already, on their first day of assessing the situation, both believed that this offensive could—and probably would—bring an end to the war, one way or another.

As they closed the conversation, Kissinger raised the prospect of a South Vietnamese collapse. Again Nixon emphasized the stakes at play, both international and domestic, and he commented: "That's the question we can't even think about . . . if they were going to collapse they had to do it a year ago." The bottom line, for Nixon, was: "We're playing a much bigger game—we're playing a Russia game, a China game, and an election game and we're not gonna have the ARVN collapse." In Nixon's eyes, the military action was only part of a much larger set of considerations. It would have to support diplomacy and domestic politics. His fate in those critical areas, conversely, would be defined by the success of military action. It made no sense to view the battle in isolation.

From this conversation, it is clear that Nixon misunderstood the operational authorities that had been issued to the forces in Southeast Asia in the month before the offensive. Recall that in early March Abrams at MACV had asked for authority to strike against the buildup visible north of the DMZ. Laird had moderated the request, recommending only three one-day strikes in a more restricted area. After Laird's recommendation crossed the river to the White House, Kissinger had rejected even Laird's minimal approach, fearful that it might jeopardize the opening with China or the impending Moscow summit. Nixon, however, had thought that the military had received clearance to resume attacks north of the DMZ after his return from China—an error that Kissinger was in no hurry to correct.

After Kissinger left for the WSAG meeting, Nixon asked Haldeman to clear his calendar, since "in the next couple of days, I've really got to get ahold of this thing, and shake them up a bit."[12] Then he turned to disparaging the cabinet members, telling Haldeman that "it's really too bad to have Rogers and Laird, two weak and vacillating men," in this crisis, and lamenting: "I shouldn't be asking them, they should be asking what can we do, how can we help?" Haldeman picked up on the theme: "Laird should be calling, I think we have a chance to make a positive out of this, this is what I propose to do, I'd like to go out, say ding ding ding, I'd like to get our goddamned bombers in there and start hitting things for a change." Nixon replied in a pensive tone: "Our bombers . . . it's a colossal joke now. We can't hit anything unless the weather's perfect—ceiling unlimited."

At that point Kissinger stormed back into the room, in a high state of frustration and concern. At the WSAG meeting he had learned of the destruction of two of the 3rd ARVN's three regiments. He was alarmed at the state of the defense in theater, and at the stagnant flow of information to the White House: "It now turns out, which they hadn't told us, which I found out by the purest accident, that two regiments of that division up there have been destroyed. I found this out by badgering them." He continued: "It's my instinct, as it was in Lam Son, there's some blight on that operation, and Moorer has to know that there's an enormous sense of urgency here and that we want this thing, I think Laird has drilled into their heads so much to do nothing, that they just don't react."

Deeply agitated, Kissinger again asked that Nixon bring in Admiral Moorer and impress two points on the CJCS. First, information on the offensive must flow directly to the White House. Second, the U.S. military response to the invasion must be aggressive and creative to a degree never yet seen in this war. Nixon agreed, and thus set the stage for a most remarkable meeting.

Kissinger went to retrieve Moorer and Rush and brought them in to speak with the president. After very perfunctory pleasantries, Nixon leaped to the point: "I am the commander in chief, and not the secretary of defense, is that clear?" He then moved on to the two points that he and Kissinger had defined earlier. First, he wanted the daily briefing reliably, on time, and unsanitized. Second, he charged that MACV had flown only a fraction of the sorties authorized: "The excuse is weather, I understand." Moorer tried to interject an explanation of the problems faced by MACV, but Nixon cut him off:

I understand, now let's come to Abrams—why didn't he think of that? What is his job out there—just do it by the numbers, or is it his job to try to see that this kind of offensive is stopped? Now, I want you to understand, there's some talk of Abrams going to chief of staff of the Army. Now, I want you to know, that I don't intend him to go to the chief of staff of the Army because of his conduct in this business—he's shown no imagination, he's drinking too much, I want you to give him the order, he's to go on the wagon throughout the balance of this offensive—is that clear?[13]

Nixon then resumed his attack on the Air Force in a rambling diatribe. After belaboring the issues of information flow and air action for a few more minutes, he calmed down and offered a useful strategic insight: "My point is, I know we don't have many assets out there in terms of ground forces—and we're not gonna have any. This has got to be said. But we've got some very considerable assets in terms of air power—but those assets have to be, they have to be concentrated, concentrated in areas that will provide shock treatment." He pressed Moorer to conduct a 48-hour strike north of the DMZ, and to do it by Wednesday, weather permitting: "There are other reasons which are supplementary, but the military reasons are the important one. If we don't whack those supplies now, they might be coming in September and October, so let's get the damned strike off, I mean if the weather is reasonable."

Returning to the matter of the Air Force's timidity, Nixon repeated: "The goddamned Air Force has to take some goddamned risk, just like they did during the Battle of the Bulge in World War II—because we were under serious attack—if the Air Force hadn't taken some risks, we'd have lost the battle." At that point Moorer had had enough, and finally he spoke up: "The Air Force is not reluctant in any sense to take risks, Mr. President. The problem is that north of the DMZ, with these missile sites, and they're moving them around all the time and you need some kind of visibility in order to get the sites out." Moorer emphasized that Abrams had "repeatedly asked for authority to attack these missile sites north and we haven't been giving them authority because you just gave it to us yesterday." The session ended with Nixon's closing direction: "From now on, you get those reports in to me. Second thing is, I want Abrams braced hard. His promotion depends on how he conducts himself. Now . . . yes, you were here at the time—he screwed up Laos—he's not gonna screw this one up."

This fifteen-minute conversation was pivotal in shaping America's response to the invasion, and it throws light on several important points about presidential war leadership. First, Nixon and Kissinger realized that the first prerequisite of command is to understand the situation. By arranging for daily briefings and insisting that the White House must receive them, in Nixon's phrase, "directly, and they must be unsanitized," Nixon had created the basis for effective command. Second, although in an unstructured way, in this conversation Nixon presented the CJCS with a picture of how he wanted this war conducted and what he expected of the military chain of command. Nixon had a strategic vision, and he outlined it for Moorer. He also demonstrated a full willingness to direct tactical operations, with his specific direction to attack the NVA missile sites that had destroyed the AC-130 near the DMZ.

The dominant theme, however, was Nixon's lack of respect for the military forces in theater, both for the Air Force as an organization and for the theater commander, General Abrams. This disrespect dated back to Lam Son 719, and it was to remain a constant theme until Abrams's change of command at the end of June. By an unfortunate chance, Laird's memorandum nominating Abrams to succeed General William Westmoreland as chief of staff of the Army had arrived in the White House almost simultaneously with the first news of the invasion. The nomination offered a focal point for Nixon's mistrust of Abrams, and the president raised it routinely, usually as a threat, over the weeks to come.[14]

This conversation was among the remarkably few in which Nixon ever directly confronted a subordinate. He was notoriously unwilling to do so, and his discomfort is evident in the awkwardness, disorganization, and bluster of his conversation with Moorer. The morning's events also illustrate the strange symbiosis of Nixon and Kissinger—the near-complete reliance of the president on this single aide, and the means by which Kissinger maintained his influence.

Moments after Moorer left, Nixon telephoned Kissinger to again discuss the March 8 memorandum in which Abrams had requested authority for strikes north of the DMZ—not to critique the decisions made then, but to be ready in case the military came "whining around" on the subject.[15] He directed Kissinger to have Haig look into the matter. Haig worked with Moorer to assemble the full course of events, and had the answer for Kissinger a few hours later. Kissinger then discussed the events with the president, taking the opportunity to put his own interpretation on the sequence of events: "The trouble is, Mr. President, as always they gave you an impossible proposition. We couldn't go in there day after day, by their own judgment, and what they wanted was unlimited authority to attack in there, and given the situation with the Chinese and the Russians—"[16]

Nixon interjected: "Your point, what we shouldn't do and put a pall on the China trip at that point, right?" Kissinger replied: "Yes, the China trip and also the upcoming Russian trip, it would be like something that was a daily campaign. Now I do not believe that they ever came to us, but I have to say I would not have been for it if they had come to us." In any event, he added, "It isn't a bad public posture to say that for a month and a half you didn't approve requests to hit North Vietnam—we watched the buildup but we wanted to make absolutely sure" of the aggressive intent behind the buildup. Clearly aware that Nixon was in an aggressive mood, Kissinger was unwilling to remind the president of the true course of events: that at Kissinger's recommendation, the White House had rejected Abrams's request to conduct an air offensive against the increasingly visible North Vietnamese buildup. His defense comprised a mix of half-truths, obscurations, and denial, but it did at least enable the president and his national security advisor to move beyond old decisions, to focus on what must be done next. The incident illustrates an observation made by Undersecretary of State Alexis Johnson: "Henry, like most geniuses, has spectacular talents but corresponding faults. He was amazingly successful juggling a profusion of balls while pirouetting atop a high wire. When some of the balls dropped, however, it was obvious that devotion to truth was not always his guiding principle."[17]

A memo Haig drafted later that day suggests that he and Kissinger had had a still stronger motive for holding air attacks in abeyance. During that stressful Monday morning Haig had offended Kissinger, and late in the day he sent the memo to explain his views and clear the air between them. He opened by reviewing the situation, stating that the U.S. leadership had reduced force levels "beyond prudence" and had "known for weeks that the enemy was going to hit hard and, in fact, hoped they would." Nixon, Kissinger, and Haig had long known of the problems existing with the Air Force and with Abrams. Nothing that had happened, in short, was beyond what they had foreseen. He continued:

> In short, we have taken all kinds of risk, with the hope and in my case the conviction, that the China initiative might substitute for more straight-forward applications of national power. The simple logic I was trying to emphasize is this. From this point on, the game is ours as are the prob-lems. They are not Abrams'. They are not Laird's but rather yours and mine, as well as the President's. I do not feel that we can, or should, do more than work together coolly and cooperative to make Abrams as ef-

fective as is humanly possible. Harassment and second guessing may be justified but we just cannot afford them.[18]

Haig, at least, had expected the Chinese to be willing and able to restrain the North Vietnamese from launching the offensive. It is likely that Kissinger shared that view, since his expectations for the effectiveness of diplomatic action were normally higher than Haig's. The reason for their decision to hold back on strikes against the NVA buildup was not just to avoid jeopardizing the China opening. It reflected as well a hope that the new relationship with China would make the strikes unnecessary.

By noon on this first day addressing the attack, Nixon had begun pulling together the military, diplomatic, and public relations components of his response. With reinforcements already en route to the battle area, and with the efforts to isolate Hanoi from its sponsors in Moscow and Beijing under way, he had begun to move the giant machine of government into alignment with his will.

As he did so, though, he paid a price for the style of government that he had adopted over the three preceding years. Nixon's midmorning conversation with Haldeman exactly described the ideal reaction of his cabinet secretaries to the invasion. They should have responded vigorously with the resources of their departments to meet the president's direction. But after years of being frozen out of the action, of being isolated from the decisionmaking process, of being sharply brought into line at any hint of independent action, neither the defense department nor the state department was in any condition to respond creatively to the new situation. Nixon and Kissinger had no faith whatever in either the secretary of defense or the secretary of state, and Kissinger in particular had no desire to restore sound working relationships with them. Instead, the White House turned to subordinates in the two departments—Ken Rush at the Pentagon and Alexis Johnson at the state department—to conduct essential business, while leaving Rogers and Laird, statutory members of the National Security Council, in the dark as much as possible. It was a strange and risky way to conduct a war.

The nation's military forces were no more ready than the executive branch to step forward with aggressive action. For the eight years of the air war to that point, the air and naval forces in theater had been subject to painfully tight control, first under Johnson and then under Nixon. The degree of detailed direction under Johnson is legendary. The level of political control over operations in Southeast Asia had not fundamentally changed under Nixon, though the tempo of the war largely rendered the close control of the Johnson years unnecessary. Only days before the NVA offensive began, General Lavelle had been recalled to Washington and relieved of command for his broad interpretation of existing operating authorities. His fate stood as a stark warning of the penalties for excessive aggressiveness. It was unrealistic to expect an instantaneous reversal of the attitudes engendered during eight years of combat.

Rush and Moorer, on returning to the Pentagon, naturally told Laird of their remarkable meeting with the president, and Laird called Kissinger to express his concern. By that point Kissinger was ready to concede that his account of the sequence of decisions in February and March had been inaccurate, and he offered to send a memo to the president setting the record straight. Laird, however, had deeper concerns. He answered: "I don't care about that. You don't need to review any of that." When Kissinger offered to take responsibility, Laird responded: "No, that's not what I'm interested in. The important thing in this town is trust. Trust between you and me, between you and the President, between me and the President and so on." He emphasized that when the White House had refused to authorize the strikes he requested in early March, he had taken responsibility for the decision within the Pentagon. He concluded: "We have got to have a greater degree of trust."[19] Laird's appeal had little discernible effect as events unfolded over the coming months.

That afternoon, action officers on the Joint Staff drafted the message that would extend air strikes further into North Vietnam, to include the town of Dong Hoi, the southernmost transportation node in the DRV. This was the second in a series of incremental steps broadening the area of American air activity over the North under Operation Freedom Train. The next day the northernmost boundary would move another twenty-five miles, to eighteen degrees north, and four days later a further sixty miles, to nineteen degrees.[20]

Meanwhile, Moorer worked to translate Nixon's direction into clear, executable guidance for operations. Late that night the JCS released Moorer's message to the Pentagon outlining the president's direction. It opened: "Secretary Rush, Doctor Kissinger and I held a discussion today with the President concerning the situation in South Vietnam. Naturally, the President is very concerned about the development of events and requested that I pass to Gen Abrams the need to execute maximum aggressiveness in the use of air power." Moorer repeated Nixon's desire that "maximum impact from air attack be achieved as soon as possible," emphasizing that the president "would like for COMUSMACV and staff to give this matter their around-the-clock attention during the current crisis. Furthermore, he requested that I investigate the feasibility of augmenting both the B52 and tacair assets." Then Moorer again stressed Nixon's desire that the strike north of the DMZ "go as soon as possible, subject to good weather which is necessary for an effective strike." He closed with a general charge to everyone in the chain of command: "I request that each of you give this air offensive your personal and continuous attention and fully utilize every opportunity to effect a massive impact on the enemy. The President has clearly stated that he expects imaginative, aggressive and continuous attention to be focused on the current crisis throughout the unified command system. Request you advise me immediately of any additional authorities and resources you require."[21]

On Tuesday, April 4, the formal government machinery for dealing with crises moved into action. Kissinger chaired another WSAG meeting, looking ahead to possible contingencies and tasking the military to review and submit its existing plans to mine Haiphong harbor. The president, too, looked ahead. By this time Nixon had contemplated a world in which South Vietnam had fallen, the United States having been defeated and discredited by a fourth-rate power. It was a world in which the Americans had no viable foreign policy, with the Soviets testing them everywhere, and with their friends having lost confidence in American backing. It was a world in which U.S. society was torn apart, with the liberals and leftists ascendant amid recriminations for the useless loss of 50,000 American lives. Given this vision, the president saw his decision about policy as clear-cut: "I don't think anybody realizes how far I am prepared to go to save this . . . we have no option but to win this . . . whatever is necessary to stop this thing has to be done."[22] Already Nixon leaned toward a blockade of North Vietnam, selectively enforced to permit food and medicine into the country. Kissinger pointed out that a blockade would necessitate physically challenging every ship heading toward Haiphong, and that during the Cuban missile crisis every confrontation with a Soviet ship had brought another round of headlines. A series of confrontations with the USSR would inevitably imperil the Moscow summit, now only seven weeks away.

As he had promised the day before, Nixon paid close attention to the unfolding action and the air attacks across the theater. He was in a more reflective mood than on Monday, as he contemplated possibilities for future events.[23] He called Moorer to check on the actions ordered the previous day, and to direct Moorer to send every destroyer and cruiser in the Pacific Fleet to Southeast Asia, ignoring nuclear alert commitments if necessary. As a side benefit of the developing rapprochement with the Soviet Union, the president felt comfortable committing the vast mass of American military power to a peripheral conflict, knowing that the USSR would not seek advantage elsewhere. On the other hand, Nixon decided to accept a standing invitation to visit Poland, despite Dobrynin's warning: "I can't tell you how this will annoy Brezhnev."[24] It was an easy way to send the Soviets a message that their backing of North Vietnam's offensive would carry a price, while also appealing to a large bloc of American voters.

By now the pieces were falling into place. The president and Kissinger had "shaken them up," and the military was moving massive reinforcements into the theater. Word had gone forth through the chain of command that the president expected an aggressive campaign. The air and naval forces in Southeast Asia were standing by for a break in the weather to begin a 48-hour strike against the North. The interagency planning process was engaged, and the planners were considering the next steps. Kissinger had begun his campaign to reinforce the diplomatic isolation of North Vietnam. The public diplomacy campaign had opened with Kissinger and Nixon agreeably surprised by the positive press they had received so far. The Pacific Command staff was working feverishly to update its plan for mining the North Vietnamese ports and to define the forces and operating authorities it would need to prosecute a more aggressive bombing campaign.

The White House's lack of confidence in its theater commanders, however, remained a problem. On Wednesday, April 5, a solution appeared. Admiral Moorer sent his director of the Joint Staff, General John Vogt, to the White House to brief Kissinger on the progress of the campaign. The men knew each other well. Their acquaintance reached back to Kissinger's days at Harvard, where Vogt had studied in a program for senior military officers. They had worked closely together throughout Vogt's tour on the Joint Staff. Vogt, having been selected for a promotion and an assignment in Europe, had been on the point of departure when the North Vietnamese struck. In his diary entry the following day, Haldeman summarized the account of the briefing that he had heard from Kissinger:

Vogt mentioned to Henry that he was terribly distressed with the way the military and particularly the Air Force were handling the Vietnam situation, particularly their failure to carry out the P's orders and an even worse failure to come up with any ideas on their own on how things ought to be handled. Vogt made the comment to K that he would like to give up his 4th star that he was about to get for going over to NATO and be assigned to Vietnam and get the thing straightened out.[25]

Back in the Oval Office, Kissinger relayed Vogt's comments to Nixon. At the president's direction, he then called Moorer to ask the CJCS to make sure they had the right man in command out in Saigon. Kissinger suggested that they think about sending General Lew Clay, a former Seventh Air Force commander, back to Saigon, or perhaps look at Vogt. He asked Moorer to have a recommendation to the president by noon. At that point Nixon took the phone to reiterate the importance of hitting the North Vietnamese hard with B-52s: "Have 'em fly at 95 or 110,000 feet and drop them in the boondocks" if necessary, but fly the sorties. Nixon closed the conversation by returning to the need to find "the most experienced, tough commander—someone with imagination and verve."[26]

Moorer quickly checked with Laird and with the Air Force chief of staff, General Jack Ryan. He then called back to recommend Vogt, and the deal was done. Kissinger urged Nixon to meet with Vogt because "he needs to get the word as to what the hell we want done out there." Nixon's vision of the significance of this battle had expanded again; by now he considered it central to "the whole future of the profession of arms." After some hesitation, he agreed to meet with Vogt the following day.

As Nixon closed his day in the Oval Office, half a world away, the morning dawned bright and clear in the panhandle of North Vietnam. The time had come for Nixon's 48-hour strike against the missile sites north of the DMZ. At bases all across Southeast Asia, the crews prepared for their missions as the maintenance crews fueled the aircraft and loaded weapons. Offshore, Carrier Task Force 77 repositioned the *Kitty Hawk* and the *Hancock* northward to join the *Coral Sea*. North Vietnamese intelligence detected the move; at 5:00 A.M., the General Staff warned the forward command post of the Air Defense Command of an impending strike against SAM and artillery positions, warehouses, and supply stockpiles. All air defense units moved to combat-ready status. The warning indicates that the North Vietnamese had penetrated the tasking network for theater air forces, even stating accurately that the strike would be conducted primarily by Navy fighters.[27]

The air wings in Thailand had long awaited this opportunity to strike the SAM sites. As early as February, the 388th Tactical Fighter Wing (TFW) at Korat RTAFB had worked through the tactics required.[28] They planned to pair F-105 Iron Hand aircraft with F-4s—the F-105s to detect the sites and suppress them with Shrike antiradiation missiles, and the F-4s to follow up with cluster bombs to destroy the equipment and the operators. They would cross the coastline low and fast, pop up to find the targets, hit hard, and leave quickly. Jamming support would multiply the confusion of the SAM operators.

The operation proceeded as planned. "Early in the morning," relates the North Vietnamese history of the Air Defense Service, "electronic jamming signals from U.S. electronic warfare aircraft blanked the screens of our radars. Then U.S. Navy aircraft streaked in at extremely low altitude toward the coastline."[29] The Second War of Destruction, as the North Vietnamese termed the air war, had begun.

The two-day attack had a devastating effect on the North Vietnamese air defenses. On the first day, strikes "hit the 274th Regiment's technical support battalion, heavily damaging our stockpile of missiles for the missile launch battalions." The next day things got even worse for the defenders, as "the enemy launched a ferocious large-scale attack against almost every one of our surface-to-air missile launch sites." The Navy tactics greatly impressed the NVA defenders:

> The enemy sent one flight of aircraft in at medium altitude to attract our fire and then sent in small flights of aircraft, flying at low altitude (below 1,000 meters) and using terrain features to cover their approach. When these small attack flights were 7–10 kilometers from our missile launch sites, they climbed to an altitude of 2,000 meters to drop cluster bombs and high-explosive bombs on our launch positions, either from level flight or in a dive-bombing run. After dropping their bombs, they dove to low altitude and turned away to escape quickly out to sea. Many units did not even have time to open fire, and they were unable to support one another. Seven of our missile battalions were struck in these attacks, and five of those battalions were rendered combat ineffective.[30]

The two-day strike was just the opening blow, and it was only part of the pressure building against the NVA air defenses. Naval gunfire support arriving offshore had begun adding its weight to the attack on the missile sites. As the North Vietnamese described the situation: "In addition to air attacks, all types of U.S. warships off the coast constantly shelled our positions. The battle was tense and extremely savage. Many of our missile battalions had their equipment destroyed, and at times our losses were so heavy that only one-third of our forces were able to fight. All efforts to repair, restore, and replace weapons, equipment, and missiles met great obstacles."[31]

It was perhaps the most effective defense-suppression effort in the whole war, and it had a profound impact on the course of the battle. It opened the DRV panhandle to attack by American fighter aircraft, and by the B-52s that Nixon was so impatient to send north. Certainly it sent a powerful signal to the North Vietnamese, exactly as Nixon had wanted. On April 9 the NVA general staff finally ordered all armed forces throughout North Vietnam to shift to a wartime footing. In response, "the Air Defense–Air Force Service Command ordered the entire service up to full combat-ready status . . . and quickly conducted training for its troops on fighting the enemy under conditions of heavy electronic jamming and on countering enemy precision-guided weapons."[32] Nixon's vigorous response to their invasion had caught the North Vietnamese off guard.

The first day's strikes were complete, and early reports had reached Washington, by the time Kissinger and Vogt entered Nixon's hideaway office a little after 10:00 A.M. on April 6. Kissinger opened the conversation with a short summary of the attacks, and then Nixon came quickly to the point of the meeting: "The performance of the Air Force has not been, in my view, adequate. The reason it has not been adequate is not because of the bravery of the people . . . but the reason it's not been adequate, it's been routine, by the numbers, there's been no imagination." Nixon postulated that this "may well be the last time the Air Force has to pop anybody," so he urged Vogt to ensure that this last campaign would be one in which the service could take pride. "Let's see some imagination and drive," he charged. "I'm gonna watch this every morning and every night—you're going out there on a rescue mission."[33]

Nixon declared that he considered Abrams a "splendid man, a magnificent record in World War II—a fine record in Vietnam—he's been there too long. He's tired, unimaginative. What's going to determine this is not what Abrams decides, because he's not gonna take any risks at this point, but what *you'll* decide." Most of all, Nixon wanted Vogt to look toward concentrating his forces. "He who concentrates his forces wins the battle; he who spreads his forces out gets the hell kicked out of him . . .

we've got to come up with some ideas to *jolt* these guys." Haldeman, who
sat in on the meeting, recounted the conversation in his diary: "The P told
him to bypass Abrams, that he did not have confidence in Abrams, that
he'd been a great commander in W.W. II, but that he was over the hill now
and that Vogt was to get things done. If he had any problems he was to let
the P know, not just let the thing simmer."[34]

Nixon asked Vogt if he needed anything. The general brought up
MACV's command structure, commenting that it would be a great help if
he could be named the deputy commander of MACV instead of merely the
deputy commander for air. The JCS had already approved that change as
part of an overall reorganization of the MACV and Seventh Air Force
staffs scheduled for the end of June. Nixon replied: "Work it out—the reason it should be worked out isn't because of personalities, the reason it
should be worked out is that all the goddamned thing is about now, is *air.*
Right, Henry?" The president had penetrated to the heart of the issue, but
had also penetrated into the most tangled of military issues: command relations. Despite Nixon's spoken support, Vogt would prove unable to accelerate the change to the new command structure once he arrived in theater. The meeting drew to a close, with Nixon again insisting on the
importance of using the B-52s in North Vietnam. Vogt promised to find
some targets, and took his leave. On April 10 he took command of Seventh
Air Force.

Nixon was an attentive though unsystematic student of military history,
and as he contemplated this situation he observed to Moorer: "More wars
have been lost through reluctance to change commanders than for any
other reason."[35] Given his sentiments about Abrams and the Air Force, it
was especially necessary and appropriate for Nixon to select one of the
very few senior Air Force leaders who enjoyed his confidence to run this
critical air war. Kissinger and Nixon badly needed to have a common
understanding of the stakes at play in this campaign with the military leadership, and with Vogt they achieved just that. For Nixon, however talented
Lieutenant General Marvin McNickle—Ryan's choice as successor to
Lavelle—might have proven, he would always be just another anonymous
general out there. It served all parties to have the president and Kissinger
comfortable with the leader on the scene.

Nonetheless, the episode left scars in several places. Kissinger was not
a universal favorite among the U.S. military leadership, and he was especially unpopular at MACV headquarters in Saigon.[36] Vogt's close ties with

Nixon and Kissinger, coupled with the process by which he gained command, did little to build confidence between Vogt and his commander, Abrams. Kissinger called Vogt to tell him informally of his selection to take over Seventh Air Force early Wednesday afternoon, April 5, and Vogt asked to see Kissinger before departing for Southeast Asia. He told Kissinger: "I definitely will have a problem at the other end." Kissinger assured him: "We will make heads roll. You do what is wanted and he's got to get out of the way."[37] Neither did Vogt's means of gaining the assignment endear him to the Air Force leadership. By Haldeman's account, Vogt had criticized another senior officer, the Air Force's conduct of the battle, and Ryan's choice of McNickle to succeed Lavelle. The subsequent correspondence among Vogt, Pacific Air Forces (PACAF) commander General Lew Clay, and Ryan shows an edginess that goes beyond what one would normally expect even in the most stressful situation.

Vogt had the president's confidence and a clear idea of what the highest authorities expected from him. He did not, however, have experience in high command or in running an air war. His last command had been at the squadron level in 1946. Since then he had demonstrated outstanding staff skills as he climbed from the rank of major to lieutenant general, but he had never had the opportunity to command. McNickle's recent experience in Southeast Asia left him far better qualified than Vogt to move quickly into command in Saigon. He was intimately familiar with Seventh Air Force operations; he knew the individuals on the staff and in command; and he had worked with the support issues of manpower and logistics on a daily basis. He had, in fact, run the air war after Lavelle's recall. In contrast, it would inevitably take time for Vogt to settle into his new responsibilities, and to master the details of day-to-day operations and the tasking process.

Few men in the history of that war faced as complicated a problem in command as Vogt. He worked directly for General Ryan in one capacity, for Clay in another, for Abrams in still another, all the while understanding that his real bosses were back in the White House. None of these commanders was reluctant to offer his views. Balancing their demands would be a delicate task.[38]

In this intense period, Nixon and Kissinger established the policy outline and put their mark on the war. Meanwhile Haig worked his usual countless hours, handling the detailed coordination necessary to execute the strategy. Already by April 5, Moorer's message to Pacific Command had yielded recommendations for a one-time strike on Haiphong by carrier-based forces, and for a mining operation against Haiphong.[39] Laird forwarded the plans to Kissinger with a memorandum reiterating his consistently held premises with respect to bombing North Vietnam. He argued that interdiction would be ineffective, since the attacks could not reach the sources of production, and so "the merits and demerits of bombing in North Vietnam are therefore primarily political." He believed that the "political value of bombing is principally in the threat, i.e., the danger to Hanoi of losing the relatively small growth base the country has . . . That value is lost once extensive operations have been conducted." Moreover, the bombing had become a negative symbol, providing a rallying point for antiwar forces. Nor did Laird favor the mining option. He added a handwritten note to his memo emphasizing that while there might be a useful political effect of these plans, "the military effect would be minor and the impact on present battle would be even less."[40]

On April 6 Haig forwarded yet another contingency plan to Kissinger, this one outlining "an intense no-holds barred air and naval campaign against the North." The plan called for "bombing of all areas of NVN (except for a buffer zone along the PRC border), including the Haiphong port area and military targets in Hanoi." There would be a "companion naval campaign with shore bombardment all along the coast, the mining of Haiphong and other lesser ports, blockade of ports and interdiction of coastal shipping." The plan included a "parallel psychological campaign against the NVN people and the leadership" along with "all possible diplomatic actions."[41]

The plan called for a three-week period for planning and moving the necessary forces into position; it would therefore be the end of April before the attacks could begin, unless the campaign opened piecemeal with the forces on hand. The contingency plan listed in detail the steps that would be necessary to prepare theater forces for an intense air and naval operation. It included military, diplomatic, political/press, and propaganda actions to be taken progressively through the preparation period and early in the campaign. It offered a very sound blueprint for the actions that would be taken during the crisis in early May. Even the plan's assumptions about the conditions that would trigger this decision precisely defined the circumstances in which Nixon was to put it into effect a month later: South Vietnam failing to stop the offensive, U.S. air and naval action unable to alter the situation, and the president accepting the domestic and international price of an expanded war. Just a week into the NVA offensive, the pathway toward an all-out air campaign was already clearly marked.

Through this period Haig also attempted to smooth the rough edges of the White House's relationship with the Pentagon, by maintaining contact with Moorer and the Army staff. On the night of April 5, for example, he spoke with Moorer, offering some advice that would relieve some of the pressure on Abrams:

> All I would suggest is I think we could really resolve a lot of these problems if Abrams had somebody giving a wrap-up to you or to Laird or to somebody for the President on the conceptual problems. I know he is being harassed but the President never gets anything concrete from the Commander . . . There is no need for him to stick his head in a meat grinder but the President keeps getting these calls from Right Wingers saying he's not doing the right thing and so on.[42]

Moorer told Haig that he had spoken to Abrams that day: "He [Abrams] kind of got all upset and he went on to say he was going to resign. I asked him 'What's the problem, Abe?' Finally he calmed down but he never told me what his problem was."[43] The two continued to discuss Abrams's nomination as Army chief of staff and the president's threat to remove him from command, Moorer offering his view that "it would cause a lot of unnecessary upheaval." The CJCS commented on his conversation with Nixon: "It is so difficult to communicate with him. I am crazy about him but he's so goddamn hard to talk to." Haig offered some degree of solace in his reply: "The problem is he waits too late at night to get to you and then he has had some reinforcements by the time he gets to you."[44] Evidently, rumors of Nixon's drinking were not limited to the NSC staff.

It had been an intense week, but by its close Nixon had set his stamp on the campaign, shaping operations to meet his vision and establishing a sound basis for further operations. The diplomatic effort to isolate North Vietnam was proceeding, and the lines for press commentary for the domestic audience had been established. A massive flow of forces was under way to the theater of operations, and North Vietnam had undergone its first air attack in response to the invasion. The process Nixon had followed to achieve these goals had little resemblance to that outlined in civics texts, but it had proven effective in allowing him to "get ahold of this thing."

Haig, Laird, Nixon, and Abrams meet at the White House, October 16, 1972.
Nixon Library.

Nixon and Kissinger confer in the president's hideaway office in the Old Executive Office Building. Nixon Library.

Nixon and Moorer celebrate the return of POWs from North Vietnam, February 1973. Nixon Library.

A B-52D on short final approach at U-Tapao RTAFB, October 30, 1972. National Archives.

An F-4 from the 388th Tactical Fighter Wing, May 28, 1972. National Archives.

A-1 preflight operations at Nakhon Phanom RTAFB, Easter Sunday, 1972. National Archives.

Preflight operations at Udorn RTAFB, September 30, 1972. National Archives.

Captured NVA T-54 tanks at Hue. Copyright John Hoffman. All rights reserved; used with permission.

A captured Soviet M-1946 130-mm gun on display at Hue. National Archives.

South Vietnamese trucks pass destroyed NVA armored vehicles along Route 1 south of Quang Tri. The tank on top is a PT-76; the one on the bottom is a PT-85. Copyright John Hoffman. All rights reserved; used with permission.

7

THE FORCES FLOW FORWARD

The first concrete manifestations of Nixon's resolve that "whatever is necessary to stop this has got to be done" came well before the offensive, in early February. As intelligence indicators increasingly pointed to the likelihood of an offensive during Tet, Nixon dispatched air and naval forces to counter the expected attack. This was the first of three waves of forces that would flow into Southeast Asia, eventually filling to capacity every available runway in the region and straining the Air Force and the Navy to their utmost.

The forces arriving in Indochina transformed the battle. Perhaps more significantly, they transformed the strategic posture of the United States. These deployments demonstrated a capability never before seen in strategic affairs. Within a matter of days, the Americans had projected overwhelming military power around the world, with the supply and logistical support necessary to sustain a high-tempo, high-technology air war. This was a turning point in contemporary military history.

The February deployments were small compared with those to follow. They were intended as much to signal Nixon's resolve as to strengthen U.S. military capabilities. On February 4 Nixon ordered the deployment of B-52s, an aircraft carrier, and fighter aircraft into the theater, and eliminated restrictions on the number of sorties the military were authorized to fly in Southeast Asia.[1]

The B-52 deployment, code-named Bullet Shot, proved to be the first of six that SAC would execute during this period. This first reinforcement, expected at the time to be for the short term, sent 29 B-52Ds to Andersen AFB, Guam, and 10 KC-135 tankers to Kadena AB, Okinawa. Behind the movement of the 29 B-52s lay an immense logistical effort. For this first increment alone, SAC deployed 182 pieces of ground equipment, 71 vehicles, and 32 extra engines. In addition to the tanker support to the deploying aircraft, the move required 7 KC-135 sorties, 23 C-141 and 5 C-5 missions, along with 9 flights by DC-8 and Boeing 707 charter aircraft.[2] Meanwhile, Pacific Air Forces (PACAF) deployed the 523rd Tactical Fighter Squadron from Clark AFB in the Philippines, splitting the unit among three bases in Thailand and South Vietnam. Nixon's order also sent the USS *Kitty Hawk* across the Pacific well in advance of its planned timeline, forcing the unit to curtail its pre-cruise workup.[3]

This first movement demonstrated an unusual willingness on Nixon's part to take advantage of strategic warning, sending forces into theater based on intelligence indications of an imminent attack. It is rare for intelligence indicators to be clear enough, and policymakers resolute enough, to act on warning alone. The movements in early February added about 90 fighter aircraft and 15 B-52 sorties per day to MACV's capabilities and demonstrated the strategic mobility of American forces. However impressive this first deployment, though, it was dwarfed by what followed. The second movement, triggered by the NVA invasion, involved nearly every element of U.S. attack capabilities—land-based and naval fighter aircraft, B-52s, and naval gunfire support—on a scale and with a rapidity never before seen in the war.

The reinforcements began with forces already stationed in the theater. On April 1, CINCPAC Admiral John McCain directed the 35th Tactical Fighter Squadron from Kunsan AB, Korea, to deploy its 18 aircraft into Southeast Asia: 9 to Ubon RTAFB, the rest to Danang AB.[4] These forces were in combat within a week.

The reinforcement by forces stationed in the United States followed very quickly after Nixon's conversation with Moorer on April 3. Within two days Abrams had requested fighter augmentation, and deployment orders had reached two F-4 squadrons at Seymour Johnson AFB and an F-105G Wild Weasel squadron at McConnell AFB, as the grinding attrition along the DMZ had made it clear that SAM suppression would have to improve in a hurry if the ARVN defenses were to hold. As the Tactical Air Command completed this deployment, code-named Constant Guard, the JCS alerted the command that further deployments would soon follow.

Meanwhile, fighter squadrons from the 1st Marine Air Wing returned to Southeast Asia for the first time since their departure in November 1971. Two F-4 squadrons moved from Iwakuni, Japan, into Danang AB on April 6, with another following by April 15. This deployment was complicated by the Japanese government's unwillingness to support combat operations in Southeast Asia from forces based on its soil. The Marines therefore executed a "training deployment" into Cubi Point, in the Philippines, before continuing after a brief pause into Indochina. In theory, logistical support for these USMC F-4s should have been simplified by the presence of the Air Force's 366th Tactical Fighter Wing at Danang. In practice, however, Air Force Phantoms were different models from those flown by the Marines, and there proved to be little commonality between the aircraft of the two services. On the bright side, because there was no Marine ground force in combat, the command and control issues that had bedeviled air operations during earlier portions of the war did not surface in 1972. The Marine units worked within the Seventh Air Force command and control system, though chafing at the perceived inefficiency of the Air Force tasking process.[5]

Nixon's direction to Moorer paid even quicker dividends with respect to B-52s than with fighter aircraft. Within three hours of their conversation, SAC issued a warning order for the deployment of 20 more B-52s and 6 KC-135 tankers.

That was still not enough to meet the commander in chief's guidance. As the SAC historians commented, "All B-52D resources available within reason had now been exhausted for Bullet Shot deployments, the sortie rate had shot up to a new record of nearly 1,900 per month and still the JCS was looking for more." That was exactly correct, except that it was Nixon looking for more, not the military chain of command. That same day SAC directed yet another deployment, this time reaching into the B-52G fleet for 28 aircraft, all directed to Andersen AFB, Guam. The deployment of the B-52G models reflected Nixon's preoccupation with numbers of B-52 sorties. These aircraft had not been modified for conventional operations and so carried only 27 bombs, as compared with the 108 normally carried by the older B-52Ds. However, their combination of an internal bomb load and efficient engines enabled them to fly their combat sorties without air refueling, saving precious tanker resources for other requirements.[6]

The naval buildup was equally dramatic. The invasion found the *Coral Sea* and the *Hancock* launching combat sorties, the *Kitty Hawk* at Subic Bay, and the *Constellation* in Japan, on the way back to the United States after its Southeast Asia deployment. Back in the United States, the *Midway* was preparing for a mid-May deployment and the *Saratoga* was nearing its departure for a Mediterranean cruise. Within weeks, all these carriers were committed to the battle. The *Kitty Hawk* began its second line period with an emergency deployment from Cubi Point on April 2, and a day later it launched missions into the DMZ area.[7] Seventh Fleet recalled the *Constellation* from Japan, and the carrier arrived on station on April 7.[8]

It was more complicated with the ships still in America. The emergency demanded that these units condense the normal pre-cruise workup, and in the case of the *Saratoga*, that the air wing reorient its preparations from relatively routine Mediterranean operations to combat in Asia. The *Midway* and its Carrier Air Wing 5 received their deployment order on April 7 and deployed only three days later, seven weeks ahead of schedule. The *Saratoga* was alerted on April 8 and was under way 64 hours later. Fortunately, the ship and its air wing had just finished their training cycle. But reorienting from a Mediterranean cruise to combat operations in Southeast Asia demanded material support from Navy units all along the eastern seaboard, and then an emergency training program for the crews as the *Saratoga* made its way toward Southeast Asia. The wing conducted its first combat operations over South Vietnam on May 18.

Surface ships quickly moved to add their firepower, both north and south of the DMZ. By April 7 the gun line off MR I included the cruiser *Oklahoma City* and six destroyers. North of the DMZ, six more ships pounded SAM batteries, supply areas, and the Route 1 corridor. CINCPAC had already identified six destroyers in San Diego, four in Long Beach, and three in Pearl Harbor, all available for deployment within 24 hours if needed.[9]

The Air Force's sortie rate was slower to increase than the Navy's, even with the rapid deployment. Although arriving units quickly began to fly sorties, they could not generate appreciable combat power until the support base arrived, days later. In the first half of April the Air Force flew an average of 206 fighter sorties per day, a very marginal improvement over the March average of 204. The land-based sortie rate doubled once the support infrastructure was in place; in the second half of April the Air Force flew more than 400 sorties per day.[10] The B-52 sortie rate showed the same pattern: having averaged 50 sorties per day in March, the B-52s averaged only 52 in the first half of April, with the rate increasingly rapidly in the second half of the month.

In the month after the offensive opened, the overall fighter sortie rate in Southeast Asia increased from 326 to over 600 sorties per day. The focus of the sorties changed even more dramatically. In March U.S. fighter forces averaged 13 sorties per day in South Vietnam, with the vast majority of the air effort being directed against the Ho Chi Minh Trail. In April the daily average over South Vietnam reached 337.[11] The wave of fighters and bombers Nixon sent to Indochina quickly had an effect on the battlefields as the situation in South Vietnam reached its most dangerous period.

The increase in firepower, though, came far more rapidly than did the ability to control it effectively. The influx of aircraft and sorties overwhelmed the command and control system in theater during the first month of the offensive, robbing the U.S. buildup of much of the effectiveness it might otherwise have had. At the most basic level, the problems reflected the drawdown in the number of forward air controllers in theater, from about 425 to 160 pilots working over South Vietnam. Beyond that, it took time for the command system, largely atrophied in the years of Vietnamization, to regain proficiency in tasking and controlling attack sorties. In the first month of the offensive, the Navy estimated, only 60 percent of its sorties were controlled by FACs. The other flights released ordnance under flight leader control, or jettisoned their bombs, or dropped them into free-fire zones. Nixon could send more forces into the theater, but he could not rebuild an atrophied command and control system so quickly.

The third big wave of reinforcements came three weeks later, as the situation on the ground grew critical and the president directed an all-out air operation against North Vietnam. Nixon and Kissinger wanted to ensure that requirements in the battle area were satisfied, even as the attacks intensified over the North. On April 26 the JCS directed the deployment of two more tactical fighter squadrons to Udorn. The next increment was already under way as these two squadrons crossed the Pacific. A week later the Air Force chief of staff, General John D. Ryan, directed the 49th Tactical Fighter Wing (TFW) at Holloman AFB, New Mexico, to conduct a four-squadron deployment to Takhli RTAFB, Thailand. The wing began deploying one squadron per day, beginning on May 7. Four days later the wing flew its first combat sorties from Thailand, over An Loc.[12]

This deployment was the more remarkable because it sent a full wing into a base that the Americans had left six months earlier, and that had been largely stripped of everything useful in the interim. The Air Force historians commented: "The base was in need of extensive rehabilitation and there were shortages of power, water, useable living quarters, air conditioners (for high heat-producing/temperature-sensitive equipment) and dining halls."[13] It was a remarkable achievement from a logistical perspective, but the need to reopen this bare base highlighted the stresses shaping the U.S. response to the invasion. In planning this move, the JCS looked at deploying the 49th TFW into South Vietnam. The drawdown had left several facilities open, close to the battle area, and ready to receive the fighters. With old bases at Phu Cat, Cam Ranh Bay, Phan Rang, and Tuy Hoa all standing available, militarily it made little sense to reopen a base and to send a fighter wing into southern Thailand. But the iron demands of domestic politics in an election year persuaded Nixon to continue the troop withdrawal despite the crisis nearing its peak in South Vietnam. His speech on April 26 featured another reduction in U.S. forces, sized to enable him to claim that he had withdrawn 500,000 Americans from South Vietnam during his presidency. That number could only be met by sending more units to Thailand, despite the cost in combat effectiveness.[14]

The new manpower ceiling also compelled MACV to move the Marine air units at Danang AB, an area where they could directly support combat operations, to an extremely austere base hundreds of miles from the combat area. The Air Force had built a 10,000-foot runway at Nam Phong, Thailand, in 1967, but it had been used only as an emergency field since that time. It had one hangar, no maintenance facilities, no logistics or weapons storage areas, a runway, a taxiway, and a parking apron. Fuel would have to be trucked from a port facility, since there was no fuel storage area or pipeline. Nonetheless, all the other working airfields in Thailand were filled to capacity with Air Force units, and so on May 11 Moorer approved the plan to move the Marines into Nam Phong RTAFB on an "austere" basis—without even the limited creature comforts normal for a Marine deployment.

The Marines began combat operations from Nam Phong on June 16. The deployment to a field 340 miles west of Danang required in-flight refueling en route to targets in MR I, and lengthened the average duration of sorties from one to two hours, increasing stress on aircraft and crews alike. The added fuel for these long missions came at the expense of bomb loads, which were reduced by 500 pounds per sortie. The need to meet draw-down figures drove a huge cost in logistical load, combat effectiveness, and stress on the men involved.[15] The only positive outcome of this move was that the Marines could reunite their squadrons, creating a composite wing of A-6s, F-4s, helicopters, and KC-130 refueling aircraft.

President Nixon directed yet another deployment of B-52s on May 19, disregarding the reservations of the Air Force and the secretary of defense. At that point Nixon's patience was even more limited than usual, and he vowed: "I want this order carried out, regardless of how many heads have to roll in carrying it out." The president recognized that the military value of this force would be limited, but he expected that "the psychological value of having 100 more B-52s on the line in Vietnam would be enor-mous."[16]

This wave of reinforcements was double the size of any previous incre-ment, piling another 66 B-52Gs into an already saturated infrastructure on Guam. The wing coped with the additional aircraft by closing a runway and using it as a parking ramp. The B-52s began arriving on May 27, with arrivals continuing until June 8. The sortie count rose to 81 on June 5, 99 on June 15, 102 on June 19, and finally reached the stable rate of 105 per day on June 21.[17] Again, the bare numbers of aircraft conceal the immen-sity of the logistics effort needed to deploy and sustain this force. This in-crement required 61 C-141s, 20 C-5s, 4 DC-8s, and 4 Boeing 707s, which together hauled about 2,000 tons of cargo and nearly 2,500 passengers.

The military logistics system had responded magnificently to Nixon's direction, though the response was far from flawless. For the Air Force, most of the more serious problems arose in the first increments. These mostly reflected the difficulty of coordinating plans across the multitude of headquarters and units involved in the movements, with the difficulty compounded by rapidly changing plans. Both the 388th TFW at Korat and the 432nd Tactical Reconnaissance Wing (TRW) at Udorn found themselves greeting incoming units on the ramp, having been unaware that the augmenting forces were inbound until the arriving aircraft were on final approach. Excessive concern for security exacerbated these prob-lems in routine coordination. In the early deployments, time and security issues prevented the deploying units from coordinating with their hosts, and most units assumed they were moving to a bare base. They brought far more equipment than they would need in the developed infrastructure in Thailand.[18] This was a manageable problem, but it added to the stress on the airlift system, as gear shipped around the world to Thailand was turned around and shipped right back to the United States.

These problems aside, in those weeks the Air Force, Navy, and Marine logisticians forged a remarkable achievement. It was, in fact, a historic accomplishment. For the first time, the U.S. military employed jet transports and air refueling to project massive power around the world, quickly, in a large and sustainable force. This has come to seem rather routine in the succeeding decades, but this was the first such effort. It demonstrated a capability that no other nation has ever matched, and one that has become an essential element in America's strategic arsenal.

The military consequences of this massive movement were equally great. The second round of deployments brought to bear firepower beyond anything the North Vietnamese had anticipated, and proved to be a critical component in the ARVN's stand against the NVA. When Nixon decided to open a full-scale, sustained air campaign against the North in May, the third round of deployments enabled him to do so while also sustaining the necessary air support in South Vietnam. The two waves met different military needs—but both supported Nixon's goals of sustaining South Vietnam whatever the cost and of using this offensive to move toward a negotiated end to U.S. involvement in the war. The bare fact that Nixon would send such a massive force into the theater sent a clear message, to friend and foe alike, that the president expected to exact a heavy toll on the North Vietnamese for this attack.

But the deployment imposed a variety of costs on the American military. Some were obvious, some were subtle, but all shared one characteristic: the longer the deployment, the greater the costs. These fell predominantly on the Air Force and the Navy, which provided the vast bulk of the reinforcements.

Secretary Laird considered the president's aggressive reaction to the invasion to be "wild," and from the beginning attempted to temper the U.S. response.[19] He was unconvinced that the massive movement of forces to Southeast Asia was wise policy for either the near or the long term. He disagreed with Kissinger's view that the campaign would be short-lived, one way or the other. He told Kissinger: "That battle isn't going to be over this year . . . I don't like to get into a position where there are no more assets to continue over a long period of time."[20] The need to maintain a rotation base in the short term complemented his worry about the long-term effects of the campaign on American readiness. His years in office had seen the burgeoning of Soviet military power as the U.S. military fought an apparently endless war. As more and more forces were deployed, he fretted that he would leave office the following January "with our readiness at an all time low because of our efforts in Southeast Asia."[21] Laird's sensitivity to domestic politics also played a role, as he sought to minimize the nation's reengagement in an unpopular war.

On April 21 Laird sent a memorandum to Kissinger in an effort to hold the force levels in Southeast Asia to those on hand and deploying at the time. Laird argued that reinforcements beyond those already en route would provide small military and political benefits, given the substantial forces already in place or on the way. Already the air forces in theater could deliver about 80,000 tons of bombs per month, about equal to the 1967 level. He pointed out that the bases in Thailand were nearing saturation, and that the military would need to maintain a reserve to provide for future rotations. Further, he argued that even the costs of the current deployments would be difficult to meet, and that the morale of the deploying forces would decay if the forces were seen to be serving no useful military purposes.[22]

Haig offered Kissinger his views, concurring with Laird's points on the whole. The crisis that erupted the following week, though, swept away any chance that the flow of reinforcements might be halted. Laird's memorandum arrived at the White House a few days before Nixon ordered the third, and largest, wave of reinforcements. The defense secretary's recommendations did not have the effect he sought, but his memorandum did alert Haig and his superiors to the need for a rotation plan to sustain the augmented American presence in theater. Haig drafted a response for Kissinger, directing Laird to submit a rotation plan and to furnish "measures required to assure that sortie levels and naval gunfire support can continue without constraint."[23]

Laird's concerns about the long-term effects of this operation proved valid. The strains on the Air Force personnel system, for example, began with the first deployments and never really ended. Both bomber and fighter units were affected by the turmoil and the inability of the system to keep up with the constant churn of "short notice deployments, large numbers of people involved, numerous bases participating, the continual movement of people, and the differing and fluctuating policies for advance pay, per diem and the like." As time went on and deployments continued to add people to already crowded bases, housing and support issues became acute. The deployments tended to feed the need for more deployments in what has become known as the "logistics snowball." As the SAC historians summarized the situation: "The great number of people and aircraft present snowballed the requirements for even more people—security police to protect SAC assets and personal property, subject now to even greater risk of loss or theft. More people were also needed for packing, crating, and shipping the mounting numbers of parts and spares."[24]

The problems were exacerbated because the men came from bases all over the world, in small groups or as individuals, without the level of command supervision that normally structures military operations. In the fighter bases in Thailand the situation was even more problematic, since many of the men deployed for maintenance support were unqualified in the aircraft they were supposed to be maintaining.[25] Their supervisors were so busy supporting combat operations that there was little time for on-the-job training. This led, in turn, to disciplinary problems, as the deployed airmen found time weighing heavily on their hands. A crew chief at Korat RTAFB later recalled: "To say that drinking was a problem there was really an understatement . . . Drinking was rampant, I mean it was just assumed that you were going to drink yourself blind every chance you got."[26]

The massive deployments and the disruption of ship schedules imposed a range of costs on the Navy as well. By April the service already felt the pinch resulting from the massive reinforcement in Southeast Asia. The Navy was stripping ordnance, sensors, and antiaircraft missiles from around the world to send into the theater.[27] In June the chief of naval operations, Admiral Elmo "Bud" Zumwalt, sent a more comprehensive list of his concerns to Moorer, requesting that the CJCS advise the secretary of defense and the president of them.

At the broadest levels, the CNO was worried about the massive concentration of naval power in one corner of the world. That concentration required the Navy to denude all other areas, weakening deterrence and creating "a period of dangerous vulnerability." Zumwalt also pointed out that if the activity in Southeast Asia continued beyond September, "world-wide ordnance inventories will be severely depleted," and that the costs of the deployment would come at the expense of modernization and personnel programs. Serving at a most turbulent time, Zumwalt alerted Moorer and the chain of command to a cascading series of problems that would follow the commitment to this offensive: personnel turbulence and extended deployments, canceled exercises, disrupted maintenance schedules and modernization programs, all contributing to a decay in worldwide readiness.[28]

This final splurge in the Vietnam war contributed greatly to the hollow military of the late 1970s. Congress never fully replenished the matériel consumed in this massive deployment and the subsequent combat. This was an invisible corrosion, though, and it took time for the effects to appear. Serious as this outcome was, the impacts on the personnel serving were both more immediate and more easily observable.

To meet the president's direction, the average ship deployment in the Seventh Fleet increased from six to nine months, with the redeployment cycle reduced to six months. The stresses imposed by longer deployments were multiplied by the problems the service had making its recruiting requirements. The result was the perfect storm: fewer ships, fewer men per ship, more tasking. As Zumwalt summarized: "The intensity of the air activity over Vietnam that the White House demanded meant that there were more casualties, more damage to planes and ships, increasing shortages of spare parts and equipment of various kinds, and routine sixteen-hour and eighteen-hour or even twenty-hour working days for weeks on end for many of the men of the Seventh Fleet."[29] The aircraft carriers bore the brunt of the stepped-up operational tempo, staying under way over 87 percent of the time from April through August.

Racial tension provided the last element in this volatile mix. At the time, prejudice was endemic in the Navy, and the CNO was passionately engaged in an effort to improve this situation. Zumwalt thought that "When the pressures of daily life are so great that large numbers of people feel aggrieved, their nerves jangled, and their tempers stretched thin, the most likely objects of the hostility they feel are people they never much cared for when times were easy."[30] Perhaps predictably, the eruption arrived in the *Kitty Hawk*. This carrier had put to sea with ten days' notice, seven weeks before its scheduled departure. Once under way, it remained at sea for eight months, launching a record number of combat sorties. Fatigue and stress gradually mounted. On the night of October 12–13, 1972, the carrier was the scene of sporadic rampages in a racial confrontation. Remarkably, flight operations resumed only three hours after the last of the disturbances.

Four days later another violent outburst occurred on a fleet oiler, the *Hassayampa*. Zumwalt considered the incidents disturbing precisely because the two ships and situations were so dissimilar: "Clearly racial animosity was not confined to an overcrowded or overworked or insensitively commanded ship, but was a condition that afflicted perhaps unavoidably, the entire Navy."[31] Race provided the spark, long hours and seemingly endless deployments provided the fuel.

The most serious incident began weeks later, and again involved one of the carriers that had deployed to meet the initial NVA surge. The *Constellation* had been on the point of returning home in late March. But the ship was recalled from Japan on April 2, and spent another three months launching combat sorties before being relieved in June. Its deployment extended, the ship's time stateside was curtailed, which in turn meant that the crew had to complete a large package of repairs in an eight-week period. During that period the ship was nearly uninhabitable, filled with din and dust, with contractors working nonstop from 6 A.M. to 10 P.M.[32] In that atmosphere, tensions gradually rose until November 3, when about ninety black sailors conducted a sit-in. Over the following week, the confrontation achieved national notoriety. Zumwalt handled the situation personally, risking his removal by a White House concerned that the uprising might spread through the fleet and the other services.[33] The incident finally subsided with little lasting effect except to alienate Zumwalt further from Kissinger and Nixon.

The U.S. military would cope with the material and personal costs of this deployment for a decade. Not until the Reagan buildup of the early 1980s did the services finally rebuild their training programs and their supply inventories. The stakes in the American response were high, as was the payoff—but so, too, was the price.

8

B-52s OVER THE NORTH

For Creighton Abrams, his B-52s constituted a central reserve, the only force he controlled that he could use anywhere he needed, day or night. Through the years of his command in South Vietnam, as U.S. forces departed, he became increasingly reliant on his greatest remaining resource, the heavy firepower provided by the bomber force, which he described as having "the punching power of several ground divisions." He had become a virtuoso at using the B-52s to flail enemy logistics systems and to disrupt enemy troop concentrations.[1]

For Richard Nixon, his B-52s constituted the highest point of American military technology, a symbol of unmatchable might and unshakeable will. His willingness to use these aircraft in the North Vietnamese heartland, as Johnson had failed to do, bore testimony to the fact that he "had the will in spades" to take any measure necessary to win this campaign.

Like the blind men examining the elephant, both Abrams and Nixon had captured an essential part of the truth. Unlike the men in that fable, they struggled for control of the elephant, in an acrimonious struggle that opened in the first days of the offensive and continued until Abrams left Vietnam in late June. Their disagreement abated a bit as Nixon flooded the theater with B-52s, but it never really ended. There were always more requirements than there were aircraft to fill them.

At its heart, the dispute represented a fundamental difference in perspective between the theater commander and his commander in chief. As Moorer noted later: "I believe it's fair to say that General Abrams was far more concerned about activities in South Vietnam, where he was operating, than he was about Laos or North Vietnam or even Cambodia. While from a Washington view, the operation was looked on as a Southeast Asia vice a South Vietnam operation."[2] Perhaps transcending his perspective from Saigon, Abrams responded as a forty-year Army officer whose first consideration was the men fighting under his command. He shared the view of the ARVN 23d Division commander, Brigadier General Ly Tong Ba, who commented: "If the B-52 strikes only strategic targets they can strike only Hanoi. From the 17th parallel south I say that the best strategic targets for the B-52s is right in front of my positions."[3]

The dispute began in the first days of the offensive. By April 3, with the first detailed reports of the NVA assault, Nixon had already resolved to send the B-52s over the North. Word of his decision quickly reached Saigon, and Abrams responded with a message recommending that B-52s be "used primarily against enemy forces in-country. The outcome of the current campaign for the next several weeks will be fought and determined with enemy forces and logistics already deployed in South Vietnam and the Laotian panhandle." Abrams proposed that the campaign "leave the full weight of the B-52 effort for in-country application."[4]

Disregarding Abrams's recommendation, Nixon pressed for a B-52 attack as soon as possible, waiting only until after the strikes against the SAM sites in the southern DRV. Once the defenses had been pounded down, the B-52s would hit North Vietnam. Detailed planning began on April 7. As with the later strikes, the specific targets were chosen in an extended negotiation involving MACV, the JCS, CINCPAC, and SAC. Eventually the JCS and CINCPAC concurred on two targets, the railroad yards and POL (petroleum, oil, lubricants) storage facilities in Vinh.

The strike force consisted of twelve bombers, with six B-52s in each of two cells. Ten of the B-52s carried a standard load of 42 750-pound and 24 500-pound bombs, a total payload of almost 22 tons per aircraft. The other two carried 66 cluster bombs each. The bombers used the Skyspot radar guidance system at Hue for weapons release. The mission launched at 2:28 A.M. on April 10.[5]

The attack took the B-52s within range of two known SAM sites, and so Seventh Air Force and Carrier Task Force 77 assembled an overwhelming defense package. To protect these twelve aircraft, the Air Force launched eight aircraft to counter MiGs, another ten to suppress the SAM sites, and another four aircraft in standoff orbits jamming the North Vietnamese radars. Most notably, for the first time the Air Force conducted an operation that was to become a signature of the campaign against the North. Fifteen minutes before the bombers arrived, twenty F-4s laid a chaff corridor, dropping strips of tinfoil across the strikers' flight path, blanketing the bombers from detection by fire-control radar. From offshore, the Navy provided another four fighters, four aircraft for SAM suppression, and another two standoff jammers.

The defenses reacted strongly if not effectively, firing 35 missiles against the attacking force. None hit, and all the aircraft returned safely to base. Post-strike analysis indicated that the raid destroyed a maximum of 50 tons of fuel, cut the rail lines in four places, and hit ten rail cars and a locomotive. As the SAC historians summarized: "Damage was described in official reports as anything from moderate to minimal—that is, rather disappointing."[6] Certainly, it was scant payoff for a 70-aircraft strike force hitting a fixed target, with surprise on its side. Two days after the raid, Laird informed Kissinger that the B-52 strike had missed its target by a kilometer—not because the ground radar was inaccurate, but because the charts for North Vietnam were off by that amount. Succeeding strikes would have to use the bombers' internal radar systems until the charts could be recalibrated.[7]

The Americans might have been disappointed with their results, but the North Vietnamese were appalled at the ineffectiveness of their defenses. The air defenders did not even know that B-52s had been in the attack force until the following day, when a team from the Air Defense Headquarters traveled to Vinh and analyzed the bomb craters. The North Vietnamese Air Force (NVAF) official history lists a catalog of sins: "Our identification and engagement of low-flying aircraft was poor, our troops were unable to detect the enemy B-52s, and mutual support arrangements between units were inadequate. We did not mass our fire against the primary enemy attack flights, our combat efficiency was poor, and we were unable to protect the targets."[8]

Three days later the B-52s returned to the North in a strike on Bai Thuong Airfield. The North Vietnamese had used this base as a staging point for hit-and-run attacks through the preceding winter, and still stationed MiG-17s and MiG-21s there. This time the B-52s used their onboard targeting radar, and accuracy improved; the eighteen bombers left 530 craters in the target area, cutting the runway in seventeen places and destroying one MiG-17. The strike had the same massive escort package as the earlier mission against Vinh, with nearly the same overwhelming effect on the defenses. The American crews reported 34 SAM launches, with one EA-6 jamming aircraft destroyed.[9]

The military value of these two raids had been limited. They had succeeded, though, in putting Hanoi on notice that the air war directed by Nixon would be a very different affair from anything they had seen from Johnson. The air attacks continued and grew more dramatic over the next week, as the crisis deepened and the diplomatic situation became more complex. Next, Nixon directed a raid into the North Vietnamese heartland, against Hanoi and Haiphong—the first since 1968.

The difference in the target reflected a difference in the target audience for the strike. On April 12, Soviet Ambassador Anatoly Dobrynin had invited Kissinger to Moscow to conduct pre-summit talks with Brezhnev and other Soviet leaders. This raid aimed to strengthen Kissinger's position during his visit, and later Nixon's in Moscow, following the invariable Nixon formula of negotiating from strength. As Kissinger said on April 17, discussing the raid: "We have to show the Soviets that we're willing to confront them—otherwise the President's bargaining position in Moscow will be a disaster—being able to hold on in South Vietnam against the North Vietnamese doesn't help us bargain with the Soviets."[10]

To an even greater degree than the earlier raids, the first round of planning for this attack reflected Nixon's desire to inflict overwhelming shock. Over the week-long planning process, though, successive versions of the attack plan whittled away at the B-52 force. The first plans called for a 40-bomber strike, with 300 fighter sorties to widen the destruction and suppress the defenses. But the number of B-52s gradually dwindled to the final figure of 18.

That erosion reflected an extended and increasingly acrimonious debate between Nixon and Abrams over priorities for these aircraft, with Moorer acting as intermediary for the discussion. The tasking for the strike came at a particularly stressing time in theater. Mid-April found the ARVN engaged in a counteroffensive in MR I, the NVA threatening an attack in MR II, An Loc under siege in MR III, and air power compensating for forces deployed out of MR IV to these other areas. General Abrams's air forces were severely stretched across these theaters. The proximate issue was the diversion of B-52s away from the primary battlefield in the South; the deeper concern was the massive investment in the protective package, which especially affected the carrier-based aircraft.

Abrams's last protest reached Washington as Nixon returned from delivering a speech in Canada. The theater commander concluded: "In my view the risks have remained unchanged and they are grave."[11] Nixon judged that Abrams's message was aimed at ensuring that the president would get all the blame if the NVA offensive succeeded, and he decided to cancel the strike.[12] The message triggered a series of bitter phone calls among Nixon, Kissinger, Laird, and Moorer. As the tension rose, Kissinger demanded of Laird: "I want two names to replace Abrams—who should replace Abrams?" And he added bitterly: "In every crisis, the President is left by his people."[13] He and Nixon called Laird to cancel the strike when the attacking force was about an hour from Haiphong. By chance, Moorer happened to be with Laird, and he intervened to say: "The military people out in Vietnam already think we are crazy. If we scuttle this flight and have them jettison the bombs . . . then if there were any doubts about us being crazy they then would be convinced of it."[14]

Moorer persuaded all concerned to go ahead with the strike, and it proceeded as planned. One B-52 turned back en route, so seventeen bombed Haiphong that night. As in the earlier raids, the Navy and Seventh Air Force put together a massive supporting package to protect the bombers. Twelve A-6 Intruders were first into the target area, conducting single-ship low-level attacks against the SAM sites protecting the port. The Intruders barreled across the Gulf of Tonkin to find the NVA defenses alert and ready. Just as with the first strikes above the DMZ on April 6, the NVA's general staff alerted the local air defenders well ahead of the impending strike. This time the warning reached the 363rd Air Defense Division five hours before the planned attack, and nearly three hours before the B-52s were launched. Worse yet for the Americans, the air defense units were in the midst of an exercise, practicing the battle plan to defend Haiphong.[15] Representatives of the air defense service headquarters were at all command centers and out at the firing positions. As the air defense service commander, Major General Nguyen Xuan Mau, later recalled: "Clearly this was a very advantageous situation which could help the unit win victory."[16]

General Mau described the sequence as viewed by the defenders. At 0215 the tactical aircraft entered the area. At 0228 "B-52 cells began appearing on the intelligence mapboard at the central radar collation center. Only later did we learn that these were actually F-4s masquerading as B-52s." The missile regiments fired a barrage of SAMs at 0232, without result. At 0256 the first bombs began exploding as the B-52s reached the city. "At this time, however," Mau recounted, "we saw that none of our units were launching their missiles. The command post encouraged the units to fire, but the units reported back that they were unable to detect any targets."[17]

The attackers could not see the confusion inside the command center, only the missiles arcing through the night sky and the radar warning strobes on their warning systems. One pilot remembered: "Our strike was about thirty miles outside of Haiphong and there were already five or six SAMs in the air and we were not even in range. The whole thing was surreal. The threat indicator looked like a sparkler. It was emitting strobes in every conceivable direction in the world."[18]

The North Vietnamese defenders launched somewhere between thirty and thirty-five missiles, shooting down one F-105 Wild Weasel as it attacked a missile storage facility. The military value of this strike, combined with fighter attacks the next day, far exceeded anything achieved in the earlier raids. U.S. intelligence reported that the strike destroyed 23 POL tanks, cut three railroad lines, and destroyed 20–30 pieces of rolling stock.[19] A month later the *New York Times* correspondent Anthony Lewis wrote that the destruction was still evident: "Dozens of twisted railroad cars can be seen, although many of the tracks have been repaired."[20]

Alone among these April strikes against the North, this raid inflicted serious collateral damage on the North Vietnamese population. To put it more plainly, the B-52s struck a number of civilian areas, killing many women and children. City officials claimed that the raids killed 244 civilians, with another 513 injured and over 2,000 homes destroyed. Lewis reported: "A large series of apartment blocks called Cau Tre Workers' Housing is almost completely smashed. The best-preserved object is a small dove house still standing on its pole in front of the shattered buildings."[21] Accounts from French diplomatic circles in mid-May noted: "Haiphong has been extremely seriously hit and . . . civilians have brought dead into the town hall of Haiphong to remonstrate with authorities over the loss of life."[22]

No one in the American chain of command deliberately targeted civilians. However, civilian deaths were an almost inevitable part of the strike plan, given the technology available to the crews and the tactical situation. A cell of B-52s normally released its bombs into a "box" about $1\frac{1}{4}$ miles long and half a mile wide. Few targets in an urban area could even theoretically fit into such a box. Further, the margin for error in such an attack was prohibitively small; with the B-52s delivering their bombs at a true air speed of 420 knots, a ten-second delay in weapons release would cause a one-mile error, enough to place a bomb load into populated areas. Even under ideal circumstances, the B-52 bombing system was imprecise—it had been designed, after all, for nuclear strike missions. And the circumstances facing the crews that night were far from ideal: a first-look attack on a heavily defended area in darkness, with dozens of missiles arcing through the sky, any of which could mean death. Finally, as one correspondent reporting on the strike noted: "The blast pressure from the B-52 raids . . . is enough to blow down flimsy houses hundreds of yards away from the B-52 targets."[23] The strike and all of its consequences perfectly reflected Nixon's direction with regard to strikes in the North: "Now, we won't deliberately aim for civilians, but if a few bombs slop over, that's just too bad."[24]

The B-52 night strikes were followed the next day by Navy and Air Force attacks on Hanoi and Haiphong. For the first time since 1968, F-4s appeared over the North Vietnamese capital, with thirty-two aircraft striking the Than Am petroleum processing station and the Gia Thuong storage area. Meanwhile, Navy fighters returned to Haiphong, striking a series of warehouse areas, the naval base, two airfields, a vehicle storage facility, and the shipyard.[25] The Air Force strike was delayed for an hour, as weather threatened the mission. Vogt finally decided to launch the strike, ready to divert the aircraft to the secondary target if necessary. The first attackers found the target area clear, and rolled in from 14,000 feet. By the time the second wave neared the target area, black oil smoke reached an altitude of 18,000 feet. Vogt considered the strike "one of the best ever conducted in the Hanoi area," especially since the Air Force escort shot down three MiG-21s during the raid.[26] A naval gunfire attack on the Dong Ha peninsula outside Haiphong further strengthened the message to Moscow.

Although Moorer had interceded to avoid the last-minute cancellation of the B-52 strike, Kissinger and Nixon considered the problem with Abrams serious enough to send Haig around the world to Saigon. He was assigned to discuss B-52 and fighter attacks on the North with Abrams, and to ensure that Abrams understood their larger purposes and the strategy at play beyond Indochina. Haig and his accompanying staff members were also expected to assess the situation, providing the president and Kissinger with an evaluation independent of the military and diplomatic reporting chains coming out of Saigon.[27] It was the first of three trips Haig would take to Southeast Asia during the offensive, as he provided the nearest equivalent to direct on-scene observation available to Nixon.

This series of strikes concluded with two more raids in the Thanh Hoa area, on April 21 and 23, during Kissinger's visit to Moscow. Like the three earlier strikes, these attacks were more useful from a diplomatic perspective than for purely military purposes, serving primarily to strengthen Kissinger's position in his talks with Brezhnev and Gromyko. Both raids struck shortly after nightfall, with the now-standard escort packages working to suppress enemy defenses. During these two raids the NVA defenders launched 55 to 65 missiles, with one SA-2 damaging a B-52 on the second raid. The bomber managed to deliver its ordnance and then diverted to Danang; the crew escaped unharmed.[28]

These B-52 raids were only the most vivid element of an escalating pattern of attacks on North Vietnam. The fighter strikes beginning in early April have been overshadowed in history by the Linebacker campaign that followed. However, they brought significant firepower to bear on the North Vietnamese as the NVA attempted to bring supplies forward into the battle area. The air attacks also wore away at the North Vietnamese air defenses in the area and reintroduced U.S. planners and air crews to sustained offensive operations over North Vietnam. In the month of April, Air Force attack sorties in the North increased almost tenfold from the March total, from 64 to 628. The Navy increase was even greater, from 68 to 1,250 attack sorties. Most of these went into the area just north of the DMZ, targeting the supplies that would flow to NVA forces engaged in MR I.

There was yet another component to this burgeoning American assault on North Vietnam: naval gunfire. In fact, this was the first weapon directed against the North. Untroubled by the poor weather that had grounded most aircraft, the *Joseph Strauss* and the *Richard B. Anderson* fired on a SAM site in North Vietnam on April 5. By April 7 the Seventh Fleet mustered a gun line of six destroyers off North Vietnam, with another seven ships, including the cruiser *Oklahoma City*, operating in support of South Vietnamese forces in MR I.[29] In April these vessels fired a total of 83,200 shells—over eight times the 10,000 they had fired in March.[30]

As with nearly all areas of the U.S. response, the naval gunfire support needed a few days to pick up its effectiveness. North of the DMZ the gradual broadening of the operating area meant that the ships continually found themselves firing into positions that they had not observed. Their direction was to take advantage immediately of every increase in their operating authorities, without any provision for surveillance or the normal targeting process. So instead of taking time to reconnoiter the new areas, the ships fired into them on the basis of maps and whatever they could observe from offshore. As the Seventh Fleet commander, Vice Admiral William Mack, commented: "We literally walked up the shore doing the same thing, just throwing of hundreds of rounds of ammunition over on the sand and the roads, just wasted."[31] The problem was exacerbated by the absence of spotters to observe and adjust the naval gunfire. In mid-April the Navy deployed five Marine TA-4s to Danang to fill that role, and the problem eased.[32]

For all the destruction wrought by the naval gunfire, it was not entirely a one-sided battle. North Vietnamese shore batteries and artillery units fired at the ships offshore, with occasional successes. The Navy deployed two ships to Danang to provide an advanced repair capability for ships damaged in the exchanges of gunfire. In the first month of the offensive they patched up four ships and sent them back into battle. Somewhat ironically, an American missile inflicted the heaviest damage on a ship in this period. During the Haiphong raids on April 16, a misguided Shrike antiradiation missile homed in on the *Worden*, severely damaging the superstructure and killing one sailor.[33]

Despite their inefficiencies, the naval gunfire attacks quickly affected the flow of supplies down Route 1 toward the southern battlefield. The NVA command therefore directed the Air Force to attack ships conducting gunfire missions off the North Vietnamese panhandle. Headquarters hoped these attacks would open up the supply lines toward the battle area and drive the naval gunfire away from the coastline.[34]

The North Vietnamese had begun preparations for this operation the preceding November, when the general staff directed the Air Force to select ten MiG-17 pilots to train in over-water navigation and ship attack. The Cuban ministry of defense sent a pilot and a technical officer to help train the North Vietnamese pilots in ship-attack tactics, and by March six pilots had qualified in this new skill. Meanwhile, North Vietnamese engineers constructed a secret airfield in the southern DRV panhandle as a staging area for the attacks. The plan was to deploy two MiG-17s south to Quang Binh Province, just above the DMZ, and strike with the advantage of surprise. The aircraft deployed secretly on April 18. They launched their attack the following day, vectored to their targets by coastal defense radar.[35] While en route the MiG pilots lost sight of each other, and they conducted separate attacks, delivering their 250-kilogram weapons using the skip-bomb techniques pioneered during World War II.

The MiGs' target was Task Group 77.1.2, with the cruiser *Oklahoma City* and the destroyers *Higbee*, *Sterett*, and *Lloyd Thomas*, which was conducting shore bombardment of the Dong Hoi area. The Navy analysis of the engagement recounted: "After one false start, an enemy aircraft closed the formation at an elevation of about 50 feet and *Sterett* fired a salvo of missiles scoring a direct hit with the second missile seconds after the hostile aircraft had attacked and bombed the *Higbee*, destroying her after gun mount." The second MiG turned and fled toward the mountains, with the *Sterett* firing another salvo. The aircraft was out of sight as the missiles neared, but "information from other sources indicate high probability of a kill of a second Mig."[36] The North Vietnamese account, in contrast, claims that both aircraft returned safely to base, after sorties lasting only seventeen minutes.[37]

This period of escalation provided an opportunity for American air forces to retune their tactical skills. For those who had been in Southeast Asia before, it was a matter of going back to basics. The same tactics and mind-sets that had kept pilots alive in 1968 worked in 1972. But many of the crews and planners, especially those on the Air Force side, were new to the theater, and this was a period for relearning painful and expensive lessons lost during the bombing halt.

For the North Vietnamese, the lessons of this period went still deeper. This series of attacks forced a fundamental reevaluation of their whole air defense posture. The Haiphong strike on April 16, especially, demonstrated beyond a shadow of a doubt that the air defenses of their heartland were nearly helpless against the B-52s. The defenders had no counter to the new tactics and equipment employed by the American strike forces.

The Air Force–Air Defense Command's lack of preparation for the attacks speaks clearly of the North Vietnamese surprise at Nixon's response. The first strikes on the North occurred, for example, on April 6; three days later, finally, the general staff ordered all armed forces units throughout North Vietnam to shift to a wartime footing. The air defense units' inability even to detect, let alone to engage, the B-52s in their first attack on the North on April 10 shocked the North Vietnamese. The attack on Haiphong on April 16 compounded this reaction, and a day later "the Air Force–Air Defense Command convened a military-political conference to develop military tasks to be accomplished during the following phase." The conference resulted in a new mission statement and operations order for the air defenders. The operations order defined three critical tasks: protecting supply lines and communications; protecting key strategic areas in North Vietnam; and providing cover for the combined-arms units fighting in the South. The tasks were daunting. As the history of the air defense forces summarized: "These three missions were to be carried out simultaneously under very urgent conditions and throughout our country at a time when our forces, equipment, and the combat skills of our troops were limited in many respects."[38]

Most critically, as the history states: "We realized that the possibility that the U.S. would use B-52s to conduct massive attacks against the North would soon become a reality. We needed to study the enemy carefully . . . to find ways to engage the B-52s effectively."[39] The search for counters to the bombers would engage the service's staff, operational units, intelligence, and scientific/technical capabilities.

This first round of attacks exposed a wide range of problems for the air defenders. First and most fundamentally, the air defense service had been overconfident going into the battle, and therefore "our preparations for combat had been inadequate." The service's strong performance during the First War of Destruction had left it unready for a resumption of war in the North. As a result: "When confronted with the enemy's rapid escalation and his new plans and schemes, the combat efficiency of our troops had been low, we had been unable to shoot down enemy B-52s, the targets we were assigned to protect had been hit, and large numbers of civilians had been killed and wounded."[40]

There were also operational errors. The air defense units were badly deployed for this new operational environment, with units widely spread across the theater. It was necessary to concentrate and thicken the air defense forces, even at the cost of leaving some areas exposed to attack. Among a series of smaller moves, the command redeployed the 377th Air Defense Division from Laos, pulling it back into lower North Vietnam to refit. It would become a new strategic reserve force. The 365th Air Defense Division moved northward to strengthen its ability to protect Route 1. As these forces concentrated, the Air Defense Command offered support to the military regions and the local militias in strengthening their air defenses. The military regions deployed 22 more air defense battalions, and the militias deployed another 603 antiaircraft guns.[41]

Two weeks later, the general staff sent an inspection team to evaluate the service's combat performance. The team included both a staff element, to look at combat tactics, and a technical element, to study the technological issues involved. Clearly, the general staff remained unsatisfied with the air defenders' performance, and with the response to the early attacks.

The delegation "saw clear evidence that this war of destruction was completely different from the first American war of destruction. This war was a rapidly escalating war, which escalated by leaps and bounds and made massive, concentrated attacks against many different areas using new or improved technical equipment, devious tactics and operational procedures, and was highly destructive and violent." The Americans had gone to a new generation of aircraft, with F-4s and A-7s largely replacing the F-105s and A-4s of the 1960s. They had introduced a range of precision weapons, upgraded their electronic warfare systems, and developed a newer and more deadly antiradiation missile, the AGM-78. Beyond the strategic surprise achieved by Nixon, the Americans' array of new weapons found the North Vietnamese ill prepared. They had been generally aware that the Americans had new jammers, but had been unable to gain "concrete and specific knowledge of the technology and tactics that the enemy air force would use." As a result, they "continued training our troops using the old training manuals derived from past experience."[42]

The North Vietnamese concluded that, in this first phase of the air offensive, they had basically accomplished their three strategic missions. It was hardly an overwhelming success, though. Because they "had not properly assessed the situation and our missions, the service had not yet been able to ensure that it would fight continuously, and the combat efficiency of our troops was still low."[43]

Both of the adversaries had been surprised in the first days of the renewed warfare in the North. As the conflict continued, its course would largely be determined by the ability of the two sides to adjust, to adapt to the ever-changing circumstances of a fluid combat environment. The Americans would always enjoy the edge in technology and numbers; the North Vietnamese would have an advantage as defenders, and in their ability to mobilize their entire society behind the war effort. The interplay between these enemies would not cease until the end of the war, months away.

9

ATTACK IN THE HIGHLANDS

Along the DMZ and north of Saigon, the NVA offensives struck like waves, crashing down and sweeping away defenses in stunning catastrophic blows. On the third front, in the central highlands, the NVA advance was more like a tide, gradually but inexorably gathering strength, slowly grinding away the outposts that protected the central core of the region.

The terrain and the ARVN defensive alignment made this approach inevitable. The highlands fell within South Vietnam's Military Region II, a vast territory that comprised almost half of South Vietnam's land area but was home to less than 20 percent of its population, with about three million inhabitants. To the west MR II bordered Laos and Cambodia in an area of sprawling high plateaus, rolling hills, and dense jungle. The highlands sloped eastward toward a long, narrow, and curving strip of coastal land. Through this coastal region ran National Route 1, connecting a series of ports along the South China Sea and extending southward the full length of the nation. Down the spine of the highlands, roughly paralleling Route 1, lay Route 14, connecting the center of allied power in the region—the garrison at Kontum, and to its south the cities of Pleiku and then Ban Me Thuot. From Pleiku, Route 19 extended to the southeast over the An Khe pass, linking the northern highlands with the port at Qui

Nhon, the critical entry point for supplies for the ARVN forces defending the highlands. Weather patterns set the pace of fighting in MR II as throughout Indochina; the period from February through May, which offered a brief interlude between the monsoons, was almost invariably the time the communists chose for offensive action.

The South Vietnamese entrusted this vast region to two divisions under the overall command of Lieutenant General Ngo Dzu. The 22d ARVN bore responsibility for the northern provinces of Kontum, in the highlands, and Binh Dinh, along the coast. These provinces both offered formidable challenges, though of different kinds. Kontum Province lay adjacent to the highly developed NVA logistics centers along the tri-border area. Binh Dinh Province was a long-standing center of Viet Cong activity, extending back into the 1940s. The area had been pacified, at least on the surface, but much remained to be seen about the solidity of that pacification effort if it should be placed under stress. A South Korean division stationed in Binh Dinh provided security for Route 19 from the coast up to An Khe pass, but by 1972 it had lost the aggressiveness that had characterized its operations through most of the war; like all the allied contingents, it was under pressure to minimize casualties in a declining cause. The 23d ARVN secured the southern portion of the region. II Corps also exercised operational command of eleven ranger battalions stationed along the western border to protect the central core of the region.

By early 1972 the American ground combat role in the region had come to an end, but the United States maintained a formidable presence in the person of John Paul Vann, the senior advisor to Dzu. A unique combination of energy, passion, deceit, courage, ambition, and talent, Vann was controversial at the time and remains so today.[1] His involvement with the war began in the early 1960s and continued, off and on, through his departure from the military and his return to Southeast Asia as a civilian working for USAID. Late in 1971, when Dzu rose to command of II Corps, Vann engineered the appointment as Dzu's senior advisor, effectively achieving the general officer status that had been closed to him while on active duty. Vann exercised a blend of formal and informal power—his formal authority as senior advisor buttressed by his long commitment to the war, his reputation, his contacts with journalists, and his long-standing influence over the ARVN corps commander.

II Corps had long been considered the weakest of South Vietnam's four corps commands.[2] The two divisions were thought to be among the ARVN's worst, and while Dzu approached his duties energetically, he had never demonstrated extraordinary talent as a combat leader. Recognizing the threat to the highlands, President Thieu sent an Airborne brigade from the national strategic reserve to bolster the command. This move brought its own problems, as the inevitable frictions across the South Vietnamese chain of command surfaced once again. As 1971 waned, Vann's deputy, General George E. Wear, offered his assessment of II Corps at a MACV staff meeting. "I wish I could be a lot more optimistic than I am about the ARVN in II Corps," Wear said. "Our experience has been, as you well know, that when the NVA well-trained units come across the border, the ARVN just hasn't stood up against them." Worse yet, there was little evident improvement despite the resources being poured into Vietnamization: "The two divisions I don't think have really improved in the 17 months I've watched them."[3] In early 1972 a CIA assessment noted: "The government forces assigned to defend Military Region 2 are among the weakest in South Vietnam, both in numbers and in demonstrated fighting prowess."[4]

These American analysts would have been still more discouraged had they known that General Nguyen Huu Hanh, the deputy commander of II Corps, was a communist sympathizer, intent on doing "nothing to harm the revolution." The full extent of his activities in support of the liberation forces remains unknown, but at a minimum they included protecting communist agents and working to minimize the aggressiveness of ARVN military action.[5]

The state of the ARVN forces was of relatively little concern through the early 1970s, as the communist forces in the region were in no better condition and action remained light. In mid-1971, however, that picture began to change. As early as June 1971, when plans for the 1972 offensive were still in work back in Hanoi, the NVA deployed heavy artillery and 85-mm antiaircraft units into the area, along with 8,000 infantrymen. MACV intelligence carefully tracked the buildup along the tri-border area through the winter of 1971–1972, watching as the communists deployed the 2nd NVA Division from Laos and the 320th NVA Division down the Ho Chi Minh Trail from its base areas in North Vietnam. By February 1972 North Vietnamese strength in the region had reached levels never before seen in the conflict, with large stockpiles of equipment in place.[6] The newly deployed divisions would join the 3rd NVA "Gold Star" Division, operating in its traditional areas in the coastal lowlands, under a campaign headquarters operating out of the tri-border area.

Observing the buildup, U.S. and South Vietnamese intelligence tried to piece together a picture of North Vietnamese objectives and capabilities. Thieu and his advisors expected the highlands to be the focus of the North Vietnamese offensive, with the NVA pursuing its old dream of shearing South Vietnam into two isolated halves along Route 19.[7] American estimates were more circumspect: the CIA expected the NVA attack to come during Tet, in mid-February, and to aim primarily at disrupting Nixon's visit to China. Prisoners and defectors told broadly similar stories, of large NVA forces moving forward from the base areas in Laos and Cambodia, expecting to strip away the firebases and border camps along the frontier, then attack the major garrison cities of Kontum and Pleiku. Other reports indicated that the NVA would contest ARVN control of Binh Dinh Province.

During the first months of 1972, II Corps worked to flesh out this broad picture of NVA intentions, with Vann and the other American advisors through the chain of command providing much of the motive force. Everyone involved expected an offensive. From an intelligence perspective, the remaining questions were at least as important: the timing, the targets, the weight, and the persistence of the attack all remained blanks. Vann threw himself into filling out this intelligence picture, and into readying II Corps for the attack, with his characteristic energy and passion. Always he felt the press of time, expecting the offensive to fall in mid-February, during Tet, or perhaps a week later, during Nixon's visit to Beijing. The demonstrated shortcomings of RVNAF intelligence and air capabilities fueled Vann's sense of urgency. Nearly all useful intelligence came through U.S. signals and communications intercepts, as ARVN ground patrolling remained remarkable mostly for its lack of aggressiveness.[8] Vann's real concern was that the South Vietnamese would be unable to provide targets for B-52 strikes or to control U.S. fighter aircraft effectively.[9]

In this case Vann was struggling with a broader issue. Control of air power was an area in which the forms of Vietnamization had been observed, with actual combat capability lagging far behind. Most observers agreed that the South Vietnamese fighter pilots, especially in the A-1 Skyraiders, were world class. Vietnamese forward air controllers, however, generally performed dismally, as did the air control system as a whole once the Americans relinquished control. The regional air control center was transferred to the South Vietnamese in July 1971, with only a small advisory group of Americans remaining to assist the transition. The head of the advisory group, Colonel Joe Joiner, reported that from that point most of the South Vietnamese sorties were "totally non-productive" because the FACs could rarely be counted on to conduct effective reconnaissance. Instead, most strikes went against known coordinates whether or not an actual target existed there.

Vann encouraged Dzu to adopt a forward defense strategy, extending the ARVN defenses along an arc north of Kontum, and then around to the west along Rocket Ridge, a height overlooking Route 14 between Kontum and Tan Canh extending northwest toward the tri-border area. At Vann's urging, Dzu directed the 22d ARVN to move its headquarters to Tan Canh, north of Kontum, stationing the 42nd Regiment there and its sister unit, the 47th, at Dak To II, a few miles southwest of Tan Canh. Vann expected these strongholds to stall the NVA offensive, holding the North Vietnamese in place to permit American B-52s and fighter strikes to punish the attacking troops. This aggressive posture suited Vann well—but it was not natural for the ARVN forces, or for their senior commanders. As March drew to a close, Vann told Abrams: "I see the current situation as an outstanding opportunity for the GVN [the South Vietnamese government], but one that is almost certain to be missed through inadequate leadership and motivation from corps commander on down."[10]

The months of careful study by U.S. and ARVN intelligence exposed the NVA's broad-scale deployment patterns very well. Allied intelligence was less successful, however, in defining the overall NVA strategy in the region and the relationships of the various operations the NVA would conduct. The high command assigned forces in the highlands the following tasks:

> Annihilate the enemy, liberate the Dak To-Tan Canh area, and, if the conditions are favorable, liberate Kontum City. The direction of development may be the direction of Pleiku; if the conditions are favorable, expand the Pleiku liberated area, liberate Ban Me Thuot City, and establish a full-fledged base area linking the highlands with the base area in Eastern Nam Bo. Since the highlands were closely related to the Zone 5 [central coastal] lowlands, the highlands main-force troops' tasks were to annihilate at all costs the enemy's forces and to draw out and pin them down, thereby creating a basis for the offensive and uprising movement in the Zone 5 lowlands.[11]

As elsewhere, the direction to prepare for an all-out offensive triggered feverish activity among the NVA and Viet Cong forces committed to the attack. Through the winter the NVA regiments trained in two tactics suited to the campaign plan outlined by the Central Military Committee: "mobile envelopment and continuous attack, and siege operations ending with an assault to overrun enemy positions using combined-arms tactics." Logistical preparations continued all winter, hindered by the fierce air attacks along the supply routes and the intensive bombardments in the NVA base areas ordered by Nixon in early February. Viet Cong logisticians and NVA engineers constructed an extensive road network to support the impending offensive, and executed a "rice campaign" to assemble the food to sustain an attacking force.[12] Nonetheless, with only two weeks remaining before the campaign was to begin, the supply services had amassed only about 35 percent of the rice necessary for the plan. "Rice, ammunition, and fuel were still lacking . . . The difficulties were piling up so much that they seemed insurmountable."[13] In spite of intense activity during these final days, the NVA managed to stockpile barely enough supplies for the campaign's opening stage.

The action in the highlands began in early April, almost simultaneously with the attacks north of Saigon and along the DMZ. As projected by the NVA high command, the attacks in three widely separated theaters stretched the RVNAF to its utmost. In MR II, the offensive opened with an assault on Firebase Delta, the southernmost outpost on Rocket Ridge, on April 3. Vann thwarted that attack almost single-handedly, repeatedly flying into the compound to kick supplies out of his helicopter to the hard-pressed defenders. That day he assumed a personal responsibility for II Corps's defenses that he would never relinquish. The following day the 3rd NVA Division erupted out of its long-held base area in the An Lao Valley, overrunning Binh Dinh's two northernmost districts. Within a matter of days, the painstaking pacification effort of the previous three years was in tatters, leaving 200,000 South Vietnamese under communist control. Facing the long-awaited NVA offensive, Dzu initially decided to strip the coastal lowlands of ARVN troops, deploying them into the highlands to strengthen the defenses north of Kontum. Vann talked him out of that move, but the stress had begun to build, both on the ARVN defenses across MR II and, more significantly, on their corps commander.[14]

Over the next few days ARVN intelligence confirmed that the next wave of attacks was imminent, with the 320th NVA Division moving into position in the west. The attack opened on Firebase Charlie on April 14, with a punishing artillery bombardment followed by two mass infantry as-

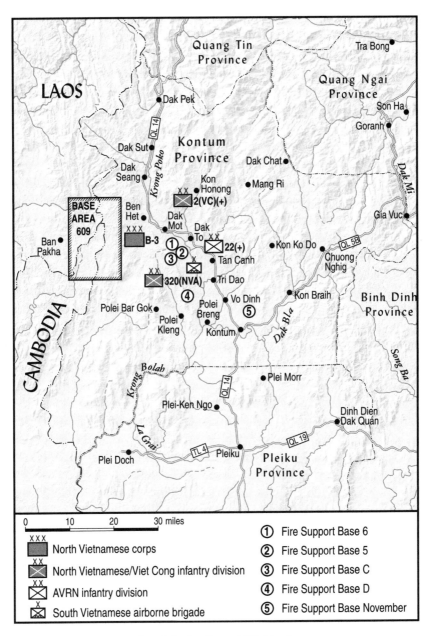

LAOS

Quang Tin
Province

Tra Bong•

Quang Ngai
Province

Son Ha•

•Dak Pek

Goranh•

Dak Sut•

Kontum
Province

Dak Chat•

•Dak
Seang

Kon
Honong•

•Mang Ri

Gia Vuc•

BASE
AREA
609

Ben
Het•

2(VC)(+)

Dak
Mot•

Dak
To•

22(+)

•Kon Ko Do

QL 5B

Ban•
Pakha

B-3

① ②
③ ⊠
•Tan Canh

Chuong
Nghig•

320(NVA)

•Tri Dao

Binh Dinh
Province

④
Polei
Breng•
•Vo Dinh

•Kon Braih

Polei Bar Gok•

⑤

Polei
Kleng•
•Kontum

CAMBODIA

Krong Bolah

•Plei Morr

Song Ba

Plei-Ken Ngo•

Dinh Dien
•Dak Quan

La Grai

Plei Doch•
•Pleiku

Pleiku
Province

0   10   20   30 miles

XXX	North Vietnamese corps	①	Fire Support Base 6
XX	North Vietnamese/Viet Cong infantry division	②	Fire Support Base 5
XX	AVRN infantry division	③	Fire Support Base C
X	South Vietnamese airborne brigade	④	Fire Support Base D
		⑤	Fire Support Base November

Attack in the Central Highlands

saults. The base fell that night, followed a week later by Firebase Delta. The western approaches to Tan Canh and Route 14 were now open.

During those weeks in early April, the NVA gradually pushed the South Vietnamese defenders of Tan Canh and Dak To back toward their main compounds, eroding the strength of the garrisons in a careful campaign to isolate the outposts. The painstaking approach left the 2nd NVA Division with overwhelming superiority at the point of attack—both numerically and qualitatively. The blow fell on April 24, with the 2nd NVA Division and four independent regiments attacking Tan Canh. The North Vietnamese multiplied the shock of their assault with their first use of wire-guided antitank weapons, Soviet AT-3 Saggers. This was hardly leading-edge weaponry, except in the context of this war. It was based on German technology from World War II, and had been exported to the Warsaw Pact countries and the Middle East in the late 1960s. At Tan Canh it won the fight with the first shots. The first Sagger fired destroyed a South Vietnamese tank. Minutes later, another collapsed the post's command bunker, killing about twenty soldiers. More important, this shot destroyed the fighting spirit of the division commander, Colonel Le Duc Dat. Physically uninjured, Dat decided that the fight was lost, and took no further part in the defense. The battle raged on through the afternoon, with the wire-guided weapons continuing to whittle away at the defenders' tank force and the NVA artillery pounding the compound. Meanwhile, NVA units closed Route 14 both north and south of Tan Canh, leaving the garrison isolated as it approached its last hours.

That night the NVA deployed tanks from the north. Once again, as along the DMZ and at Loc Ninh, the first sight of tanks shocked the ARVN defenders and dissolved their resistance. The senior American advisor, Colonel Phillip Kaplan, called in AC-130 gunships, and they took station over the outpost, working around low clouds and avoiding fire from the antiaircraft units around the perimeter. Finally four helicopters arrived to evacuate the American advisory team, as Tan Canh fell to the North Vietnamese. The defenses at Dak To II disintegrated quickly under NVA pressure, and the firebase was in North Vietnamese hands by nightfall on April 24.

At that point the way to Kontum was open, had the NVA only seized the opportunity. Once again, though, they followed the pattern they had established in early fighting on the other two fronts. They failed to exploit their dearly bought early victories, giving the ARVN and their American supporters the chance to shore up defenses. Along the DMZ, north of Saigon, and finally in the central highlands, the NVA shredded the defenses with their initial onslaught. In the highlands as in the other two areas, their hesitation proved fatal, leaving them at the mercy of massed American air power.

The ARVN, too, fell into fatal patterns in this engagement. As they did along the DMZ, in MR II they settled into firebases, which then became set-piece targets for NVA artillery. The ARVN troops were unready to face the NVA tanks, despite the months of warning. As a result, two regiments had disintegrated, and the entire defensive strategy and alignment for the central highlands lay in ruins. Vann had encouraged Dzu to adopt an aggressive forward defense, against the repeated advice of his deputy. Now his gamble had failed. Vann and Dzu would have to devise a new strategy and find forces to hold the highlands, working against time to reconstitute the defense before the NVA could resume its advance.

Of more immediate material concern, the ARVN soldiers multiplied their subsequent problems by failing to destroy the equipment in their evacuated positions. In Tan Canh and Dak To they left behind 23 105-mm howitzers, 7 155-mm field pieces, 10 T-41 tanks, and 16,000 rounds of artillery ammunition. American gunships and fighters would destroy what they could, but much of this equipment would be turned against the ARVN in the weeks to come. This, too, was a tendency established in earlier battles; an advisor in MR III estimated that during the first two weeks of the offensive the United States used 80 percent of its tactical air strikes in the area destroying captured ARVN equipment.[15]

Most of all, though, the combat in this sector resembled the fighting elsewhere in exposing weaknesses among the ARVN senior commanders. At the end of April Vann submitted a report summarizing the results of the campaign to that point and giving his prognosis for future events. As he viewed it: "The attacking enemy units gained momentum, not because of their effectiveness, but because of the collapse of friendly opposition." He attributed that collapse, in turn, "not to a good enemy effort, but rather from the effects of years of ineffective leadership in many RVNAF units. Soldiers, witnessing the timidity and incompetence of their leaders developed an irrational fear of the enemy."[16]

In a perverse way, that offered a ray of hope. Vann noted that new leaders had been assigned to the 22nd Division, and that the defenses of northern MR II now came under the command of Colonel Ly Tong Ba of the 23rd ARVN. There was nothing wrong with the equipment, or even with the fighting spirit of the soldiers, if properly led: "Throughout the region,

GVN forces are superior in numbers, equipment, and support . . . The GVN problem is morale rather than military capacity."[17] The key lay in the new leadership, and Vann was energetic and capable enough to compensate for any ARVN shortcomings in that area. In fact, at this juncture he and his American staff assumed effective command of the defenses.

Vann commented on the psychological aspects of the defeat among the populace. In early April, he reported, there had been a widespread confidence that the ARVN and its American backers would easily defeat the enemy. The disasters at Tan Canh and Dak To had instilled "almost a psychotic dread of NVA tanks that afflicts the GVN troops as well as the citizenry." This fear reflected a larger concern, that the United States had bargained away South Vietnam in the new triangular diplomacy, a suspicion that caused "extreme fear and lack of confidence in the GVN in Kontum and Binh Long. The already prevalent attitude that Vietnam is a pawn being manipulated by the US, the People's Republic of China, and the USSR, further compounds public pessimism."[18]

The flow of refugees from northern Kontum Province heightened the sense of fear and disintegration; by the end of April, Vann estimated, 38,000 had fled the battle area and taken refuge in the city. The initial government response had gone well, with refugees receiving adequate food and shelter. As their numbers grew and the fear of NVA forces increased, "food shortages, the general exodus of frightened civil servants, and the lack of strong refugee camp leadership became problems."[19] Vann took steps to reduce the refugee load on the garrison, flying out civilians on the return legs of the supply sorties into Kontum. As he saw it: "Although the backhaul does impose some delay and slowdown of resupply, it is considered well worth the effort and justified just from the standpoint of reducing the resupply requirement."[20] Over the next two weeks the evacuations lifted 20,000 civilians out of the city, 14,000 of them on CH-47 helicopters. The soldiers who remained braced for the attack they knew would come soon.

The attacks of April had worn away the region's perimeter defenses, leaving the critical core open to attack. The NVA stood on the verge of achieving its objectives in the central highlands, overrunning Kontum and extending the attack toward the south, while reversing South Vietnam's pacification programs along the coast. The campaign would turn on the ARVN's ability to reconstitute the defenses, and on Vann's ability to marshal American air power effectively in their support.

10

THE FALL OF QUANG TRI

When dawn broke along the DMZ on Monday, April 3, the drama of Easter Sunday had subsided overnight, as the North Vietnamese paused to reposition and resupply their forces. This marked a pattern that was to recur throughout the offensive. The NVA attacked with resolution and courage, at a high cost breaking the South Vietnamese defenses. At the moment of victory, though, they paused to regroup, releasing the pressure on the defenders and losing the operational momentum they had purchased at such a high price. New to mechanized warfare, the NVA had neither the logistical capability nor the command and control they needed to sustain their assault. The lull gave the South Vietnamese a respite, and brought nearer the moment when improving weather would permit the full exercise of American air power.

There was no secret about what was happening. American sensors picked up the NVA logistical buildup in progress, and General Kroesen reported its progress regularly; on April 5, for example, he noted an estimated 3,000 crates, probably artillery ammunition, in a single storage site northwest of the battle area. The NVA air defense network, too, was deploying farther south, with a missile transporter having been sighted well south of the DMZ. Kroesen also reported the losses of ARVN equipment, which at that point included sixty artillery pieces, and noted the advisory team's inability to judge the effectiveness of air attacks to that point. All in all, the pause offered some relief from the chaos of the previous days, but little basis for long-term optimism.[1]

The NVA resumed offensive action on April 9, sending a tank and infantry force against the South Vietnamese Marine base at Firebase Pedro, west of Quang Tri City. The attack was designed to outflank the South Vietnamese defenses along Route 1; a successful assault would likely have dissolved the South Vietnamese defenses north of Quang Tri. Instead, the South Vietnamese Marines' resolute defense represented a remarkable reversal of the events of the previous weeks. In a two-day battle the South Vietnamese, fighting largely without American air support, met and turned back the NVA's thrust, destroying fifteen tanks in the process.

It was a convincing success, in some ways perhaps too convincing. Even before the engagement the I Corps commander, General Lam, had decided to take the offensive; Kroesen notified Abrams on April 8 that Lam "has reiterated orders to his major subordinate commanders directing them to be prepared to initiate the offensive within one week. The primary objective will be to regain that part of Quang Tri lost to the NVA." As always, Kroesen remained diplomatic in his evaluation, but he was dubious about this proposed counterattack.[2]

Shrugging off Kroesen's views, Lam decided that the successes around Pedro signified I Corps's readiness to return to the attack. Initially he and his staff planned to counterattack directly toward the north, to retake the ground lost along Route 1 all the way back to the DMZ. Only after long deliberation did he decide instead to move out toward the west, to avoid exposing his flank to the strength of the NVA forces. Finally he decided to direct an offensive that would reestablish the former line of defenses in the high terrain to the west.[3]

If nothing else, the plan demonstrated Lam's detachment from the situation actually facing his soldiers in Quang Tri Province. As his eventual successor Ngo Quang Truong noted, Lam "monitored the progress of battles through reports and he issued directives and orders from his headquarters. He never personally observed the 3d Division line of defense to determine the problems being faced by unit commanders."[4] The result was inevitable. The plan badly overestimated the offensive capabilities of the 3rd Division's forces and underestimated the strength of the NVA units opposing the counteroffensive.

Most of all, perhaps, it overestimated the cohesion of the ARVN forces at the command level. As stresses mounted on the ARVN defenses, the 3rd ARVN Division had gained forces from both the national and the I Corps reserve. These forces were invaluable in stabilizing the defense, but they posed a massive problem in command and control for the 3rd Division commander, General Giai.

Even under the best of circumstances, the vast span of control exercised by Giai would have proven problematic. By this point he was exercising command over two infantry regiments of his own, and operational control over two Marine brigades, four Ranger groups, one armor brigade, plus all the territorial forces of Quang Tri Province. Giai faced circumstances, though, that were far from the best. In a long-standing and frequently re-peated pattern, the Ranger units and the Marines deployed into the 3rd Division area only formally acknowledged his command authority. At best, these relationships would rob the ARVN defense of its responsiveness. At worst, they would generate corrosive mistrust among the elements of the defense, as it came under increasing stress. Lam exacerbated the problem through his willingness to bypass Giai and issue orders directly to subordi-nate brigade commanders—a recipe for confusion and discord. The situa-tion deteriorated in short order, leading to a total disruption of command and control at the front.[5]

Kroesen continued to report on planning for the offensive, summariz-ing the final plan on April 13. The attack would start the following day, with four task forces sweeping toward the west. Although his advice about the offensive had had little effect on Lam, Kroesen could still perform the increasingly central role of American advisors at all levels: coordinating the massive fire support available from U.S. air and naval forces. On the eve of the offensive, he assured Abrams that the attack would be preceded by sixteen B-52 strikes, along with intensive artillery and fighter attack missions.[6]

The attack began as scheduled the next morning, but it bore little re-semblance to the broad advance envisioned by General Lam. Instead of the four task forces rolling forward toward the high terrain, it consisted of little more than an air and artillery bombardment. The troops, weary from weeks of constant fighting and bombardment, showed little offensive spirit. Their commanders showed even less. The offensive quickly settled into a costly, static battle of attrition. Lacking confidence in the plan, Giai's subordinates took advantage of his inability to keep track of so many attached units. Daily they reported new reasons to delay their attack—

logistical problems, personnel attrition, troop fatigue, whatever necessary to avoid combat.[7] Over the first four days of the offensive, as the U.S. Air Force carried out a total of 407 attack sorties, the front lines moved two kilometers eastward.[8]

The offensive reconfirmed the superiority of the NVA artillery over their ARVN counterparts. The ARVN artillery pieces destroyed and captured through the first days of the offensive were speedily replaced, though some of the replacement equipment proved inoperable.[9] During the period immediately preceding this South Vietnamese offensive, the ARVN artillery fired about 11,400 rounds per day. These expenditures were unsupportable, given that all ammunition had to be hauled up Route 1 on trucks. General Giai therefore set a limit of 1,580 rounds per day through the offensive.[10] Perhaps more seriously, the ARVN artillery failed to adapt to the new conventional tactics being employed by the NVA. Through the counteroffensive, as the U.S. artillery advisor to the 3rd Division noted, "The fundamentals of conventional warfare were violated by ARVN in almost all cases. No alternate positions were selected, there was very little centralized control, and for the most part, the artillery remained in static positions."[11] ARVN targeting was erratic, and the ARVN artillery failed to develop procedures for counterbattery fire.

By contrast, the NVA artillery forces earned the respect of the Americans observing their tactics. The American after-action report, after commenting on the careful preparation and camouflage of the NVA artillery units and their protection by antiaircraft units, summarized: "Generally speaking the NVA utilized their artillery to the maximum and in accordance with conventional doctrine."[12] As in the opening days of the offensive, artillery proved to be the NVA's most effective and lethal arm.

The 3rd ARVN Division struggled to overcome its problems with fire coordination. There was rarely a problem in massing enormous firepower; the issue lay in finding and targeting the enemy. The clearest example, and perhaps the most damaging, was in targeting the B-52 strikes that offered such great potential for crushing the NVA strength in the confined areas west of the ARVN defenses. The air liaison officer for the 3rd ARVN, Captain David Brookbank, later recounted his frustrations with the haphazard approach taken to directing this powerful asset:

I witnessed ARC LIGHT targets being put on the map and then moved around "checkerboard" style in an effort to guess which targets might be

approved by higher headquarters. This was almost impossible to determine since priorities shifted constantly, lists piled on top of lists, and
then I Corps would also modify and reorder priorities. Most of the ARC
LIGHT strikes were extremely effective due to the numerous concentrations of NVA. But, in my opinion, many targets were poorly selected
and merely provided the NVA ready made foxholes. The effectiveness of
the B-52 strikes were not so much a function of planning but rather a
product of not being able to miss hitting "a wave in the ocean."[13]

The command's attempts to coordinate the work of the artillery, naval
gunfire, American air forces, and South Vietnamese air support also left
much room for improvement. It was intrinsically a very complex function,
as the commanders and their staffs worked to integrate the firepower from
at least five separate chains of command, operating in an increasingly confined space. In principle, the Americans and the Vietnamese reached an informal agreement as the defenses stabilized in early April. U.S. fighters
would control strikes deep in enemy territory, with U.S. observer aircraft
operating forward of the battle area. Vietnamese forward air controllers
would operate directly over the battle, controlling strikes in close coordination with the ground commanders below. As the antiaircraft fire became
more intense, however, Vietnamese controllers were less willing to operate
in any area not occupied by friendly forces. Brookbank charged: "The
VNAF FACs in my opinion failed miserably. Either they failed to go to
their assigned areas or they would not make contact with the ARVN
ground commander . . . the FACs were orbiting well inside friendly lines
and not making contact." Finally the American controllers assumed responsibility for the battle area.[14]

The ARVN offensive foundered under the weight of all these problems.
It was not a spectacular failure; there were no scenes of mass casualties, or
of units breaking and fleeing to the rear. The failure was subtler and more
serious. The focus on this impractical offensive to the west distracted the
corps and division commanders from the more essential tasks of organizing the defenses and resting and refitting the troops after the trials of the
previous weeks. There was no attempt to rotate the 3rd ARVN Division
soldiers, only ceaseless exhortations to attack. Meanwhile Giai's effective
command over his subordinates in attached units continued to fade.

During this period, to the west and the north, the NVA used this pause
to reposition and resupply its forces, and to study the new defensive pat-

terns established by the ARVN. American sensors detected the NVA re-supply efforts very quickly, but the specific thrust and weight of the im-pending offensive remained unclear to the defenders. For the next phase of the NVA's offensive, three divisions—the 308th, 304th, and 324th, with artillery and tank support—would execute a campaign-level flank attack against the ARVN firebases clustered along Route 1. The NVA moved tanks forward and redeployed air defenses into position to cover the next phase of operations. The 64th Battalion of the 236B Antiaircraft Regi-ment, an SA-2 missile unit, moved forward under the cover of darkness, through "a newly liberated area, an area of bare hills still covered with en-emy bombs and mines, terrain with which the unit was not familiar, and with enemy aircraft constantly overhead."[15] The unit moved over a period of three nights, a battery crossing the Ben Hai River each night from April 23 to April 25.

As the NVA deployed their air defense cover forward, they moved to cut the lifeline connecting the 3rd ARVN Division and its attached forces from their logistics sources to the south. The NVA offensive opened on April 27, with attacks closing Route 1 along a seven-kilometer stretch near the provincial border. Lam first ordered ARVN supply columns to break through the roadblocks, then directed relief efforts from both the south and the north. None succeeded. The fatigue and the stress of combat con-tinued to build in the defending units; as Truong later recalled: "Gone were the last shreds of self-assurance and cohesiveness. Units of the 3d Di-vision fought on without much conviction and were practically left to fend for themselves."[16]

Over the ensuing days, the situation grew increasingly chaotic for the South Vietnamese as the fabric of the defense unraveled. By April 29 the defense forces had contracted to a narrow corridor along Route 1 with ma-jor elements no longer effective. Problems in gunfire coordination and in targeting, present since the beginning of the campaign, became acute as the confusion grew and the defensive perimeter contracted. By the third day of the renewed NVA offensive, naval gunfire support was being with-held 80 percent of the time, to avoid endangering fighters conducting air strikes. Finally the naval squadron offshore threatened to pull ships off the line unless they were used more effectively.

It was even worse for the FAC force coordinating air strikes. With the defense perimeter shrinking daily, the airspace became dangerously crowded, to the point where adding additional FACs and fighters became counterproductive—with the constant danger of midair collisions and friendly fire, no one could offer fully effective support. Nor had the 3rd ARVN Division's ability to handle the demands of conventional war improved significantly since the opening of the NVA offensive. One American advisor noted "a lack of mutual support, coordination and integration of defensive measures between adjacent units," which had left gaps between units uncovered by fire, patrols, or observation. The ARVN remained unready to fight this new sort of conventional war.

The leadership issues that had been evident from the beginning of the campaign grew more bitter and more damaging as the combat became more intense and the situation more desperate. Giai's grip on subordinate commanders progressively slipped as the stresses increased. His advisor, Colonel Donald Metcalf, commented: "The last five or six days that we were there the command and control of the 3rd ARVN Division became less and less and less . . . The point being that [Giai] could give an order, he could come up with a plan, implement instructions, but he never really knew whether they were going to be complied with."[17]

On April 30 the dysfunctional command structure in I Corps finally destroyed any hope of holding Quang Tri City. That evening Giai called his subordinates together and briefed them on his plan to withdraw the bulk of his forces south of the Thach Han River. He had kept the plan secret until then, fearing that the units under his command would stampede to the south if word got out. As Truong summarized: "Basically, the plan consisted of holding Quang Tri City with a Marine brigade, establishing a defense line on the southern bank of the Thach Han River with infantry and Ranger troops and releasing enough tank and armored cavalry units for the pressing task of reopening Route QL-1 to the south."[18] It was a risky plan, but no better alternative existed.

Whatever chance for survival Giai's scheme might have provided vanished, though, when Lam countermanded the order the following morning. Lam's direction amounted to a straightforward repetition of President Thieu's order to hold existing positions at all cost. The impending reopening of the Paris peace talks motivated Thieu's order, but it proved disastrous when applied on the battlefield. Giai dutifully reversed his order to withdraw, but his subordinates claimed to be unable to reverse the movement of their units, or in some cases flatly refused to comply. In Truong's words: "And so within the space of four hours, the ARVN dispositions for defense crumbled completely. Those units to the north manning positions around Quang Tri Combat Base streamed across the Thach Han River and continued their way south with the uncontainable force of a flood over a broken dam."[19] Some individuals and units continued to fight bravely, but the overall structure of the defense dissolved quickly and completely.

By early afternoon of May 1, with effective opposition at an end, Metcalf ordered the extraction of the U.S. advisors from the Citadel at Quang Tri. As the NVA closed in, four Jolly Green HH-53 helicopters pulled out the advisors and General Giai in an extraordinarily skillful and brave action. The nearly miraculous extraction minimized American losses, but otherwise did little to reduce the sting of this defeat. Quang Tri was the first provincial capital lost to the North Vietnamese in the course of the war. Worse yet, the road now seemed clear for the NVA forces to press through the ragged remnants of the ARVN units and take the old imperial capital of Hue. NVA possession of Hue would mean the complete success of the offensive in MR I, and probably would bring the end of President Thieu's government. The North Vietnamese objective of a coalition government, transitioning quickly to a structure under their control, appeared within reach.

Through this period, as the South Vietnamese defenses weakened and then collapsed, General Abrams sent three personal assessments of the situation back to Washington. Requested by Secretary Laird, the messages apparently were originally intended to provide background for Nixon's use in a speech to the nation on April 26. The first message, dated April 24, offered a decidedly positive assessment of South Vietnam's political and military reaction to the offensive: "Overall the South Vietnamese have fought well under extremely difficult circumstances. There has been a mixture of effective and ineffective performance, as in any combat situation, but on the whole the effective far outweighs the ineffective." On the verge of the NVA's rapid conquest of MR I, Abrams characterized the leadership in that area as "outstanding; aggressive and confident. They have been and continue to be offensive minded." He was much more critical of the leadership in MR II, judging that "the performance of the 22nd Division commander has been inadequate"—a judgment that reached back well before the offensive. Abrams commended the leadership of President Thieu, detailing the series of redeployments Thieu had directed to counter the NVA moves. His assessments of the ARVN leadership filtered out much bad news that had been evident for nearly a month.[20]

A week later he forwarded another assessment, more somber given the events of the intervening days. At that point the details of the ARVN's defeat in MR I were unclear, but the scale of the disaster was evident. The days of late April had also brought a rapid collapse of the 22nd Division in MR II, and the situation in MR III remained serious though not critical. Problems among the senior commanders had become obvious in all three regions. At this turning point Abrams considered South Vietnam's prospects to be "now a function of two intangibles." The first was the South Vietnamese military's will to fight, especially as there were "serious problems in this regard at the lower levels and command and control is becoming increasingly difficult to maintain." The second was the damage that had been done to the enemy, not precisely measurable but certainly significant. "There is no doubt that the enemy has been badly hurt, primarily by US air power, but the extent of damage must for the time being remain one of the intangibles." Abrams took this opportunity once again to argue for employment of B-52s over the battlefield and the suspension of raids over the North: "It is imperative that our air support be focused on the battle for RVN. We must have the authority and flexibility to employ all available air assets to decisively deal with major threat areas incountry as a matter of first priority over requirements in areas outside the battle zone."[21]

Abrams's summary reflected the gloom attending this low point in South Vietnamese fortunes. He closed with an ominous overall judgment: "I must report that as the pressure has mounted and the battle has become brutal the senior leadership has begun to bend and in some cases break. In adversity it is losing its will and cannot be depended on to take the measures necessary to stand and fight . . . In light of this there is no basis for confidence that Hue or Kontum will be held."[22]

Gloomy as Abrams's assessment was, there was still more bad news just appearing on the battlefront. On April 29, as the defenses deteriorated amid the chaos at the ARVN command level, an F-4 crew operating over the battle area returned to report that a small missile fired from North Vietnamese positions had appeared to track the Phantoms. There had been no damage, and the aircraft returned safely to base. On May 1, an O-1 light observation aircraft operating near Quang Tri City was hit by a missile. The rescue effort brought the normal package of propeller-driven A-1 Skyraiders to suppress the defenses, and shortly before dusk another fell victim while orbiting ten miles south of Quang Tri at 3,500 feet.[23] The next morning North Vietnamese missiles destroyed two more A-1s as they searched for the crews that had been downed the day before.

This was the first confirmed use of the SA-7 Strela by the North Vietnamese. The shoulder-fired surface-to-air missile was unsophisticated; its technical capabilities were severely limited by the design trade-offs necessary to create a man-portable SAM. But it had a dramatic effect on the battle. In fact, it remains a factor on battlefields around the world today, over three decades later.

The missile was only 57 inches long and carried a warhead weighing about two and a half pounds. Because it guided on heat emitted by the target aircraft, it was limited to launches against receding targets. The launch envelope was further restricted by the weapon's small rocket engine, which limited the system to maximum altitudes of about 9,000 feet. High-performance aircraft could outrun the missile by maintaining their speeds above 450 knots; the missile could be defeated by decoy flares and by maneuver. The rocket motor emitted a characteristic blast of white smoke on launch, simplifying visual detection, and the missile flew in a very characteristic corkscrew path, making identification easy once air crews detected the launch.

But despite all these limitations the SA-7s caused a near-crisis in air operations throughout the theater. The new threat could appear almost anywhere and destroy any slow-moving aircraft operating below 9,000 feet. Forward air controllers, the heart of the air support system, could no longer operate at low altitudes to find enemy forces. The most effective ground-attack aircraft, the A-1 and the A-37 Dragonfly, were peculiarly vulnerable to the SA-7 because their tactics and their success were based on slow, low flight. Gunships were forced to higher altitudes or out of confirmed SA-7 areas entirely. The airdrop altitudes being used by the C-130s supplying the besieged defenders at An Loc were no longer safe. Helicopters faced even worse problems: by nature they were slow and low-flying, with no excess weight devoted to protection against missiles. The effect on operations was multiplied by lack of knowledge about the new system and the lack of firm intelligence reaching the air crews. Gunship crew members, for example, were firmly convinced that the officially stated maximum altitude for the missile was an understatement.

American intelligence quickly moved to acquire a Strela, and by May 21

MACV had found a "controlled source" willing to sell one for $50,000. Before money changed hands, however, South Vietnamese Rangers captured two missiles in MR I and provided one to the Americans for study and exploitation. This followed rapidly, with the CIA, Army, and Navy jointly publishing a report on the missile on June 1. The immediate need in the field, however, could only be met by tactical adjustment and improvisation. Helicopters were forced to adopt low-level "nap of the earth" tactics, and fixed-wing aircraft generally moved to altitudes above 10,000 when operating in known SA-7 areas. C-130 crews flying in such areas flew with their cargo ramps open, with the loadmaster lying on his stomach, looking toward the ground and ready to fire a flare if he sighted a missile. Similarly, FACs were forced to high altitudes and constant turns in an effort to spot the missiles in time to out-maneuver them. While these tactics reduced the risk to air crews, they came at a high price in mission effectiveness. The higher the FACs operated, the less likely they were to detect enemy activity, and the more time they spent watching for SA-7s, the less time they spent on directing strikes.

As the Americans adapted their tactics, so did the North Vietnamese. The Seventh Air Force director of operations, General Alton Slay, later recalled that the NVA gunners appeared to gain proficiency both in handling the weapon and in tactical subtlety. In his assessment, at first the NVA crews overestimated the Strela's capabilities, and were as willing to fire at an F-4 at 10,000 feet as at a FAC well within their range. Later they became more discriminating, and developed more effective tactics. For example, they would execute what Slay termed "propaganda launches," firing a missile just to demonstrate its presence in an area, expecting the Americans then to restrict their operations. Or in Slay's terms, they "would lay low for days without shooting any SA-7s and then all of a sudden they would shoot 8–10 at once. They were attempting to lure the FACs down to the lower altitudes to get at them—laying traps."[24]

It appears, in fact, that the losses near Quang Tri resulted from exactly this tactic. The Strela launch on April 29 was the first missile mentioned in American intelligence—but it was not the first fired by the North Vietnamese. In the initial surge at the beginning of April, they had fired five missiles and destroyed two aircraft. After those early successes they had restricted their use of the missiles until the next opportunity to have a direct effect on the battle, with the American air operations confined to a small sector around the city of Quang Tri. The NVA would further refine this ambush tactic as the offensive continued, combining it with the use of terrain features to improve their targeting of enemy aircraft.

Slay concluded: "We were unprepared for the advent of the SA-7 . . . We did not anticipate it and we were not prepared. We didn't have the tactics to cope with it and had to devise them on the spot."[25] The "threat in being" of the missile would have a confining effect on American air operations through the remainder of the offensive, far beyond the bare number of aircraft struck by the system.

11

THE PATH TO LINEBACKER

The White House's intense activity of early April gave way to a brief pause, as Nixon and his staff awaited developments on the ground and on the diplomatic front. Nixon decided that it was time for a press conference focusing on Southeast Asia, then switched to a speech, and finally concluded that the time was not right for either.[1] On April 12, with the offensive nearly two weeks old, Dobrynin invited Kissinger to Moscow to prepare for the impending summit; after some hesitation and with some misgivings, Nixon approved the trip.

The president sent Haig to Southeast Asia from April 16 to April 18, specifically to talk to Abrams about the need for B-52 attacks in the North and their place in the White House's overall strategy. He was also to perform his normal function as the president's eyes, getting a first-hand view of events in Indochina and bringing his impressions back to Washington. Haig met with Thieu, Bunker, Abrams, and Hollingsworth, and on his return submitted a basically upbeat assessment to Kissinger and Nixon. He noted the "strength and vitality of allied efforts" in countering the NVA offensive, which according to him was "stalled and is behind schedule." He warned against "the erosion of U.S. support for U.S. and ARVN forces through declining sortie rates, ammunitions expenditures and other funding constraints," a thinly veiled criticism of Laird's recourse to those measures over the previous years.[2]

Immediately after Haig's return, Kissinger left for Moscow for what was to develop into one of the most contentious and stressful periods of his tenure as national security advisor. Nixon was consumed with Vietnam and insisted that Kissinger focus strictly on that issue while in Moscow. Kissinger considered that narrow focus to be both impossible and foolish, given the opportunities open for progress in other areas with the Soviets. The two engaged in an intense exchange of messages throughout Kissinger's four-day stay, with Haig acting as intermediary.[3]

As Kissinger's visit drew to a close, Nixon sent a message expressing his concern that on the domestic front the administration would face a "rising chorus of criticism from our political opponents on the left and our hawk friends on the right for going to Moscow and failing to get progress on the main issue." Already Nixon was projecting his response to the next round of peace talks, scheduled for May 2, anticipating that the North Vietnamese would not give much more ground than they had before, and that the United States would "have to go all-out on the bombing front." He compared the Moscow summit to his visit to China, in which "we made a decision, which I think was right, not to be provocative in our bombing of targets north of the DMZ even though we knew from all intelligence reports that an enemy buildup was in progress." But Nixon was convinced that it would be necessary to bomb Hanoi and Haiphong again after the talks on May 2, risking the summit and "possibly damaging it irreparably if that meeting turns out to be a failure."[4] At the time, he contemplated a massive two-day attack on Hanoi and Haiphong, with B-52s and as many fighters as could be spared from the battle area. It was the germ of the process that would lead to the sustained air campaign known as Linebacker.

Kissinger returned home on April 24 and submitted a trip report to Nixon emphasizing his achievements in Moscow. He had gotten the Soviets engaged directly in the negotiating process, annoyed the North Vietnamese, and positioned the United States for any further military action that might be necessary. For the first time, the Soviets dispatched a representative to Hanoi to relay Kissinger's peace proposals, thus adding to the pressure on the North Vietnamese.[5] It was the second time within an eight-day span that Soviet diplomats had passed American peace proposals along to the North Vietnamese; the Soviet ambassador to Hanoi, I. S. Scherbakov, had met with Pham Van Dong and Le Duan in mid-April to communicate messages Kissinger passed through Dobrynin. Those earlier messages had included a thinly veiled threat that after North Vietnam had sent nearly all its regular forces to fight in the South, "it might fall into a most difficult situation, should the opposite side open a large-scale operation on the DRVN territory itself."[6] Nixon and Kissinger would work to build the credibility of this threat in the weeks to come.

The rapid pace of events continued after Kissinger returned home. He arrived to find that Nixon had decided it was finally time to address the American people on the situation in Vietnam, another reflection of the anxiety the president felt over Kissinger's stay in Moscow.[7] The speech would include another announcement of a troop withdrawal, as a means of quieting the antiwar movement despite the war's new intensity.

Washington solicited Abrams's views on the drawdown. He responded with a review of ongoing operations, concluding that any reduction of the existing 69,000-troop ceiling would eliminate his forces' ability to give the South Vietnamese the support that was essential during the crisis. He noted that any reduction from current troop levels would require the tactical fighter forces still based in Vietnam to relocate to Thailand, with an unacceptable loss of combat capability. He recommended therefore that he himself, as the theater commander, define the rate and timing of any further reductions, without any specific schedule.[8] Laird forwarded Abrams's message to the White House, with his own memorandum outlining four options with different rates of withdrawal and final force levels. None of these matched Abrams's recommendation.[9] Kissinger, in turn, recommended yet another option, a withdrawal of 20,000 men over the next two months. This level would permit the president to announce that he had withdrawn half a million American troops from Vietnam since coming to office.[10] Nixon accepted Kissinger's proposal and incorporated it into his speech on April 26. The whole process reflected the domestic pressures driving the administration and the low regard held in Washington for the views of the theater commander, who was facing the greatest crisis in his tour of duty.

News arrived the day after Nixon's speech of the NVA's renewed offensive in MR I and the deterioration of the ARVN defenses along Route 1 south of the DMZ. With the speech behind him, Nixon flew to Key Biscayne to spend time relaxing with his longtime friend Bebe Rebozo. From Florida the president sent a belligerent message back to Kissinger, directing that "the absolute maximum number of sorties must be flown from now thru Tuesday . . . if at all possible 1,000 sorties per day." Nixon expected these attacks to have "maximum psychological impact on your hosts [the North Vietnamese] Tuesday." He demanded a report "soonest by message as to how this order is being specifically executed," and closed peremptorily: "There are to be no excuses and there is no appeal."[11]

That same day Nixon turned his thoughts to a broader evaluation of the strategy to be pursued over the coming months. The next round of peace talks would be the first Kissinger-Tho session since the previous September, after a long minuet of cancellations and postponements as the two sides jockeyed for advantage. Now Nixon looked toward the negotiations in the context of international diplomacy, domestic politics, and the state of the battlefield, and dictated a memorandum to Kissinger outlining his views. He emphasized the need for a three-day strike against Hanoi, beginning Friday, May 5. It should involve at least 100 B-52s, with all the tactical aircraft that could be spared. This strike, he said, was essential to reduce the NVA's potential for offensive action later in the year, and would speed negotiations and impress American public opinion. But the time window for such a strike was limited:

> We have to recognize the hard fact—unless we hit the Hanoi-Haiphong complex this weekend, we probably are not going to be able to hit it at all before the election. After this weekend, we will be too close to the Russian Summit. During the Summit and for a couple of weeks afterwards, our hands will be tied for the very same good reasons that they were tied during and after the Chinese Summit. Then we will be in the middle of June with the Democratic Convention only three to four weeks away and it would be a mistake to have the strike at that time. Another factor is that the more time that passes there is a possibility that Congress will act to tie our hands. Finally, support for taking a hard line, while relatively strong now, will erode day by day, particularly as the news from the battle is so viciously distorted by the press so that people get a sense of hopelessness, and then would assume that we were only striking out of desperation.[12]

And so the strike would have to go in the first weekend of May. The only event that would alter this decision would be a definite move by the North Vietnamese to reach a settlement before the Moscow summit. Given the situation on the battlefield, this was highly unlikely. The greatest deterrent to a strike remained the risk of losing the Moscow summit. Nixon, however, had already reconciled himself to losing this meeting. He decided at that point to continue with the summit only if one of two conditions was met: either there was substantial improvement in the battle, or he received a firm commitment from the Soviets to join the Americans in an effort to end the war.[13]

The next day saw the collapse of the ARVN defenses in MR I and the dramatic rescue of the U.S. advisors from the Quang Tri citadel. Kissinger was focused on preparing for the negotiating session, so Haig dictated a memo outlining the situation and the fundamental questions that would face the administration if the negotiations continued in a stalemate, "the likelihood of which increases with each North Vietnamese ground success." The options he suggested for consideration ranged from doing nothing up to blockading Cuba while mobilizing the reserves and occupying Haiphong and Hanoi. He also offered the pointed question of whether the president should "meet with the Joint Chiefs of Staff as a body to ensure that he has, for the record, tapped their views"—an action never taken during the whole course of the offensive, let alone during this crisis. This memorandum serves as a microcosm of Haig's role within the NSC—offering far more aggressive military options than anything considered acceptable by Kissinger, and helping to orchestrate the staff action necessary to stay abreast of onrushing events.[14]

On May 1 the president met with Secretary of State Rogers, who was soon to depart for meetings in Europe. The conversation swept over a range of issues, especially the Strategic Arms Limitation Treaty (SALT), which was nearing completion. Nixon then updated Rogers on the situation in Southeast Asia and described the plan for an intensive series of air strikes at the end of the week.[15]

Nixon, Kissinger, and Haig continued their talk after Rogers left. Haig reviewed the situation in South Vietnam and offered his assessment of the ARVN's performance: "I just think they didn't fight very well." The conversation wandered into a discussion of infantry tactics, and Nixon asked: "Why not get out of it now? What do you think, Henry?" This gave Kissinger an opportunity to display his expertise on infantry warfare: "Well, my philosophy has always been to make the enemy concentrate and then get the hell out . . . we don't want to lose provincial towns, but we're losing a division in each provincial town on top of the provincial towns, and I think it's a stupid strategy."

Nixon turned then to Haig: "What's your opinion, Al? *You* run the war." After a moment, Haig replied: "I don't think they can leave Kontum, simply because if they do, they're gonna get caught on the roads and cut up.

Gotta stand there and fight . . . and again, it's the development of the targets . . . and again, to the degree they fold we can put all the airplanes in the world in there and it's not gonna change the battle." To this Nixon commented: "I just wonder how much the air power is doing, that's all. I have grave doubts." After another round of assessments of the North Vietnamese ability to sustain the offensive, Nixon again emphasized: "We will do what is necessary, believe me if we have to level the goddamned place, we will do it . . . we've got to crack it, and crack it hard . . . I want 100 B-52s, is that understood?"

Kissinger's next suggestion integrated the military, diplomatic, and domestic political strategies that would be at play if the situation continued to erode. He proposed that the president adopt a two-pronged strategy, ordering aggressive air strikes while continuing preparations for the Moscow summit—using the summit to buy himself some relief from attacks by his liberal critics. Then, if the ARVN reached the verge of collapse, the United States should impose a blockade against North Vietnam to provide negotiating leverage, and cancel the summit.

Later that evening Nixon and Kissinger met again to review events, discuss Kissinger's negotiating position for the Paris talks, and study General Abrams's assessment, which was expected momentarily from the Pentagon. Both were in a reflective mood as they contemplated the implications of the possible ARVN collapse.[16] They again rehearsed their frustration with the military performance in Vietnam, and Kissinger summarized: "Mr. President, we have to redo our military establishment as soon as the election is over—because by '77 it won't be worth being credited to this country any more." They agreed that John Connally, then nearing the end of his tenure as secretary of the treasury, would be the ideal secretary of defense in 1973, if he could be spared from other responsibilities.

When Abrams's report finally arrived, Kissinger paged through it, noting: "His main point is that the commanders are not cooperating with each other." The men discussed the leadership failures that had become evident in the ARVN, raising the specter of a disintegration of the South Vietnamese military. Nixon mused: "I wonder if you really don't have to go to a blockade—not now but if this thing collapses . . ." Kissinger replied: "If this collapses, we have no choice but to go to the blockade—so they know the prisoners must come back—and blockade them." Nixon: "That'd be the basis for it—we'd get our prisoners back—but then we're defeated." Kissinger: "Then we tighten our belts—then we should make the Russians pay for it." Nixon: "Well, we're sort of at that day, May 1, 1972, and just the question of the damned—everyone puts it too much in terms of this immediate thing, this battle, but I think the Abrams report is an honest report, it's pretty goddamned sobering, don't you think?" Kissinger: "That's what's been worrying me for the last week to ten days. Losses of these capitals we can handle. If these units will stand and fight then the North Vietnamese will lose the war because there are too many capitals for them to take."

The meeting ended with an exchange that reflects the strain and frustration of this interminable war. Nixon closed with a summary: "This is rougher in a sense, because all the chips are on the line. They weren't in Cambodia, they weren't in Laos. And frankly, it's better that way, it's better to get the son of a bitching war over with." Kissinger replied: "It's got to be over now by summer, by July, August, it's gonna be, one way or the other. I mean clearly, the South Vietnamese can't keep this up for another three months." Nixon interjected: "And the North?" The two decided that neither side could keep up the battle through the summer.

There matters stood as Kissinger departed for Paris and his first meeting with Le Duc Tho since the previous September. As might have been expected, this round of negotiations proved the least fruitful yet. The North Vietnamese saw little reason to compromise, since they were dealing from strength; the Americans similarly refused to compromise out of weakness. The three-hour session was "thoroughly unproductive on substance."[17] Kissinger had anticipated little progress, and he had gotten exactly that.[18]

A series of mini-dramas unfolded as Kissinger returned to Washington. Nixon told Haig of his decision to direct a massive two-day strike, and of his conviction that it was time to cancel the Moscow summit—that given the strike he planned to direct against Hanoi, the Soviets would cancel it in any case, and it was essential to preempt them. As Kissinger flew back across the Atlantic, Haig informed him of the president's mood and his intentions. Finally Nixon told Haig to have Kissinger, on his arrival from Paris, meet them on the presidential yacht, the *Sequoia*. While on the flight Kissinger received Abrams's report of his conversation with Thieu. That day Abrams had called on Thieu to offer his assessment of the battle, pointing out the inadequacies of South Vietnam's senior military leaders and suggesting, in Haig's summary, that "the South Vietnamese had lost their will to fight and that total capitulation might occur at any moment."[19]

Kissinger exploded, "appalled" by Abrams's action, which he described as "a self-serving, egg-sucking, panicky lecture." Kissinger feared that Thieu would construe this as the preparation for a sellout. He directed Haig to send a message to Bunker, telling the ambassador to visit Thieu immediately and express full U.S. support. Haig complied.[20]

That evening, on the afterdeck of the *Sequoia*, Nixon, Kissinger, Haig, and Haldeman discussed the day's events and planned for the immediate future. Afterward Kissinger returned to his office to set in motion the decisions that Nixon had taken on the yacht. A phone call to Moorer triggered the tasking order to Seventh Air Force to plan a massive two-day strike for the following weekend.[21] Kissinger then telephoned Moorer and Laird to arrange for a high-level logistics team to go to Vietnam no later than the next evening. The team was to "look into the replacement needs and modernization needs on the most urgent crash basis."[22] Laird protested that they could put this list together right in Washington, and that in any case "They don't need equipment, what they need right now is a kick in the ass." Nonetheless, Kissinger and Nixon valued the symbolism of a public visit, and Laird pulled together the team within the next twenty-five minutes. Finally, Kissinger broke the news to Laird that Nixon had directed a further reinforcement of the B-52s in theater. Laird protested: "Why, Henry, that is just crazy . . . you know there is just no sense in sending any more B-52s."[23] In Laird's view, the B-52Gs already sent had proven of little value, carrying the bomb load of only two F-4s, and with very few suitable targets. The president's order stood, however, and Laird set about finding bases for the next flow of B-52s to Southeast Asia. Kissinger's activity on this long day—beginning with a negotiating session with Le Duc Tho, then working with Bunker and Haig on the trip back to Washington, later meeting Nixon on the *Sequoia*, and finally conducting these late-night phone conversations—demonstrated once again his extraordinary energy and stamina.

Thursday, May 4, saw President Nixon delivering the eulogy for J. Edgar Hoover, the longtime director of the FBI, who had passed away early Tuesday morning. After the funeral service, Nixon and Kissinger gathered to decide the next steps for the Vietnam campaign. As always, Haldeman attended as the silent note-taker. Right at the outset the president announced that he had decided, finally, to drop restraint in his air campaign against North Vietnam. He commented that his greatest mistakes as president had come when he failed to follow his instincts—specifically, when he had failed in early 1969 to respond to the North Korean shoot-down of an EC-121 aircraft, and later that year to order a massive bombing campaign against North Vietnam on the first anniversary of the bombing halt. Then he had limited the incursion into Cambodia in 1970, and finally he had let Laird manage the Laotian operation in 1971. He mused: "If we'd put three-fourths of the energy into Laos that we're using now, we'd be out of the war."[24]

Now it was finally time, Nixon concluded, to follow his instincts, which had never been wrong yet. He would unleash strikes on Haiphong and Hanoi, and if they hit Soviet ships, it would just be too bad; they wouldn't aim at civilians, but "if some bombs slopped over, that was just too bad . . . We cannot lose the war. Now understand me: the South Vietnamese may lose the war. But we cannot lose this war . . . if the summit is cancelled, and we win the war, we're still in business . . . We're gonna cream them, now that's what we're gonna do. This isn't in anger or anything—this old thing that I'm petulant and everything, that's bullshit . . . they [the North Vietnamese] may decide they'll try to wait us out until the election—and if they do, that's too goddamned bad—because then I'll be in office after the election, too, and I really will go wild."

For the next hour and a half, first with Kissinger, then adding Connally and Haig, Nixon refined his decision to use decisive force and created the rough outline of the campaign that would follow. Kissinger suggested: "If we're going to go all out, why not blockade first?" Nixon replied: "Let me understand—the likelihood of the Soviets canceling the summit is enormously increased by a blockade." Then Kissinger worked through the options, noting: "If you bomb more than two days—they cancel the summit—but we're past the point where a two-day pop does any good." Kissinger further noted that a blockade could be conducted with little investment in air forces; they could keep the planes operating in the South, and so they "wouldn't run up against Laird and Abrams." They could conduct a surgical operation against North Vietnam, striking oil and fuel and electrical networks, sending sorties against the rail lines to China, but still keeping their air forces primarily concentrated on the battle area. Kissinger summarized: "We wouldn't have to have these massive strikes in any one blow because what we would be doing is just wearing them down."

The two then discussed the outlines of the announcement for the action and the themes they would use to justify the blockade. Finally Nixon said, as if to ensure that he had the right understanding of the plan: "The blockade will be with mines, of course." That launched a short discussion of the means of closing shipping into North Vietnam and the measures the North Vietnamese might take to counter a mining campaign. Primarily, as Kissinger noted, they could undertake lightering operations, downloading ships outside the harbors and using smaller vessels to move the cargos to shore. Therefore, he concluded, you would have to use a combination: mines to close the harbors plus naval patrols to reduce the lightering operations. And with that, the pieces were all in place: mining, strikes against the road and rail network from China, naval patrols to close off attempts to circumvent the mines, and a sustained, gradual campaign against North Vietnam's power network, oil and gas supplies, and national infrastructure.

This decision made, Nixon and Kissinger returned to their recurrent discussion of the inadequacy of the military chain of command, right from Laird down into Indochina. They touched on the possibility of replacing Laird with Connally, and then the options for replacing Abrams. In Nixon's view, however, the problems were as much institutional as they were personal. He vented his frustration with the command structure he had inherited from Johnson, vowing to rework the chain of command to run from Saigon to Moorer, and then directly from the JCS to the White House. Alert to the political risks inherent in crossing Laird, Haldeman suggested that instead of replacing him, Nixon could just relieve the secretary of defense of his responsibility for the war in Vietnam.

At that point John Connally and Al Haig arrived to join the conference. By now Nixon considered Connally the only man capable of succeeding him as president, and Haig had become, effectively, the primary military advisor to the commander in chief. Nixon wanted their views and, more significantly, he wanted their reassurance on the course he had chosen.

For a few minutes the meeting took on the air of a Kiwanis Club luncheon as the Texan spun anecdotes of oil men he had known. Once they got down to business, Nixon took Connally through the history of decisions in which he had failed to follow his instinct to hit hard. He recounted the constant opposition of Rogers and Laird to any decisive use of force, and emphasized the importance of the Cambodia and Laos incursions in limiting American casualties. Finally reaching the present, Nixon gave the same broad policy objective that he had earlier with Kissinger: "The South Vietnamese might lose, which means I've made the decision that whatever happens in South Vietnam, we are going to cream North Vietnam."

He continued: "Bombing is expected—they're ready for it. Now in my view, there's only one way to finish North Vietnam. It's to blockade—and bomb. Bombing is essential for taking out the railways into China—the roads into China—and destroying the POL and other supplies. Al, you agree on that—you sold me on that, right? . . . I think that over four or five months a blockade for that period of time will effectively destroy the enemy's ability to mount another offensive—don't you think so, Al?" Kissinger commented that a blockade would permit Soviet ships to leave Haiphong—after which, air strikes could "turn Haiphong into a shell."

With the lines of military action established, Nixon returned to the question of the commanders who would execute the plans, and then to the alignment of personalities within the executive branch. Turning to Haig, he said, "I think we have to remove Abrams. I think we ought to send you out." Connally interjected that Abrams faced a terrible dilemma in working for a secretary of defense who had fundamentally different views from the president. Again Nixon and Kissinger worked through the options open to them—what to do with Abrams, who might be available to replace him at MACV, how to work around Laird and control Rogers. Nixon even suggested that he might send Haldeman to the NSC to help Kissinger control Rogers. He told Kissinger: "Someone's got to kiss Rogers's ass, and you're no good at ass-kissing." Kissinger controlled his enthusiasm at the prospect of having such a powerful subordinate, then turned back to the subject of Abrams: "Abrams doesn't understand, he's proven totally insensitive to the political environment . . . Abrams has done nothing—he's not taken care of the Vietnamese." Nixon added: "And he drinks too much." In the end, they decided not to replace Abrams, but to send Haig out, in Nixon's phrase, "to look over Abrams's shoulder." As for Laird, they once again decided to leave him in position. Kissinger commented: "I think Laird will be more trouble on the outside than on the inside." They would just have to work around the secretary of defense, since, as Nixon announced: "I'm not gonna have Laird leak this all over the place."

Finally Moorer arrived, raising the curtain on the last act in the afternoon's drama. Nixon began by repeating his catechism, that the president was the commander in chief and that Moorer worked for him, not for Laird. Then he swore the CJCS to secrecy—"Nothing is to go to the secretary. Nothing is to go to Vietnam"—and directed him to form a small planning cell to work out a plan for a blockade. Moorer assured him that the plans were already in hand and that they had been updated repeatedly since 1967, when as CINCPAC he had come back to Washington to urge the mining of Haiphong. Nixon told Moorer to generate plans for an amphibious feint against the North Vietnamese panhandle as well.

With the major decisions made, it was time for the execution phase. Kissinger returned to his office to dictate a message to Bunker, alerting the ambassador: "The president is nearing the end of his patience with General Abrams on the issue of air action against North Vietnam." After recounting the massive reinforcements sent to the theater by the White House, Kissinger said: "The fact that General Abrams would dispatch an on-the-record cable to the effect that the diversion of some of these assets for a 48-hour effort in the north jeopardizes our security is increasingly difficult to comprehend. As you know, General Haig was sent to Saigon for the specific purpose of making these broader political considerations clear to General Abrams." Kissinger asked Bunker to discuss this problem with Abrams at the earliest possible minute, and added that, in the meantime, "the President has, in the light of General Abrams's official recommendation, deferred action on the 48-hour Hanoi/Haiphong strike." This last comment was partially true, and on the whole misleading. The deferral of the strike had not been related to Abrams's recommendation, but to a general shift in the war strategy—about which the theater commander had not been consulted or even informed.[25]

The process leading to the mining operation and the air offensive offers some fundamental insights into strategic decisionmaking in the Nixon White House. To begin with the obvious, the decisions were made by a tightly constricted circle of trusted intimates—at this time extending from Nixon and Kissinger only as far as Haig and Connally. The president and the national security advisor actively excluded the state department and the department of defense. The secretary of state entered the conversation only as someone to be mollified to prevent later complaints, and the secretary of defense as one from whom this massive reorientation of military action must be kept secret.

The statutory responsibility of the Joint Chiefs of Staff as military advisors to the national command authorities was not even a memory. Neither Nixon nor Kissinger accepted Haig's hint that they convene the JCS, even if only for form's sake. It was Haig who advised Nixon on the need to combine the mining with attacks on the railroads, Haig who assessed the field commanders and the command structure, Haig whom Nixon trusted to execute this operation with the proper vigor. The president called Moorer into the discussion only to execute a decision already made; the face-to-face discussion with the CJCS was not to explore military options, but only to emphasize the importance of keeping the secretary of defense in the dark.

The decisionmaking process reaffirmed the deep division between the civilian policymakers and the military leaders and operators who were responsible for executing policy. The frustrations of early April had remained latent during the weeks of relative equilibrium on the battlefield, but the recent reverses reemphasized the sharp divisions among the White House, the Pentagon, and MACV. The staffs at the defense department, the Joint Staff, the services, CINCPAC, and MACV continued to churn out analyses, recommendations, studies, and projections, but in the end it was one major general with an office in the basement of the White House who enjoyed the confidence of the president.

The North Vietnamese Politburo's calculus that the summits and the presidential election would restrain Nixon's response to the invasion was exactly opposite to Nixon's thought patterns. The Moscow summit was, in fact, one of the stimulants to the decision to take tough action; the timing of the conventions and the electoral campaign imposed urgency on aggressive action that might not otherwise have existed.

Nixon viewed this moment as a fundamental turning point, not just a new approach but a new beginning, and he wanted to sweep away all the impediments that had constrained his application of military force in the past. The strategy would change; so would the command structure and the people executing the strategy. The next day Nixon called Haig into his office and declared: "I want to set up a new command for the whole area—I don't think it should be CINCPAC—and I don't think Abrams can handle it."[26] His plan was to establish a unified command in Saigon, restructuring MACV and taking it out of the control of CINCPAC. This new command would have responsibility for South Vietnam, North Vietnam, Laos, and Cambodia. The commander would report directly to Moorer, who would report directly to the president. Only in this way, reasoned Nixon, could he end the destructive and frustrating competition for attack missions between the war in the North and the war in the South. There would be one commander with authority over all forces and over the entire region, and one simple chain of command to the national leadership.

The president and Haig sorted through the candidates to replace Abrams and exchanged suggestions on what to do with the general after his dismissal. Nixon sketched out a command structure with General Bruce

Palmer, then the Army's vice chief of staff, installed as the regional commander, and with General William DuPuy commanding Army forces in theater. General Vogt would assume command of theater air forces, and they would get "the best admiral we've got" to run naval operations in theater. They again discussed getting the secretary of defense under control, with Nixon pointing out: "See, I shouldn't be put through the emotional stress of having [to make] a goddamned cabinet officer do what I've ordered."

Now prepared to cross his own Rubicon, Nixon departed for Camp David to prepare the nationwide address that would accompany the mining operation. The two events would take place at the same moment, half a world apart, at 9 P.M. May 8 in Washington and 9 A.M. May 9 in Haiphong Harbor. The president left his advisors to work out the ticklish task of executing his direction without setting off a bureaucratic firestorm and without letting the secretary of defense know about this fundamental change in strategy.

The advisors' effort opened with Kissinger meeting Laird for breakfast on Saturday, May 6. It was a delicate moment. As Haig's talking paper for Kissinger warned: "Because Secretary Laird is not aware of what actions have taken place between you, Under Secretary Rush and Admiral Moorer, it is necessary that you approach this topic gingerly"—one of the great understatements of bureaucratic history. Haig outlined the military actions to be taken the following week—presenting them only as a planning exercise—and summarized the president's decision to revamp the command structure in Southeast Asia. Haig's paper provided a framework for the new command structure, along with the president's preferences for commanders. It also noted that Nixon had called Haig the night before to confirm that he definitely wanted to recall Abrams. The president would agree to naming Abrams to a two-year tour as the chief of staff of the Army "providing General Abrams is in agreement with the other provisions that you are aware of and providing that you concur."[27] The full range of these provisions can only be speculated upon, but they included an agreement that the appointment would only be for two years, and another not to air publicly the internal squabbling that had marked the relationship between the theater commander and the White House.

Kissinger met with Laird and, as expected, Laird offered firm resistance to the idea of a thorough reconstruction of the chain of command. His most effective arguments were technical: that the message and communications structure could not be altered instantly, and that massive changes at a time of crisis would only add to the risk. Kissinger agreed, and sold that reservation to Nixon later that morning.[28] Laird also advised against the changes in commanders, and over the next two days, through a series of phone conversations among Nixon, Kissinger, and Laird, that idea vanished as well.

Nixon's vow to abolish the existing command structure for Indochina diagnosed and addressed one of the great flaws in the American war effort. With the failure to change it, the dysfunctional structure continued to plague operations through the end of the war, eight months away. It was probably beyond the capability of the U.S. civil-military command structure to undergo such radical change at a time of crisis. Had Nixon's proposed structure been in place from the start of the war, however, it might have imposed a unity of effort on the fighting that was lacking through the whole course of the war.

That Saturday morning Kissinger and Nixon discussed the problem of getting the secretary of state to agree with this new strategy. Earlier Nixon had asked Kissinger to try to elicit Laird's help in persuading Rogers, but Kissinger had failed to broach the subject during his breakfast meeting with Laird. Finally, Nixon decided to call together the whole national security council "rather than to get Rogers in and have a debate about the thing."[29]

Early that afternoon, Nixon called Kissinger again, to discuss the speech he was drafting and to get an update on the bureaucratic struggles in progress. The Joint Chiefs were to meet at 2:00 to address the president's proposed changes in the command structure, and Kissinger had scheduled a 2:30 meeting with a CIA working group to explore North Vietnam's alternatives should the ports be closed. Nixon stressed that air attacks would follow the mining operation: "We must go after the rail lines, which is part of the blockade basically, immediately. I think that should go on Monday night—see what I mean—it is part of the blockade." Kissinger replied: "We will get that done right away." Thus the largest air battle of the war in Indochina was set in motion.[30]

Kissinger and Laird met again for breakfast on Sunday, May 7. Since the meeting the day before, Laird had sent the president a "compendium of papers outlining limitations on effectiveness of the earlier air interdiction program," still in hopes of dissuading the president from resuming a large-scale bombing campaign. By that point Laird and Moorer had persuaded Nixon to keep Abrams in place until the crisis had subsided, but the president remained adamant about changing the command structure.[31] Kissinger informed Laird that the president had recalled Rogers from Europe to participate in an NSC meeting scheduled for Monday morning, May 8.

With these meetings, the stage was set for introduction of the new strategy to the wider interagency planning apparatus. The confrontation began at a WSAG meeting the evening of May 7, and centered on CIA director Richard Helms's opposition to the mining operation—a position consistent with CIA positions taken since the first days of the war. Kissinger recounted the discussion to Nixon the following day: "Well, it turned out he [Helms] was really quite emotional. I gave him unshirted hell. I said let me tell you one thing, if you ever talk that way to the president, you'll need another job that evening because you're our intelligence officer—we don't need you for policy judgments." Nixon asked: "What's he emotional about?" Kissinger answered that Helms expected the North Vietnamese to reorient their logistics from ships to railroad lines from China. In Kissinger's estimation that was theoretically possible, but it would be difficult, time-consuming, and costly for the North Vietnamese. Summarizing the mood of the meeting, Kissinger predicted: "We will have a murderous problem with the bureaucracy . . . they're all against it except Moorer and [Deputy Secretary of Defense Ken] Rush." He reported that for most of those at the meeting the real objective of the combat at this point was to save South Vietnam. The general belief was that given the NVA's logistical stockpiling, anything done in the North could only have effects beginning, at best, three months away, and if South Vietnam could withstand the current shock, it would be a win.[32]

Kissinger summarized the arguments for the mining in military terms, shifting from the largely diplomatic perspective he had taken in earlier discussions. In his view, even if the blockade failed to isolate North Vietnam from its sources of supply, the effort required to keep supplies flowing would multiply the stresses on the regime, the society, and its economy, while providing a shot in the arm for the South Vietnamese and strengthening the U.S. position in the case of an ARVN collapse. The bombing would not directly affect combat for some time, but it would help ensure against a resurgent North Vietnamese offensive in the fall or the following year.

On Monday morning Nixon conducted the NSC meeting, finally calling into session the group formally charged with deliberating about national strategic matters. He opened with an overview of a theoretical range of policy options. One such option was "bugging out," withdrawing U.S. forces while blaming Congress for undermining the administration at the negotiating table and the South Vietnamese for not being able to "hack it."[33] Another was to continue at the current level of effort. Finally, they could choose some combination of bombing and mining. Each of these courses had risks; the question was which course would minimize them. Moorer outlined the mining plan and the current flow of goods into North Vietnamese ports, and then Helms offered his assessment of the effects of the mining. Nixon and Laird entered a collateral argument over the impact of the North Vietnamese tank force on the campaign. The debate then broadened to a discussion of strategy for the next phase of the war.

Laird led the opposition, arguing as he had before that the mining would not affect the current campaign and would be tremendously costly: "I am limited to 2.4 billion dollars annually. I have put in 2.9 billion dollars already, hiding it under the table. I am taking it out of the hide of the Services." The real fighting, Laird asserted, was in the South, that was where the war needed to be won, and operations against North Vietnam were risky and irrelevant to the combat that mattered. Connally and Vice President Agnew took an aggressive stance, Connally arguing: "If Vietnam is defeated, Mr. President, you won't have anything. I agree it won't happen in three weeks but it is a mistake to tie our hands as we did in the mid-1960's." After more than three hours, Nixon adjourned the meeting without announcing a decision. His closing commitment, though, was to "weigh Mel's options," to "weigh the bombing option which I don't like," and to "weigh the operation we have discussed today which does not take so much from General Abrams." There could be little doubt of the outcome.[34]

It is noteworthy that, in this discussion of a strategic interdiction campaign, no one ever mentioned the precision weapons that offered the best opportunity for success in restricting the North Vietnamese road and rail systems. These weapons were to prove the most important element of the campaign against the railroads; they had been operational since 1968, and they were to feature prominently in the strikes in the following days. Nonetheless, even Moorer, a strong advocate of the air campaign, failed to mention them in the overview he provided for the NSC.[35]

It is also significant that Nixon and Laird engaged in a fairly direct debate on the causes of the South Vietnamese failures. For Laird, the question was not one of equipment, but of "whether they are willing to stand and fight and search out the artillery." Nixon, in contrast, focused on the NVA's use of tanks: "Regarding the tanks, all but nine of ours were knocked out. Our small tanks are no match for the T-54s." He also used the discussion to advance his criticism of the aid that the department of defense had provided to the South Vietnamese: "The ARVN had 48 tanks—they have 500; I saw the figures."[36] In fact the figure of 500 tanks was an overestimate, and the 48 included only the M-48s, the most advanced tanks in the ARVN arsenal. In any case, the extreme infrequency of tank-on-tank engagements rendered the whole discussion rather pointless except as revealing the president's perception of the campaign.

With the NSC session over, Nixon and Kissinger met to discuss the next steps. Should they delay the announcement for 48 hours, asked Nixon, to give the impression of consultation and consideration of the opposing arguments? Kissinger recommended against that step, given the likelihood of leaks. Further, news had arrived that Kurt Waldheim, the secretary general of the United Nations, was planning to call a special session to discuss Vietnam. This was another impetus toward prompt action before this new diplomatic front could complicate the situation. Nixon and Kissinger were uncertain whether Waldheim's plan had been prompted by the Soviets or the state department, but they knew it must be countered. So they decided to hold to the previously defined schedule. The principals would be notified of the decision at 2 P.M., and the announcement to the nation would follow at 9. Connally then joined the two men, and they reviewed the decision once more.[37]

That afternoon there were innumerable implementing actions to be taken. Kissinger convened a WSAG meeting to pull together the military, diplomatic, and legal components of the mining. As the 9:00 speech approached, he contacted Moorer to ensure that plans were in progress for the air campaign to follow the mining operation. He had two major points. First: "We want to make absolutely sure that we are not going to fritter our stuff away . . . No air defense except for the minimum necessary." Second, there was to be an air attack on Hanoi the next day, before the North Vietnamese could begin working out alternative transportation routing. The strike force should first attack the petroleum and fuel in storage, then go to work on the bridges and the road/rail network.[38]

A few minutes later Laird called to confirm these directions, and to get reassurance that his position in the NSC meeting had not angered the president. Kissinger assured him, with artful ambiguity: "I thought it was absolutely essential you did what you did."[39] At Nixon's direction, Kissinger then contacted Deputy Secretary of Defense Ken Rush and Assistant Secretary of State William Sullivan to direct the opening of a massive leaflet campaign against North Vietnam and the NVA troops in the South, making sure the soldiers knew about the actions being taken against their supply lines.[40]

Two hours before the speech, Nixon called Kissinger, wondering whether the peace offer had been cleared with Thieu. The answer was no, but as Nixon said, "I'm all for it, and if he doesn't agree, that's too bad, huh."[41] Kissinger assured the president that Thieu would have a few hours' warning, though he was already inside that timeline, and the two men put the issue aside. As they spoke, out in the Pacific, the mines had been prepared and loaded onto the aircraft, and the crews were preparing for their mission.

12

CLOSING THE PORTS

The mining operation that closed Haiphong harbor on the morning of May 9 marked a rare milestone in the long history of American military operations in Southeast Asia. At long last, after eight years of frustration, U.S. forces conducted an operation suited to the American way of war. It was quick, it was strategically significant, it took advantage of numbers, technology, and firepower. There was good intelligence on the threat, and the command structure permitted the development of an elegant and powerful operation. The strategic direction was clear and executable, and so for once there was unity of action extending all the way from the White House to the time settings on the mines that settled into the harbor mud. It was indeed a rare moment in this frustrating war.

It was all so clean and quick that in retrospect it came to seem inevitable, as if the air-delivered mines were the obvious and immediate choice. But in fact there was an enormous amount of analysis conducted during the planning of this operation, as military planners sorted through all the feasible ways of shutting down the flow of supplies into North Vietnamese ports. At the strategic level a blockade held favor right up to the end, when Nixon opted for a mining operation supplemented by naval patrol. Debates at the military planning level paralleled these strategic deliberations. Intelligence looked at the possibility of shutting down Haiphong harbor by dropping objects into the water to speed up the silting process. There was another proposal, a Pacific Fleet concept calling for the scuttling of two or three cargo-laden hulls at strategic locations in the Haiphong approach channel.[1] As mining became a more prominent option, naval planners considered a submarine delivery, but ruled it out because of the harbor's shallow waters. A surface delivery would face formidable defenses, and would be risky even if the mines could be modified for delivery by high-speed boats. As other options fell away, aerial delivery emerged as the most feasible choice.[2]

Plans for mining Haiphong had been completed by 1965, and they had been repeatedly updated and reviewed since then. The detailed plan could be found in Mine Field Planning Folder 21 (MFPF 21), which outlined the configuration for twenty-one separate minefields along the coast of North Vietnam. MFPF 21 defined the locations for all the mines for each field, and the settings—arming delay, sensitivity, ship counts, and so on—for each mine. The plan included a delivery folder, which contained navigation and intelligence information for each target area. This delivery information was designed to assist units in determining the tactics, courses, and identification features necessary to carry out the operation. Seventh Fleet maintained OPLAN 121, a contingency mining plan based on MFPF 21.[3]

In theory, it could have been just a matter of pulling these plans off the shelf and turning them over to the units for execution. In practice, existing plans provided a solid starting point for a frenetic planning exercise extending from the White House to the Pentagon, out to Honolulu, and finally to the waters off Indochina. The plans needed updating to account for the current state of North Vietnamese defenses. They also needed adjustment for the political requirements established by the president, and for the likelihood that the U.S. Navy would someday be required to clear the fields. These considerations drove a number of changes to the plan as envisioned in 1971.

Strategic requirements prompted the most significant changes. The MFPF 21 minefield included three types of mines: the Mark 52–2 magnetic mine, the Mark 52–3 pressure-magnetic mine, and the Destructor (DST)-36. The Mark 52 models were purpose-designed mines, very sophisticated and very expensive. It was clear that they could close the harbor, but it was much less clear that the Navy would be able to clear them when the conflict was over, should that be part of the peace settlement. So the Mark 52–3 model, with its pressure-magnetic sensor, was eliminated from the plan. It was replaced by the simpler Mark 52–2, with a magnetic fuse. The DSTs were much simpler systems, essentially incorporating a magnetic fuse on a 500-pound bomb. They could only execute a 24-hour delay before arming, and so they, too, were eliminated to permit the 72-hour delay in arming that Nixon directed.[4]

It was the attention from the "highest authority," and not these relatively straightforward technical changes, that drove the staffs right through the chain of command. When given this tasking, Moorer had promised that it could be done quickly, and that it could be kept secret from Laird. Well aware that his credibility was on the line, he took a personal interest in the shape of the minefields. Moorer took the problem to Zumwalt, in order to take advantage of the Navy's expertise. The CNO gathered five senior officers around him on the floor of his office and set to work, using "a chart of the waters of North Vietnam, a ruler and a pair of dividers." "By midnight," he recalled, "we had the concept done and I was able to hand it to Admiral Moorer first thing next morning."[5]

It is a mark of the eventual success of this plan that so many people claimed authorship. The Seventh Fleet commander, Admiral William Mack, insisted: "It was our plan, a Seventh Fleet plan, in spite of the fact that it's been written in certain books that this plan was made in the CNO's office and so forth. That's a bunch of baloney. It was not. It was made right there by the Seventh Fleet staff."[6] The mine warfare office, for its part, emphasized that all these adjustments merely changed the basic plan, MFPF 21, "which was used (essentially intact) as the basis for the mining operation."[7] In fact, given the stakes and complexity of this operation, it naturally engrossed the attention of officers from the CJCS and the CNO on down, as they reviewed and adjusted the plan.

After all the staff-work and the detailed involvement of the admirals, it all came down to the men on board the carriers. Carrier Task Force 77 carried the responsibility to maintain a mining-ready carrier on station at all times, with the *Coral Sea* and Carrier Air Wing 15 filling this role in May 1972. The wing commander, Captain Roger Sheets, selected the commander of Marine attack squadron VMA-224, Lieutenant Colonel Charlie Carr, to lead the mission, calling him up to the air intelligence center when the mission order arrived on the carrier. There Carr encountered a Marine sentry, a rarity aboard ship, epitomizing the emphasis on secrecy that began at the Oval Office. Carr later recalled: "I knocked on the door, and

Lieutenant Commander Harvey Ickle, . . . the mine warfare officer on the Coral Sea, opened up the door. He had a coal miner's helmet complete with a little light on his head. I said, 'You're shitting me,' and Harvey said, 'No, I'm not.' We then started planning the mission . . . using a marvelous old French map as a guide."[8]

Carr decided to lead three A-6s to drop Mark 52s in the inner channel, with six A-7Es mining the outer segment of the channel. They had two primary concerns as they planned the mission. First, the timing was critical. Their direction came straight from the White House, and it was very specific. They were to drop the mines as President Nixon addressed the nation, twelve time zones away, at 9:00 P.M. on May 8. That would be exactly 9:00 A.M. on May 9 in Haiphong harbor.

The defenses around Haiphong posed a more lethal problem. The mines that the A-6s and A-7s carried were heavy, and they could have been designed specifically to increase drag on the aircraft. The aircraft would execute the attack run at 375 knots, 300 feet above the water. The missile threat would not be significant at that altitude, but a North Vietnamese fighter intercepting that formation could wreak havoc on the plan.

The naval forces offshore put together a formidable defense for the mining aircraft, taking advantage of the fact that there would be no other friendly aircraft in the area. Two guided-missile cruisers and a destroyer set an antiaircraft screen thirty miles offshore. Each of the guided-missile cruisers, the *Chicago* and the *Long Beach*, controlled a flight of F-4s as back-ups. Confident that there would be no friendly aircraft over North Vietnam as the operation started, they established a free-fire zone for any aircraft flying above 500 feet.

The mission would employ overwhelming force, near Haiphong and elsewhere. The *Kitty Hawk* would launch two diversionary strikes, hitting Nam Dinh just before the strike went into the harbor. Four ships would open naval gunfire on the Do Son Peninsula, about six miles southwest of the harbor, from 8:25 until 8:55. Finally, the carriers would fly the normal electronic countermeasure and electronic support aircraft to detect and jam enemy radar. In total, about 150 aircraft and two naval task forces would back the nine aircraft laying the mines. Thirty-six mines would close the harbor.[9]

The strike on May 9 went remarkably close to the plan. The mining flights launched at 8:10 and circled the carrier at 200 feet above the water until 8:40, then began the attack run. To the south, the diversionary flights diverted from Nam Dinh, attacking Thanh Hoa and Phu Qui instead. The North Vietnamese launched several MiGs, which headed southeast toward Haiphong. At 8:49 the *Chicago* launched one Talos surface-to-air missile at a range of 48 miles, followed by another a minute later. The missiles destroyed one MiG, and the others turned away.

As the mining force approached Haiphong, the NVA defenders fired three SAMs, which detonated harmlessly 6,000–8,000 feet above the water. The flights reached Haiphong precisely on time and dropped the mines starting at 8:59. The last mine was in the water by 9:01. All were set with a seventy-two hour delay, a 116-day sterilization time, and a ship count of one.[10] They would detonate on detecting the first merchant ship that passed after the time delay. With luck, that would never be necessary, and it was never the intent. As Admiral Mack commented: "The threat was what stopped them from going out through the field, not the number of mines."[11] Thirty-six ships were moored in the harbor. Nine left during the three-day grace period, all without pilots, as the North Vietnamese tried to discourage departures of ships that were not yet offloaded. The other twenty-seven ships would remain in Haiphong for the duration of the war. In the following days, A-7s and A-6s mined the ports at Thanh Hoa, Dong Hoi, Vinh, Hon Gai, Quang Khe, and Cam Pha. The North Vietnamese would make some fitful attempts at minesweeping, but for all practical purposes, these major ports were now closed.

Nixon began his speech as the mines sunk to the harbor floor. He finished by the time the strikers had all returned to their carriers. Nixon had foreseen from the first days of the offensive that, one way or another, this spasm of violence in Vietnam would lead to peace. The clarity and urgency of that possibility had risen through the succeeding month, as the death toll mounted and the North Vietnamese advanced in every sector of attack. Now he outlined a strategy comprising diplomatic, informational, and military elements—all working toward extricating the United States from the war. He opened by reviewing the situation, building the case for the escalation he had ordered. He justified the decision to mine the harbors partly as a defensive measure for the Americans still in Indochina, and partly as a matter of national credibility and honor, a refusal to topple the government of an ally. He omitted the more fundamental reason, that the strong action was necessary to support his own position in Moscow.[12]

Nixon presented the choices remaining to him as starkly as he did the issues. "We now have a clear, hard choice among three courses of action: Immediate withdrawal of all American forces, continued attempts at negotiation, or decisive military action to win the war." There were, of course, other choices, most obviously the focus on supporting the ARVN that Laird had advocated. After dismissing his first two options, Nixon announced his decision: "There is only one way to stop the killing. That is to keep the weapons of war out of the hands of the international outlaws of North Vietnam." Then came the stunning announcement:

> I have ordered the following measures which are being implemented as I am speaking to you. All entrances to North Vietnamese ports will be mined to prevent access to these ports . . . United States forces have been directed to take appropriate measures within the internal and claimed territorial waters of North Vietnam to interdict the delivery of any supplies. Rail and all other communications will be cut off to the maximum extent possible. Air and naval strikes against military targets in North Vietnam will continue.

Listeners around the world focused on this dramatic announcement and the escalation it portended. But like a magician, calling attention to one hand while performing a trick with another, Nixon then offered new negotiating terms that, in any other context, would have seemed like surrender. He managed to do so, moreover, in the form of an ultimatum. He stated the new American terms for settlement as follows:

> These actions I have ordered will cease when the following conditions are met. First, all American prisoners of war must be returned. Second, there must be an internationally supervised cease-fire throughout Indochina. Once prisoners of war are released, once the internationally supervised cease-fire has begun, we will stop all acts of force throughout Indochina, and at that time we will proceed with a complete withdrawal of all American forces from Vietnam within four months.

The address closed with brief comments "directed individually to each of the major parties involved in the continuing tragedy of the Vietnam War." He briefly addressed the people of South Vietnam and North Vietnam. Then he turned to the Soviet Union, at greater length, with remarks he had drafted himself. The essence of his remarks to the Soviets came toward the end of his address:

> We do not ask you to sacrifice your principles, or your friends, but neither should you permit Hanoi's intransigence to blot out the prospects we together have so patiently prepared. We, the United States, and the

Soviet Union, are on the threshold of a new relationships that can serve not only the interests of our two countries, but the cause of world peace. We are prepared to continue to build this relationship. The responsibility is yours if we fail to do so.

The president artfully aimed at the tensions between the Soviets and the North Vietnamese and the tension among the Soviet Union's strategic goals. In doing so, he also placed the burden of the summit's possible cancellation squarely on the Soviets, for both their consideration and that of the American public. The ball was in the Soviets' court, and only time would tell whether they would permit the summit to proceed.

The response in the United States was immediate and vivid. Nixon's talent for polarizing America was never in bolder display than in this decision. The speech reawakened the antiwar movement, greatly attenuated since the late 1960s. There were scattered protests, some violent. But there was nothing of the sustained, bitter uproar that had characterized the antiwar movement during earlier crises, and the limited violence subsided in a couple of days. As the students took to the barricades, the op-ed writers took to their typewriters. Nixon had expected rough treatment from the press, and he got it. War fatigue and personal antipathy toward Nixon played a role. So did the speech's odd juxtaposition of tough military measures, conciliatory negotiating terms, and grim and unyielding tone. From all across the nation the president's decision came under attack. Some writers focused on the risk of superpower confrontation, others on the marginal legality of the mining and escalation of the war, others on the vast risk accepted by Nixon for the marginal gains he stood to achieve through success. The Democratic presidential candidates added their predictable, almost ritual condemnation.

Nixon could discount the press, the protestors, and the Democratic candidates. Their reactions were expected and created little threat to his major interests. With regard to domestic politics, he had long ago concluded that he would never be treated fairly by the left, and that his real political imperative was to preserve his hold on the right. Polls taken immediately after the speech reported that 59 percent of the listening public approved of Nixon's decisions, quickly defusing any concern he might have had for the political cost of the escalation.[13]

From an audience extending around the world, only a few listeners really mattered to Nixon. These were concentrated on Capitol Hill, in the

Kremlin, and in the Politburo in Hanoi. Little as Nixon may have valued the opinion of the senators and representatives, they offered some threat to his policy through their control of the purse. The day after the speech, the Senate Democratic Caucus condemned Nixon's actions and voted 35 to 8 to cut off funds for the war, contingent only on Hanoi's agreement to release the American prisoners of war. A second vote, condemning Nixon's escalation of the war, passed by a vote of 29 to 14. In the House, as the *Washington Post* reported, "the Nixon announcement set off more than an hour of impassioned oratory pro and con. It was interrupted three times by outbursts from the visitors' gallery, where young people shouting antiwar slogans were hustled off by police."[14] The next day, Haldeman noted that Nixon "wants us to go all out on the Southern Democrats, so that this doesn't become a party line deal."[15] Whether because of that effort or not, the votes showed a deep regional split in the Democrats' attitudes. Southern Democrats accounted for 7 of the party's 8 rejections of the proposal to cut funding, and 12 of the 14 Democratic votes against a condemnation of Nixon's escalation.[16] The administration once again contained congressional frustration, averting a major crisis.

There was little realistic likelihood that Hanoi would accept the terms Nixon offered in the speech, and there is no indication that the president ever really thought the Politburo might stop its offensive to negotiate on these terms. There existed a whole array of obstacles to peace at that point. To begin with, Nixon's speech offered little that was new, only accelerating the timeline for a U.S. pullout after the cease-fire. The NVA enjoyed every advantage on the battlefield at the moment, and a cease-fire would strip their forces of the momentum they had gained at so high a cost. Nixon specified that any cease-fire would have to extend throughout Indochina; the North Vietnamese could not have delivered the Cambodian communists even if they had tried. The "international commission" Nixon proposed to oversee the cease-fire offered endless opportunities for delay, during which the South Vietnamese would have time to regain their balance and strength. Most fundamentally, Nixon's proposal offered only a military settlement to the war, without addressing the political issues that caused and shaped the fighting.[17]

The composition and the decisionmaking process of the North Vietnamese Politburo probably offered significant obstacles to their acceptance of this proposal. The Politburo worked on a consensus basis, and the strategic decision to launch the offensive had been hard fought and delicately balanced. Ironically, the American president, working within a democratic system, had vastly more power over national decisionmaking than any single member of the Politburo. Le Duan, to be sure, was first among equals, but he could not have engineered so rapid and fundamental a redirection of the North Vietnamese strategy even had he wished to do so. It was a fleeting opportunity, and opportunistic decisionmaking was not a strong point in the North Vietnamese system. The North Vietnamese considered Nixon's speech as presenting an ultimatum, not an opportunity, and they responded accordingly. They denounced Nixon's actions as an ultimatum "not only to the Vietnamese people but to the Socialist camp and the entire world."[18]

So it all came down to the USSR. How would the Soviets respond to this direct challenge? For two anxious days, the White House awaited their decision. The answer arrived on May 11, not directly, but through statements not made and actions not taken by the Soviet leadership. Ambassador Dobrynin delivered a formal protest of the mining, but it carefully avoided any ultimatum or direct response to the closure of the ports. More directly, the Soviet minister of trade, Nikolai Patolichev, visited Nixon at the White House, accompanied by Dobrynin, for a cordial and productive meeting oriented toward the trade agreements to be reached at the summit. The Soviets had not even adopted the face-saving compromise natural to any bureaucracy, an indefinite delay. The summit would proceed as planned, on the original schedule. This was a major triumph for Nixon, and a clear reward for the careful diplomacy that he and Kissinger had conducted over the previous years.

The last strange note occurred in Saigon. On the night of May 8, as naval forces offshore prepared for the mining operation, Abrams hosted the delegation that Nixon had sent to South Vietnam to assess the ARVN's logistical status, five flag officers led by an assistant secretary of defense, Barry Shillito. In the course of the dinner conversation, a member of the delegation, Admiral Charles S. Minter, asked Abrams how he planned to use one of the ships then deploying to Southeast Asia. The innocent question triggered a profane outburst, Abrams complaining that he had no idea how the ship would be used since the Navy was fighting its own war. That very day, the gun line deployed offshore had redeployed without notice, canceling its gunnery missions in support of the battle area. It was a prolonged and bitter diatribe, shocking the guests, one of whom described Abrams as "an inebriate and a tyrant."[19]

Afterwards, Shillito called the Pentagon to report the incident to Laird. It developed that the naval task force had deployed northward to support the mining and blockade operations, and no one had thought to inform the theater commander. The White House had finally informed Abrams of the change in the theater strategy through a back-channel message to Bunker on May 7, asking the ambassador to brief COMUSMACV. But no one had told Abrams of the naval forces' involvement, and the deployment northward without his knowledge had reopened old wounds.[20]

The mining operation off Haiphong that morning was only the opening move in an operation that would continue until the following January 14, when an A-7 would drop the last mine delivered by U.S. forces.[21] Operations against the ports were conducted under the code name Pocket Money. They complemented mining operations in inland waterways, which were executed as part of the Linebacker air campaign against the North Vietnamese transportation infrastructure. The two operations naturally intersected in some areas, but were kept distinct in recognition of the political sensitivity of Pocket Money operations. These were carefully controlled at the White House and JCS level; new minefields and even reseeding the mines in Haiphong required Kissinger's approval, and Laird and Moorer received daily briefings on the status of the minefields. Moorer, in fact, carried an index card in his pocket that summarized the self-destruct and sterilization time for all the minefields in North Vietnamese harbors.[22] The mines delivered inland, however, offered little diplomatic threat, and so these were under less centralized regulation.

Between May 1972 and January 1973, Navy and Air Force aircraft delivered 11,603 DST mines throughout North Vietnam.[23] Navy fighters dropped a total of 108 Mark 52s into Haiphong harbor, as CTF 77 worked to close gaps in the fields and to reseed mines once their sterilization periods had expired.[24] Overall, Pocket Money can be considered one of the few unambiguous successes of the American war effort in Southeast Asia. Once the mines were activated, nothing left the ports and nothing arrived.

It came as no surprise that the mines stopped traffic through the ports. American policy and intelligence analyses since the first days of the war had predicted they would have that effect. The issue since the 1960s, however, had been whether the North Vietnamese could work around the closure of the ports by using small water craft and by increasing rail and road traffic from China. The CIA and civilians in the defense department had consistently predicted that mining would have no practical effect on the NVA war effort, since railroads could pick up the traffic with little loss of time or capacity. The bombing campaign over the next months would test that analysis, as Air Force and Navy forces executed a sustained attack on North Vietnam's transportation infrastructure.

13

LINEBACKER PLANNING AND DIRECTION

As policy guidance goes, Nixon's vow to "bomb those bastards like they've never been bombed before," to "cream them," was unusually clear, leaving little room for doubt about the sort of campaign he wanted to see.[1] The discussions that led up to the air campaign also made it clear that the mining would be followed by the interdiction of the railways connecting North Vietnam and China, and by operations against lighters off the coast. But there remained a huge gap between that level of guidance and the specific tasking necessary to put the right bombs on the right targets in the right sequence.

It was the job of the military chain of command to translate the president's policy guidance into direction to the operators, increasingly detailed as it worked down the chain of command. Ultimately, the work of every pilot rolling in on a target, every crew chief pumping fuel, and every munitions specialist hanging bombs on aircraft would have to support the policy direction established in the Oval Office. The campaign can be seen as a massive management function, as the large, multilayered bureaucracy that governs U.S. military operations sought to create the effects directed by the commander in chief.

While Nixon viewed this air operation as a completely new departure in the war, administratively it was built on the foundations of the Rolling

Thunder campaign conducted under the Johnson administration. Nixon's air operation would retain the general command arrangements devised in 1965. CINCPAC, in Hawaii, would exercise overall command of the air offensive against the North, except for the area just north of the DMZ, where MACV would have that responsibility. Within North Vietnam, the Air Force and Navy air forces would divide their attacks geographically.

Planning for the 1972 air operation also took advantage of policy reviews and operational planning conducted earlier in the Nixon administration, as decisionmakers, both civilian and military, repeatedly addressed options that might end the war. The first of these explorations had occurred a month after the new administration entered office. On February 21, 1969, Kissinger directed the Pentagon to assess "potential military actions which might jar the North Vietnamese into being more forthcoming at the Paris talks." The first reply from the JCS offered suggestions that Kissinger considered to be beyond what the international and domestic situation would permit. The refined options, now known as the "indicator actions," provided a series of steps that could be taken to signal that a resumption of U.S. attacks was imminent. Kissinger went so far as to direct an increase in naval reconnaissance flights over the North and to direct CINCPAC to "position search and rescue and positive identification radar advisory zone ships in a manner to indicate resumption of air and naval bombardment for psychological purposes and to test NVN reaction."[2]

The Joint Chiefs assessed a series of options provided by the NSC. These included repositioning naval gunfire ships into the Gulf of Tonkin; moving CTF 77 back toward Yankee Station, the launch point for carrier-based air attacks on the North; embarking Marine forces to threaten an amphibious action against North Vietnam; changing the operational patterns of USAF and VNAF aircraft to indicate the resumption of air attacks against the North; conducting leaflet drops over Laos and the South China Sea, avoiding overflight of North Vietnam; and reinstating harassment raids against the North. On the whole, the Chiefs were quite unimpressed by the prospect of these limited actions, and Laird, if anything, was even more skeptical than the JCS. As the Chiefs summarized: "Any military 'indicator' actions without military follow-up of sufficient magnitude, such as bombardment of NVN, will have little if any effect on the enemy's combat activity in South Vietnam or his attitude at the Paris negotiations."[3]

Kissinger's first foray into military planning was relatively tentative, an attempt to nudge the North Vietnamese into serious negotiations. In that first summer in office, he and Nixon sought a far more aggressive way to bring the war to an end, one aimed at bludgeoning the North Vietnamese into serious negotiations. Through the fall of 1969, as the conflict in South Vietnam subsided into protracted warfare, military planners in the Pacific and in Washington developed detailed and comprehensive concepts for these attacks. The initiative combined a Navy mining operation, code-named Duck Hook, with a series of air campaign options under the umbrella designation Pruning Knife.[4] Nixon planned to unleash this campaign in early November 1969, the anniversary of Johnson's cessation of air attacks on North Vietnam.

Perhaps even more than Linebacker as finally executed, Pruning Knife reflected the purest use possible at the time of air attack as a coercive weapon. There was no focus on strictly military targeting and no emphasis on interdiction of military forces or material. The objective that had governed attack planning in the first years of the war, of limiting NVA capabilities to operate in the South, was gone. Instead, Pruning Knife was intended to impose as much damage as possible on North Vietnam's economic and war-supporting facilities in an intensive bombing campaign, followed by a sustained campaign against the transportation infrastructure to isolate North Vietnam and disrupt efforts to rebuild its economy.[5]

The planners built four options: 7- and 14-day attacks for both monsoon seasons: in the northeast from October through March, and in the southwest from April to October. All the options incorporated the same general sequence. The incrementalism of the Johnson years would be rejected, with the first attacks aimed at surprise and overwhelming power. Initial operations would target the North Vietnamese air defenses, to minimize losses and improve the effectiveness of subsequent strikes. These defense-suppression strikes would be followed by early air strikes against high-value targets that could be readily dispersed, then by strikes on "economic and war-support targets" and by mining of North Vietnam's deep-water ports. As the campaign developed and as the enemy adapted to the mining, there would follow naval gunfire and air strikes against coastal traffic and associated logistical targets, and air attacks against the northeast rail line connecting Hanoi and China. These follow-on actions would reinforce North Vietnam's isolation from its external sources of supply. In the absence of large-scale commitments to supporting combat in South Vietnam, planners expected to commit 740 sorties per day to the attacks on the North during the intensive initial phase, with the pace slowing to 250–300 sorties per day during the follow-on phase.[6]

In light of later controversies, it is interesting to note that the planners explicitly addressed the idea of striking the system of dikes that stretched throughout North Vietnam. Their conclusion was that "as a target system, this category requires an inordinate weight of effort, and it is doubtful that any meaningful results could be achieved. More than 2000 miles of dikes are spread out over the broad Red River Delta area. Any attempt to breach this system would require a large scale effort and the results would be minimized by the extensive system of secondary and tertiary dikes and dams."[7] Even before issues of morality and the laws of war entered the picture, basic considerations of military utility ruled out a concentrated attack on the dikes.

Long, hard experience during Rolling Thunder had tempered the strike planners' optimism about the effects of the interdiction effort. The JCS memorandum forwarding the plan to Laird included, for example, a table summarizing the results of a concerted, extended effort to shut down the northeast rail line in the summer and fall of 1967. Over that period, Air Force and Navy aircraft had flown 1,458 sorties against the railroad. These had managed to close the line for a total of seven days between June and October. The North Vietnamese had been forced to shuttle supplies for 79 days in that period, but had successfully accommodated to the attacks.

In forwarding the attack options, the JCS clearly worked to avoid raising unrealistic hopes about the effectiveness and speed of the campaign. Their assessment provides a clear, succinct summary of the obstacles that would face strike forces in any extended campaign against North Vietnam. It summarized the upgrades to North Vietnamese defenses since the end of Rolling Thunder, and projected that the attacks on the DRV's logistical structure had no prospect of shutting down the flow of essential supplies: "While the plan would create very serious problems for Hanoi, the nation's viability would not be critically impaired." Most critically, the Chiefs pointed out: "In order to achieve general destruction of the economy and of North Vietnam's capability to continue as a viable entity, an expanded air and naval campaign would be required . . . such a campaign would require at least two good weather seasons . . . it is estimated that at least twelve to eighteen months will be required to achieve decisive results."[8] The limited-duration offensive contemplated by Nixon, in short, offered little prospect of real military value.

These plans followed the normal path of military planning: they absorbed thousands of hours of staff effort with no immediate result. In the absence of a specific trigger event for such a dramatic escalation, and deterred by massive antiwar demonstrations, Nixon turned away from military action, instead delivering his "Silent Majority" speech calling on Middle America for sustained support of his policies.[9] Pruning Knife and Duck Hook went back on the shelf, and the staff officers who had been planning these options in deep secrecy resumed their normal duties.

Still, the Pruning Knife planning options remain of interest on several counts. They offer a clear view of the sort of concentrated, ferocious air action Nixon and Kissinger contemplated. They depict a doctrinally pure approach to a strategic air offensive against North Vietnam, beginning with a focused attack on air defenses and then moving to take out all elements of value in the national infrastructure. They provide a good analysis of the problems air and naval forces would face in this endeavor—problems that would worsen over time, as North Vietnam continued to recover from the three-year offensive it had suffered from 1965 to 1968. The Pruning Knife plans, modified somewhat over time, remained on the books until 1972, and provided some of the planning basis for Linebacker.

The cast of characters involved in Pruning Knife reappeared, to a striking degree, three years later in Linebacker. In the fall of 1969, Moorer was the Chief of Naval Operations, and he signed one version of the Pruning Knife plan as acting CJCS. The Air Staff's Director for Plans and Operations in 1969 was Lieutenant General John Vogt, who later worked his way into command of Seventh Air Force and directed the land-based portion of Linebacker. Alexander Haig, then a lowly colonel on the NSC staff, worked long hours in reviewing the plans; by 1972 he had become a major general and, more significantly, the president's most trusted advisor on military affairs. The plans gave Nixon and Kissinger a template they would remember in 1972. All the major participants, in short, were there for both operations.

Nixon recalled this sequence in May 1972, as he contemplated actions in response to the NVA offensive and the impending Moscow summit. As he viewed his presidency, this was one of the four times he had turned away from decisive military action. In retrospect, he viewed all four as mistakes. With each serious consideration of military action, with each detailed study of the options available, the psychological and organizational friction against such bold action weakened. Each repetition brought him closer to the final decision to unleash the Linebacker offensive.

Over the next few years, planners in Hawaii, Saigon, and Washington continued to turn out concept plans for short-duration strikes against portions of the North Vietnamese logistical and air defense systems. By December 1971 these included three plans derived from Pruning Knife, outlining strikes against Hanoi and Haiphong. Outline plans also addressed the target sets below 20 degrees north (Fringe Index), 19 degrees north (Frame Gap), and on the coastline, from the DMZ to China (Fracture Blow). Friday Train outlined a two-day strike against the southern extension of the POL pipeline, Freeway Race offered three options for one-day strikes against complexes in the Panhandle, and Baron Sword focused on targets near the DMZ. In the winter of 1971–1972 the JCS added Fracture Baron, outlining a one-day strike against truck concentrations in the Hanoi area.[10]

As the threat of an NVA offensive grew increasingly evident that winter, the existing plans for air operations against the North were first rationalized and then extended in preparation for the combat expected to follow. On January 26 the JCS directed MACV to prepare plans for air attack against air defense radars south of the 20 degree line (Freedom Dash); attack against SAM threats immediately north of the DMZ (Freedom Block); and attacks against "staging areas, enemy troop concentrations, logistic support facilities, and all other supply and transport activities in support of the land battle in South Vietnam" (Freedom Play).[11]

These concept plans reflect again the old adage "Plans are useless, but planning is essential." None was ever executed exactly as written, but all served in some form, as they were adapted to meet the mission and threat as they existed in the spring of 1972. It was still necessary to refine these earlier plans and adjust them to meet Nixon's guidance, and this process took place in a feverish burst of activity beginning on May 8. The specific interface between civilian decisionmakers and the military chain of command occurred within the NSC offices, as Kissinger and Haig reviewed the messages drafted by the JCS to provide operational direction to CINCPAC and its subordinate commands.

Moreover, these messages were broadly based on direction provided by the NSC through a series of telephone calls to the Pentagon. As an example, in the early evening of May 8, in the interval between the climactic NSC meeting, the WSAG follow-on gathering, and Nixon's speech to the nation, Kissinger called Moorer to set the post-mining events in motion. Kissinger outlined the targets he wanted struck the day after the mining operation, and emphasized the importance of a rapid and decisive follow-up to the closure of the ports. He directed the air attacks to follow "within 24 hours so that they don't even begin considering what to do about alternative routes and then right after that POL again. From then on you just go ahead on these bridges, etc."[12]

Kissinger also provided direction that was to have a long-term effect on the campaign, telling Moorer: "We want to make absolutely sure that we are not going to fritter our stuff away . . . No air defense except for the minimum necessary."[13] Nixon and Kissinger had been concerned in the opening days of Freedom Train that the first air attacks on North Vietnam had focused almost entirely on the SAM threat, without striking the supplies just north of the DMZ. Now they took steps to prevent a recurrence. Kissinger's broad guidance was to find its way into the operations orders outlining the Linebacker campaign, explicitly directing that the weight of effort expended on defenses should be limited to the amount necessary to permit immediate accomplishment of the mission.[14]

Having worked its way through the military planning process, Kissinger's guidance yielded JCS direction to execute a one-day strike on May 10. The JCS message assigned the specific targets to be struck by both Air Force and Navy fighters and outlined the general flow of the air strikes. The initial strikes would be code-named Rolling Thunder Alpha, a revival of the air campaign conducted in the late 1960s.[15]

On May 9 there followed a series of JCS messages, extending this opening strike into a broad, sustained air campaign. One provided public affairs guidance, changing the operation's name to Linebacker.[16] The Pentagon also defined the campaign's objectives and the operating authorities—most importantly, the geographic restrictions—to be met by the theater commands, along with the weight of effort expected by the White House.[17] The JCS direction went to CINCPAC, Admiral John McCain, at his headquarters in Hawaii. During Rolling Thunder and again during this air operation against North Vietnam, CINCPAC would be the command responsible for conducting the offensive against North Vietnam, with MACV retaining responsibility for attacks in South Vietnam, Laos, Cambodia, and the area of the DRV just north of the demilitarized zone. McCain and his staff then amplified and transmitted the guidance to its components at Pacific Air Forces (PACAF) and the Pacific Fleet. These commands, in turn, sent their guidance cascading down to the next levels of command, where the operational decisions would be made—for the Air Force, Seventh Air Force, and for the Navy, Seventh Fleet and CTF 77.

PACAF directed Seventh Air Force to execute a four-phase air offensive, emphasizing that the Seventh Air Force commander would have complete flexibility to adjust priorities as required by the tactical situation. The plan would require about 75 to 100 tactical sorties per day, subject to MACV's requirements for air support in South Vietnam. The overall campaign would open with operations against the northeast railroad, with strikes against key command and control facilities to be included if authorized by higher authorities. The next phase would include "primary storage areas and railroad classification yards." Then would follow another phase attacking "storage, support, and transshipment areas developed by the enemy to bypass or negate the effect of damage achieved in phases I and II." Phase IV would consist of strikes against "enemy defenses, such as command and control facilities, AAA repair areas, and airfields."[18]

The initial concept of operations bore two interesting features. First, it explicitly minimized attacks on enemy defenses. The planners in Hawaii specified: "The nature of these targets is such that they will be struck as necessary during all phases to protect friendly forces. The hardening of most of these targets, coupled with the dispersal of enemy aircraft, however, makes heavy strikes less productive; therefore, weight of effort should be limited to that which will satisfactorily harass or inhibit enemy defensive activity while phase I, II, and III targets are struck."[19]

This amounted to an elaboration of Kissinger's guidance offered the night of May 8, and it was to fundamentally affect the conduct of air operations through the first months of Linebacker. It is of interest that Nixon and Johnson both arrived at the decision to limit air attacks on the North Vietnamese defenses, but through very different routes. Johnson and his secretary of defense, Robert McNamara, had forbidden strikes on the SAM sites in early 1965 for fear of killing Soviet advisors.[20] Nixon, in contrast, feared diffusion of effort in endless attacks against dispersed and hardened defense forces.

The second noteworthy aspect of this plan is its emphasis on precision weapons, both to maximize damage to the enemy, and to limit civilian casualties. The plan specified: "Terminally guided munitions should be employed against these [phase I] point targets to assure destruction."[21] The extensive use of precision weapons, however, conflicted with Pacific Command's guidance on the weight of effort to be applied. CINCPAC's direction to fly 75 to 100 strike sorties a day, 32 in the immediate future, reflected Nixon's emphasis on the mass of effort rather than on specific

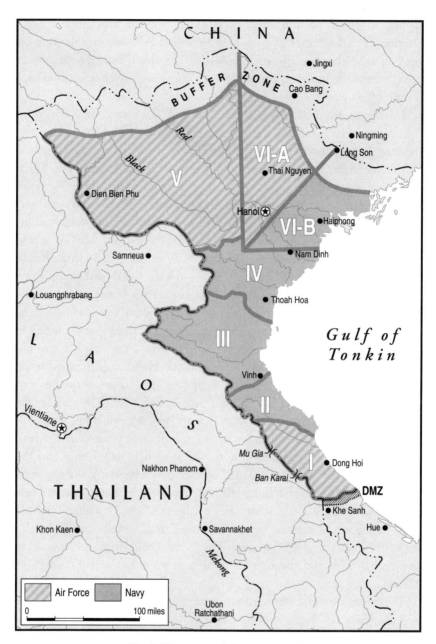

North Vietnam and the Route Packs

damage imposed on the enemy. With laser-guided weaponry, a small fraction of that number of aircraft could inflict the necessary damage on the North Vietnamese infrastructure—but that strictly military measure of effectiveness did not account for the political and psychological effects sought by Nixon.

Having received all this guidance, Seventh Air Force then issued an operations order providing a single source of direction for the wings conducting the campaign. Most significantly, this order provided a detailed definition of the route package boundaries that would define Air Force and Navy areas of responsibility for operations within North Vietnam. As noted earlier, Linebacker operations defaulted to the same system used throughout Rolling Thunder, with land-based and carrier air operations separated geographically in operations over the North. MACV would control strikes in Route Pack (RP) 1, directly north of the DMZ. Route Packs 2, 3, and 4 extended northward through the DRV panhandle. They would be primarily Navy responsibilities. Route Pack 5 covered the northwest quadrant of North Vietnam, most notably the rail line leading northwest out of Hanoi; the Air Force, operating out of Thailand and coming in from Laos, would conduct operations in that area. Route Pack 6 covered the North Vietnamese heartland of Hanoi and Haiphong, along with the critical northeast rail line leading to Lang Son. This area was the heart of the North Vietnamese nation and was fiercely defended. The services divided this area into two attack areas, Route Pack 6A and Route Pack 6B, with the northeast railroad line marking the boundary between the two. The Air Force took responsibility for RP 6A, including Hanoi and the northeast railroad. The Navy would operate over Haiphong and the critical links in the Hanoi-Haiphong railroad. Thus the Air Force assumed primary responsibility for closing both of the rail lines to China, and for keeping the sort of intense pressure on Hanoi that formed an essential element in Nixon's strategic concept. The Navy would primarily operate in the coastal areas and through the long transportation corridor south of Hanoi.

Within this general framework of geographic separation, the Air Force and the Navy developed means of cooperating in some aspects of operations. For example, they coordinated procedures for weather diversions from one area to another, and Navy picket ships provided radar coverage of North Vietnam for both Navy and Air Force strike forces. A joint communications network, the Southeast Asia Tactical Data System, enabled the different forces to exchange radar and intelligence information.[22]

Nixon's determination to avoid his predecessor's mistakes was reflected in major differences between this air campaign and Rolling Thunder. First, he expected an aggressive campaign from the start, without the creeping escalation of the Johnson years. Second, he expected the commanders in theater to direct the war, without the micromanagement of the Johnson-McNamara White House. He wanted a decentralized campaign, aggressively pursued, subject to as few restrictions as feasible. Higher authorities would impose constraints only where necessary to protect overriding diplomatic or political objectives. The operational framework for the campaign reflected these preferences in the geographic structure governing air operations, and in the procedures for validating targets and scheduling attacks.

Nixon and his staffers wished to minimize the geographic sanctuaries offered the North Vietnamese in Rolling Thunder, and so shrank the restricted areas around Hanoi and Haiphong from the 30- and 10-mile circles of the Johnson years to 10 and 5 miles respectively. Moreover, under Nixon these circles did not define completely restricted areas but areas in which all targets would have to be validated by the JCS. Once validated, they could be struck as the field commanders decided. Where Johnson and his advisors had parceled out strikes in these cities very carefully, Nixon was repeatedly frustrated by the military commanders' inability to hit these targets as hard as he wished.

The restrictions along the border with China were much more stringent. The restricted area along the Chinese border remained precisely as it had been defined in Rolling Thunder: 30 miles deep from the Laotian border to 106 degrees west, and 25 miles from there to the China Sea. Targets within that area would have to be validated by the JCS, and then could only be struck with specific authorization. Field commanders would not have the authority to strike targets in this large area at need, nor could they send armed reconnaissance sorties into the area. The fears of direct Chinese intervention had nearly vanished with the diplomatic opening to China, but Nixon and Kissinger sustained these restrictions in order to protect the still-delicate relationship with the PRC. This deep buffer zone came at a high price in military effectiveness, severely limiting the interdiction operations along the road/rail network northeast of Hanoi.

CINCPAC had the authority to validate fixed targets through the rest of the campaign area. Targets, once validated, could be struck whenever weather and defenses permitted. Finally, the JCS authorizations provided for armed reconnaissance strikes against traffic and lines of communications. Except under unusual circumstances, Seventh Air Force and CTF 77 would decide on their targets and schedules for daily operations.

The series of initial planning messages established the framework of the campaign. That same period saw a blizzard of messages among the commands' intelligence agencies, nominating and validating targets.[23] These messages all worked toward the next critical step in the planning process: finding and targeting the critical nodes in the North Vietnamese economic and logistical systems. There would be little time for reflection or careful selection at the outset of the campaign, as the intelligence and operational staffs worked to approve the targets necessary to prosecute the sort of aggressive campaign Nixon expected. Instead there was a crash program, as the Pacific Command staff built the structures and processes necessary to provide validated targets for attack. At the outset of the campaign there were 53 authorized targets. By the end of May the command had validated 590, and by October that number had reached 1,138.[24]

The effort to find, identify, and attack targets was critical to the campaign, and the American forces called on a range of systems to perform those functions. Space-based imagery systems still relied on film-return capsules, with average flight duration in that period of about two weeks. These systems were not useful, therefore, in tracking mobile targets. However, the CIA used space-based reconnaissance to keep track of the status of airfields in North Vietnam, and to detect and describe new installations.[25] These reports fed through intelligence channels into targeting cells for eventual attack. Manned strategic reconnaissance systems were not widely used over North Vietnam; the U-2s could not penetrate the areas of interest because of the missile threat, and the weather patterns normally prevented high-altitude systems from being effective in any case. Unmanned systems, then called "drones," able to fly low-altitude penetration sorties, performed the bulk of the strategic reconnaissance over North Vietnam. These aircraft, owned and operated by SAC, were subject to squabbles over tasking and responsiveness, as Seventh Air Force intermittently bid for more direct control of mission scheduling. Procedures remained basically stable through this period, however, with SAC mission planners programming the drones. During 1972 the drones flew a total of 498 missions, losing 52 aircraft. The missions targeted a total of 6,335 high-priority points for photos, succeeding with 2,543 of these. As with most weapons systems in theater, the drones' operational tempo accelerated dramatically from 1971 to 1972, with sorties increasing from 286 to 498.[26]

This initial series of messages established a sound framework, one that lasted with little adjustment until the end of the campaign. The adage that no plan survives initial contact with the enemy, however, proved valid as the campaign progressed. For one thing, the broad geographic latitude provided in the basic campaign plan often faced restrictions due to various political requirements. Available evidence indicates that Haig directed these restrictions in secure phone conversations with Laird's military assistants.[27] Just during the first two months of the campaign, in May and June, Kissinger forbade operations in the Hanoi and Haiphong areas from May 20 until June 5, as the president visited Moscow, Tehran, and Warsaw.[28] Kissinger authorized strikes on four targets in the Chinese buffer zone for the four days before Nixon's departure.[29] Restrictions on strikes in Hanoi and Haiphong were imposed again on June 13 as Soviet President Podgorny visited North Vietnam. Meanwhile, the PRC agreed to receive Kissinger for his fourth visit. In order to eliminate any chance of diplomatic embarrassment, Kissinger called Moorer to direct a further prohibition on all strikes north of 20 degrees 25 minutes effective on June 13.[30] This restriction remained in place until June 17; those on Hanoi and Haiphong lasted until June 24.[31] Though never as extensive as the bombing halts during the Johnson years, these adjustments repeatedly released the relentless pressure envisioned by Nixon at the campaign's outset.[32]

Other adjustments to the basic plan reflected deeper issues. They arose from two sources: the North Vietnamese reaction to the attacks, and the never-ending effort to balance the various diplomatic and military objectives being sought in the bombing. The first of these resulted in an adjustment of operational priorities; the second yielded increasingly specific direction on the weight of strikes to be sent into RP 6.

The priorities defined by CINCPAC at the outset of the campaign evolved quickly. On May 24 the command established a new scheme, increasing the emphasis on the lines of communications to China and reducing the original focus on POL. The new scheme was much more specific than the one issued earlier, especially in providing the operational commanders with priorities in the attack effort. First would come the rail lines from China to Hanoi, and then the road and rail network from Hanoi southward to the DMZ. Petroleum products were given the next priority, and then the power network. Last would follow armed reconnaissance missions, attacking targets of opportunity.[33] Broadly speaking, these target categories would maintain their priorities until the end of the campaign.

The second general adjustment to the targeting guidance reflected Nixon's impatience with the tempo of attacks against Hanoi and Haiphong. To some degree, this frustration resulted from a tension between the political and the military objectives of the air campaign. Attacks against the railroads north of Hanoi could certainly impede the flow of material from China, but attacks there had neither the visibility nor the psychological effect that the president sought. Nixon had promised in April that he would "watch this every day and every night." He did exactly that, each morning and evening receiving updates on the number of sorties flown and the targets being struck. His dissatisfaction, transmitted through Kissinger and Haig to the Pentagon, led eventually to messages focusing on the geographic distribution of sorties instead of the target sets defined in May. By July and August the apparent diffusion of the air effort led Admiral Moorer to admonish CINCPAC: "You should note that the picture as seen from here is that a disproportionate share of the air effort is programmed in the NVN panhandle at the expense of targets in the northern route packages. To illustrate my point, less than 25 percent of the validated targets in RP V and VI have been struck . . . While the need for strong operations in the lower route packages is certainly appreciated, the limited weight of effort against key targets in the northern area of NVN raises questions as to whether we are holding our priorities."[34]

Moorer's exhortation reflected the basic tension between the campaign's political and more narrowly military objectives. Field commanders, driven by weather, defenses, and conflicting priorities, had not focused the campaign as directed by the commander in chief. Attacks on vehicles traveling in the North Vietnamese panhandle might, in fact, have more effect on NVA logistics than attacks farther north, but in Nixon's view they did not offer the coercive impact he sought in this decisive air offensive.

While the weight of effort was susceptible to direction from the highest authorities, the division of Air Force and Navy air operations along geographic lines proved to be less so. The basic structure stood through the end of the campaign, though problems with the concept eventually led

CINCPAC to direct an "integrated strike zone" in the Hanoi-Haiphong area. This decision came in October, far too late to affect operations during the heart of the air offensive, in the summer months.

Vogt later offered his views on the geographic distribution of air operations, as the services wrestled over command arrangements to be constructed for air operations after the cease-fire in Vietnam. Careful to define the air campaign as an overall success, he noted two inherent problems with the geographic division of air operations. First, it had prevented Air Force and Navy forces from combining to saturate and overwhelm the defenses on any given attack. "I can only conclude," he summarized, "that both the Navy and ourselves lost airplanes which need not have gone down had defense saturation tactics employing both forces been utilized." While increasing the air forces' vulnerability to North Vietnamese defenses, the arrangement had weakened the Americans' ability to disrupt the flow of material along the NVA's lines of communications. The command arrangements used in Linebacker, commented Vogt, "made a coordinated campaign impossible." By allocating the interior road network of the North Vietnamese panhandle to the Navy fighters, which rarely operated that far inland, the command structure had essentially created a sanctuary for NVA logisticians: "The enemy was able to move virtually untouched along the inner road networks away from the coastline."[35]

But as the campaign opened, these results lay far in the future. There was, in any case, no opportunity to address these fundamental issues in the few hours available between the president's decision and the start of the campaign. For better or for worse, the air operation would begin at once, with all the power and drama that Nixon could instill.

14

THE INITIAL STRIKES

However dramatic, the mining operation in Haiphong on the morning of May 9 was only the opening step in a larger campaign. In fact, it was by far the simplest in a series of actions that would be required to have a real effect on the course of events in theater. The opposition to the mining by the CIA and Laird's office was based as much on its likely futility as on the diplomatic risks it entailed. It would be an empty gesture to close the ports without shutting down the other means of moving supplies into North Vietnam, and analysts concluded that there was no feasible way to do so. The sad experience of Rolling Thunder seemed to confirm this analysis. As Nixon viewed it, his political future, and America's world position, depended on the ability of U.S. air forces in theater to reverse that history.

That reversal would depend to some degree on new technology that would be employed in the campaign. But most of all, the president's driving will was what would make this campaign fundamentally different from anything seen under Johnson. A few hours after his speech announcing the harbor mining, in the evening of May 8–9, Nixon dictated a note to Kissinger, outlining the difference as he saw it.

> Now that I have made this tough watershed decision, I intend to stop at nothing to bring the enemy to his knees . . . We have the power. The

only question is whether we have the will to use that power. What distinguishes me from Johnson is that I have the will in spades. If we now fail it will be because the bureaucrats and the bureaucracy and particularly those of the Defense Department, who will of course be vigorously assisted by their allies in State, will find ways to erode the strong decisive measures I have indicated we are going to take.[1]

The initial attacks in the new campaign were designed to highlight that difference from the Rolling Thunder days. Where Johnson had directed a gradual escalation in strength and locations of attacks, with strikes creeping northward over a period of months, Nixon would take the war straight to the enemy's heartland, with heavy attacks on Hanoi and Haiphong on the first day. On May 6 the JCS sent out the order to prepare for strikes on the two cities. The extended air war would open on May 10, with a series of attacks on Haiphong, the coastal ports, and Hanoi. The day would begin with the three carriers offshore—the *Constellation*, the *Kitty Hawk*, and the *Coral Sea*—launching Alpha strikes, coordinated attacks on fixed targets in Haiphong. Each carrier would generate a separate strike, and the force would thus attack in three waves at ten-minute intervals. The *Constellation*'s strike group would hit the oil tanks on the west side of town; the *Coral Sea* was assigned the city rail yard, and the *Kitty Hawk* would take down the main bridge leading out of Haiphong toward Hanoi. Later the Air Force would attack from the west, coming across Laos. They would hit the rail yard at Yen Vien, and perhaps the most visible target in North Vietnam, the Paul Doumer Bridge connecting Hanoi with points east. In the afternoon the Navy would execute another two series of attacks. The first would go against the Hai Phuong bridge linking the port city to Hanoi. Late in the day there would follow a final strike against the ports northeast of the city at Cam Pha and Hon Gai. On that first day U.S. strike forces would hit the most visible and critical targets in the North Vietnamese logistical system. They would strike in mass, and they would use every weapon in their arsenal.[2]

As would recur throughout the campaign, the Air Force and Navy strike forces reflected the forces' different operating philosophies. These, in turn, reflected their basing modes and their key technologies. The Navy strike forces would come from single air wings, units that had trained together, deployed together, and flown together in combat. The pilots planned and briefed the missions together, and had the opportunity to discuss every contingency that might arise. Each carrier provided nearly all the elements of an integrated strike force, relying on outside support only for radar warning and intelligence support. Obviously these were tremendous advantages as men reacted to the rapid and stressful events of the day. However, the naval air forces lagged behind the Air Force in adopting the laser guidance technology that had revolutionized Air Force capabilities. The Navy's reliance on "iron bombs" further shaped its strike forces. Where the Air Force strikes relied on a few very precise bombers, plus a massive support package, the Navy attacks would employ fewer escorts and more bombers, relying on mass to achieve necessary levels of damage.

The strike packages this day were fairly typical of those used throughout the early months of the air campaign. The *Constellation*, for example, launched thirty-three fighters for the first strike against Haiphong. Of these, sixteen—six A-6s and ten A-7s—carried 500-pound bombs. These weapons were adequate for a soft area target like an above-ground petroleum storage facility. Nine F-4s would provide defense against the air threat. Another flight of four F-4s would attack the antiaircraft artillery in the area, and two more A-7s would provide "Iron Hand" support, suppressing the surface-to-air missiles in the area.[3]

The strike package would receive intelligence support from various specialized aircraft, listening to North Vietnamese radios and picking up radar signals from the defenders. They would relay their information through the radar picket ship, the *Chicago*, which would provide radar coverage for the strike force. The picket ships operating in the Gulf of Tonkin maintained the rotating call sign Red Crown, and the crews fighting in the North universally considered them the most credible and timely source of warning support.

The Air Force strike, by comparison, would launch from every fighter base in Thailand. The different elements would be orchestrated by the Seventh Air Force fragmentary order, or "frag," which would task the wings and direct the overall composition of the strike—the timing, call signs, radio frequencies, tanker information, and general flow of the mission. There was no single face-to-face briefing for the strike package. Neither was there an opportunity for the crews to study the plan beforehand and think through the contingencies of this mission; the crews learned of the targets and the plan in the predawn briefings conducted at each base.

Already with this first strike, the units fell into roles defined by their specialized equipment. The attack force would come from the 8th Tactical

Fighter Wing (TFW) at Ubon RTAFB, with its laser-guided and electro-optical precision weapons. The strikers would rely on a chaff corridor for protection as they entered the high-threat area of Hanoi; the chaff bombers, another eight F-4s, would also come from Ubon. The air-to-air protection would come from the 432nd TRW at Udorn RTAFB; this was the only wing that had aircraft equipped with the Combat Tree system, enabling them to pick up North Vietnamese fighters far more effectively than did the basic F-4 radar system.[4] SAM suppression and jamming support would come from the 388th TFW at Korat, with its Wild Weasel F-105 squadron and EB-66 jammers. The search and rescue (SAR) package would come from Nakhon Phanom RTAFB, and the tankers from U-Tapao and Takhli. Like the Navy forces, the Air Force strike package received support from intelligence aircraft orbiting over Laos and offshore, and it relied on Red Crown for support in the target area. In all, the strike would include 120 aircraft, with 88 penetrating North Vietnam. Thirty-two aircraft would conduct the actual attacks; the rest were there to get those aircraft safely to the target area and back.[5]

The Alpha strike from the *Constellation* was the first launch of the day. By now the complex process of launching thirty aircraft in a ten-minute span was well practiced, though never routine. First to go were the tankers, which climbed to 15,000 feet and established orbits off the carriers. The fighters launched, topped off their fuel, and assembled the package at the tanker rendezvous, pushing inland from there. At 8:00 the strike force turned toward Haiphong and began its ingress. The strikes from the *Coral Sea* and the *Kitty Hawk* followed at ten-minute intervals. The *Constellation*'s strike force reached the coast east of Haiphong, and as it turned west on its attack run, the support elements deployed into position. The escorts split out toward the north, south, and west of Haiphong; the Iron Hand force weaved behind the strikers; an EKA-3B, a bomber converted for use as a tanker and electronic warfare aircraft, set up its jamming orbit outside the SAM zone. As the attack force reached the target area, the defending SAM sites and the Iron Hand A-7s conducted their duel, with the A-7s launching Shrike antiradiation missiles to suppress the sites. There were a few SAM launches, but no hits, and it was evident that the SAM operators were stymied, for this engagement, by the Shrikes. The bombers reached the west side of the city and the antiaircraft batteries there opened fire, triggering attacks by the flak-suppression flights accompanying the bombers. Finally the bombers rolled into their 45-degree dive bomb passes, released their bombs at 7,000 feet, pulled out at 3,500 feet, and jinked their way out of the target area. Behind them, the bombs touched off a series of explosions and fires as they struck the oil storage.

As the Navy strikes marshaled off the coast, well off to the southwest the Air Force units in Thailand prepared and launched their contributions to the strike on Hanoi. The tankers from U-Tapao were the first to take off, at 7:30. At 9:20 air-to-air flights from Udorn RTAFB were the first to enter North Vietnamese airspace, quickly engaging MiG-19s defending the western approaches to Hanoi. First blood went to the F-4s. Vectored by Red Crown, the crews used their Combat Tree interrogators to find and identify the North Vietnamese defenders. The Phantoms launched their radar-guided AIM-7 missiles head-on, at a range of eight miles from the MiGs. Results were about normal for the notoriously unreliable AIM-7. One missile fused when its motor burned out, exploding harmlessly in front of the F-4s. Two others dropped off their launch aircraft like rocks as their motors failed to ignite. But the two that worked, worked spectacularly, smashing into MiGs and destroying them instantly. Before the flights even reached each other, the Americans had two kills.

As the Americans maneuvered to destroy the remaining two MiG-19s, another flight of MiGs entered the fight unobserved. Two attacked the lead F-4, flown by Major Bob Lodge. Lodge was probably the most respected Air Force pilot in Southeast Asia at the time, an acknowledged expert with two kills already to his credit. But at that moment his concentration on getting another victory cost him his life, as two MiGs camped behind him and blanketed his aircraft with 30-mm cannon fire. Lodge's aircraft burst into flame and entered an inverted spin; backseater Captain Roger Locher ejected and landed on a wooded ridge overlooking the NVAF fighter base at Yen Bai. There he would stay until an epic rescue mission pulled him out more than three weeks later.

To the southeast, the Air Force strike package reached Hanoi at 9:40. First in were the SAM-suppression flights, launching their antiradiation missiles to keep the SA-2s from entering the engagement. The flights of chaff bombers followed, executing the least enviable task of anyone in the strike force. Their job was to lay a chaff corridor into the heart of the city, blinding the North Vietnamese radars. It was a thankless and dangerous task. The chaff flights needed to enter the Hanoi area at 26,000 feet, with the drag and airspeed limitations of the chaff dispensers greatly reducing the Phantoms' already-limited performance at that altitude. To lay an adequate corridor, the chaff flights were forced to fly at slow speed in a straight line over the most highly defended target area in Indochina, with their position at the front of the chaff corridor announcing their presence to every defending missile site. The Air Force had used chaff corridors in earlier strikes on Haiphong and Thanh Hoa, but this would be their first use during daylight hours. These were some very long moments for the crews involved.

The chaff bombers reached their final turn point eighteen miles south of Hanoi at 9:49 A.M. and turned toward the target area. As they turned, defenders fired two missiles that detonated near the flight but inflicted no damage. Finally the F-4s began their carefully timed release of the chaff bombs. Every fifteen seconds for two minutes they released another bomb, until they were all gone. The aircraft departed to the southwest as the metallic strips of chaff drifted toward the earth, blanketing the North Vietnamese radar scopes and protecting the strikers who would soon enter the area.

The chaff provided a broad highway for the strike flights, which now entered the fight from the southwest. They would strike two different targets in Hanoi, with four flights of four targeted on each of the target areas. The plan was to attack the Paul Doumer Bridge with precision weapons, a mix of electro-optical and laser-guided bombs. The second strike would then follow, with another sixteen aircraft attacking the Yen Vien rail yard with 500-pound bombs.

The attackers would hit the bridge with the electro-optical (EO) weapons from the south, coming out of the sun to give the weapons' seeker heads the best possible look at the target. The laser-guided bombs would be delivered from the east, along the axis of the bridge, to increase the chances of a hit. Their ingress through the chaff corridor was an act of faith, trusting the invisible chaff and their equally invisible electronic protection to see them safely to the target, now visible in the distance. Despite the Shrike launches, the jamming, and the chaff, the North Vietnamese defenders fired freely at the inbound aircraft.

Finally came the moment of truth, the payoff for all the effort taken to that point. One of the EO bombs failed to come off the aircraft. The other seven arced away, and then went their separate ways as their guidance systems failed to track their targets. Some went long, some fell short, some swerved into the city. None hit the bridge. It was a miserable performance.

As the first set of strikers turned away toward the west, disgusted with their weapons, the laser bombers edged off toward the east, then rolled in to deliver their bombs, with the lead aircraft designating the target with his laser pod. These worked far better than the EO weapons, pummeling the bridge but failing to drop a span into the river—the normal measure of success for a bridge attack. Severely damaged, impassable to rail or road traffic, the bridge still stood. As the first strike exited across Hanoi, the second group pressed ahead toward the rail yard. Climbing to 20,000 feet, they rolled into their attack dives and delivered their bombs at 8,700 feet, completing their attacks through heavy antiaircraft fire. Once again, the vigorous defenses were ineffective except in forcing the aircraft to maneuver, disrupting the attack geometry. Like the flights that had struck the bridge, the second strike exited toward the west; as one flight lead recalled: "We went out scalded-ass fast and it took a while to get the flight back in order."[6]

Nonetheless, the aircraft all exited the area safely, heading west toward home. Four Phantom flights covered the withdrawing strike force, with Harlow flight operating northwest of Hanoi, near the MiG base at Yen Bai. With the air action quiet, the flight lead took the aircraft over Yen Bai to take a look. Suddenly a MiG-19 materialized behind the flight, and there ensued a flurry of hurried radio calls. The MiG opened fire, and 30-mm shells ripped away the Harlow 4's left wing. The Phantom burst into flames and crashed to earth, killing both members of the crew. The flight lead turned behind the MiG and fired three missiles, all outside of range; the MiG escaped.[7] The other F-4s recovered safely, concluding the day's activity in the west.

Through the afternoon, the carriers offshore launched two more waves of attacks. The first struck the railroad/road system connecting Haiphong and Hanoi and triggered the largest air battle of the Vietnam war. As the strikers pulled off target, at least eight MiG-17s swept in from the east, somehow undetected by the armada of American intelligence platforms. Caught at an initial disadvantage, the Navy crews quickly mastered the situation, taking advantage of the training programs constructed since the days of Rolling Thunder. Once they lost the advantage of surprise, the MiGs settled into a low-altitude defensive wheel, and as opportunities presented themselves, the Americans shot down five of these Korean War–vintage jets. In this swirling engagement, Phantom crew Lieutenant Randy Cunningham and Lieutenant Willie Driscoll of VF-96 claimed three kills. These victories gave Cunningham a total of five kills, making him the first American ace of the war.[8]

The last wave struck the ports northeast of Haiphong. By this time, having contested three earlier strikes, the North Vietnamese defenses were largely exhausted, and the strikers recovered without a loss. Over the long run, probably the most significant result of these attacks was the destruction of the Soviet collier *Grisha Akopyan* in the attack on Hon Gai. A 500-pound bomb struck the ship, killing the bosun and injuring the captain. However unintentional, these casualties would inevitably complicate the already complex interplay of motives surrounding the Moscow summit. The Soviets' response to Nixon's offensive would no longer play out strictly along the abstractions of policy and economics, but must account for the loss of life.

At last night fell, closing the action after the most intense air battles of the ten-year American war in Indochina. Both sides assessed the results of the first day. Certainly the strikes had achieved the shock and weight that Nixon had directed, massing repeated attacks directly into North Vietnam's heartland. For the Air Force, results were mixed. The strike on the rail yard had sliced all the through lines, but the Paul Doumer Bridge, the centerpiece of the day's action, was badly damaged but still standing. The Navy attacks had knocked down spans on three bridges linking Hanoi and Haiphong. More significantly, the Navy could claim the first air ace in the war, a significant boost to morale and an edge in the perennial rivalry between the Air Force and the Navy. Less visibly, the overall conduct of the mission and the Navy crews' dominance of their engagements reflected the value of the improvements in air-to-air training that had been instituted since the Rolling Thunder days. On the whole, the day's action constituted a very effective opening to the interdiction campaign directed by the president.

Certainly the air defenders in Hanoi viewed it as such. On the night of May 10 the commander of the Air Defense–Air Force Command personally briefed North Vietnam's defense minister, General Vo Nguyen Giap, on the day's activities. Giap "commended the resourceful, courageous, and steadfast combat spirit" of the Air Force personnel, but directed that the Air Force must move to "secret, surprise attacks sure to achieve victory and he criticized the erroneous concept of seeking 'one for one exchanges.'"[9] At the end of the first day of renewed warfare in the North, it was already clear that the massed formations the North Vietnamese had employed had operated to the Americans' benefit. The losses taken that day could not continue. The North Vietnamese would have to adjust their tactics to execute smaller, hit-and-run attacks, and engage only when they could minimize the chances of losing aircraft. This discussion on the first night of the campaign began the process of action and reaction, as the adversaries adjusted to each other's tactics and equipment, that would not cease until the end of the war.

The strikes continued over the following days, though without the weight or the drama of the attacks on May 10. On May 11 Vogt sent another strike force out to finish the job of destroying the Paul Doumer Bridge, this time with 3,000-pound bombs as opposed to the 2,000-pound weapons used in the first attacks. He also tasked strikes on the North Vietnamese Air Defense Command center at Bac Mai, on the southern outskirts of Hanoi. Air Force F-4s executed the first in a series of strikes against bridges on the northeast rail line, attacking a bridge at Cao Hung.[10]

MiG-21s from the 927th Air force Regiment employed the tactics directed by Giap to conduct hit-and-run attacks on the Air Force package, downing an F-105 and an F-4 without loss.[11] The attack on the F-105 demonstrated growing refinement in the coordination of the NVA air defenses. Vogt reported: "As the flight of F-105s were approaching their target area, they noted six SAMs launched in front of their flight. The SAMs were apparently used to divert the attention of the pilots as two MiGs attacked the flight from the six o'clock position downing the F-105."[12]

Bad as that was, it could have been even worse for the Air Force. The weather that was always the strongest element of the North Vietnamese air defense returned on May 11, and Vogt delayed the launch of the strike against the Paul Doumer Bridge. In the process, the coordination of the strike package broke down, as the command system failed to ensure that all the participating units got word of the revised plan. By the time the attack force reached Hanoi, they were all alone: there was no chaff corridor, no SAM suppression, no escort against the MiG threat. Astonishingly, the strike force flew across the city, rolled into its attack, and dropped the bridge. Although this is speculative, it is probable that the NVA air defense system misidentified the flight as a reconnaissance sortie and held its fire, conserving its missiles for attack missions expected to follow. It was a case of rare good fortune for the strike force, and although this incident ended harmlessly, it did point out the serious coordination issues associated with orchestrating forces from so many units and bases.

The next day the Air Force struck two bridges on the northwest rail line, at Lang Bun and Lang Trip. At this point, Vogt believed "that we have stopped the flow of rail traffic between China and Hanoi"—a level of optimism that would quickly disappear as North Vietnamese countermeasures began to take effect. In the same message in which he reported that success, he felt compelled to defend the weight of effort he was scheduling against targets in North Vietnam. Vogt noted that it was "a little less than planning guidance indicated," but explained that the ongoing tactical emergency in the An Loc battle, combined with the threat to Kontum, "compels us to keep adequate air handy to deal with these critical situations in-country."[13] That day the Air Force sent 177 fighter sorties into the An Loc area, along with 48 B-52 strikes. The massive effort around An Loc may well have saved that situation, but it came at the expense of the sort of effort over North Vietnam that Nixon demanded of the Air Force. The old conflict between the use of air assets in the theater battle and over the North had grown, if anything, more intense. Vogt was caught in the middle, forced to balance the demands of the theater commander and the commander in chief. It was not a comfortable position.

It was made still worse by the weather, which frequently precluded strikes north of Hanoi and even more often resulted in delays and disruption of the strike package. On May 13, for example, Vogt sent the Air Force strikers against the Thanh Hoa bridge, the most famous and most costly target of the Rolling Thunder air campaign. The bridge had withstood strike after strike beginning in 1965; it was strongly built and well defended, a mark of its role in the North Vietnamese logistical network. The bridge spanned the Song My river, connecting the nation's heartland with the main front along the DMZ. Abrams and Vogt expected its destruction to go far toward denying the North Vietnamese forces now marshaling in front of Hue the matériel they would need to continue their offensive. If anything, the symbolic value of its destruction would be even greater. The bridge's ability to withstand repeated strikes, while its defenders exacted a toll from the attacking aircraft, gave it a symbolic importance exceeding its actual role in the logistical system.[14]

A Seventh Air Force strike had damaged the structure on April 26, but Vogt decided that "since the span is not down, repairs could conceivably be quickly made."[15] He reported on May 12 that he planned a strike for the following day, designed as much for psychological effect as for military impact. Once the strike was airborne, Vogt was faced with a familiar dilemma, as unfavorable weather obscured the target. He had the strike aircraft hang with the air refuelers, waiting for a change in the weather, until finally he directed the attack to proceed, hoping there would be a break in the clouds over the target. There was, and the strikers dropped a span into the river. It was cause for much celebration through the American chain of command, but the North Vietnamese logistical system continued to find ways to funnel supplies toward the battle area.

Over the following weeks Vogt continued to schedule strikes against the major choke points in the North's transportation system. However, he faced unremitting demands from the battle in the South, and the weather continued to close off attacks in the North. On May 14 the Air Force conducted no Linebacker raids, and on May 15 an attack scheduled in the Hanoi area diverted into Route Pack 1 to attack the Dong Hoi bridge. May 16 passed with no Air Force package in RP 6. On the next day an attack struck the Viet Tri bridge on the northwest rail route, and May 18 saw a return to Hanoi with yet another strike against the POL storage area. The strikes against the two major bridges continued to be the highlights of the air campaign, but the momentum had died and the Air Force lagged in creating the overwhelming attacks envisioned by Nixon.

Through that period, as the Linebacker air campaign took shape, the Navy wings offshore launched strike after strike against targets extending from the DMZ to the Chinese buffer zone. CTF 77 settled into a rotation, with three carriers executing strikes against the North while a fourth operated in support of the theater battle in the South. Of the three carriers operating against North Vietnam, normally two launched coordinated Alpha strikes against fixed targets while the third conducted cyclic operations, pushing out sorties to fly armed reconnaissance sorties. These Navy strikes lacked the precision weapons and the masses of defense suppression characteristic of the Air Force missions, but they compensated through their weight of effort and the range of the attacks they conducted. On May 13, for example, as Seventh Air Force closed the Thanh Hoa bridge, Navy strikes hit five different bridges in the North Vietnamese panhandle, two POL storage and processing facilities, a SAM storage area, and a power plant, flying a total of 276 sorties over North Vietnam.[16] The following day Seventh Air Force sent 83 sorties over the North, all striking in RP 1. CTF 77 strikes hit eight bridges, a boat factory, a power plant, and a POL storage area, sending a total of 213 strikers against North Vietnam.[17] On May 15 the Air Force struck the Dong Hoi bridge in RP 1, as the Navy attacked nine bridges and two railroad siding areas. On May 16 there were no Air Force strikes above RP 1, while the Navy sent 244 sorties northward. These attacked twelve bridges, three POL facilities, and a power plant, among other miscellaneous targets.

As with the carrier-based attacks, the Air Force strikes at the outset of the campaign established a pattern that would persist through the next few months. Vogt selected tactics reflecting a delicate interplay among policy, technology, logistics, and tactics. The general had a perfectly clear idea of the sort of air campaign the president and Kissinger had in mind. What was less obvious, though, was how to create a detailed structure to integrate all the elements necessary to conduct an effective operation—especially in the face of a resilient defense such as that he faced over the North.

Vogt enjoyed two huge advantages over his predecessors of the Rolling Thunder days. First, he had been given wide latitude to strike targets as the weather and defenses permitted, rather than having to respond to specific, time-limited direction from Washington. Second, he would have the opportunity to use the precision weaponry developed during the first part of the war, which had been grossly underutilized through the relatively quiet period between 1968 and the return to operations over the North.

Without question, the precision weapons provided a great advantage in this air offensive. Aircraft could strike accurately from a higher altitude, avoiding the antiaircraft fire that had always been the greatest threat to strike aircraft. More significantly, perhaps, a single aircraft could attack with greater assurance of destroying a target than had been possible for entire strike forces in Rolling Thunder. Instead of relying on masses of aircraft, all releasing bombs manually, planners could depend on a single laser designator to guide the bombs of a few strikers to an aim point.

For all these advantages, the use of precision weapons posed challenges that had to be resolved through the hard experience of combat. To begin with, the laser beam was easily blanked by haze, fog, or clouds, and so demanded even better weather conditions than those necessary for visual strikes.[18] Also, the detailed tactics necessary to integrate the laser designator with the strikers, and defend the strike package in a heavily defended area, had yet to be worked out. It was especially critical to do so, because the advanced pods that permitted operations in high-threat areas were extremely scarce—at the start of the offensive, only four were available in theater, with no more on the way. To conduct the strikes to full advantage, above all else, these pods must be protected. The basic operational strategy for the campaign depended on preserving them for use in the Hanoi-Haiphong area.

Beyond this need to protect the laser pods, Vogt understood that this would be an extended campaign against tough defenses. For compelling reasons, ranging from preserving the crews' morale to sustaining public support for the operation, it was essential to control the loss rate. In principle, that would be possible either by adjusting tactics or by choosing to attack targets in less defended areas. For the near term, given Nixon and Kissinger's focus on attacks in the Hanoi-Haiphong area, it was necessary to strike in that region and devise tactics to control the attrition rate.

Vogt therefore built his strategy around "mass gaggles," with a few precision strikers protected by layers of defenders. When everything worked as planned, the array of SAM-suppression assets, air-to-air patrols and escort, jammers, chaff, intelligence aircraft, strikers, picket ships, and radar sites, all supported by dozens of tanker aircraft, combined to overwhelm the defenses and suppress the loss rate. The large packages provided an integrated set of capabilities, with mutually supporting elements able to neutralize the different threats posed by North Vietnamese defenders. When it all came together, it was a thing of beauty: a quick and accurate strike, and everyone in and out safely.

There were costs associated with this approach, though. First, and most obvious, was the complexity of marshaling the components from bases scattered across Southeast Asia. The larger the package, the more components employed by Seventh Air Force, the more difficult and the more important was effective coordination among the widely separated forces that would have to operate as a unit over Hanoi.

In theory, and often in practice, the frag order issued by Seventh Air Force provided all the information necessary to coordinate the mission: tanker data, frequencies, call signs, target information, and so on. The frag was the engine driving all preparation, from loading and preparing the aircraft to the detailed squadron tasks of scheduling air crews and developing detailed tactics. It worked, normally, in getting everyone onto and off the tankers, in the proper airspace, and oriented properly. What it could not provide was a detailed mutual understanding, among all the elements of these complicated packages, of how to respond to the lethal, fast-developing situations inherent in battling weather and an experienced, capable enemy. Some of that understanding could be built by telephonic briefings among the flights operating from the different bases, but even that approach was often limited or impossible because of the unpredictability of the telephone system across Thailand. Given its central importance to the whole range of supporting tasks that were required to create an effective strike, it was imperative that the frag be sent to the wings as early as possible—but this proved very difficult for the Seventh Air Force staff, as they worked out their procedures for this new level of warfare.

Combat experience over the centuries has driven the development of innumerable axioms providing rules of thumb for warfare. Many of these boil down to the importance of "keeping it simple, stupid." The more complex a plan, the more interfaces built into the flow of information, the more fragile it becomes. The pathway of logic traced above may have driven the conclusion that these complex, large packages were necessary; but their consistent success put a premium on experienced air crews, used to working together, with reliable and clear communications.

As it happened, none of these three essential elements was present. Over the years leading up to this offensive, the experience level of the air crews in Southeast Asia declined. By 1971 this had become a serious problem, though in the absence of sustained operations over the North, complaints from theater commanders received little hearing from the stateside training establishment. The standard squadron air crews were young, and the training they received before deploying overseas did not give them the basic background they needed to operate in a fluid high-threat environment.

Neither were they used to working together. In the months before the offensive, despite the fairly clear view of what was coming, there was no effort through the chain of command to develop the tactics or training programs to ready the forces to return to high-intensity warfare. In addition, personnel policies precluded crews from serving multiple tours overseas and defined a one-year tour for everyone in the units. Over the three years since Rolling Thunder, the Air Force had seen three generations of pilots go through Southeast Asia, with relatively little experience in operations in high threat areas. Each of these three generations was highly focused on the task at hand: stopping the flow of traffic down the Ho Chi Minh Trail, and responding to tactical situations in the South, Laos, and Cambodia. The corporate memory of operations in the Red River Delta was lost. The formula would have to be developed all over again, and that would be a costly process.

The problem was compounded by the rapid, massive influx of people and units deploying in response to the tactical situation. It was good to have the extra sorties and firepower, and in most cases the air crews deploying from the Tactical Air Command had far more experience than those based in Southeast Asia. But they would have to be integrated into theater and wing operations, and that would take some time.

The radio was the third essential element and, in a way, the most frustrating. The basic UHF radio was far simpler than many other technologies brought to bear in this air war, and its deficiencies had been known since the first days of Rolling Thunder in 1965. Seven years later, with a new arsenal of weapons and avionics, the crews operating over North Vietnam again found themselves hamstrung by weak and unreliable radios. Furthermore, their communications were not secure. Over and over again, from the first days of the war, it had been clear that the North Vietnamese were listening to American tactical communications, using the intelligence gained to direct their fighters against vulnerable elements of the force. On a few occasions the Americans attempted to use that capability against their enemies, swapping around call signs, for example, to lure the North Vietnamese fighter forces into ambush.[19] Over time the U.S. research and development community had fielded a secure voice system, but it was slow and unreliable. It was also unusable in a tactical setting, since for anyone to use it, everyone had to have the capability—and not everyone did.

These three factors operated together, whether for good or ill. The more experienced the crew members, the more used everyone was to working together, and the more comfortable everyone was working with the plan, the less communication would be required. When the plan broke down, though, that was precisely the time when good communications discipline and technology would prove essential.

There were other costs, more subtle and less predictable, to this general mission approach. First, the very complexity of the mission packages made it very difficult to change the pattern of operations. Once everyone got used to a certain way of doing things, it was hard to adjust the pattern and make sure everyone got the word. The vast chain of squadron scheduling, mission planning, and logistical preparations necessary to make these missions work reinforced the reluctance to change. The more predictably these functions could be performed, the more efficiently they would operate. So there was a vast momentum to be overcome in order to change the rhythm of operations. There would be a real danger of falling into a set pattern of operations that could be understood, and exploited, by the North Vietnamese.

The structure of these missions placed a heavy load on the maintenance troops, upon whose work the whole effort depended. The Linebacker missions had the highest priority among the wing operations and placed the highest demands on maintenance. However, especially during the first days of the campaign, South Vietnam was at real risk of collapse under the weight of the NVA offensives. However massive the reinforcements ordered by Nixon, the sortie count remained basically a zero-sum game. Flights into North Vietnam came at the cost of coverage of South Vietnamese forces. Seventh Air Force built its daily flow by scheduling the Linebacker sorties, subtracting them from the total available for operations throughout the theater, and then scheduling the rest for sorties in the South and over Laos and Cambodia.[20] The large packages for Linebacker built a huge requirement for aircraft, concentrated in a very small, precise time window. This would become increasingly problematic as the campaign continued, and as wear and damage to the aircraft accumulated.

The "mass gaggles" concentrated immense power that could overwhelm the defenses fielded by the North Vietnamese. That power came at the cost of a certain degree of fragility and inflexibility, inherent in the concept and exacerbated by the inexperience of the crews undertaking the missions. The success of the campaign, and ultimately of Nixon and Kissinger's strategic concept, would be determined by the ability of the forces to mature into this new, demanding mission area and adapt to the demands set by the defenses and the weather.

15

THE DRV RESPONDS

The North Vietnamese response to Nixon's speech on May 8, and to the opening of the Second War of Destruction, covered the range of their nation's capabilities. Having miscalculated the power that Nixon was willing to exert, the Politburo now reached for every tool at hand to counter the overwhelming forces being employed against them. In broad terms, these tools can be categorized as diplomatic, economic, military, and informational—and the North Vietnamese used them all, with varying degrees of success.

The first task facing the Politburo, however, was to assess the situation and plan the actions to meet this crisis. The Politburo tasked the Party Secretariat and the cabinet's Current Affairs Committee to survey the situation, and to present recommendations. After a very intense week, the working group was ready with a report summarizing current stockpiles, the transportation and labor situation, and the steps that would enable the regime to continue the struggle through the coming months.

The mining operation had caught the North Vietnamese short of reserves in critical areas. Consumer goods would not be a problem, with sufficient stocks on hand, but "as for our other types of key, vital supplies, such as food, fuel, iron and steel, wood, etc., our stock levels are low and we must be very economical in our expenditures of them if they are to last us through the next several months."[1] Petroleum and diesel were not a problem, with five months' supply on hand, but gasoline stocks would only last for three months, even if the regime reached into its strategic reserve. Food stocks were worrisome, extending only for four or five months. The working group did not consider the industrial sector critical, except insofar as it produced basic material necessary to support the transportation sector. For example, a shortage of sheet metal threatened to limit the state's ability to build ferries and repair the transportation infrastructure under attack.

The problems imposed by these material shortfalls would be multiplied by the strain on the transportation infrastructure imposed by the American bombing. Already the attacks of April had crippled the ability to unload material in Haiphong and move supplies southward toward the battlefields. By mid-May there was a backlog of 60,000 tons of supplies in Haiphong, but the punishment inflicted on the transportation infrastructure meant that the regime could only move about 2,600 tons per day. The nation's leadership had attempted to provide for the possibility of air attack in the southern regions, but had seriously underestimated requirements, providing road construction material at only about 10 percent of the level established during the Rolling Thunder air campaign. Worse yet: "As for our northern lines of communication, it seems there was no preparation at all of supplies, labor resources, transportation equipment etc. to ensure the continued flow of traffic and supplies, so the work of repairing roads and bridges has run into difficulties."[2]

The stress of providing manpower for production, transportation, and military purposes had created a "very tense and difficult" situation. The basic task of repairing the Red River dike system absorbed about 200,000–250,000 workers per day; the Army needed about 90,000 new recruits to meet its requirements; and transportation and supply operations under air attack would double the number of laborers needed to move supplies through the system—from 40,000 at the outset of the attack to an eventual total of 80,000. Many of these would come from production enterprises shut down or evacuated under the bombing.

Any logistical system consists of basic elements: the supplies to be moved, the transportation infrastructure, the workers who keep the supplies moving, and the command system knitting everything together. Nixon's shocking assault had stressed each of these. How should the state respond?

The committee specified the first requirement: "At present the work of supporting transportation and supply operations is our central, Number One priority. This work is of the greatest importance for us on all fronts: military, economic, political, and diplomatic. It is one of the conditions that will decide our success or failure in production and in battle."[3] To ensure success, the regime would have to concentrate its strength to protect the flow of traffic along rail and roads. It would be especially important to protect the railroads extending northeast and northwest of Hanoi into China, the connections between Hanoi and Haiphong, and the routes from the heartland southward to the battle area. Further, they would have to complete oil pipelines from the Chinese border into the Red River area, and then on toward the battlefield.

The committee projected that it would be necessary to import between 1.6 and 1.9 million tons of supplies during the eight months remaining in 1972. Under the circumstances, with the ports closed and the lines leading to China under determined attack, this was a remarkably aggressive program. Of this total, 280,000 tons were to be military supplies, the remainder economic imports. About 1.35 million tons would have to come across the rail and road complex northeast of Hanoi. It would be imperative to find a way, even in the worst case, to bring 5,000 to 5,500 tons per day across this route, regardless of American attacks. Within this massive undertaking, the most pressing task would be to find a way to bring in 600,000 tons of supplies expected from the Soviet Union and Eastern Europe. Until supply lines could be established and reserve stocks built up, it would be necessary to economize on materials, particularly gasoline. The national response to Nixon's offensive, in sum, would demand a wrenching series of actions as the DRV imposed rationing, allocated the material on hand, and reoriented its entire system of transportation.

While the regime could take decisive steps internally, in the end its success would rest on its ability to sustain the support of its superpower allies in Moscow and Beijing. Immediately after the attack, without awaiting a detailed assessment of the situation, the Politburo turned to Moscow and Beijing for help in surmounting this crisis.

The North Vietnamese requested that the Soviet Union cancel the upcoming summit with the Americans and send a naval task force into Haiphong harbor, directly challenging the U.S. blockade. The Kremlin was no more eager than the White House to create a superpower military confrontation, and so quickly dismissed the proposal for a naval task force. The question of the summit was much more complicated. The mining had placed the Soviets in a very difficult position, caught between the demands of their role as leaders of the communist world and their need for a range of benefits from a summit with the Americans.

Soviet Ambassador Anatoly Dobrynin flew back to Moscow to participate in the deliberations. He later recalled that the summit hung in the balance, with opposition led by the military leadership and by President Nicolai Podgorny. Brezhnev hesitated, while Kosygin and Gromyko favored continuing with the summit. In the end, the decision hinged on the Soviets' long-standing frustration with the behavior of the North Vietnamese as allies—their secretiveness, their scarcely concealed suspicion of the Soviets, and their unwillingness to consult or even inform the USSR about their strategic decisionmaking. It took much to override the Soviet leaders' almost instinctive support for international solidarity and their desire to maintain close ties with the North Vietnamese as an element of the Soviet-Chinese rivalry. Simple national pride added to the difficulty, as Nixon forced them to publicly turn away from allies suffering an all-out military assault. Further, the decision to proceed with the summit threatened the credibility of the Soviets as allies: "Not only the Vietnamese but other Soviet allies and clients might conclude that their alignment with the Soviet Union might result in their interests being given short shrift if they conflicted with the common interests of the two superpowers."[4]

The Soviets stood to gain much from the Moscow summit—an arms control agreement with America, trade advantages, and perhaps most important, general acceptance as America's peer on the global scene.[5] Beyond the concrete advantages they expected to reap from the meeting, Brezhnev had tied his personal prestige to the summit; its cancellation would have come as a serious blow to his leadership position. Nonetheless, the decision to continue with the summit came hard.

The Chinese were spared such a dramatic decision, having already hosted the U.S. president six weeks before. In their case, there was no visible, symbolic event tied to very important incentives to be weighed. They were able to meet the forms of solidarity with their North Vietnamese allies through a *pro forma* condemnation of the bombing, without having to make more fundamental choices about the larger framework of their relationship with America.[6] Still, as the DRV leadership noted, the Chinese conspicuously failed to reverse, or even to slow, the process of rapprochement with the United States that had progressed so rapidly over the past year. There would be no repetition of the experience of 1970, when the

U.S.-ARVN incursion into Cambodia had brought the still-tentative warming to a halt. Nixon's maneuvers had succeeded to some measure in isolating the North Vietnamese.[7] By May this cannot have come as a surprise to the DRV leaders. They had seen Nixon receive a Chinese Ping-Pong team in the White House on April 18, two days after the B-52 strikes on Haiphong.[8]

Both the Chinese and the Russians moved toward an understanding with the Americans. They would continue sending material support to the North Vietnamese, but would not jeopardize their broader national interests—specifically, their improving relationship with the United States—to do so. Both attempted to make clear to the key Americans the limits on their diplomatic freedom of action and on their influence over the Vietnamese. Both of the communist superpowers, at different times, staged theatrical outbursts against American visitors, evidently to provide their North Vietnamese allies with a record of tough-minded support of their interests.[9] For their part, Nixon and Kissinger were willing to score debating points over the Russian and Chinese support of North Vietnam's offensive. They were unwilling, however, to allow this issue to reverse the complex diplomatic process they had set in motion. The three great powers moved to a level of accommodation that met their allies' minimum needs while preserving their own central interests.

In the eternal pattern of international affairs, the North Vietnamese were forced to accept their position. Unable to galvanize their allies to greater diplomatic support, they at least ensured access to the material support that would enable them to continue the war. In broad terms, they needed a continuation of the economic and military aid that supported the war effort; assistance in moving this material into the battle area; and improved air defenses to protect the nation, the fighting forces, and the supplies en route to the battle.

The PRC set out to help meet these requirements. Through the mid-to late 1960s, the Chinese had deployed seven engineering groups into North Vietnam, specifically to build an integrated, redundant transportation system capable of withstanding an American air offensive. They had supplied antiaircraft troops and combat engineers to keep the roads open during Rolling Thunder, focusing their efforts in the northern areas of North Vietnam.[10] In 1972 there would be no repeat of this large-scale deployment of Chinese troops. Within that limitation, the PRC moved to meet the emergency created by the attacks on North Vietnam.

The very day of the Haiphong mining operation, May 9, the DRV's ambassador to China met with Zhou Enlai to request Chinese assistance in clearing the mines. Zhou agreed, and by late May a Chinese mine investigation team deployed to Haiphong to gather information on the mines. Chinese minesweepers were in operation by July, and they stayed at work until August 1973. In total, twelve minesweepers and four support ships participated in the effort, clearing a total of 46 mines.[11] In light of the thousands of mines laid by the United States, and the significant forces employed by the PRC, that meager yield testifies to the complexities of mine-clearing operations.

With the harbors firmly closed, it was essential that the DRV develop new methods of delivering the bulk supplies now unable to arrive by sea. Probably the most pressing requirement was oil—which had previously arrived through Haiphong, and which was indispensable not only to the ongoing combat but also to the civilian economy and the transportation infrastructure. The PRC agreed to build a series of pipelines to the DRV border, where they would meet up with others built by the North Vietnamese to move the oil southward toward Hanoi.

The pipelines were not a panacea for the North Vietnamese. There remained problems with storage and secondary distribution; the pipelines were subject to attack, though they were very difficult to shut down by air action. But once they were completed, the North Vietnamese had at their disposal a distribution system that extended from southern China all the way to the battlefields, and that was almost invulnerable to long-term air interdiction. The Americans had fought doggedly to close down the pipelines across Laos in previous years, and had failed. Chances of succeeding in cutting the lines deep within North Vietnam were very slim. If the Americans were to halt the NVA offensive, they would have to do it by means other than shutting off the supply of oil. The Chinese also increased their allocation of trucks delivering supplies to North Vietnam by 2,200 to help compensate for the loss of seaborne imports.[12]

In addition, the PRC agreed to provide massive amounts of antiaircraft artillery to the North Vietnamese. In late August and early September the Chinese delivered the guns and support equipment to equip ten antiaircraft regiments. As the official history of the Air Defense Command summarized: "The receipt and shipment of these weapons proceeded rapidly. Every day, truck convoys carrying antiaircraft artillery equipment moved down from Lang Son [along the northeast railroad] through the chokepoints on Route 1 North to A34 for maintenance, adjustment, and removal of storage grease before being sent to the units. In a short period of time, ten antiaircraft artillery regiments equipped with weapons and equipment provided to us by China were deployed within the combat formations of the Air Defense Command and other friendly units."[13]

The Soviets, too, maintained the flow of supplies to their Vietnamese allies. As had been the pattern throughout the war, the equipment they provided complemented Chinese aid with high-tech weapons, especially for air defense. Most significantly, in May the USSR's Politburo approved the transfer of SA-3 surface-to-air missiles to North Vietnam. On May 30 the Air Defense–Air Force Service Headquarters formed the 276th Missile Regiment and the 277th Missile Regiment; these units were to be deployed to the USSR for training in this new missile system.[14]

It would be months before the units could be trained and the equipment deployed, and in the end the new system would become operational just as the war ended the following January. Nonetheless, this decision showed the deep ambivalence of the Soviet leadership over the ongoing air campaign. The SA-3 was by no means a state-of-the-art system. Still, it offered far better capabilities at low altitudes and against maneuvering targets than the old SA-2. More important, the system operated on entirely different frequency bands than the SA-2, and so, at a stroke, nearly the entire array of self-defense systems that the Americans had created over the previous eight years would be rendered useless. Every element of the U.S. air forces operating over North Vietnam had oriented its tactics toward defeating the SA-2 threat. That was the basis for the chaff corridors, and for the Iron Hand escorts that shaped both the land-based and the carrier-based air operations. Against the more maneuverable SA-3, which would be untouched by the jamming systems carried by American fighters, the entire air campaign might have been placed in peril. Evidently the Soviets decided they could not deny this defensive system to their allies as the North Vietnamese underwent a crushing air attack, regardless of the penalty the USSR would pay with respect to its relations with the United States.

During the deliberations leading to the decision to mine the harbors, Kissinger had emphasized the difficulties the North Vietnamese would face in rerouting the flow of supplies from the ports to overland delivery. This seemingly straightforward, though massive, logistical effort was complicated by the fact that the Soviet Union and the PRC were by now bitter rivals, rarely able to cooperate on anything. The flow of Soviet supplies across China had been an irritant for both nations as early as 1967. That year the Sino-Soviet quarrel over the passage of Soviet equipment across China reached such a pitch that the Vietnamese were forced to take custody of the Soviet equipment at its entry to China and accompany it to Vietnam.[15]

However, the multinational logistical response to the U.S. mining proved remarkably quick. In part this responsiveness reflected the diplomatic pressure exerted by the DRV. In addition, the urgency reflected the simple imperatives of supply-chain management. The pipeline of supplies heading into Haiphong and the other ports was full, and that material needed a destination and handling on arrival. There was little time to spend on the luxury of superpower squabbling. A week after the mining, on May 17–18, the Chinese hosted a meeting in Beijing at which PRC and Soviet officials worked out the rerouting of supplies across China.[16] For the moment, the two communist powers set aside their quarrel, meeting with such civility that some observers feared Nixon's aggressive campaign would yield a broad Sino-Soviet reconciliation.[17] That fear faded quickly, though the two powers continued to cooperate effectively in a very trying logistical task.

The North Vietnamese were thus able to ensure the continued flow of material into their logistics network, despite the disruption caused by the mining. The next challenge was to protect the material as it made its way from the Chinese border to the battlefront, and there the initial results were deeply disturbing. The DRV's expectations of this air war were shaped, in part, by their analysis of Rolling Thunder. Those expectations evaporated immediately under the violence unleashed by Nixon.

Already in April, it had become clear that the North Vietnamese air defense system was unready for the generation of weaponry now fielded by the Americans. The general air offensive that began in early May triggered another series of assessments and adjustments, as the DRV sought to sustain an effective defense. The process began on May 9, only hours after the naval strike had closed Haiphong harbor. The high command met that day "to study the situation, to assess the situation, to determine the enemy's plans and goals and the level of intensity of his war of destruction." The multiple waves of attacks on May 10 and 11 went far toward clarifying Nixon's plans and goals, and left no doubt whatever about the level of intensity that the Americans had in mind. Moreover, they confirmed again the U.S. forces' advances in technical sophistication. The 361st Air Defense Division, responsible for the defense of Hanoi, launched 41 missiles in those two days, but "no enemy aircraft crashed on the spot. Many of our missiles flew right past the target and detonated themselves at the end of their flights, and our combat efficiency was low."[18]

In the aftermath of these strikes, "after a number of unsuccessful battles in all areas," the North Vietnamese conducted an assessment of all aspects of their air defenses: personnel and training programs, technology, and deployment patterns, both on the national level and locally. The inspection team consisted of both Party members, from the service party Current Affairs Committee, and the military, from the Air Defense–Air Force Command. Given the unhappy results of the early combat, it is unsurprising that they found problems in every area they examined.

The air defenders shared the problems in personnel policy of their American adversaries. They, too, had lost many of the skills formed at such expense during the Rolling Thunder era. The expert SAM operators, their skills honed through years of engagements in the mid-1960s, had moved on to other assignments or had been promoted. In the 361st Air Defense Division, "only two of their operators have personal experience in combat operations during the first war of destruction, and all the rest of the division's operators are brand new."[19] The inspection team noted that "the problem now was to quickly provide supplemental training" that would improve both the operators' combat skills and the coordination of the defenses at the command centers and headquarters. As early as mid-May, the service conducted live-fire training, emphasizing tactics against the new weapons and tactics being employed by the Americans.

The air defenses faced a series of interrelated problems on the technical and tactical levels. The U.S. forces had devised new electronic techniques and equipment, which had overwhelmed the North Vietnamese defenses in the initial engagements. To some extent, this reflected a failure of North Vietnamese intelligence: "Before the beginning of the second war of destruction, our military technology and military science research agencies had some limited knowledge that the enemy would use new types of electronic countermeasures equipment . . . but we did not have concrete and specific knowledge of the technology and tactics that the enemy air force would use, and so we continued training our troops using the old training manuals derived from past experience."[20]

Thus the North Vietnamese found themselves well prepared to fight the last war, but badly deficient in handling the new U.S. tactical and technical concepts. The problems with jamming were compounded by the strike forces' employment of the improved Shrike antiradiation missile. The Americans had used this weapon during Rolling Thunder, but in the intervening years had improved the basic model and introduced a more powerful, longer-range successor, the AGM-78. The defenders' problems were multiplied by the Americans' new tactic of firing the antiradiation missiles preemptively, not waiting for radars to transmit but just firing the missile into the target area as the attacking aircraft approached. If a radar did come on line, the missile would detect and attack it. If the radars stayed quiet, the strike operated unopposed. The Shrikes took a heavy toll on the air defenses, and the Air Defense–Air Force Service worked urgently to develop countertactics.

The North Vietnamese Air Force (NVAF) conducted its own review of its tactics on May 12, immediately after the massive air battles that opened the Linebacker offensive. The officers assessed the Americans' new tactics and equipment and debated what tactics would be most appropriate in this new situation. At the opening of the campaign the NVAF had committed the bulk of its strength to the combat, hoping to inflict heavy losses on the U.S. attackers. Many of these attacks had been bold, head-on engagements, with little attempt to employ surprise. The results had been unambiguous. While the North Vietnamese achieved two air-to-air kills, those had come at a prohibitively high cost of eleven aircraft. Clearly that was an unsustainable loss rate, especially against an enemy that was so lavishly equipped with aircraft and crews. The Air Force would have to strike a new balance "between destroying the enemy, protecting the target, and preserving and strengthening our own forces. With respect to tactics, the conference decided we would fight primarily small and medium-sized engagements, always seizing the initiative in every situation and maximizing the element of surprise."[21] There would be no more massive, swirling dogfights over North Vietnam; the NVAF moved toward hit-and-run attacks, seeking to draw blood and disrupt American air operations while sustaining their own strength.

At that same time, and with the same sense of urgency, the general staff was reviewing the military situation and establishing priorities for the Air Defense–Air Force Service units. The highest priority would go to protecting the supply lines from the Chinese borders to the entry points to the Ho Chi Minh Trail. The next priority would go to "important targets with direct links to our lines of communications," including Hanoi, Haiphong, Thanh Hoa, and Vinh.[22] Next came a number of independent targets, including the steel mills at Thai Nguyen and the smaller ports northeast of Haiphong; logistics storage areas received that same priority. Then came the effort to combat the blockade, and finally the mission of protecting the flow of supplies along the Ho Chi Minh Trail and to the combat area in the northern provinces. The Air Force would concentrate its forces in the Hanoi area and defend the important lines of communications from Thanh Hoa northward.

In practice, this decision meant a large-scale redeployment of the missile units away from the combat area and the immediate rear area of the units fighting south of the DMZ. The general staff clearly believed it was essential to concentrate its forces, but this movement entailed two risks. First, it would deprive the forces south of the DMZ of the defensive umbrella they relied upon. Without the missiles, the area would open up to B-52s and AC-130s, with disastrous results for the NVA units there. Second, the movement entailed great risk for the men and matériel moving back to the north. In static positions, they could be carefully camouflaged, dug in, and protected by antiaircraft networks. Once the SAMs were flushed into motion, all these defensive measures would be weakened.

The service also adjusted its tactical deployment patterns, looking for a counter to the laser-guided weaponry that had taken down the Doumer and Thanh Hoa bridges. Little could be done technically to counter the laser guidance, and so the service primarily tried to disrupt the delivery by anticipating the attack patterns and establishing gun positions in three areas: where the U.S. attack forces marshaled while coordinating the attack; where they dived to their bomb-release position; and at the bomb-release point. The only other solutions within their capabilities were limited: "releasing smoke clouds to cover the target, and perhaps also deploying barrage balloons at the target we were defending."[23] These defense measures from the World War II playbook offered little hope of countering laser-guided weapons, but in the absence of alternatives, the NVA forces prepared to give them a try.

The intensive attacks of early May forced the regime to accelerate its civil defense measures to ensure the population was protected and that basic governmental and transportation functions could continue. On May 16 the weekly report by the British consul in Hanoi, Joe Wright, summarized the situation in the city as Linebacker opened. At that point, the raids had caused "the evacuation plan to move from Phase 1 (evacuation of women, children, and old people; partial evacuation of administrative services) to Phase 2 (evacuation of all personnel not directly involved in 'Production' or the war effort, of cooperatives, and of more administrative service personnel)." It also triggered "a massive program of shelter construction . . . hundreds of holes have now been bored in the gaps between existing individual shelters. Trees have been torn up to make room for shelters, which are being personalized by the addition of names, supplementary sandbagging, and other refinements." The next phase of the evacuation plan would entail the "partial evacuation of all enterprises and factories, and the remaining civil population." Phase 4 would see the total evacuation of the city, "leaving Hanoi to its defenders."[24] In the longer run, the evacuation of the cities would create a very large labor pool for transportation tasks, but that massive organizational task still lay ahead.

So the North Vietnamese population repeated the experience of the Rolling Thunder years, evacuating the major cities into the countryside. The evacuation disrupted the country's economy and its social patterns, requiring that the government institute measures to ensure that the evacuees found shelter in the country, and that the normal functions of production and education continued as far as possible. The armed forces, the government, and the people of North Vietnam, all of them surprised by the suddenness and the violence of Nixon's air offensive, settled in for a long, hard campaign.

16

NIXON TRIUMPHANT

Through the first days after the mining, Richard Nixon anxiously awaited word on the domestic response and, especially, on Moscow's reaction to his escalation of the war. Haldeman set up a team to track and influence the reception of Nixon's announcement, and he and the president repeatedly reviewed the news from around the country.[1] On the whole, Nixon was pleased with the response, but it still was an anxious time as he waited for a Soviet decision and dealt with the ferocious attacks in the press. By May 12 it was clear that the summit would proceed, and that his careful diplomatic spadework of the previous months had succeeded. The Moscow summit, the crowning achievement of his presidency, was imminent. It was on track despite the worst predictions of the press, the attacks in Congress, and the resistance from the bureaucracy. In Nixon's view, he had triumphed once more over the same elements that had opposed him throughout his career.

John Connally's departure from the cabinet on May 15 heightened the drama and tension of the period, as Nixon's most trusted cabinet member left to return to Texas. The shooting of George Wallace that same day further multiplied the stress. Last-minute summit preparations occupied much of the president and Kissinger's time and generated yet another fierce interagency scrimmage as the last issues in the SALT treaty were addressed. The conflict involved the Nixon administration's normal mix of personal, institutional, and substantive issues, as Kissinger and the state department struggled for control over the final stage of the negotiations.[2] Meanwhile, Nixon and his inner circle feared a JCS-led revolt against the terms of the treaty. While not directly related to the combat in Southeast Asia, the arms control negotiations increased the tension between the White House and the military at a critical time. It was an incredibly busy and vivid period.

Nixon spent much of the interval between the mining and his trip to Moscow away from Washington, with trips to Camp David and Key Biscayne. In this ten-day period he dictated a series of astonishing memoranda to Kissinger and Haldeman. These addressed the fundamental change in the character of the war that he had set in progress. From a personal perspective, the memos reflected a blend of bitterness over the attacks he had sustained with a sense of triumph over his adversaries. Once again, in his view, he had proven smarter and tougher than those around him. Substantively, the prevailing theme is the absolute need to seize the moment, to press ahead aggressively against all his enemies and with all the tools at his disposal. These enemies included the press, Congress, the military, the CIA, the state department, and the North Vietnamese. The memos provide a glimpse into the Nixon administration's pathology. On a more positive note, they offer a view of a president attempting to orchestrate all the instruments in his power to achieve his strategic objectives.

Nixon fired the opening salvo on May 10, the day after the mining, with a memo to Kissinger addressing an issue that he would repeatedly revisit over the coming days. He believed that the real value of the military operations he had ordered lay as much in their psychological effect as in their direct military results, but that the CIA-led effort to build a psychological-warfare campaign was half-hearted, unimaginative, and completely ineffectual. He opened the memo: "As you know, I have very little confidence in the CIA insofar as in developing programs that are imaginative on the propaganda side such as we used so successfully to discourage the enemy in World War II." He proceeded to suggest a series of themes that could be used against the enemy's soldiers and populace—themes of the "massive public support for the President's decision, of the damage that is being done to installations in North Vietnam, of the ships that are with the Marine Division on it that are menacing the coast of North Vietnam."[3]

In Nixon's view, the CIA's psychological operations were mechanical: "I just have a feeling that they are more interested in numbers of hours of broadcasts, numbers of leaflets—in other words, simply how much they are doing—than the quality of what they are doing."[4] Kissinger sent the memo along to Haig, who commented: "The President is, of course, exactly right here except he thinks CIA does it all. These operations are controlled by [Ambassador William] Sullivan's Interdepartmental Group. I think we should brutalize Sullivan at tomorrow's WSAG." Haig added that they should direct Sullivan's working group to develop a "specific plan to implement the President's directive."[5]

Nixon's long-standing frustration with his military commanders triggered a memorandum to Kissinger and Haig on May 15, proposing that Abrams consider "amassing what tanks we have left for at least one surprise offensive against the enemy in some area where they can effectively be used." He continued: "I do not pretend to have any knowledge or experience whatever in military matters. But I do know that military men generally are noted for the courage and loyalty of their character and notorious for the plodding mediocrity of their strategy and tactics . . . we will have to admit that while the bravery of our forces in Vietnam has been far beyond the call of duty, our military leadership has been a sad chapter in the proud military history of this country."[6]

Beyond demonstrating the degree of Nixon's frustration with the military, this memorandum illustrates some strange misunderstandings of the conflict that was raging half a world away. At the most fundamental level, even had this tactical move been feasible or advisable, Abrams had no tanks of his own. He would have to work through Thieu to assemble an armored force, and that relationship had proved very fragile a year earlier, in Lam Son 719. Thieu was an instinctively cautious man, and one very reluctant to interfere with the autonomy of his corps commanders—as he would have to do if the South Vietnamese were to stage this massed armored attack. Neither did the terrain, the tactical situation, or the ARVN logistical system support this concept. Nixon was always fascinated by the principles of mass, concentration, and shock, and these are valuable general principles, but it was not easy to find appropriate applications of them in this campaign, at least in the ground fighting.

That same day Nixon turned his commentary on the press, pointing out to Haldeman that the media had largely retreated from their predictions of disaster immediately after the May 8 speech. Instead, they "now have the gall to say that the Monday decision was wrong and reckless but that the

Soviet Union is showing great restraint in continuing the summit none-theless." Nixon concluded: "This is really the most devastating proof of the fact that whatever we do and however it turns out, we are going to be torn to pieces by our liberal critics in the press and on television." He noted: "What really matters now, of course, is how it all comes out. We shall continue to pour in the military action that is necessary to bring about a negotiated settlement as soon as possible." While doing so, though, it would be important to "hammer hard on the personal factors of courage, coolness in crisis, and putting country above political and parti-san and personal considerations." Because of the press's inveterate bias against him, Nixon believed, the campaign would need to "hammer home the necessity to put this hidden goal up front and center and hammer it home from now until election." Harking back to the Kennedy administra-tion, Nixon recalled that Kennedy had reaped the benefits of the press coverage of the Cuban missile crisis. He saw Kennedy as having enjoyed the advantage of the media's liberal bias. And so Nixon was determined to "see that we double the effort that he had due to the fact that our problem is doubly as difficult because of the opposition of the press."[7]

As the trip to Moscow neared, Nixon returned to the theme of the inef-fectiveness of American information operations. On May 18 he wrote to Kissinger: "I am still totally unsatisfied with the efforts we are making on the propaganda front in Vietnam." The president remained concerned about the lack of energy and creativity displayed by the CIA. By now, how-ever, he had begun to look beyond the immediate failures to the larger structural impediments to effective public diplomacy during wartime: "My study of every war in this century indicates that a propaganda chief was an almost indispensable adjunct to the military and political leaders." He mused: "It is too late perhaps to do anything except on a patchwork basis as far as this present operation is concerned . . . But looking to the future I think we have to have a topflight man probably on the White House staff and of course as a direct deputy to you at the NSC to advise on and to di-rect where necessary the propaganda offenses which are always needed to complement our military and political actions." Nixon planned to find "someone full time who will direct his attentions to how we handle things in a propaganda way, both covertly and overtly." He planned to take care of this problem immediately after his return from Moscow.[8]

Like so many of Nixon's plans, this initiative was ultimately derailed by the electoral campaign and the entanglement of Watergate. To this day,

there exists no effective structural approach to fixing the awkward relationship among military, diplomatic, and informational activities. Like
Nixon, later presidents have attempted to address this requirement by ad
hoc arrangements, but these have almost invariably proven unsatisfactory.
This remains a weakness in American strategic affairs.

His focus on propaganda activities and psychological warfare again
turned Nixon's attention to the CIA. Already frustrated by director Richard Helms's opposition to the mining and the escalation of the war, Nixon
decided it was time to take action against the agency. He dictated a memorandum to Haldeman with the striking opening section: "One department
which particularly needs a house-cleaning is the CIA. The problem in
the CIA is muscle-bound bureaucracy which has completely paralyzed the
brain and the other is the fact that its personnel, just like the personnel
in State, is primarily Ivy League and the Georgetown set rather than the
type of people that we get into the services and the FBI."[9] Nixon asked
Haldeman to commission a study "immediately as to how many people in
CIA could be removed by Presidential action." The reduction would be
justified on budgetary grounds, but Nixon expected Haldeman to understand the real reason for the cuts.

The next day, May 19, Nixon flew to Washington from Camp David in
midmorning.[10] He stopped off to visit Wallace at Walter Reed Army Me-
morial Hospital, and then continued to the White House to meet with
Kissinger and Vice President Spiro Agnew. Agnew was just back from a
tour of the Far East, structured around the ceremonies surrounding the
return of Okinawa to Japanese sovereignty. As Nixon and Kissinger chat-
ted, Agnew asked for the opportunity to debrief his trip. The vice president then offered Nixon and Kissinger a *tour d'horizon* of the Far East and
of the impressions he had gained on his visit.

In the process, Agnew inadvertently triggered one of the most extraordinary outbursts in a long series of outbursts captured by Nixon's taping
system. On the way back from Asia, Agnew had spoken with an Air Force
general about the bombing campaign then just beginning. Now, in the
Oval Office, Agnew innocently remarked: "Evidently there is some re-
morse about the restrictions on the bombing." He then listened in silence
as Nixon and Kissinger vied with each other to heap abuse on the Air
Force and its leadership. In the end Nixon vowed to remove the Air Force
chief of staff, General John Ryan, yelling over Kissinger's voice: "Ryan is
out, out, out, out, out!"[11] In a conversation that afternoon with his coun-

terpart at the office of the secretary of defense, General Robert Pursley, Haig briefly described the scene: "The President called Henry and they immediately called the Chairman in and a session went on like you never heard."[12] It was indeed unique, even in the context of this strange set of characters in this time of intense pressure. Summoned by the president, Moorer walked into the meeting to find Nixon and Kissinger as angry as he had ever seen them; he had no idea what had triggered the outburst or what the facts of the matter were. Agnew was unable, or unwilling, to identify the specific complaints he had heard, or to say where, when, or from whom he had heard the comments on the bombing restrictions—not even whether he had heard them in Saigon, on Guam, or in Hawaii. So that afternoon Moorer spent much time on the phone to the Pacific, trying to find out who had said what to the vice president. Perhaps unsurprisingly, no one owned up to the comments, and everyone in the chain of command professed satisfaction with the strategic direction coming from the White House.[13]

That afternoon Nixon dictated yet another memo to Kissinger and Haig, triggered by Agnew's comment and summarizing the frustrations the president had stored up over the previous weeks. He opened: "I am thoroughly disgusted with the consistent failure to carry out orders that I have given over the past three and a half years, and particularly in the past critical eight weeks, with regard to Vietnam. It is easy, of course, to blame the bureaucracy for failing to carry out orders. But we always have the problem of the bureaucracy."[14]

Nixon emphasized his long-standing direction to provide the South Vietnamese with an increase in the quantity and quality of weapons, which had led nowhere: "All that we have gotten from the Pentagon is the run around and a sometimes deliberate sabotage of the orders that I have given." He returned to the issue of psychological warfare: "The performance in the psychological warfare field is nothing short of disgraceful. The mountain has labored for seven weeks and when it finally produced, it produced not much than a mouse. Or to put it more honestly, it produced a rat."[15] Finally the bureaucracy had produced a program, but the president was unimpressed with its creativity and had no confidence that it would be carried out with any vigor.

The commander in chief then turned to the performance of his military forces. Agnew's comment still rankled, and Nixon vented once again in the memo. "The crowning insult to all this injury," he began, "is to have the military whine around to Agnew that they were not getting enough support from the Commander-in-Chief in giving them targets they could hit in North Vietnam." His anger focused on the Air Force, as it had since the beginning of the offensive. He directed Kissinger and Haig to "convey directly to the Air Force that I am thoroughly disgusted with their performance in North Vietnam." He announced his intention to remove strikes around Hanoi and Haiphong from Air Force jurisdiction, and give command authority there to "a Naval commander whom I will select." He vowed: "If there is one more instance of whining about target restrictions we will simply blow the whistle on this whole sorry performance of our Air Force in failing for day after day after day in North Vietnam this past week to hit enormously important targets when they had an opportunity to do so and were ordered to do so and then wouldn't carry out the order."[16]

The next morning, May 20, Nixon directed the last of these memos to Haig. In a few hours he would leave for Salzburg, and then travel to Moscow for the summit that would redefine the Cold War. After that he would continue on to Tehran and then Warsaw. He was well aware that while he was on the road his grip on the war would weaken. He therefore left detailed instructions for Haig, "so that you will have guidance for the period that we are gone on our trip to Moscow." Nixon summarized his overriding concern:

> It is vitally important that there be no abatement whatever in our air and naval strikes while we are gone. It is particularly important that any stories in the press indicating that we are letting up during this period be knocked down instantly, preferably in Saigon, if necessary at the Pentagon and if necessary even by you at the White House. There is nothing that could hurt us more in the minds of public opinion than some suggestion that we made a deal with the Russians to cool it in Vietnam while trying to negotiate agreements with them in Moscow.

Nixon proceeded to direct sortie counts and locations for the period that he would be in Moscow, going to the length of adjusting the count when the *Saratoga*, then nearing Southeast Asia, began sending sorties over the North. He directed "a relentless air attack on our targets in North Vietnam during this period—particularly on rail lines, POL and power plants. Concentrate on those targets which will have a major impact on civilian morale as well as accomplishing our primary objective of reducing the enemy's ability to conduct the war."[17]

He then returned to the propaganda front, with another variation on his previous proposal for organizing this function. He now favored placing a new office in the White House, along the model constructed in Eisenhower's administration. He was still working out his thoughts on this subject, and his new version differed in two major respects from that proposed a few days earlier. First, this new office would be located in the White House, not in the NSC; second, its purpose was no longer to integrate the administration's propaganda programs but to ensure that the administration got the credit it deserved for its work. In both respects, the new proposal weakened the power of the concept for foreign policy purposes. It seems likely that Nixon's suspicion of Kissinger played a role in his new desire to move this office out of the NSC, which from a substantive perspective was its more logical location.

On a more immediate aspect of this issue, the White House had just received a report from the French consul in Hanoi describing the effects of the early air attacks on North Vietnam. The report described the shock of these bombings, especially in Haiphong. It indicated that while the regime showed no sign of losing control of its population, the bombings had levied a great level of stress on the government and the population, far exceeding anything seen in Johnson's air war. Nixon directed Haig to ensure that this report was leaked to the press, explicitly to counter the "sickeningly pro-communist stories appearing in the New York Times from Tony Lewis."[18]

Nixon then changed the topic: "On another subject, we face a critical problem in terms of avoiding a massive right-wing revolt on the SALT agreement." He directed Haig to "develop a team, consisting of yourself, Moorer, Rush and Laird when he returns, to pick off individual Senators and very important opinion makers who are on the right to mute their criticism when the announcement comes in from Moscow." Timing would be of the essence: "I think our case can be sold to some of the more sensible hawks, but it must be done on an individual basis before they get the announcement from Moscow and make up their minds and dig in against us." He concluded: "It is no comfort that the liberals will praise the agreement, whatever it is. But let us always remember that the liberals will never support us—the hawks are our hard-core, and we must do everything we can to keep them from jumping ship after getting their enthusiasm restored as a result of our mining operation in the North."[19]

That afternoon, May 20, Nixon departed for the Moscow summit. He would not return to Washington until June 1. During his stay in Moscow he kept in touch with the war effort by telephone conversations with Haig, who remained in Washington as Kissinger accompanied the president. Nixon's greatest concern was that the North Vietnamese would overrun Kontum or Hue during the summit, embarrassing him and weakening him in the eyes of his Soviet hosts. He and Kissinger had prepared for this contingency, directing the Joint Staff to prepare plans for "heavy TACAIR and B-52 strikes against military targets in the Hanoi/Haiphong area."[20] These strikes proved unnecessary, however, as the South Vietnamese defenses held.

By the time Nixon returned to the United States, the crisis in Southeast Asia had crested and there was no longer any imminent danger of a South Vietnamese collapse. The air campaign over North Vietnam had settled into a rhythm and had begun to have visible effects on the North Vietnamese logistical system. The reinforcements dispatched in May had arrived in theater and were contributing to the battle. With the situation finally under control, the president turned his attention increasingly to domestic issues and the electoral campaign. The effort to contain the damage of the June 17 Watergate break-in also consumed increasing portions of the president's time through the summer. Not until October did the progress of the negotiations again demand that Nixon pay sustained attention to the fighting.

For this brief period between the mining of the harbors and his departure for Moscow, however, Nixon wrestled with the government he led, still working to impose his sense of urgency on a bureaucracy he deeply mistrusted, one whose role he had attempted to minimize through his three years in office. He and Kissinger sought to orchestrate the military, diplomatic, and informational instruments of power in this wholly new phase of the war, facing the limitations and testing the powers of a commander in chief in wartime.

17

THE SIEGE OF AN LOC

There was no shortage of horrifying moments for the soldiers engaged in the Easter Offensive. One thinks of ARVN infantrymen undergoing the initial artillery barrages along the demilitarized zone, or their counterparts ambushed on the road from Loc Ninh. The NVA soldiers subjected to B-52 bombardment or gunship attacks knew their own brand of suffering. But for sustained misery, nothing in this campaign surpassed the siege at An Loc, which extended from mid-April until the end of June. For weeks on end the garrison inside the city suffered intense artillery barrages while cut off from resupply and denied basic medical care. Their adversaries outside the town dug deeper and deeper into their shelters as B-52 raids, gunship attacks, and fighter aircraft whittled away at their numbers. This was a sustained battle of attrition, which would be won by the combatant with greater staying power—both moral and material.

It began when North Vietnam's COSVN high command reassessed its strategy following the two unsuccessful attacks of mid-April. The assaults on April 11 and 13 had failed to overwhelm the garrison, though they had left the northern half of the city in NVA hands. That gain had come at high cost, including the almost complete destruction of their armored forces. Now COSVN directed that the NVA settle into a siege, eroding the defending garrison through artillery attack and starvation while awaiting reinforcements. Once the defenders had been sufficiently weakened and the NVA losses of mid-April had been replaced, COSVN would direct another major assault, seeking to overwhelm the defenses and finally claim the town.

With the South Vietnamese troops cut off from the outside world, and with their artillery forces destroyed or ineffective, the defenses of An Loc relied almost entirely on air support for the firepower that would keep the NVA at bay, and for the supplies that would keep the garrison alive and fighting. If South Vietnamese and U.S. air forces could meet the requirements for firepower and resupply, the battle would be won. If not, it would be lost and An Loc would fall. The result was by no means a foregone conclusion. At the outset of the battle, as described earlier, the tactical air control system was in disarray, both inefficient and ineffective. B-52 targeting had been problematic throughout the war. The tactical airlift forces that would have to resupply the garrison faced a degree of opposition never before encountered in the conflict. The battle's outcome would pivot on the ability of theater air forces to respond to these conditions.

COSVN's campaign headquarters ordered a series of smaller-scale attacks in mid-April to consolidate the NVA's siege positions and to isolate the ARVN garrison within as tight a perimeter as possible. On April 18 the NVA 9th Division conducted an attack from the north, supported by three T-54s from the 20th Tank Battalion. The attack fizzled quickly, however, as two tanks mired down in bomb craters and the attacking armor was rendered ineffective.[1]

That day the South Vietnamese gained an extraordinary intelligence windfall, capturing a six-page letter from the NVA 9th Division's political officer to COSVN. The letter attributed the failure to take An Loc to two factors: repeated failures in tank-infantry coordination, and the pounding the division had taken from B-52s.[2] Of more interest, the letter outlined the plan for subsequent activity. On April 19 the 9th Division would launch an attack on the South Vietnamese outpost on Windy Hill, southeast of the city. That would be followed by an attack on the city itself, with the main blow striking from the rubber plantations southwest of the city.

The NVA action unfolded precisely as outlined in the captured letter. Three T-54 tanks supported an attack on Windy Hill, seeking to gain a position overlooking the city and to tighten the noose around the garrison. The attack opened at 3:30 A.M., but the tank crews found their advance hampered by the darkness and the heavy vegetation. Forced into a column formation, the armored force was weakened when the lead tank got stuck between two large trees; the other two continued the assault but were quickly knocked out by ARVN infantrymen using light antitank weapons. The North Vietnamese infantry carried the position by the early afternoon, and the surviving ARVN defenders retreated into An Loc or to the south. However, the assault on the city itself made little headway, and ended on April 22 with the South Vietnamese still in firm control of the southern portion of An Loc.[3]

It was time for the NVA armor to rest, refit, and regroup. The 20th Tank Battalion had fought five engagements and lost the bulk of the forces it had committed to battle. It withdrew to its base area on April 20 to reconstitute its forces. Only three days later, however, the 9th Division issued orders for the next assault, to occur in early May. The 20th Tank Battalion "hurriedly repaired damaged vehicles and guns, regrouped its personnel, and reorganized its organizational structure" in preparation for the next phase of the campaign.[4]

Meanwhile the adversaries settled in for the siege. As with perhaps all siege operations since the first days of land warfare, the North Vietnamese plan involved a combination of isolation and attack. The NVA would maintain its land blockade of the city—a relatively straightforward task, given that there was only one major artery, Route 13, leading into An Loc. With road traffic denied, the NVA would ring the area with antiaircraft artillery, cutting off aerial resupply and reinforcement. The surrounding artillery would whittle away at the garrison, eroding its numerical strength and its will to resist. This combination of pressures yielded the ghastly conditions faced by the city's defenders, and its remaining civilian population, in the coming weeks. In all there were about 20,000 people isolated in the city, about two-thirds of them civilians.[5]

The NVA 7th Division blocked Route 13 on April 7. Expecting to reopen the road quickly, the allies undertook to supply the garrison on an interim basis with helicopters and C-123s. This continued until April 12, when NVA gunners destroyed a helicopter in the landing zone with a mortar round.[6] The C-123s operated a bit longer, but the technological limitations of the VNAF aircraft required that they deliver their supplies during daylight, from low level, in the teeth of thickening NVA antiaircraft fire. No amount of courage could keep aircraft flying in this situation, and the South Vietnamese crews compounded the problem by using the same ingress route, sortie after sortie. The results were inevitable. North Vietnamese gunners destroyed one aircraft on April 15, and on April 19 a second C-123, loaded with ammunition, was hit and crashed three kilometers southwest of the city. The VNAF command canceled all further airdrops.[7] If the garrison was to survive, the Americans would have to sustain the airlift.

To do so, the American crews of the 374th Tactical Airlift Wing would have to overcome obstacles they had never before faced. The threat environment was nearly prohibitive, with dense small-arms fire interlaced with .51 caliber, 23- and 37-mm antiaircraft fire. The small perimeter defended by the ARVN complicated matters. By mid-April only one small drop zone, a soccer field 200 meters square on the south side of town, remained open, and it was under observation and constant bombardment by the NVA artillery overlooking the city. In the next few weeks the Americans would undertake a series of tactical and technical innovations, seeking a survivable delivery profile that would deliver enough supplies to sustain the South Vietnamese defenders.

The search opened on April 15, with two C-130s conducting daylight low-level airdrops. The first made it safely, taking only two hits from ground fire. As the second made his run fifteen minutes later, ground fire smashed into the cockpit, killing the flight engineer and wounding the navigator and the copilot. The crew aborted the approach, and miraculously nursed the aircraft back to Tan Son Nhut AB. Convinced that classic low-level delivery was untenable in the threat environment surrounding An Loc, the airlifters and FACs met that night to work out new tactics. They established six different ground tracks into the drop zone to give the aircraft some flexibility and an element of surprise. FACs would choose the entry and exit routes based on their observation of the ground defenses, and they would direct the C-130s. This worked for a single day, with two successful missions into the city. But on April 18 the first mission into An Loc took ground fire on the approach run and the right engine burst into flame. The pilot jettisoned the cargo and turned to the south, hoping to reach Tan Son Nhut before the aircraft disintegrated. Losing control, the pilot crash-landed the C-130 in an open field along Route 13. The crew survived, rescued quickly by Army helicopters, but that marked the end, for the time being, of the daytime low-level resupply missions. The price had become prohibitive.

The NVA defenses thus forced the resupply efforts into a high-altitude delivery profile. This was a decision born of desperation. Neither the

equipment nor the training programs on hand supported this profile; tactics would have to be worked out in the field, under fire. Technical problems ranged from how to rig the pallets of supplies to the ballistics and
wind drift of loaded pallets dropped from high altitudes. All had to be
solved if An Loc was to survive, and the initial results were very discouraging. The pallets so laboriously loaded and dropped to the garrison went, in
large measure, into North Vietnamese lines; on April 20, for example, the
Americans dropped 26 tons of supplies, 24 of them to the North Vietnamese. A range of operational and command issues compounded the technical problems. After days of misdirected airdrops, it turned out that Army
advisors had given the wrong coordinates for the drop zone to the Air
Force—so the more precise the drop, the less likely it was to reach friendly
hands.

Finally the intractable problems of high-altitude delivery forced a return to low-level operations, this time at night. There were good reasons,
however, why the crews had been reluctant to resort to this alternative:
they were insufficiently trained in night operations and lacked proficiency
in the specialized skills involved. Night operations also posed a new series
of technical challenges. Nonetheless, in the absence of any other option
that might save the besieged garrison, the C-130 crews decided to give the
low-level night missions a try.

Within a week this tactic, like its predecessors, proved unworkable. The
night drops were canceled after NVA gunners destroyed two C-130s on
their approaches to the city. By that time half of the missions flown into An
Loc had resulted in battle damage; 3 C-130s had been lost and 37 damaged, with 15 dead servicemen.

Not only were the losses prohibitive, but the missions delivered very little to the city's defenders. Through this time, Army advisors estimated that
only 8–10 percent of the supplies dropped by the C-130s reached the defenders. The 90 percent of the airdrops not recovered by the ARVN went
to the NVA; advisors estimated that by early May 567 tons of supplies had
been delivered to the North Vietnamese forces. This was an incredible
boon to the attackers, especially given the long and difficult supply corridor linking the COSVN area with its sources of supply in the North. The
point was driven home when an NVA officer was captured on the eastern
side of the city in May. Americans on the scene noted: "The first thing he
asked for was a can of fruit cocktail . . . had been eating it for weeks from
misdropped supplies by the USAF, most likely C rations." The Army of-

ficers, who had been surviving on canned rice and brackish water, were not amused.[8]

Problems with resupply by no means ended when the supplies hit the ground, even when they landed in a designated drop zone. The North Vietnamese naturally made a practice of shelling the recovery areas within minutes of the drops, inflicting casualties and destroying the supplies. During the most perilous portion of the siege, through mid-May, the more serious problem was that there was no internal distribution system within the garrison to ensure that supplies reached the right recipients. Instead the garrison commander directed his subordinates to "square away" the supplies landing in their areas. Inevitably that led to hoarding and major inefficiencies in the use of supplies that were dangerously scarce to begin with.[9]

Distribution of supplies was a major function of command, and the failures there were symptomatic of larger issues. The 5th ARVN Division commander, General Le Van Hung, succeeded in holding the defenses together despite the ceaseless pounding and the short rations. Beyond the problems forced on him by the NVA, Hung had to cope with the command issues endemic to the South Vietnamese military. Though he was formally in command of the garrison at An Loc, Hung's control over the Airborne, Ranger, and provincial units of the garrison was fragile at best. An American advisor later commented: "To this day I do not know (nor do I think any one else does) what the command relationship is or is supposed to be."[10]

As casualties mounted, medical care became increasingly critical, and this exposed a second disastrous failing in the command structure. Once the city was isolated, medical supplies dwindled to nothing. The North Vietnamese artillery destroyed the hospital on April 28, leaving the garrison without even a clinic to care for the wounded. Neither could they be evacuated, since the VNAF refused to fly medical evacuation missions into the city. American helicopters occasionally reached the city, rotating personnel and bringing in supplies, but attempts to use them to evacuate wounded deteriorated into chaos in the landing zones. Colonel William E. Miller, the senior U.S. advisor to the 5th ARVN Division, said in an interview: "I charge the division commander with criminal negligence for not putting an officer or officers out on the ground in charge of the operations for getting the people on the choppers." The wounded had little chance for care and less for evacuation. It was a grim situation, with predictable results. In Miller's words: "We had mass graves . . . truckload after truck-load—civilians, ARVN, RF/PF, enemy—they had front loaders in there . . . dug a hole, put them in and covered them up."[11]

The lack of medical treatment ate away the strength of the garrison, and, more broadly, the situation placed stringent limits on Hung's operational flexibility. The lack of medical care played into every operational decision, large or small, that the garrison commander faced. In theory it would have been possible, for example, to conduct a helicopter-borne attack from the city, destroying the NVA artillery that was torturing the defenders. Hung refused to order the attack, however, unless it was conducted with American helicopters and with assurance that the United States would evacuate the wounded. This was impossible given the constraints governing the use of U.S. forces, and so the idea faded away.

Slowly the NVA artillery whittled away at the garrison. By early May, An Loc's defenders numbered only about half their strength at the outset of the siege. General Hollingsworth, senior U.S. advisor to the commander of South Vietnamese forces in MR III, tallied the strength of the garrison on May 6, and later recalled that the 5th ARVN Division had dwindled from its original strength of approximately 6,500 men to 3,100 soldiers, about half of whom were wounded. The RF/PF forces now numbered about 700 men capable of fighting. The decline in strength, however, was even greater than these numbers suggest. Hollingsworth polled the garrison's officers on the capabilities of their units. Their replies were bleak: "The Division Commander, Province Chief, and their respective advisors told me that they could not hold against another attack. They further stated that the failure of VNAF to evacuate seriously wounded casualties during the month of April, the continuous incoming rockets, artillery, and mortar fire and resultant low morale of the remaining forces, had brought the troops to a point where they feared to move, shoot, or expose themselves."[12]

Clearly, under these conditions, the city's fate would be decided by the effectiveness of the air forces committed to its defense. There the news was good. As the siege continued, the Army and the Air Force worked out the procedures necessary to control the masses of fighter-bombers committed to the area. The FACs had had a problem with task saturation: often the airspace over the city would become saturated with fighters—usually when Navy aircraft appeared in large groups because of carrier cycle requirements. Seventh Air Force addressed this problem by assigning several controllers to the area, with one acting as a "King FAC" with overall control over allocating sorties in the battle area. When too many aircraft approached, the excess would be sent south to work with other controllers over Route 13.

B-52 targeting, too, improved under the unique conditions of this battle. For one thing, the NVA attackers were forced to operate in a relatively confined area. The Americans no longer had to seek out the enemy across miles of Laotian roads or in deep jungles; the enemy's assembly areas lay all around the city. More significantly, the garrison could take advantage of a flood of human intelligence, from refugees and local occupants, that helped to pinpoint NVA assembly areas. The bombers exacted a constant psychological and material toll on the attackers, though specific casualty counts were rarely available; as an American advisor noted: "We did not worry about BDA [bomb damage assessment] too much because with all those bombs we felt we were hitting something anyway."[13] In April the Air Force sent 363 B-52 sorties into MR III, nearly all in the immediate area of An Loc, with the B-52s dropping 8,119 tons of bombs.

Over An Loc the AC-130 gunships returned to their original mission, providing support to troops and outposts under attack, after years of focusing on truck interdiction over Laos. It took a few days for the air control system to employ the gunships effectively. Initially neither the headquarters planners nor the FACs operating over the battlefield had a clear view of the gunships' capabilities or the sort of support they could provide. After some days of frustration, the gunship squadron deployed crews to Tan Son Nhut AB to meet with the FACs and discuss tactics and capabilities.[14] The situation then turned around quickly, with the gunships assuming a central role in the city's defenses. The latest version, with the onboard 105-mm howitzer, proved to be especially valuable. It essentially replaced the garrison's artillery, which was progressively destroyed by the NVA guns outside the town.[15]

The situation provided an unusual interval of personal involvement by the air crews in the fate of the garrison on the ground. Returning to the same battle day after day, talking with the same controllers over and over, air crews came to take a personal interest in the battle. Over time, the combination of the system's accuracy and firepower and the crews' intimate familiarity with the area enabled the aircraft to put rounds into specific stories of specific buildings, an immense advantage in the street fighting characteristic of that battle. The aircraft achieved this accuracy while flying at 9,000 feet, impervious to the light antiaircraft artillery employed by the NVA in the area.

Even with all this support, the garrison continued to waste away. The air support could shield the city, but it could neither suppress the NVA artillery nor ensure the delivery of supplies. In early May, however, the situation began to change. The turnaround arrived with dramatic suddenness, just at the point when night drops were canceled on May 4. The solution demanded a range of tactical and technical developments. The Army and the Air Force deployed parachute riggers to Saigon—first to advise the South Vietnamese, then in larger numbers to take over the parachute rigging. The accuracy of the airdrops improved as the 474th TAW refined the ballistics data for pallets dropped at high altitude, and then devised the tactic of having AC-130 gunships fire test rounds against truck hulks near the drop zone to obtain accurate wind data. Finally, the wing adopted the practice of dropping the pallets in multiple releases, testing results with a small drop first and then refining the aim point. Within a week, deliveries reached a recovery rate of 90 percent. The crisis in supply was at an end. The fate of An Loc, and perhaps of Thieu's government, had rested on the ability of Air Force and Army parachute riggers to work through the problems posed in this new tactical environment. Their perseverance and ingenuity now offered the garrison a chance of survival.

It was only a chance of survival, though, and by no means assured. The North Vietnamese remained massed around the defense perimeter, patiently conserving their strength, waiting for reinforcements and for the effects of the blockade to fatally weaken the garrison. In early May the defenders began to pick up signs that the climactic battle was soon to come. The clearest indication came from an NVA lieutenant who defected on May 5. On questioning, the lieutenant stated that the 5th VC Division commander had criticized the 9th Division for its failure to take the city, and had claimed that he could do it in two days if given the mission. The lieutenant further stated that COSVN had then assigned the 5th Division responsibility for taking the city, with the 9th Division acting in support. Early in May a series of tactical adjustments by the NVA forces tightened the ring around the city and offered clear evidence that the next attack would come soon.

Through this period COSVN awaited reinforcements that were en route from North Vietnam. These were necessary to replace the forces destroyed in the operations against Loc Ninh and An Loc in early April. The

NVA armor command deployed the 21st Armored Battalion down the Ho Chi Minh Trail on the long journey to An Loc. The unit operated PT-85s, the Chinese-built version of the Soviets' PT-76 light tanks. It was inherently a very vulnerable system. Nor did the unit's background offer any great hopes of success. The NVA armor command's history of the battle noted: "Most of the battalion's soldiers were former Ha Nam Ninh province local troops who had just been transferred to the armored branch. After a short period of training they were immediately sent to the front."[16]

The available sources do not indicate that the III Corps defenders detected this movement. However, by now the NVA operations had fallen into a recognizable pattern, and Hollingsworth used this predictability to his advantage. On May 9 the NVA launched strong probes all around the defensive perimeter, as the attackers looked for soft areas to exploit in subsequent attacks. As the attack ebbed away, the artillery bombardment intensified. Hollingsworth expected that "following the heavy probes on the morning of May 9, the enemy would probe again in the same fashion on the morning of the 10th, withdraw, and start his assaults for the main battle on the morning of the 11th." Hollingsworth defined eighteen Arc Light target areas for use against the attack, and asked Abrams for priority for bomber support when the attack occurred. Abrams agreed, and asked Hollingsworth his views on a plan he had been considering, to rotate the total B-52 effort from military region to military region on a twenty-four-hour basis, with all the available strikes on any given day going to a single region. The command would keep this up for three days, and then revert to the normal even division of sorties across the regions. Hollingsworth agreed on the condition that he would get the first use of the concentrated strikes.[17]

Abrams sent direction to Kroesen, Vann, and Hollingsworth on May 10, notifying them of his decision and providing broad guidance for their planning. He opened with an outline of the situation and of the enemy actions he expected between then and Ho Chi Minh's birthday on May 19. He then directed the corps advisors to concentrate the bomber strikes on NVA troop formations and not use the B-52s against logistical targets. Abrams expected the advisors to supervise this effort personally.[18] Clearly he considered this disruption of the normal allocation pattern a major opportunity, one that must be seized by the entire command. That same afternoon, Hollingsworth informed Abrams that he expected the enemy attack the next day, and would take the B-52 strikes starting at 0530 local time. They would follow at 55-minute intervals through the rest of the day.

As Hollingsworth expected, the North Vietnamese triggered their attack that night. The NVA history records: "At exactly 0130 in the morning of May 11 our attack on An Loc City began. Our artillery pounded An Loc. Our tanks and armored vehicles in all sectors were ordered to move forward to their assigned assault positions."[19] The NVA artillery barrage totaled 8,300 rounds, according to American counts; one advisor noted that "for anyone to go outside of a bunker that night was certain death—at least in our particular area where the rounds were exploding so quickly that it was impossible to count them." Abruptly the barrage stopped, as the advisor recalled, "bam—just like somebody dropped down a baton. Everything stopped at once."[20]

The NVA plan was straightforward. As summarized in the Armored Command history: "The intent was to concentrate superior infantry, artillery, and tank forces to attack from four directions straight toward the center of the enemy's defenses, drive the enemy back, divide enemy forces in order to annihilate them one by one, and in this way eventually destroy the entire enemy force defending the city." There would be two assault spearheads. Spearhead One, the primary attack, would come from the west and employ three medium T-54 tanks and two light PT-85 tanks. The other spearhead, from the northwest, would include three T-54s and one PT-85.[21] As in the April attacks, the NVA commanders divided their tank support into small groups, attached to units all around the city, rather than concentrating them for a decisive blow.

The attacking force compounded this error with bad luck and poor proficiency in executing the assault. The lead tank in the Spearhead One column struck a mine well before encountering the city's defenses. The second tank pulled around the disabled lead tank to continue the attack, and promptly struck a second mine. The third tank, the company commander's vehicle, got stuck in a bomb crater. The two PT-85s were both hit and disabled by shoulder-fired antitank weapons.[22] There was no armored reserve, and so the attack in the west continued as an infantry assault. In Spearhead Two, in the northwest sector of the town, the attack went somewhat better and the tank-infantry force penetrated the defenses.

Colonel Walter Ulmer had replaced Miller as the divisional senior advisor less than twenty-four hours before this final assault; Miller's frustration over the performance of the ARVN garrison and its leadership led

Hollingsworth to replace him on the verge of the expected culminating attack.[23] Ulmer reported the first indication of the attack shortly after midnight. At 0210 he asked Hollingsworth's staff to look into what air support might be available if this attack continued, and by 0300 he predicted that this would be the NVA's big push to take the city. Fifteen minutes later he radioed: "It is obvious that this is the enemy's main effort. I feel at this time the U.S. personnel are in immediate danger. We must plan and consider possible extraction." As he had with Miller during the earlier assaults, Hollingsworth decided to keep the advisory team in place. He went further, initially denying Ulmer's request to declare a tactical emergency as the NVA ground assault began. Around 0430, as the assault gathered energy, Ulmer began to piece together a picture of the attack pattern and requested that "everything to include the kitchen sink" be sent to provide support. Over the next few hours, as day dawned, Ulmer reported the heaviest attacks as coming from the southwest and the west, at 0625 calling in: "Entire perimeter in contact. Ammo dump on fire & exploding."[24]

By that point the air support had arrived, nearly every sort available to the U.S. forces. The first B-52 strike went in at 0530, a few minutes after a flight of Cobra helicopter gunships lifted off from Lai Khe and headed toward the battle. By then six flights of F-4 fighter-bombers were already inbound. The first gunship on station, an AC-119, returned to base with mechanical problems, but it was soon replaced by an AC-130. By 0715 the defenders had identified fifteen tanks inside the city or on the perimeter, with smoke from the battle shielding the NVA armor from air attack.[25] The attackers continued to build momentum, but the defense was holding and the air support had already begun to take its toll. Just then, to the anger and disgust of the Army advisors, an A-37 went down and the FACs on station immediately changed their focus to assisting in the pilot's rescue. Even worse, they diverted an inbound B-52 strike to preclude any possibility of striking the downed pilot. Weeks after the battle, the memory still rankled for the Army advisors whose key weapon had been taken away at the height of the battle.[26] Fortunately only one strike was diverted, and by 0915 the sequence of B-52 strikes had begun again.

The defenses held in most sectors, but in the west and the northeast the NVA pressed into the city, creating salients as they reached toward the ARVN command centers. The AC-130 again proved its worth in this crisis, with one advisor calling it the "saving grace" for the defenses. In the early afternoon, with the attacks largely stagnated, the defenders counter-attacked, but the NVA forces managed to hold the positions they had captured that day.

On that single day, American air forces committed 297 fighter and 15 gunship sorties to the defense of An Loc. The air support had saved the city, but it came at a cost. NVA forces shot down two FAC aircraft, an A-37, and a Cobra gunship, successfully employing their new tactic of clustering 23-mm, 37-mm, and .51-caliber antiaircraft weapons. Three pilots lost their lives. Late in the day, it became clear that worse was soon to follow. At 1915 a FAC reported the first confirmed sighting of an SA-7 in the An Loc area. With that single radio call the battle changed.[27] It is possible, perhaps even likely, that the heat-seeking missiles had destroyed the aircraft lost that day. In any case, confirmation of its presence meant that the tactics employed to that point over the battlefield were instantly obsolete.

Night fell with the NVA in possession of two new salients, but no longer a real threat to overrun the city. The constant grinding attrition they had suffered through weeks of air attack, plus the response of air forces during the crisis, had so weakened the attackers that the continuation of the offensive was more a mark of the Politburo's insistence than of any real possibility of success. The NVA mounted attacks the following two days, but they lacked the weight and energy of the assault of May 11 and made no further penetrations into the city. The air support from gunships proved especially useful with the NVA and ARVN troops so tightly engaged; only gunships offered the accuracy necessary to attack in this situation.

The NVA continued to employ the SA-7s through May 12. In the early evening a gunship on station reported four near misses by the missiles, and finally, the fifth struck the aircraft. One crew member recalled: "The stress bent the tail over about 7 degrees. It just wiped out the airplane as far as being able to use it again."[28] That night the NVA sought to take advantage of bad weather and staged yet another attack on An Loc, led by PT-76s. Six B-52 strikes halted this assault.[29] Later Vogt cabled back to Washington: "While it is still too early to tell, we may have broken the back of the enemy offensive capability in the An Loc area."[30] He was right.

The official history of the NVA closes its discussion of this campaign: "On 15 May, after 32 days of ferocious combat, our troops ended the attack on Binh Long city [An Loc]."[31] That was true to some extent. There were no more major assaults, and the forces executing the siege gradually began to move back toward their base areas to refit. That did little, however, to relieve the suffering of the garrison. The NVA still occupied sectors of An Loc, and the ARVN troops in the city were still isolated. The NVA continued to block Route 13 to the south, and the SA-7 once again placed in jeopardy the high-altitude airdrops of supplies. Artillery rounds still pounded the defenses.

With the destruction of the NVA tank force and the failure of this third major attack, it had become clear to the Politburo and COSVN that it was time to move to a new strategy. On Politburo direction, General Tran Van Tra ordered his units "to change tactics and surround the city, at the same time organizing forces to hold blocking positions along Route 13." He intended to "attract and tie down the enemy in order to allow the soldiers and civilian populations of the provinces of the Cochin China lowlands to expand their attacks and uprisings."[32] It was a clear example of the interplay among the elements of the North Vietnamese strategy, as COSVN used the main forces along Route 13 to open up opportunities to attack the pacification program west of Saigon. COSVN withdrew the 5th VC division from the An Loc area in late May to redeploy it in support of the counter-pacification efforts in the lowlands to the west. The unit withdrew to its base area in Cambodia, where it refitted and regrouped. Within two weeks it was again moving, marching westward toward the Elephant's Foot area along the Cambodia–South Vietnam border.

It was a remarkable display of the resilience of the communist forces, given the intensity of the 5th VC Division's operations over the preceding months. Hollingsworth estimated that the division had taken 90 percent casualties during the siege of An Loc; while this is probably an overstatement, it does measure the intensity of the action the unit had seen.[33] An after-action analysis by MACV pointed to this redeployment as an example of the NVA's "capacity to move long distances with security and with speed," and continued: "The NVA, long considered second to none in this area, have fully justified their reputation."[34] It was especially remarkable given that it involved disengaging from intense combat and moving through areas under nearly constant surveillance and attack by the Americans and the South Vietnamese. Nonetheless, while the 5th displayed considerable resilience and mobility, it never showed the same capabilities after its pummeling at Loc Ninh and An Loc that it had early in the campaign. It was possible to refill the division numerically, but its fighting skill and spirit would take longer to rebuild.

Finally, on June 12, the last North Vietnamese were driven from the city, and on June 18 General Minh declared that the siege was over. Combat operations along Route 13, however, continued for months as the South Vietnamese attempted to break the NVA's hold on the highway. It became an embarrassment to the ARVN and to the Nixon administration, which repeatedly urged Thieu to remove Minh from command. News accounts publicized the slow pace of the relief columns along the route and the languorous operational tempo of the 21st ARVN Division as it fought its way northward. Nonetheless, Thieu resisted Abrams's and Bunker's entreaties that he fire Minh. A subsequent MACV assessment commented: "General Abrams' efforts to have Minh relieved were to no avail . . . The possibility exists that his lack of aggressiveness was not entirely his fault, but was caused by pressure from higher commanders."[35]

However embarrassing it was to the White House, the struggle along Route 13 did not compensate the NVA for its failure to take its primary objective of An Loc. The NVA postmortem on the campaign offered unsparing criticism: "The primary reason for our failure . . . was that the combined-arms force commanders and their staff assistants for armor did not know how to use their forces correctly, leading to the use of our armor in small, isolated increments." This fundamental deficiency was compounded by the hurried preparation for each assault: "On occasion, there was not even time to reconnoiter the terrain and mission orders had to be issued and combat coordination arrangements made using only a battle map." The rush to battle violated the meticulous training cycle normally employed by the NVA. It was especially costly given the lack of basic training and combat experience on the part of all the forces involved. The history emphasized the exceptional rigidity of the NVA tactics: "All five battles used the same tactics . . . Combat organization was not sufficiently tight and the tactical movements of our soldiers were not intelligent or flexible."[36]

More broadly, the history also noted deep-seated flaws in the execution of the campaign strategy. The original intent was "to use siege tactics to besiege An Loc for an extended period of time, after which our forces would be massed to overrun the target in one single combined-arms battle." Instead, the on-scene commanders frittered away the shock and firepower value of armor in small attacks, permitting the garrison to grow accustomed to fighting the tanks: "In a situation where our tank force was small, we needed to retain the element of surprise, because this would be our first use of the armor on the battlefields of Cochin China . . . the use of tanks in a siege situation was not appropriate." To this list of problems we may add the fundamental inability of the armored forces to employ their weapons systems effectively, or often even to drive them safely to the point of attack. The mistakes all added up. Of 51 sorties by armored vehicles in the battles at An Loc, 36 ended with the vehicles destroyed or ineffective. By mid-May the NVA "combat forces in all three attack sectors were combat ineffective."[37] The hurried and secretive upgrade to an armored force had come at a very high price, in low crew proficiency and in the inability of the campaign commanders to coordinate armored, artillery, and infantry tactics. The lessons were costly, but the NVA set about learning them for later use.

The main-force offensive in MR III was finished, crushed under the weight of American air power. But through the summer the Politburo continued to press COSVN for renewed and widespread rural uprisings, seeking to move to the second phase of the grand offensive. In mid-June Le Duan sent a message directing COSVN to accelerate its attacks against pacification. In his view, the key was "to have a specific, detailed plan to quickly develop local force units and a guerrilla military force, including to provide them with additional personnel and to strengthen their equipment."[38] He did not provide any guidance on where COSVN could conjure up these forces. Six weeks later he followed this with further direction critiquing COSVN's leadership and operations through the summer. The Politburo repeatedly offered suggestions on igniting rural and urban uprisings, continually emphasizing the urgency of the situation. By late September, however, with the stagnation in the offensive, COSVN's leadership admitted: "Our basic shortcoming still exists. Subregion and Province Party Committees have not been able to transform the morale of cadres and party members into concrete action nor bring them into agreement with the Party."[39] The Politburo could exhort and direct, but like its demands for intensified main-force action, its insistence on the fomenting of popular uprisings represented a combination of wishful thinking, ideology, and distance from the scene of combat.

American air power had halted COSVN's main-force offensive short of its primary objective, and the rural uprisings envisioned by the Politburo never gained any real momentum. Nonetheless, the NVA's sacrifice of thousands of troops had enabled the communists to crack Saigon's defenses along the Cambodian border, and had captured terrain that would never be regained by the South Vietnamese. The threat to Saigon had also forced Thieu to weaken ARVN's presence in MR IV, creating an opportunity for NVA and VC counter-pacification efforts. Moreover, the tactical errors by the NVA armored forces provided a rich menu of lessons learned for later operations, bringing irreplaceable experience in combat that would yield important benefits in campaigns to come.

18

THE DEFENSE OF HUE

The fall of Quang Tri on May 2 brought an end to the second phase of the North Vietnamese offensive in MR I. All across South Vietnam, the communist offensive stood on the verge of achieving its goals. In the north, Hue was in peril with the 3rd ARVN Division fleeing in disarray. South Vietnam's strategy for the central highlands had been exposed as grossly inadequate with the fall of Tan Canh and the disintegration of the 22nd ARVN Division. Kontum stood next in the pathway of the NVA tanks, and no one could be confident that its defenders would do any better than those who had fought earlier in the campaign. Farther south, An Loc lay under siege, with supplies dwindling as casualties mounted. It appeared that the massive American investment in South Vietnam might be lost in a matter of days.

The population of Quang Tri, fleeing south along Route 1, fell under NVA artillery fire as they mixed with the military units retreating toward sanctuary; thousands died. The panic extended south to Hue, where the population maintained keen memories of the brief Viet Cong occupation during the 1968 Tet Offensive. Disorder reigned in Hue, with ARVN deserters looting freely and refugees pouring down the roads to the south. The structure of the society and the government unraveled. Over the first three days of May, the American advisor John Graham estimated, the population shrank from 350,000 to 70,000. Graham wrote of the refugees making their way out of town, "endless silhouettes of bent figures, carts, bundles, bicycles, wheelbarrows and babes in arms plodding toward an elusive safe haven. Law and order suffered gravely. There was a virtually total breakdown in military discipline." Morale in the city was further undermined by the widespread belief that the NVA gains reflected a deal struck between Nixon and the Chinese during his February visit to Beijing, in which the North Vietnamese would take control of Quang Tri and Hue in return for permitting the Americans to pull out "with honor." Graham noted the vicious rumors circulating, of "lack of US air support, failure to provide modern weapons, and the premature pull-out of advisors." The situation reached its lowest point, by Graham's account, on May 3.[1]

The emergency was dramatic and serious enough to force Thieu to replace Lam as commander of I Corps. On May 3 the president named Lieutenant General Ngo Quang Truong, commander of IV Corps in the Mekong Delta, to command of I Corps. For Truong this represented a homecoming and a move he had awaited for some time. He had watched the situation deteriorate in the north, aware that "neither General Lam nor his staff were competent to maneuver and support large forces in heavy combat."[2] Truong had commanded the 1st ARVN during the Tet Offensive. Now he returned to Hue with selected members of his staff, whom he had previously selected as he prepared for this assignment.

The task he faced was monumental, but in its broad outlines very simple. In short order he would have to restore order in the city, structure an organized defense north of Hue, and rationalize the command structure to enable the South Vietnamese forces to take advantage of the overwhelming firepower available from U.S. air and naval support. Most of all, he would have to infuse a new spirit into the city and its defenders, dispelling the sense of doom that had settled over MR I in the previous weeks.

The disorder and confusion that had characterized I Corps operations thus far now vanished, as Truong took firm control. By May 5, on his third day in command, Truong established a clear, workable plan for the defense of Hue. He assigned the Marine Division responsibility for the north and northwest approaches to the city, with its lines running along the south shore of the My Chanh River to Firebase Sally, and then southeastward to the Bo River. There the 1st ARVN Division's sector began, with the division primarily responsible for the southwestern area guarding the corridor

from the A Shau Valley. "My concern at the time," Truong wrote, "was to
provide for a defense in depth, to economize force, to create a realistic
chain of command, establish strong reserves for each major unit, and integrate the regular and territorial forces, which so far had operated with little coordination, into the corps defense plan."[3] Truong was able to con-
vince Thieu and the Joint General Staff to send reinforcements to replace
the 3rd ARVN Division, shattered in the previous fighting; the JGS committed the 2nd Airborne Brigade on May 8, followed by the 3rd Airborne
Brigade on May 22. Once the full Airborne Division had arrived, Truong
assigned them an area of responsibility between the Marines and the 1st
ARVN.

Graham witnessed Truong's return to Hue, and commented: "The effect of the new leadership on both the military and civil situations in Hue
was, without exaggeration, electric." He continued: "To the people of
Hue, the team that had lost Quang Tri was out (3rd Division Commander
Giai also having been sacked) and a team of known winning prowess had
taken its place. This was the hinge around which the turn-around in the
City's outlook took place."[4]

It was as dramatic a demonstration of the power of leadership as one
could ever find. On Tuesday Hue and its defenders were a panicky, disorganized mob. On Thursday there was purpose and hope. In fact, the turn-
around was too complete, as complacency quickly replaced the panic. Graham noted: "In one week, Hue City had gone from a state of panic and
chaos to one of lethargy and indifference with only a short stop at the in-
termediate stage of productive activity."[5]

The psychological transformation among the defenders was instantaneous, but it would take time before it could be translated into combat effectiveness. In the first days of May there was little organized defense
north of Hue, nothing that could have stopped a determined NVA push
toward the city. The defense was preserved through that period by two
factors. First, the NVA was no more ready to exploit this opportunity than
it had any of the others it had earned through the offensive. The NVA's
forces were disorganized and there was no logistical preparation for a further advance. The North Vietnamese were also hamstrung by their long-
standing decision to await the results of the early campaign along the
DMZ before planning for follow-on attacks. Given the slow and meticulous NVA planning cycle, that sequence would mean an inevitable pause
in the tempo of operations. Nonetheless, recognizing the opportunity

open to them and under intense pressure from the Politburo, the NVA campaign headquarters pushed troops and supplies forward as quickly as possible.

These deficiencies in the NVA planning process were unknown to the ARVN and American defenders, who did everything they could to slow and complicate the NVA advance. Under the circumstances, that meant throwing every available aircraft at the battle. Vogt put together the most concentrated interdiction campaign of the war, taking advantage of the confined and open operating area between Quang Tri and Hue. On May 1 the Americans flew 342 attack sorties into MR I, controlled by 91 FAC sorties. Another 35 B-52 strikes added to the deluge of firepower. The next day the numbers increased to 421 tactical aircraft (TACAIR) strikes and 37 B-52 sorties. Vogt kept flare-equipped F-4s over the area through the night to detect advancing NVA forces and coordinate strikes on them, and in the daylight hours slow FACs orbited every road, ready to call in strikes. On May 5 Vogt reported an "intensive campaign to disrupt the movement of enemy units and supplies southward toward Hue. This has been an around the clock effort with TAC AIR present on virtually all the major arteries leading south from inside North Vietnam itself right on down to the defensive line north of Hue." Vogt claimed to have destroyed 110 trucks within the past 24 hours and damaged another 16. In addition to hitting the trucks, Vogt sent bombers after the road infrastructure, claiming: "We have destroyed every bridge on QL-1 from friendly positions north to the DMZ." He even sent F-4s with laser-guided weapons against the fords across the Ben Hai River.[6] Clearly the commander in chief's sense of urgency had percolated down to the tactical level.

Assessing the situation, Vogt noted the "crash nature of the enemy's re-supply effort."[7] It was a desperate and dislocated effort, without the normal careful precautions taken by the NVA to minimize exposure to air attack. The NVA forces could not use their well-practiced measures of camouflage, concealment, and deception in this open country, where rapid movement was imperative. Vogt reported the NVA's attempt to rebuild, in broad daylight, the Quang Tri bridge, using large cranes for the purpose. Laser-guided bombs quickly destroyed the cranes and stymied the attempt. The North Vietnamese campaign history also notes this incident, far more vividly than did Vogt: "In just a short period of time, by the use of high explosive, cluster, white phosphorous, and napalm bombs, the enemy destroyed vegetation and turned an area of dozens of square kilometers into a wasteland, and he destroyed all bridges, ferries, and every piece of equipment that could be used to cross the river."[8]

The NVA history testifies to the dislocated planning process that was driving this deployment. The crossing point across the Quang Tri River was a crucial link in the campaign's logistical network, and the campaign headquarters had not anticipated the need to protect it with air defense forces. By the time the headquarters directed the 367th Air Defense Division to clear the bottleneck, "the situation had already become extremely difficult." The division ordered the 230th Antiaircraft Artillery Regiment to secure the crossing, but by that time only two small ferries survived, and they were unable to carry the regiment's guns to the south side of the river. As a result, the regiment was forced to deploy all its forces on one side of the river, weakening its coverage of the area. The antiaircraft and engineer forces fighting to keep the crossing open faced nearly constant air attack, along with naval gunfire and artillery fire: "Every night entire companies of engineers and assault youth were killed as they worked to prepare the river crossing point." Finally the campaign headquarters formed a "Composite Engineer-Artillery Headquarters" to coordinate the efforts to clear the ford. Not until late May, though, did the NVA manage to clear the crossing.[9]

On May 6 the NVA forces demonstrated again their determination to press the attack, along with the increasingly evident problems with their command and control structure. Vogt reported to Washington that late in the morning FACs had detected about 25 amphibious PT-76 tanks moving into position east of QL-1. The controllers called in fighters to attack, both Air Force Phantoms with laser-guided bombs and Navy aircraft armed with cluster bombs. By the late afternoon they counted 11 tanks destroyed and another 12 damaged. Vogt commented: "The fact that the enemy would risk these tanks in broad daylight in the face of all this tacair once again reveals his determination to seize his objective at all costs."[10] The NVA tactics were nearly suicidal, causing heavy losses with little prospect of gain. Along with the determination cited by Vogt, they indicate the General Staff's serious lack of appreciation for the tactical situation facing its forces north of Hue. It seems likely that the costly push forward reflected the lessons learned from the NVA's lost opportunities through the first weeks of the offensive. The inability to pursue the enemy had repeatedly proven very costly, and now, so did the attempt to learn from earlier errors.[11]

Despite the attention drawn to the battle north of Hue, it was the invasion corridor southwest of the city that most worried Truong. In that sector the firebases Bastogne and Birmingham, controlling the western approaches to Hue, had fallen in late April, as the 3rd ARVN Division disintegrated north of the city. As Vogt reported: "Truong is most concerned about an attack from the southwest along Highway 547 and possibly from trails and river beds south of 547. He asked for extensive photo coverage of this area, which I intend to provide ASAP."[12]

Truong also asked for Vogt's help in countering the NVA artillery force, especially the 130-mm gun, which had been the single most important factor in the enemy's successes to date. Intrinsically difficult to hit and destroy, the artillery pieces were employed intelligently and effectively by the NVA to minimize their exposure to aerial attack. Well concealed and emplaced, the artillery troops would normally cease fire when aircraft were overhead, denying the Americans the ability to detect and target the guns. Vogt reflexively turned to a high-technology solution to the problem, sending AC-130 gunships out to attempt to isolate the artillery with infrared sensors. He complemented the gunships by stationing FACs over the general areas where the artillery was emplaced, hoping for visual sightings as well. The effort succeeded in silencing the guns when aircraft were overhead, and Vogt claimed gun kills on several occasions; however, these were unconfirmed. The artillery threat could be managed but not destroyed.

The SAMs being deployed southward into the battle area were Vogt's other major priority. The first days of the invasion had hammered home the lesson that air support in a SAM zone would be a costly and ineffective endeavor. On May 4 Vogt reported that reconnaissance indicated that there were eight operational SAM sites in southern North Vietnam and in Quang Tri Province. On May 5 he wrote: "We have been making a special effort to prevent the movement of SAM coverage toward Hue and are hitting sites as soon as the earth scratching indicates their attempt to construct these sites."[13] Air Force and Navy aircraft also continued to hit the SAMs and their support equipment as they were transported forward. By May 6 Vogt provided another update, this one still more optimistic; his pilots had seen an appreciable decline in the number of SAM launches over the past few days, and had seen evidence that the NVA was simply abandoning much of its damaged and destroyed air defense systems.[14]

Nixon's speech on May 9, the resumption of a sustained air offensive

against North Vietnam, and the decision to mine the North Vietnamese
ports quickly affected the course of events in MR I. The first effect was
psychological, with the mining operation convincing the population of
Hue that the United States was committed to staying the course with
South Vietnam. Graham commented on the complacency of the populace:
"If the tables were reversed and Hue was Hanoi with the enemy at the
gates, every man, woman and child would be filling sandbags. Not so here
. . . So fickle was the spirit of resistance in Hue that a few lazy spring after-
noons and the apparent absence of an explicit and immediate threat served
to dilute it vastly."[15] Nonetheless, the mining contributed to a general
sense that events were beginning to go in South Vietnam's favor.

The military effects were indirect but also worked, on balance, in South
Vietnam's favor. Sorties against the North came out of a fixed sortie count,
and so in a way were drawn from the campaigns in the South. However,
the massive reinforcement of air forces ordered by Nixon largely overwhelmed that effect. Conversely, the initiation of a sustained air campaign
against the North Vietnamese heartland led the Politburo and the General
Staff to recall a significant portion of the air defenses operating in the
Quang Tri campaign, back to the North. Two of the campaign's four air
defense divisions began redeploying to the North on receiving their orders
on May 20. A third, the 377th Air Defense Division, maintained its responsibility for defense of the supply routes to the west. Only the 367th
Air Defense Division remained to provide cover for the combined-arms
force and defend the immediate rear area. So, as the climactic attack on
Hue neared, the NVA forces conducting the offensive found their air defense protection weaker than at any time since the offensive opened.[16]

The ferocious interdiction campaign gave Truong the time he needed
to reconstitute his defenses and turn to the attack. On May 13, I Corps
showed the first offensive spirit of the campaign, as the 369th Marine
Brigade executed a heliborne assault 10 kilometers southwest of Quang
Tri, then swept southward to return to its positions along the My Chanh
River. Two days later, 1st ARVN followed suit, lifting forces into Firebase
Bastogne and retaking that position, along with Firebase Birmingham. For
the first time, the South Vietnamese had begun to take the initiative in the
fight in MR I.

The NVA made a brief bid to resume the offensive on May 21, launching a tank-infantry attack against the northeastern sector of the defenses.
They succeeded in punching through the lines and advancing about ten ki-

lometers along Route 1, but a series of counterattacks by the Marines threw the NVA back to their starting point by nightfall the next day. The Marines followed with a combined heliborne-amphibious attack on May 24, sending two forces behind the NVA lines and again sweeping southward to the My Chanh.

The North Vietnamese had planned to resume their offensive against Hue on May 21, but the difficulties imposed by the South Vietnamese spoiling attacks and the American interdiction campaign forced the campaign headquarters to order a month's delay.[17] During that period the NVA would work to bring its forces and supplies into position for an attack strong enough to unseat the South Vietnamese defenses along the My Chanh, planning then to sustain its momentum long enough to sweep into Hue and drive out its defenders.

The NVA plan for the assault on Hue projected attacks from the north by two divisions, the 304th and the 308th. Simultaneously the 324th Division would strike from the southwest along Route 547, and the 320th would attack in the east, advance to the south, and be prepared to surround the city in coordination with the 324th.[18] Clearly the odds against success for this multidivisional operation were lengthening as the stalemate along the My Chanh continued. Nearly constant aerial and naval attacks punished the NVA troops and disrupted the flow of supplies. Meanwhile, reinforcements flowed forward to I Corps, and the ARVN units worn out during the battles of April were refitted and retrained. Every day brought another incremental swing in the balance of forces, as the South Vietnamese forces recovered from the disasters of the first month of the campaign.

19

THE CENTER HOLDS

In late April, with the collapse of the forces in northern Kontum Province, John Paul Vann turned his inexhaustible energy to the task of rebuilding the defenses of Kontum City. The first task was to marshal the firepower needed to hold the NVA long enough for reinforcements to flow forward. Vann assumed personal control over his most powerful asset, the B-52s, assigning targets for those sent to MR II and tirelessly lobbying to increase his allocation of strikes. Under the umbrella of the B-52, gunship, and fighter sorties, General Dzu redeployed the 23rd Division headquarters and one regiment from its area of operations in the southern highlands, to take over the defense of Kontum. This was an unusual decision in several respects. Short of a strategic emergency, few ARVN divisions ever left their home areas to serve elsewhere. This case was even more remarkable since the national strategic reserve had been exhausted and the defense of the southern highlands was left to territorial forces. The willingness to take this step reflected the improvement in the territorial forces' performance in the years since the Tet Offensive. Conversely, the long years of punishment meted out to the Viet Cong infrastructure in the pacification programs lessened the risk. Vann's judgment of the NVA's offensive capabilities played a role as well. At the end of April he noted: "The NVA has limited manpower resources. NVA forces are completely committed elsewhere, and no reserves are on hand."[1] In this situation there was little prospect of the territorial forces being seriously challenged. By April 28 the 23rd Division headquarters staff was en route to Kontum.

The operational risk of sending the 23rd Division northward was acceptable. It remained to be seen, though, whether it could arrive in time. Neither was it clear that the 23rd would perform any better than the 22nd Division had, once it faced NVA armored forces. The situation would be complicated by the mixture of forces that would fall under the command of Colonel Ly Tong Ba, commander of the 23rd Division. The new defensive structure incorporated four battalions of rangers, sector forces, an Airborne brigade, and one ARVN regiment, all under Ba's command. The defending units reported through a total of nine different chains of command. It was a recipe for confusion at best, paralysis at worst.

Ba assigned the rangers the mission of delaying the NVA advance north of the town, with his 53rd Regiment defending the east and the south. Territorial forces held the southern defenses, protecting the airfield that lay on the south side of the city; Airborne troops manned defenses along Rocket Ridge. The alignment made sense on paper, but placed a premium on cohesion and integration among disparate units, which had never been a hallmark of South Vietnamese military operations. The situation created the threat of the now-familiar command and control issues, a threat that materialized quickly and severely. In his May 1 assessment of the campaign, Abrams commented: "There is evidence of dissension among unit commanders that may cause this sizeable combined force to cave-in in the early stages of any heavy enemy pressure."[2] More specifically, an Army observer recorded that even before the enemy brought any pressure to bear, Colonel Ba had "an increasingly difficult time attempting to get these commanders to respond to his orders."[3] Vann noted that the division commander and the corps commander were "both becoming less effective as they continue without adequate rest and the crisis deepens."[4] The subordinate commanders complained that "their orders are too general and subject to frequent change." The various units even refused to send representatives to coordination meetings, a problem Vann solved by having a senior American present at the staff meetings.

The command issues ran throughout the chain of command, and they started at the very top. Vann owed his unique position to Dzu's presence in command. Nonetheless, toward the end of April and into May he continually called Abrams's attention to Dzu's shortcomings and his flagging morale. By April 28 he informed Abrams: "Increasingly I am finding it difficult to leave Gen Dzu without apprehension that he will overreact and issue orders that are either detrimental to the effort or impossible of accomplishment."[5]

The Army advisors worked feverishly to help the South Vietnamese forces establish a defense and learn the conventional warfare skills they would need against the attack that would come within days. In the immediate aftermath of the 22nd ARVN's disintegration, Vann focused every available air attack mission on the area north of the defenses, seeking to delay and weaken the NVA forces as they moved toward Kontum. Initially the air effort was weakened by bad weather and by the presence of retreating ARVN soldiers, with over a thousand friendly troops in the area, no longer in cohesive units but moving back toward Kontum in small groups.[6]

The North Vietnamese, however, maintained their methodical preparations for the battle to come, taking days to bring up supplies, redeploy their forces forward, and plan. They planned to take Kontum in two phases—first sending in the infantry to establish springboard positions for following operations, and then in the second phase committing the full strength of the armor and infantry to strike into the heart of the city. The NVA relied upon its armored forces to provide the decisive punch that would overwhelm the defenses. This would be a tall order for the 297th Tank Battalion, which by then numbered twenty tanks divided among three companies. The attack would come from the north and northwest, with the three tank companies under the operational command of three different NVA divisions committed to the battle. As at An Loc, the tanks would be engaged in small packages around the perimeter of the defenses.[7]

The defenders took full advantage of the time provided by the NVA. Through late April and early May the ARVN forces moved forward and established a credible defense of the city. Meanwhile, their American advisors arranged for an emergency effort to reequip the forces that had lost so much equipment in the early fighting. They also requested, through Abrams, a range of equipment and support to help them cope with the North Vietnamese armored forces. On April 27, only three days after the fall of Tan Canh, Abrams dispatched a message to the JCS requesting the deployment of helicopter- and ground-fired wire-guided weapons, along with training teams. He planned to station these weapons in Pleiku to defend the U.S. installations and the II Corps headquarters there. Abrams specified that the soldiers sent forward to operate and support these systems would strip their shoulder patches and unit insignia from their uniforms, and would be "forbidden, repeat forbidden, to discuss this subject with the press."[8] Abrams's well-established reluctance to deal with the press was reinforced by the extreme sensitivity entailed in sending Americans back into ground combat. Regardless of the political risk, the Army responded quickly, sending helicopter-mounted antitank weapons that would prove critical in the engagements to come. Nixon's continued pressure to provide every possible advantage to the South Vietnamese was paying off. The U.S. military and the national defense industry had become the "great rear area" for the South Vietnamese. There were bottlenecks in theater—on May 4 Vann complained to Abrams: "Requisitions have been in CLC [Combined Logistics Center] for a week and little or no equipment has been received . . . There is a critical shortage of major items of equipment."[9] But the movement of supplies into theater was accelerating, and authorities from the president down were paying close attention to supply issues. The situation would improve rapidly.

The NVA resumed its advance in late April, moving its armored vehicles into staging areas around Kontum. As May arrived, the dark picture forced Vann to define an evacuation plan for the 2,500 Americans in Pleiku. He submitted the plan on May 3, expecting that the evacuation might begin as early as May 6.

In the aftermath of the loss of Quang Tri on May 2, the defense of Kontum received another blow, this one administered in Saigon. President Thieu called all his corps commanders to a conference at the presidential palace. There he ordered that all Airborne forces in MR II and MR III would be extracted and sent to Saigon within three days. They would be reconstituted and then employed as a counterattack force in MR I, to retake the city of Quang Tri, which Thieu considered to have both military and political importance. Dzu returned to Pleiku late that night and immediately visited Vann in his quarters to recount the story of the meeting with the president. He told Vann that he had protested that the decision to redeploy the Airborne troops would lead to Kontum's fall, since his troops would desert if the Airborne forces were withdrawn; and further, he predicted that An Loc would fall and the NVA would move on Saigon if the Airborne troops left MR III. Nonetheless, Thieu was now intent on allocating his forces to meet the larger political purposes behind the flow of events on the battlefield. Dzu told Vann that he had been ordered on April 30 to hold Kontum City until May 4, a date which Dzu assumed to be significant with regard to secret U.S.-NVN negotiations.[10] Interestingly, Dzu reported that Thieu had shared with the corps commanders the assessment of ARVN performance that Abrams had sent to Laird.

That same night, as Dzu flew northward from Saigon to his headquarters, another element of his forces underwent another stunning defeat. Near the coast, the South Vietnamese regiment defending LZ English, the last ARVN stronghold in northern Binh Long Province, evacuated the post and made its way to the coast for a seaborne evacuation. It was so orderly a departure that U.S. advisors suspected that the garrison had struck a deal with the NVA. Vann consoled himself over the loss with the thought that 2,000 soldiers had survived to fight another day. They had done so, however, at the price of leaving behind a vast store of supplies for exploitation by the NVA—or destruction by American air strikes. Closer to Kontum the NVA continued its methodical advance, eliminating the firebase at Polei Kleng in a three-day battle ending on the morning of May 9. Its loss opened the western approaches to Kontum and represented the last preparatory attack by the NVA as it readied its assault on the city.

By then, though, two weeks had passed since the fall of Tan Canh and Dak To. The South Vietnamese had needed every day and hour of that time, but finally had managed to pull together a structured defense of Kontum. The same day that Vann reported the fall of Polei Kleng, he commented: "The defensive plan for Kontum is finally taking coherent form. The 23rd Division is achieving results in their efforts to establish an integrated defense."[11] The division's three regiments held sectors along the arc from the northwest of the city—held by the 44th Regiment, blocking Route 14—then the 45th Regiment in the north and the 53rd in the northeast. Territorial forces held the southern and southeastern sectors. The swap-out of defending units was complete, and the feverish training programs on conventional defense were well under way. Equally important, the supply situation had begun to improve. American helicopter and C-130 missions flew daily, bringing supplies into the city and removing refugees and the wounded.

The last necessary prerequisite for an effective defense fell into place on May 10, when Thieu finally removed Lieutenant General Dzu from command of II Corps. The only surprise with the replacement lay in its timing. Two weeks earlier Dzu had told Vann that he had a serious heart condition and needed hospitalization, and had asked if Vann could recommend a replacement. Vann assessed that the illness "might be a cover for his relief. I would have to say, however, that he is not in good physical shape and has been too nervous and highly strung to get any sleep for nearly a week."[12] By early May Vann cabled Abrams that Dzu had become convinced that he was "being set up by the President of SVN as a fall guy when and if Kontum falls." He expected to be court-martialed if Kontum fell, and expressed the hope to Vann "that he could be relieved before Kontum City fell so that he could only be charged with the loss of the Tan Canh/Dak To area and northern Binh Dinh." Dzu predicted the loss of nine provinces to the NVA, across all four corps areas; further, he expected these losses to lead to Thieu's resignation. Vann commented that while Dzu "flashes hot and cold," these remarks were more the mark of a "beaten and betrayed man," and stated that, in his view, Thieu needed either to back Dzu visibly and strongly or to relieve him.[13]

Never the boldest or most decisive commander, Dzu had lost his self-confidence with the fall of Tan Canh and, in Truong's words, "spent his time calling President Thieu on the telephone day and night, begging for instructions even on the most trivial things. The big challenge had not come but the pressure had taken its toll."[14] With the fall of Polei Kleng, Thieu replaced Dzu with Major General Nguyen Van Toan, an armored officer. Toan had been under house arrest for raping a 15-year-old girl, but in the national emergency of mid-May 1972 such considerations were viewed as secondary to his combat leadership.

Through this period, American air forces continued to wear down the NVA. Most of the reinforcements that Nixon had ordered into theater had arrived, and the sortie rate rose for both fighter sorties and B-52s. Once the lines stabilized in late April, B-52 targeting in particular seems to have become much more effective than at any earlier point in the war. Vann took direct control of the B-52s and ordered his deputy, General John Hill, to coordinate the other firepower support available to the garrison. Between them, and with the re-Americanization of the air control system, the Americans assumed the critical role of controlling the most effective assets available to the defense. In the short run this was probably necessary, and certainly it worked. The nearly constant bombardment of the NVA reached a peak on May 11. That day, Abrams's concept of rotating the B-52 strikes from corps to corps delivered all the bomber strikes to II Corps. Twenty-five were scheduled. Six were diverted to the An Loc area in response to the crisis there, but nineteen strikes went into the area surrounding Kontum, Vann adjusting them in progress "so as to take advantage of best and most recent intelligence."[15]

The NVA finally launched the attack on May 14. ARVN and U.S. military intelligence had picked up the indications of an impending attack, down to the push time, and the defending forces stood ready. Five NVA regiments, supported by two companies of tanks, prosecuted the attack. In a striking departure from the nearly unvarying script of the past weeks, there was no preparatory artillery barrage, just the forward movement of tanks and troops toward the city.

The major axis of attack came from the northwest, with two regiments of the 320th NVA Division attacking along Route 14. An NVA regiment attacked in the north, with two more from the 2nd NVA Division striking in the northeast and the south. The defenses were prepared, and they quickly shattered the tank force attacking from the northwest. The tanks ran a gauntlet of weapons—infantry teams, Cobra gunships with wire-guided weapons, fighters, and gunships all played a role in turning back the assault. That night the NVA launched a follow-up attack and, in the confusion of the night fighting, achieved a deep penetration in the defenses between the 44th and 53rd Regiments. The NVA continued to pour forces into the gap, and the South Vietnamese countermeasures had little effect. Finally, in desperation, Colonel Ba decided to turn the B-52s against the attackers, despite the urban setting and the close-quarter fighting in progress.

The Kontum defenders had been allocated two B-52 strikes that night. Ba decided to pull back the ARVN defenders in the contested sectors, relying on artillery fire to hold the attack at bay until the B-52s arrived. Truong described the sequel thus: "The two B-52 strikes came exactly on time, as planned, like thunderbolts unleashed over the masses of enemy troops. The explosions rocked the small city and seemed to cave in the ribs of ARVN troops not far away. As the roar subsided, a dreadful silence fell over the scene. At dawn, ARVN search elements discovered several hundred enemy bodies with their weapons scattered all around. Kontum was saved."[16]

The garrison held, but it was a narrow escape. Both sides studied the first attack and adjusted their tactics as they neared the next engagement. Ba realized that the NVA penetration had nearly disintegrated his defenses, and he and Vann decided to tighten the defensive perimeter. The NVA, once its headlong attack had been repulsed, adopted a more subtle strategy than had been employed anywhere else in the offensive. While targeting the command centers and airfield with artillery, the NVA infiltrated sappers and other reconnaissance elements into the city, attempting to create a multi-front problem for the defenders.[17] At intervals they launched tank-infantry assaults against the northern sectors of the defense, on May 20 penetrating the city and forcing Colonel Ba to commit his armored reserve.

The North Vietnamese attempted to cut the flow of supplies into the city, but never succeeded to the extent they had in An Loc. The NVA 95B Regiment maintained a tenacious hold on Route 14 between Kontum and Pleiku, denying all attempts to clear the road. On May 21 General Toan launched a vigorous attack on the blocking force, supported by B-52 fighter strikes. The relief force foundered at the Chu Pao Mountain, known to the Americans as the Rockpile; the road remained closed. One U.S. advisor compared the defenses at the Rockpile to those of Monte Cassino in World War II, with caves up to eighteen feet deep providing shelter even against B-52 strikes.[18]

Airborne resupply for Kontum, though, never faced the sustained crisis that it had over An Loc. The NVA never managed to create the concentrated ring of antiaircraft forces around Kontum that it had near An Loc. It did, however, bring the airfield under artillery fire, and managed to destroy several transports in the weeks after the initial attack. On May 17, for example, an Air Force C-130 was unloading its cargo of ammunition when artillery rounds began striking the airfield. The pilot attempted to take off, but the rear ramp was open, dragging the runway, and the aircraft never reached flying speed. At the end of the runway the aircraft struck a building and the 3,000 rounds of 105-mm ammunition on board detonated. Seven men died in the crash. The airfield reopened on May 18–19 for night resupply missions, and these continued for about a week until the airfield came under direct NVA fire. At that point the garrison reverted to C-130 airdrops and helicopter lift missions for resupply, gradually constraining the supply situation inside the city.

On May 17 Abrams hosted Vice President Spiro Agnew in Saigon. Agnew was in the Far East to attend the Okinawa reversion ceremony, as the United States turned the island back to Japan. He flew to Saigon for a brief meeting with Abrams and Bunker in the Tan Son Nhut Air Base VIP lounge. In their discussion, which lasted about fifty minutes, Abrams offered his views on the conduct of the fighting and the near-term future of the campaign. He gave Agnew a capsule summary of the situation in each military region and in the air campaign, and offered his view that "although it was too early to be certain he was beginning to feel that the thing is turning . . . Although the enemy was still determined to the point where he would attack with companies of only 25 men, his capability for offensive action was greatly decreased."[19]

By that point the situation in MR I had largely stabilized, with Hue no longer in imminent danger; in MR III the garrison in An Loc had turned back the NVA's mass assault two days earlier. Now only Kontum remained in peril, and Abrams planned to concentrate his firepower on the forces threatening the central highlands. "Up until now," he told Agnew, "the situation had been such that he had been required to split the B52 effort fairly evenly between the threatened military regions. However, now he would like to put about two thirds of the effort in Kontum and then, assuming the enemy situation changed as he felt it might, he would move the B-52s north to include North Vietnam where he could start working on the whole enemy system."[20] In the next few days he was to follow precisely that course of action, committing the bulk of his B-52s to MR II to crush the last active NVA offensive thrust.

Meanwhile the monsoon rains were setting in over the central highlands, and the aerial bombardment continued to wear down the NVA forces. A quick decision became imperative for the attackers, and so on May 25, shortly after midnight, the NVA launched its bid for a decisive victory in the highlands. This time the attackers reverted to their normal pattern, opening with an artillery bombardment featuring the 105-mm and 155-mm pieces captured earlier in the campaign. At 0300 the NVA began infiltrating forces through the southern defensive sector held by the territorial forces. About 0830 a conventional tank-infantry attack struck from the staging areas north of the city, penetrating the defenses. Most seriously, the NVA artillery silenced the ARVN batteries inside the city. Vann's deputy, General Hill, circled the city in his helicopter and decided to declare a tactical emergency as the situation deteriorated. The emergency brought an influx of fighters to the city's relief.[21]

The NVA forces followed their initial penetration with night attacks the following evening. At 0115 tanks and infantry again attacked the 53rd Regiment. By 0300 this attack breached the regiment's defenses, but then it ground to a halt about 100 meters inside the breach point, the tanks' passage blocked by the casualties among the NVA infantry, struck while forcing their way through the defenses. The tank crews climbed out of their vehicles to seek a detour, but could find none. Finally, three hours later, the dead and wounded were removed, and the NVA tanks and troops reached within 50 meters of the 44th Regiment's command post. By then, however, day was breaking, and air forces turned the tide of the battle: B-52s, fighters, helicopters with their wire-guided weapons, combining to punish and stall the NVA assault. Helicopters destroyed the last two T-54s, and the attack ground to a halt.

At nightfall on May 26 the NVA mounted yet another assault, this time sending the 64th NVA Regiment into the seam between the 53rd and the 45th ARVN regiments on the north side of the city. Once again the B-52s arrived to demolish the attacking force, enabling the ARVN defenders to seal off the penetration. The sustained attacks had left the NVA lodged deep in the city, however, with more forces moving to the attack. The next morning brought renewed combat, with two NVA regiments supported by tanks moving forward, triggering a melee in the city. The ARVN defenders countered the tank attacks, but the NVA fanned out to form pockets of resistance through the northern part of the city. The North Vietnamese held their positions tenaciously, refusing to be dislodged despite the aerial bombardment. A North Vietnamese mortar round ignited the main ARVN ammunition dump, detonating about 60 percent of the ammunition stored there. That evening Vann persuaded Ba to pull the 45th Regiment from its forward position and use it to bolster the defenses in the town. This also provided more freedom of action for the B-52s now conducting massed attacks in the area.[22] By this point, though, the NVA held the east end of town and many of the compounds across the north side of the city, along with the entire south side of the airfield.

The tide began to turn toward the evening of May 28. That morning Vann, expecting bad weather, arranged for radar-controlled attack sorties every twenty minutes, from midafternoon until after midnight. The North Vietnamese attempted no major attacks that day. The ARVN garrison began to conduct counterattacks, and the NVA attackers began to face increasingly difficult problems with supply, with B-52s repeatedly striking their storage and transport network. The radar strikes contributed to a total of 203 attack sorties flown around Kontum during a 36-hour period between the afternoon of May 27 and the early morning of May 29. As May 29 came to an end, Vann estimated that most of the attacking NVA infantry units were at about half their strength at the outset of the campaign, with B-52s having inflicted the vast majority of NVA casualties.[23]

The NVA history of this campaign recorded the end of the offensive, summarizing: "There were no tanks left, there was a shortage of supplies and equipment, the arrival of the rainy season made transportation of supplies much more difficult, and the enemy was conducting concentrated air and artillery attacks and launching counterattacks." In its aftermath, the North Vietnamese conducted their usual cold-eyed assessment of the failure, attributing it primarily to their dispersal of the armored forces and their tactical error in committing it to battle before the preparatory attacks were complete.[24] As in the other campaigns of this offensive, shortfalls in crews' basic skills played a role in their failure as well.

On May 31 Vann terminated the tactical emergency at Kontum, and by the following day the NVA was reduced to three pockets of resistance in the city and a completely defensive posture. The crisis in the central highlands was over, though hard fighting continued along Route 14 and in operations clearing the NVA from the city. On June 8 the American air control system at Pleiku recorded the end of NVA resistance in Kontum. That night resupply operations resumed at the airport, and six C-130s landed safely.

The NVA offensives in MR I and MR III opened dramatically and ended quietly. There were no culminating battles and mass retreats, just the gradual erosion of NVA strength and the release of pressure against defending ARVN troops. In MR II, though, the situation was exactly opposite. Here the opening of the campaign was gradual, with a methodical, incremental approach to the primary objective; and the end of the campaign could be clearly marked with one climactic event. The event did not occur in Kontum, however, but near a lonely road connecting Kontum and Pleiku to the south. There, in the moment of victory, on the night of June 9, John Paul Vann died in a helicopter crash—not caused by enemy action, but apparently by his pilot becoming spatially disoriented and flying into the ground. His death marked the end of the campaign in the highlands, and the end of an era in the American involvement in Southeast Asia. Vann died at the highest moment of triumph in his long career, before the gradual decline of South Vietnam's fortunes. He had achieved his lifetime goal, commanding massed forces in battle, and had emerged victorious despite his initial miscalculations. Vann could legitimately claim to have played an irreplaceable role in the crisis of April–May 1972.

20

STALEMATE AT THE MY CHANH RIVER

$\mathcal{B}$y mid-May the battle north of Hue settled into a standoff, with both sides building forces toward an offensive they expected to launch in late June. Like any standoff, this one intrinsically favored the side commanding superior firepower. Despite the continued effectiveness of the NVA's 130-mm artillery, this was an area of massive South Vietnamese advantage, and Truong did everything he could to take advantage of that superiority. Immediately upon taking command he established the command centers necessary to coordinate the many sources of firepower support available to him—organic artillery, Vietnamese Air Force attack aircraft, USAF and Navy fighters, naval gunfire support, and B-52s—seeking to eliminate the chaos and inefficiency that had plagued this function under his predecessor. Truong established his headquarters in the Hue Citadel and requested that the American Direct Air Support Center (DASC) for I Corps be moved from Danang to that location. Seventh Air Force initially hesitated, reluctant to undergo the expense and disruption of relocating a major command center. The DASC commander initially attempted to meet Truong's request by sending two underqualified officers to Hue as a forward liaison element.[1] This quickly proved militarily inadequate, and at Truong's repeated request, Vogt agreed to send the command center forward. Truong also instituted a tactic he named "Loi Phong" (Thunder

Hurricane), which he described as "a sustained offensive by fire conducted on a large scale. The program scheduled the concentrated use of all available kinds of firepower . . . for each wave of attack and with enough intensity as to completely destroy every worthwhile target detected, especially those files of enemy soldiers and materials that were streaming toward staging areas near Hue."[2]

Meanwhile, south of Hue, I Corps worked to reconstitute the units shattered in the NVA attacks of late April. The material requirements were massive, especially when considered in the context of the simultaneous call for support in the other two military regions. Truong later listed the major equipment items needing replacement: 43 M-48 and 66 M-41 tanks, another 103 M-113 armored personnel carriers, along with a total of 140 artillery pieces.[3] In addition to these weapons, the 3rd ARVN Division needed nearly complete replacement of its complement of command and control gear, trucks, individual and crew-served weapons, gas masks, ammunition, and so on. Supplies poured by ship and plane into Danang for redistribution to the units in combat, and to those undergoing refitting in the training centers around Hue.

The psychological component of this reconstitution was as massive and important as the material aspect. The troops and units that had been routed by the North Vietnamese had, naturally enough, lost confidence in themselves and in their leadership. The debacles of late April reinforced the long-standing South Vietnamese sense of inferiority, and of the invincibility of their North Vietnamese enemies. The limited offensives that Truong ordered in mid- and late May were directed as much at psychological gains as at any direct destruction they might cause the enemy. By his account, they had a powerful effect, unsettling the North Vietnamese and reinvigorating the confidence of the South Vietnamese at all levels. The sight of South Vietnamese forces sweeping through the North Vietnamese rear areas and overpowering the disorganized resistance provided visual confirmation that the tide of battle had turned in MR I. The restoration of confidence reached the citizens of Hue, who in early June began returning to the city from their refuges along the coast.[4]

By the end of May the North Vietnamese had been stymied on all three fronts, and the demands of the ground commanders for air support subsided. Finally Abrams had the opportunity to put a counter-logistics campaign into motion. Planning for this effort had begun weeks earlier, as Abrams anticipated the end of the crisis period that had existed since the start of the offensive. Once the battlefield situation had stabilized, he expected to punish the NVA logistical system, from the immediate rear of the attacking forces outward into the base areas and transit routes in Laos. To execute this campaign, though, he would have to maintain his tasking authority over the B-52s, and over the bulk of the tactical attack sorties flown by Seventh Air Force and Carrier Task Force 77.

Abrams had high expectations for this offensive, and so reacted strongly when McCain proposed a competing plan, focused on cutting the flow of supplies southward through the North Vietnamese city of Dong Hoi. McCain and the Pacific Command staff correctly assessed that Dong Hoi constituted a bottleneck for the North Vietnamese road and rail systems, and suggested a concentrated campaign against that point, employing the sensors previously used over the Ho Chi Minh Trail. These sensors would detect movement and provide targeting information for the American attack forces.[5]

McCain issued the message proposing the sensor field the day after the initiation of Linebacker, expecting the sensor and interdiction operations in the North Vietnamese panhandle to provide a logical complement to the campaign being conducted farther north. Abrams rejected the proposal, however, pointing out the difficulties in achieving sensor read-outs in a high-threat area, and in making use of any information that might be derived from the sensors. In clear weather, visual attacks would provide much more effective interdiction than the sensors, and in bad weather, attacks would be prohibitively risky given the need for defense suppression. The sensors would therefore be militarily useless, and an overall detriment given the effort and risk that would be invested in implanting them.[6] The interposition of Pacific Command in the chain of command had always been an inconvenience for Abrams, an irritation compounded by his dislike of McCain. The attempt of the headquarters in Honolulu to intrude into the details of tactical operations was notably unwelcome.

Abrams issued the operations order for the counter-logistics campaign on May 21, three days after rebuffing McCain's proposal and eleven days after the opening of Linebacker. The plan outlined a four-phase campaign aimed at interdicting the North Vietnamese forces' logistical structure throughout the immediate battle area, stretching from the A Shau Valley and the front lines, and back into the logistical areas in southern North Vietnam and Laos. The campaign would be a continuing, coordinated effort incorporating every attack asset in theater. In the first phase, the de-

struction of all significant bridges, ferries, and fords in MR I would continue, along with interdiction of traffic through the A Shau Valley.[7] The
second phase would extend the destruction into Route Pack 1, with attacks on bridges, ferries, watercraft, and fords throughout the area by tactical aircraft. The fighter attacks would be complemented by B-52 strikes
against area logistical targets. In the third phase, Air Force and Navy
forces would establish a choke point in the Dong Hoi area, with attacks on
bridges, waterways, transshipment points, and transportation repair facilities. Finally, in phase four the campaign would extend into the logistical
network in Laos.

The plan projected the employment of thirty B-52 sorties per day, attacking five targets. This sortie count represented about one-third of the
available heavy bomber strikes, a proportion only possible because of the
weakened state of NVA forces on the battlefield. Abrams wanted to concentrate the strikes, and so directed that each attack would employ six
bombers instead of the three-ship cells that had previously conducted
strikes. The bombers would saturate area targets, and would be supplemented by tactical forces attacking point targets and moving forces. Naval
gunfire would continue to operate against the coastal highways, and inland
waterways would be mined. Over time, this investment of forces offered
the prospect of throttling the flow of supplies and troops forward to the
NVA units along the My Chanh.

Abrams expected to open the campaign on May 27, but the crisis at
Kontum required a delay in the program. The first B-52 strikes struck
RP 1 on May 31, signaling the opening of the offensive. Almost before his
air offensive had begun, Abrams faced another threat to his use of the
bombers. On June 9 Admiral McCain proposed a B-52 strike against Hanoi, to be conducted on June 12 by 24 bombers with the lavish support
package necessary to control the defensive reaction. The plan raised again
the old contention about the use of B-52s. Abrams vigorously protested
against the disruption this strike would impose on his counter-logistics
campaign, arguing that, directly or indirectly, it would come at the cost of
75 sorties and "a loss of 2,574 bombs on targets in the MACV area."[8] Ten
weeks into the Easter Offensive, the old issue of B-52 employment still
served as an irritant despite the intervening events, the flow of forces into
theater and the bleeding of the North Vietnamese forces. Abrams was protecting his interests as he had all along, but with two weeks until his
change of command, this exchange seems as much a product of principle

and personal frustrations as of military criteria. Abrams was under no illusions about his standing in the White House, and was unwilling to accommodate a diversion in his most valuable resource in order to court favor that would never come. In the end, the strike was canceled, and the B-52 sorties that day were distributed fairly evenly across the theater—21 in the North Vietnamese panhandle, 30 in MR 1, 15 in MR 2, still others in Laos, Cambodia, and in southern RVN.

Three days later, on June 15, CINCPAC issued guidance for air operations that once again threatened to divert air attack sorties from the MACV area of operations. Concerned about the lack of pressure against the North Vietnamese heartland, McCain asked his subordinate commanders to forward plans that would increase the proportion of strikes in northern North Vietnam to half of all Linebacker missions. Abrams's reply was brisk and to the point: he had no objection to trade-offs within the overall Linebacker strikes, "as long as the total effort in RVN and RP-1 remains the same, and COMUSMACV retains authority to divert USAF tacair sorties from Linebacker to support tactical emergencies in RVN."[9]

Abrams did not delve into the military merits of the proposal, concerned only that it should not affect his operations. The Seventh Air Force director of operations, Major General Alton Slay, attacked the idea directly on its merits. Slay assessed that the only way to achieve that balance would be to fly two Linebacker missions per day—a completely unfeasible proposal, given the limitations on air refueling support. Slay also pointed out that the practice of counting sorties failed to account for the vastly greater effectiveness of precision weaponry—estimating that each sortie dropping guided weapons had the effect of eight conventional attacks. He contended, finally, that mechanically multiplying sorties against the North Vietnamese heartland would detract from the attacks in RP 1, which had a "direct and immediate impact on the ground battle in MR-1."[10] It is interesting that Slay, instead of Vogt, signed the Seventh Air Force position on this issue. His message aligned the command with Abrams, prioritizing the directly useful strikes against the North Vietnamese panhandle over the politically useful attacks against the Hanoi-Haiphong heartland. It is possible, though not confirmed by the evidence available, that Vogt approved the message but avoided identification with a position opposing the clear intent of the White House. In any case, the arguments against an expanded campaign in RP 6 carried the day for the moment, leaving the vast majority of strikes in RP 1.

Abrams thus maintained control over the overwhelming majority of the firepower available in theater. That would yield little benefit, however, unless this power could be directed effectively at the enemy. From the start of the war, the North Vietnamese had proven their ability to counter American firepower by their mobility and concealment. If this operation was to prove any different, the U.S. forces would have to find a way to uncover the North Vietnamese supplies and transport in RP 1, and strike them despite the formidable defenses in the area.

One component of the answer was clear, though it was not an easy choice. It was impossible to operate slow observation aircraft in a high-threat environment such as existed in RP 1, or in the area of South Vietnam north of the My Chanh line. Only fast movers could survive in that sort of arena, and even their operations came at a high risk. F-4s operating as fast FACs faced loss rates several times that of normal attack missions. Seventh Air Force had suspended the fast FAC program in January 1972 as the risk to air crews came to seem too high. The emergency facing South Vietnam, and the inability of other methods to find worthwhile targets, forced its resumption in April.[11] The risk-gain calculus shifted when South Vietnam's existence stood in the balance.

Commanders minimized the risk as best they could, scheduling their most experienced air crews for the mission. But repeated operations into the defenses in that area could only be justified as the best of a series of bad choices. The most-used alternative was to send flights out on armed reconnaissance sorties, assigned a stretch of road or an area to search and attack any targets discovered. Over time, however, it became clear that the fast FACs were more effective in finding targets, and that the added risk of fast-FAC operations had to be accepted.[12]

The constant search for a more survivable and effective means of operating in RP 1 catalyzed a partnership between the fast FACs and the sole remaining reconnaissance squadron in Seventh Air Force, the 14th Tactical Reconnaissance Squadron at Udorn RTAFB. These daytime efforts were complemented by night missions flown by the "Owl FACs" of the 497th Tactical Fighter Squadron, from Ubon RTAFB. The Owls nightly launched three two-ship flights to cover MR 1 and RP 1, working to deny the NVA logistics units the sanctuary of darkness. Seventh Air Force and its units had come a very long way from the shabby intelligence support and the clumsy command and control that characterized the first days of this campaign.

The American attackers always sought the opportunity to strike the NVA air defenses, and the North Vietnamese histories offer abundant testimony to their effectiveness in disrupting the deployment of SAM batteries in support of NVA offensive action. The Air Defense Service history, for example, recounts the trials of a unit marching continuously for 13 days, with troops sometimes receiving only 40–80 grams of rice per day. Another unit recorded running out of gasoline for their generators and being forced to send out a three-man cell to steal fuel from an enemy base. Yet another battalion was forced to cannibalize vehicles destroyed by B-52 strikes in order to continue their deployments. In the end, as the attack on Hue neared, none of the missile units was able to deploy into position to support the offensive.[13] The movement of supplies forward to the campaign staging areas, likewise, suffered grievously from the continuing air attacks. In the face of this constant attrition, NVA logisticians were able to provide only about 30 percent of the supplies called for in their plan.[14]

The North Vietnamese artillery, especially the 130-mm M-46, remained Vogt's main concern. He had not yet found a satisfactory means of detecting and targeting the NVA artillery, though U.S. air forces could temporarily suppress them while orbiting overhead. In mid-June Vogt turned to yet another approach, this time attempting to adapt an acoustic sensor system to locate the artillery as it fired. The plan seemed feasible, consisting basically of an extension of technologies employed before along the Ho Chi Minh Trail. The concept was to use acoustic sensors seeded through the artillery's operating areas to triangulate the guns' positions. The sensors would feed data into the system at Igloo White, which would then relay the information to I Corps so that the guns could be struck. In practice, the plan ran into an array of technical and tactical problems. The system could not discriminate between outgoing and incoming fire, and was plagued with the same problems of sensor reliability that had affected operations along the Laotian infiltration routes. In the end, the acoustic system recorded a lot of "booms," but did not contribute to the destruction of a single gun.

Meanwhile, Truong continued his methodical preparations for the offensive he expected to kick off on June 28. Over the first ten days of June, with the tactical situation eased, he repositioned his forces across the front. From June 11 to June 18 he ordered attacks westward toward the A Shau Valley, while the Marine and Airborne divisions probed the NVA defenses north of the My Chanh, testing their strength. From June 19 until June 27

I Corps executed a deception plan, preparing for an airborne assault on Cam Lo and an amphibious attack near the DMZ.

With about two weeks to go before the offensive opened, Truong submitted his plan for the attack to the U.S. advisory team and through the South Vietnamese chain of command. The Americans reviewing his proposal considered it too risky, particularly in view of the threat posed to Hue from the southwest. Truong flew to Saigon to present his plan to Thieu and his advisors, both Vietnamese and American. Thieu rejected the plan, and Truong flew back to Hue. The next day, according to his account, he called Thieu's national security advisor, General Dang Van Quang, and told him that I Corps would submit no further plans. If Saigon wanted Truong to do anything, he said, "they should give me a Vietnamese translation of whatever plan they want me to execute and I would comply."[15] Thieu called back, requesting another review the following day. Truong complied, and this time Thieu approved the plan. Preparations could proceed for the offensive, still planned for June 28.

Meanwhile the NVA struggled to prepare its units for its own offensive, still scheduled to begin on June 20. The 367th Air Defense Division decided, as the day neared, to send an SA-2 battalion into northern MR 1 to participate in the combined-arms offensive. The battalion began its deployment on June 17, but its fate captures in microcosm the destruction and dislocation imposed by the air forces operating overhead. Forced to deploy at night, the unit was crossing the Ben Hai River when "the battalion's transceiver vehicle ran off the edge of the underwater road at the ford and flooded with water, the fire control computer vehicle rolled over, and then an enemy attack knocked out the battalion's command vehicle."[16] The direct and indirect effects of the air operations prevented the unit, or any SA-2 unit, from participating in the eventual offensive.

The NVA sought to break the grip of the counter-logistics campaign by any means possible. Probably the greatest obstacle to successful attack on Hue lay in the interdiction efforts along the A Shau Valley and the routes leading toward the city. These roads were under almost constant observation and attack from the AC-130 gunships. The NVA air defense history noted: "Because of the limited firepower we had in the area, our effectiveness in night combat was low, so the enemy was able to block operations along this route for a considerable period of time. The movement of our mechanized vehicles was suspended."[17] The campaign headquarters decided to send an SA-7 unit down to the A Shau Valley to ambush an AC-130 and open the roads.

The 241st Antiaircraft Artillery Regiment assigned the mission to a combat team under the command of Le Van Truc. The team spent twenty days "slogging over mountain trails, wading through streams, studying the enemy's pattern of operations, and developing attack tactics," before shooting down an AC-130 over the A Shau Valley in the early evening on June 18.[18] The missile hit the right inboard engine; the aircraft, burning, cartwheeled in the air and broke apart. Twelve of the fifteen crew members died.

However remarkable this success, it was too little and too late to regain an acceptable logistical position before the attack. The long-awaited North Vietnamese offensive broke on June 20 and continued for several days. It was so anemic, however, that the American leadership did not even recognize it as the NVA's climactic effort. Vogt did not comment on the NVA offensive until its fourth day, when his daily report noted: "Activity in MR I in the last 24 hours appears to be a major attempt by the enemy to preempt General Truong's planned offensive. The enemy used a large number of tanks against the airborne defense positions, and lost 17 of them." He concluded, "The initial encounter, however, has turned out most favorably for the friendlies, and if anything, should aid the chances of a successful RVNAF offensive."[19] Vogt then turned to a review of the day's Linebacker missions and his plans for the following day's attacks against North Vietnam.

The NVA history briefly summarized the results of the offensive: "Because we had been slow to change our campaign tactics as the enemy strengthened his forces and solidified his defenses, our assault against the My Chanh defensive line from 20 to 26 June was unsuccessful, and we suffered losses that were twice as high as those we suffered during the two previous attacks."[20] It is unclear what tactical adjustments might have enabled the attack to succeed, in the face of a prepared defense with overwhelming material superiority. The defeat, and the heavy losses it entailed, reflected more the inappropriate obsession with the offensive by men back in Hanoi than any failings on the part of the men doing the fighting. As Vogt suggested, it all worked to the advantage of the South Vietnamese offensive, drawing down NVA forces and diverting them from preparing for the ARVN offensive that was soon to come.

General Truong unleashed the South Vietnamese counteroffensive, code-named Lam Son 72, as scheduled on June 28. His objective was to recapture Quang Tri City and eventually the whole province, as a political and diplomatic necessity. With the NVA under equally strict orders to hold on to the city, the campaign would consume most of the summer and impose an incredibly high cost on both North and South Vietnamese forces.

The opening of Lam Son 72 snuffed out the last offensive threat posed by the NVA. On the night it opened, the Central Military Party Committee directed the campaign headquarters to shift to a counterattack campaign. The campaign would now be "aimed at killing large numbers of enemy troops, firmly maintaining control of the liberated zone, and resolutely defeating all enemy counterattacks."[21] Although the high command continued to treasure the prospect of a renewed offensive, that became increasingly unrealistic.[22] First at An Loc, then at Kontum, and now finally north of Hue, the North Vietnamese forces had stagnated, had been fatally weakened, and finally had been forced into bitter retreat. The Politburo, far away in Hanoi, would continue to press for action, especially in the countryside, but its direction and exhortations would have little effect. The Easter Offensive was over. The events it had set in motion, though, would continue to be played out on the battlefields, in the air over North Vietnam, and at the negotiating tables in Paris.

21

REACTIVE ADVERSARIES

Through late May, as Nixon traveled to Austria and then to Moscow, the air campaign intensified and spread. Seventh Air Force continued its massive strikes, though still struggling against weather that frequently denied access to primary targets. As Nixon noted to his disgust, the weather prevented any attacks in Route Pack 6 from May 14 through May 16. But on the 17th Air Force fighters struck the bridge at Viet Tri, the single most critical bottleneck on the northwest railway. The next day F-4s returned to the Hanoi POL storage facility, this time with precision weapons, while another strike group knocked out the Lang Giai bridge in the Chinese buffer zone. Weather again prevented strikes on the 19th and the 21st, but a brief clear spell on the 20th permitted Vogt to direct a strike against the Hanoi transformer station—the first strike against North Vietnam's power grid. The next two days brought crippling attacks against the North Vietnamese rail links with China. On May 22 one flight of F-4s destroyed several bridges on the northwest railroad, and the following day Phantoms from the 8th Tactical Fighter Wing attacked the Bac Giang bridge on the northeast railroad. Problems with weather and with coordination persisted, but the attacks now were beginning to take a toll on the North Vietnamese infrastructure.

Meanwhile, the carrier-based strikes continued. Smaller and more flexible than the Air Force strike packages, Navy strikes were able to attack a much wider array of targets throughout the DRV's transportation system, and were far more able to work around marginal weather conditions than the multi-wing "mass gaggles" employed by Seventh Air Force. On May 16, for example, bad weather kept the Air Force out of northern North Vietnam, but Navy fighters struck a total of twenty-five transportation targets—bridges, sidings, refueling facilities, and so on—in the DRV. The next day the Air Force destroyed the Viet Tri bridge on the northwest rail line, as the Navy attacked thirty fixed installations. As on the previous day, these were predominantly associated with the rail and road networks, but flights struck petroleum storage and military installations as well.[1]

The crescendo of violence mounted as the month progressed. In April the Americans had launched 1,644 attack sorties, land- and sea-based, against North Vietnam. In May that number more than tripled, to 5,438 sorties.[2] Despite all the rapid adjustments made by the North Vietnamese at the outset of the offensive, the air attacks continued to grind away at the transportation infrastructure. The NVA Air Force–Air Defense Command counted 68 bridges destroyed by the end of the month, and commented: "Our air defense forces achieved poor results in their efforts to counter the enemy's use of laser-guided bombs." This ineffectiveness reflected, in the command's view, still deeper failures: "Our analysis of the enemy was weak, our efforts to find ways of dealing with the enemy attacks were not sufficiently comprehensive, and we had not fully employed the principle of military democracy."[3] After nearly two months of the U.S. air offensive, the NVA's efforts to analyze and respond to it had not yet resulted in effective counters. The Americans had seized the initiative on all levels—strategic, tactical, and technical—and the North Vietnamese air defense system was staring at the prospect of catastrophic failure.

As the NVA gained experience, however, and became more familiar with the new American tactics and technologies, it began to reach toward technical and tactical solutions. In mid-May senior members of the 361st Air Defense Division, responsible for defending Hanoi, hosted a conference to discuss the lessons learned thus far. At the end of the conference the deputy division commander, Tran Xanh, presented an overview of the new tactics being employed over Hanoi, with proposed solutions. His presentation covered the new jamming techniques used by the Americans, their effects on NVA equipment and displays, and means of countering them with the equipment on hand. He emphasized the importance of improving the ability to track targets using optical systems instead of radar tracking. Optical tracking and guidance would partially neutralize the new American electronic warfare capabilities, both by avoiding the jamming and by delaying warning to U.S. fighters that they were under attack.[4] Meanwhile another inspection team visited warehouses and machine shops to ensure that matériel was being dispersed as ordered by headquarters.

By the end of May, however, the North Vietnamese air defenders had still not found effective countermeasures to the new U.S. tactics. None of their three major elements could claim success. The antiaircraft artillery had not yet been able to defeat the Americans' laser-guided weaponry. The Air Force had managed to control its loss rate and had aggressively attacked the enemy, but was "having problems categorizing and selecting the correct targets." Most seriously, the surface-to-air missile forces continued to fire "large quantities of missiles" ineffectively, because "they were still fighting mechanically using old fighting methods that were not suited to the equipment and flight formations currently being used by the enemy." As with all military forces, old habits of training and employment died hard. In particular, the missile operators had not adjusted to the higher jamming power of the new American pods, which enabled wider spacing among the aircraft in a flight: "In this situation, if we aimed at the center of the jamming signal, as we had before, the missiles would not pass close enough to an enemy aircraft to set off the radio frequency fuse, so our missiles were flying right past their targets."[5] While a technical solution to the jamming might not be feasible, this understanding would at least give missile operators some chance of tracking and engaging their real targets.

On May 30 the Central Military Party Committee issued a new directive governing air defense against the ongoing campaign. In essence, the directive called for greater flexibility and adaptability: "We must quickly adjust and update our battle plans . . . quickly review and derive lessons learned from the recent wave of battles and provide timely guidance in selecting suitable fighting methods."[6] It also called for improved training programs, and for better coordination between the services and technical branches.

The Air Defense–Air Force Command conducted a careful study of its recent operations, sending headquarters teams out to the units to compile a "preliminary review of Air Force combat operations from 8 May to 2 June." As summarized in the official history: "This review clearly spelled out the enemy air force's tactics and schemes, the situation and the capabilities of our own Air Force, and raised a number of issues regarding combat guidance formulas and concepts, command organization, technical support, and tactics used by our different types of aircraft against each specific combat opponent."[7]

The missile forces, too, used recent combat operations to guide their deployment and employment patterns. On June 10 the Air Defense Command issued direction on the next phase of operations, emphasizing the use of optical guidance and new tactical deployment patterns to strengthen their ability to engage enemy aircraft in a jamming environment. The command directed that all SA-2 missile systems were to be modified to enable optical guidance by June 30, and additionally called for a series of tactical measures, including "increased use of a combination of mobile and static forces, spreading out our combat formations to provide forces on the inner and outer perimeter and forces to engage the enemy at long range, on both flanks of the enemy jamming signals, attacking the enemy both during his approach to and his exit from the target, engaging the enemy from the front and from the rear, etc."[8]

These analyses and directives would propel an ever-evolving tactical array for the North Vietnamese air defense. Ultimately, though, there was no chance that the defenses could turn back the U.S. air offensive. The combination of numbers, technology, and driving political will exerted by the Americans would inevitably overwhelm any defenses constructed by the DRV. These defenses could multiply the cost to the U.S. forces, they could force a massive diversion of effort to defense suppression, and they could reduce the damage done to the North Vietnamese war effort and infrastructure. Through the summer months, they succeeded in those limited objectives. But in the end, the attackers would reach their targets and impose an ever-increasing amount of damage. The North Vietnamese would therefore be forced to complement their active defenses with a range of measures that would reach into every aspect of their society and economy.

The air raids, for example, necessitated a continuous upgrading of civil defense measures. In this endeavor, the experience gained in the earlier air war stood the North Vietnamese in good stead. They had survived an earlier onslaught, they had practiced their procedures, and they had been preparing for a new air war in the years since the bombing halt. The evacuation that had begun in mid-April continued; by May 30, the British diplomat Joe Wright reported, the evacuation was more complete than that conducted in 1966–1968, and the population more disciplined. A local in-

formant told Wright that about two-thirds of the factory workers in Hanoi
had been evacuated, along with their machinery. The informant noted that
about a third of the machinery for the city's production facilities had been
left in the countryside when the factories returned to Hanoi in 1968.[9]

Nonetheless, again according to Wright's informant, the evacuation
imposed significant hardships on the population and stresses on the government. The families evacuated might be split among several reception
centers, depending on the availability of schools for any children sent into
the country. The need to feed, shelter, and protect the evacuated population in itself stretched the capabilities of the government. It also proved
difficult to maintain the supply chain for production facilities and to ensure that the people evacuated found productive employment.

Through the summer, the municipalities also took measures to create
shelters for all citizens, both at home and at work. The government directed that evacuation centers provide "an air raid shelter wherever there
is a person . . . Earth must be built up around the walls of classrooms and
operating rooms to resist the impact of bombs and bullets when the enemy
attacks suddenly, and there must be communications trenches to the air
raid shelter area." The guidance, disseminated in *Quan Doi Nhan Dan*, also
specified: "The evacuation area should also be dispersed, and not be in a
place of concentrated population or of assemblies of people. Houses must
be small, with enough room for only 10 people or less. All houses, classrooms, and places of work must be dispersed and hidden over a broad
landscape . . . If meetings are held at night, it is essential that lights not be
visible from the outside. Every way must be found to maintain the secrecy
of the evacuation area."[10]

Outlying cities came under attack as well as Hanoi and Haiphong, and
they responded vigorously. For example, Thai Nguyen, north of Hanoi,
was the site of the DRV's single steel works and also a transportation link.
The area was a frequent target of the Air Force aircraft operating out of
Thailand. By November "nearly every family has from one to two air-raid
shelters." Making medical care quickly and widely available became a municipal priority. *Quan Doi Nhan Dan* reported: "The municipal infirmary
has just opened an advanced training course in first-aid, in preventing
cave-ins of shelters, and at the same time, it has organized hundreds more
of fully equipped units with medicine, cotton and standard utensils, and
every week, it practiced rescue procedures to react quickly and effectively
in case of emergency."[11]

In Quang Binh Province, just north of the DMZ, the population assumed a more or less subterranean existence. Under the constant threat of attack, the population implemented exhaustive civil defense measures. *Quan Doi Nhan Dan* summarized these measures:

> The cooperatives are all divided into small groups when they go to work, bringing with them stretchers and medicine in order to provide quick assistance during a surprise attack. The militia forces and the Youth Group chapters . . . have dug thousands more shelters in the fields so the people of the cooperative can produce in complete safety. Anti-aircraft units have been placed in fields which are often attacked by the enemy, ready to destroy the American planes and, at the same time, to protect production.[12]

Production was important, the security of the population was important, but the real crux of the war at this point was the regime's ability to keep its supply lines open. With the harbors mined and the rail system under attack, it was imperative to find new means of moving supplies, food, and petroleum into the DRV and onward to the battlefield. The Americans aimed at closing off the flow of supplies into the DRV, then destroying the supplies in storage or in transit. In mid-May Moorer outlined his projected time lines and operational strategy for Secretary Laird: "It will probably take the enemy several months to accommodate to the loss of his port facilities and the disruption of his principal overland lines of communication. Our primary effort in the early phases of Linebacker will be directed toward delaying this accommodation . . . The enemy is now faced with the enormous task of completely readjusting his supply and distribution system to handle increased rail shipments from China. It will take 4 to 6 months of uninterrupted effort for the enemy to complete the adjustment."[13]

Moorer knew well enough that the need for readjustment would not be limited to the North Vietnamese. He continued: "Our forces and tactics will require continuous adjustment based on the enemy's efforts to accommodate the closure of the ports, and his ability to reconstitute his defenses and develop alternative LOC [lines of communication]. As new targets are developed, they will be struck with available air assets and [naval gunfire]."[14]

Moorer's projections reflected the Americans' tendency to underestimate the logistical resourcefulness of their NVA adversaries. The North's accommodation to the new operational situation appeared within weeks, not the months projected by the CJCS.

First and always, the North Vietnamese could call on their long-established expertise in road and rail repair and their ferries and road bypasses. The NVA pre-positioned repair supplies and equipment along the rail and road lines, and normally could repair a dropped bridge span in two weeks. They had also acquired floating pontoon bridges, and could use those to substitute for fixed bridges that had been destroyed. These expedients imposed penalties in time and manpower, but normally permitted the movement of traffic even under attack.

Against the power being wielded by the Americans, however, more fundamental measures would be required. As an initial response, the DRV instituted a shuttle system, using trucks to bypass the cuts in the rail lines. By early June, though, the railroad had been so thoroughly battered that a shuttle system was no longer effective. The North Vietnamese then established an equivalent of a port facility at Lang Son, near the Chinese border on Route 1. There the DRV logistical system received material from China, categorized and stored it, and transshipped it to onward destinations. Assault youth provided the additional manpower necessary to sustain this operation, working along with construction, engineering, and transportation units of the army. The North Vietnamese established a new air defense division, the 375th, to protect this compound and Route 1 north of Hanoi.[15]

American intelligence detected the first indicators of this logistical reorientation in late May, as sources in China reported three shipments of trucks located about 500 miles north of the Sino-Vietnam border. The intelligence assessment also noted published reports that "backlogs of material for NVN were occurring on rail lines in China" with more than a thousand cars holding at the border. Two weeks later there arrived the first accounts of trucks in use, working off the backlog of supplies that had awaited onward movement. On June 6 Navy fighters sighted "many truck headlights" along Route 1. The next day a reconnaissance flight found 8–10 trucks per mile in the area. Three days later a flight of Navy A-7s on a night reconnaissance mission estimated a traffic density of 30–40 trucks per mile along a 77-mile stretch of Route 1 extending from China to Hanoi. The intelligence appraisal commented: "This type of shuttling activity using from 2000 to 3000 vehicles is highly unprecedented and may signal the beginning of severe supply needs."[16] More likely, it indicated the need to distribute the backlog at the border and the desire to move the material before American countermeasures appeared in force.

Although the movement along the Route 1 corridor accounted for the bulk of the traffic from China, the North Vietnamese road network included "15 to 20 road connections [that] cross the China-Vietnam border with a combined capacity of 10,000 tons per day in the dry season and 3,000 tons per day in the wet season (June-September)." The CIA estimated that the North Vietnamese needed about 2,700 tons per day to meet their economic and military requirements, which could be met by this means alone if necessary.[17] Some of these roads were part of the original infrastructure built under French colonial supervision; others had been built by the Chinese to counter the first air war over North Vietnam; still others had been built in the intervening years in preparation for another air offensive.[18] This distributed road network denied long-term interdiction. Nor would it be easy to eliminate the trucks moving the cargo: according to CIA estimates, the DRV possessed between 18,000 and 23,000 trucks at the outset of the offensive and received another 3,000 from China by the end of June.[19] The U.S. air offensive would impose a toll on the truck fleet, as would the hard use along the primitive North Vietnamese roads. There was no possibility, however, that the Americans could choke off the movement of supplies by eliminating North Vietnam's supply of trucks.

As the trucks began to assume the load from the rail system, the North Vietnamese worked to construct the POL pipeline connecting their heartland with sources in China. The Soviets had designed the pipeline to be used by maneuver forces, and to be rapidly reparable under attack; as the CIA summarized: "the parallel-line, check-valve construction, coupled with handy stockpiles and nearly repair crews, enabled the enemy to have the line back in operation within hours." Construction began in early June on three parallel pipelines, which would provide a minimum capacity of 3,000 tons per day.[20]

The North Vietnamese paralleled these land-based measures with complementary steps in their maritime lines of communication. Mines had closed the main ports, but there remained innumerable smaller anchorages and the possibility of lightering material from larger ships to shore. Through the summer, U.S. intelligence detected eight Chinese ships lightering off the southern coast of North Vietnam. The Chinese ships were strictly off-limits to Navy fighters, but the small North Vietnamese vessels that ferried the supplies to shore were fair game, and were extremely vulnerable to attack. The Navy closed off lightering operations so effectively that the North Vietnamese were forced to throw bags of rice off the vessels and pick them up when they drifted ashore.[21]

As the Americans had projected, this array of countermeasures demanded a heavy investment of manpower on the part of the North Vietnamese. The government met these new requirements in part by using evacuees from the cities and industrial employees put out of work by the bombing. The CIA estimated that the combination of economic dislocation and large-scale evacuation had released between 300,000 and 400,000 workers from their normal jobs. The government moved to systematize its use of manpower, issuing a directive on June 1 mobilizing national manpower for the ongoing emergency. The CIA expected the DRV's logistical counteroffensive to be as much a means of social control as a way of moving cargo to the front.

The threat of U.S. amphibious operations in the North Vietnamese panhandle forced the Politburo to strengthen the nation's homeland security, increasing the need for manpower. Nixon was emphatic in ordering amphibious feints against North Vietnam's coastline, beginning in the first days of the offensive and continuing into the summer; the rapid increase in Marine amphibious capability offshore further reinforced the threat. By late May the 9th Marine Amphibious Brigade fielded the largest wartime amphibious landing force since the Inchon landings of the Korean War.[22] The brigade staff worked feverishly to construct operational plans covering a range of contingencies that would send the Marines ashore in the panhandle, which was defended by the NVA's Military Region Four; the operations officer later recalled that there "was scarcely a single square meter of the North Vietnamese coastal littoral of any value whatsoever which was not the subject of at least one plan."[23]

The Politburo's measures to meet this threat demonstrated once again the North Vietnamese mastery of mobilization and organization. During the summer the NVA doubled the number of main-force units assigned to homeland defense and quintupled the forces assigned to Military Region Four. In order to create a mobile reserve, the high command readied the 320th and 325th Infantry divisions and six independent regiments and placed them on reserve. The high command also organized the 312B Division, building on the cadre formed from training schools and from cadet officers, meanwhile strengthening its technical base by forming "dozens of new battalions and regiments of artillery, armor, sappers, engineers, and signal troops."[24]

The North Vietnamese thus moved to meet the U.S. offensive through a range of countermeasures, securing the homeland and redistributing the logistical flow away from the main arteries. The Americans had proven capable of summoning overwhelming force at any time, overpowering the defenses and destroying fixed targets almost at will. U.S. air forces had demonstrated that capability in the mining operation, and again in the air attacks that had destroyed the bridges along the railway lines. As the campaign developed, though, the Americans would need to detect, track, and target the new logistical system developed by the North Vietnamese. This reconstructed system fundamentally countered the primary strength of the U.S. air forces: their ability to bring unmatchable power to bear in a single crashing blow. Now the Americans would have to undertake the subtler, continuous process of stopping the more distributed flow established by the North Vietnamese. There would be no dramatic solution, but instead a long, wearing battle of attrition.

The American response would be complicated by the conflicting objectives to be met through air operations. At the operational level, the reinforcements Nixon sent into Southeast Asia offered much relief, but there remained a keen competition for sorties among the different users. The White House wanted constant, heavy pressure against North Vietnam's heartland; MACV wanted air power in support of South Vietnamese operations. In addition, the demands of interdiction and the wars in neighboring Laos and Cambodia required strikes throughout the North Vietnamese panhandle, in northern Laos, along the interdiction routes in southern Laos, and into Cambodia.

The tensions around objectives reached the strategic level, where the demands of diplomacy required limiting the geographic range and the timing of air operations. Nixon and Kissinger repeatedly denied that they had imposed limitations on the bombing, but in fact they did exactly that in defining the buffer zone south of the PRC-DRV border. The zone may have been essential from a diplomatic perspective. Kissinger certainly thought so, reacting furiously to any reported violation by air crews. However, it seriously limited the theater commanders' ability to dig out the North Vietnamese logistical system. It also helped to channel air operations into restricted corridors and enabled the North Vietnamese to concentrate their defenses. Additionally, the air campaign was subject to intermittent restrictions to accommodate diplomatic missions: Nixon in Moscow, Kissinger in China, and Podgorny in Hanoi, all necessitating the imposition of restricted areas around Hanoi and sometimes Haiphong. The North Vietnamese had long practice at taking advantage of these lulls, and they turned them to good advantage.

The air campaign continued into June, following roughly the lines developed from the beginning. The Air Force predominantly struck the bridges along the routes northwest and northeast of Hanoi, using large packages and precision-guided weaponry. As the rail lines closed, the focus shifted to other target sets, especially the power grid and military storage areas. Seventh Air Force sent the great preponderance of its sorties over North Vietnam against the logistical facilities and LOC just north of the DMZ, in June flying 1,734 sorties against those targets. By way of comparison, that month the Air Force recorded 278 attack sorties over the North Vietnamese heartland in Route Pack 6.

Carrier-based air forces, meanwhile, worked all along the length of the DRV, flying the majority of the U.S. strike sorties over the North. In May and June the Air Force flew 1,919 and 2,125 attack sorties into North Vietnam; the carrier wings flew 3,920 and 4,151. The carrier-based air wings also flew the bulk of the attacks into Route Pack 6, with 734 attack missions into that highly defended area.[25]

While the general pattern of operations remained constant as the campaign matured, targeting priorities underwent subtle but important shifts. Commanders detected the changes in North Vietnamese operations and logistics, and sought to find counters. For example, the Air Force and Navy forces quickly detected the redeployment of SAMs northward after the first strikes on May 10. As the redeployment continued, American intelligence tracked both the density and the widened tactical deployment pattern established by the DRV air defenders. On May 25 Vogt reported that crews had been tracked by SAM radar systems in the Chinese buffer zone, northeast of Hanoi: "We have been concerned that the enemy would move his SAMs out to cover the rail lines, and this now seems to be borne out. Henceforth, we will have to consider all operations on the northeast and northwest rail lines as being within high-threat areas." This new deployment pattern would greatly complicate the already difficult task of interdicting the DRV logistic system in the northern mountains.[26]

The move to trucks posed an especially intractable problem for the Americans, promising an unattractive replay of the Commando Hunt operations of the previous years. Chasing trucks around the roads in RP 6 was clearly not an option, so Vogt looked for other ways to counter this traffic. In early June he tried a combination of approaches. The best opportunity to destroy trucks was to be found in the marshaling and repair yards, so he sent aircraft to attack the Van La vehicle storage area on June 6 and the Hanoi vehicle maintenance center on June 8. Then on the 9th he sent strikes against highway bridges in the northeast corridor.[27] At the end of the month, after a long hiatus due to Kissinger's visit to China and a spell of bad weather, Air Force fighters again attacked the vehicle repair facility in downtown Hanoi.

Ultimately, though, Vogt conceded to his wing commanders: "We all know we can not stop truck traffic."[28] At best, air forces could slow and disrupt the flow into North Vietnam, as was also precisely the case with POL. American intelligence had expected the North Vietnamese to rely on trucks to sustain the flow of fuel after the ports were closed; the pipeline was considered a possibility, but not the most likely.[29] By early June the signs of pipeline construction were clear, however, and CINCPAC asked his subordinate commanders to propose courses of action. The general consensus was that there was no good answer. There were opportunities available to inconvenience the North Vietnamese: it might be possible to strike the pipeline itself, the storage areas, the pumps, or the stocks of repair and construction equipment. But there was no long-term means available to cut off the flow of oil.[30] Neither did the POL storage system offer a better target for attack. It, too, was distributed so widely that it was practically invulnerable to large-scale interdiction.

It appeared, then, that the NVA had successfully countered the American air strategy. The trucks and pipelines, supported by other measures, could deliver the essential supplies that had previously arrived through the ports. But there was still a long way to go between the northern frontier and the fighting forces south of the DMZ, and the material brought in from China would be subject to attack throughout that distance. From Hanoi southward, the primary arteries ran along the coastal lowlands, well within range of the carrier-based fighters. The North Vietnamese, forced to make hard choices in deploying their forces, had pulled their missile and fighter defenses farther north, enabling the Americans to reduce the proportion of their strike forces devoted to defense. On the other hand, the DRV had its usual advantage of a distributed road network offering many alternate routes through the area. The regime also made its usual investment in road repair crews, mobilizing them from the populace when necessary.

Air raids in the North Vietnamese panhandle did not provide the drama of those conducted farther north, and they did not provide the immediate pressure on Hanoi that Nixon considered essential to his strategy. However, these attacks promised much more success against the NVA logistical flow than did the strikes around Hanoi and along the northern railroads. The bare numbers indicate the intensity of the attacks in the panhandle. RP 1, about sixty miles long, absorbed 1,734 Air Force tactical attack sorties in June, and another 224 by the Navy. B-52s returned to this area as well, contributing 271 strike sorties. Fighter aircraft from the two services dropped 13,799 tons of bombs on North Vietnam, with the B-52s delivering another 6,892 500-lb bombs and 11,000 750-lb bombs.[31] It is little wonder that the North Vietnamese took such comprehensive civil defense measures.

Bomb damage estimates by American forces cannot be considered reliable in detail. Like sortie counts, though, they offer perspective on the fury of the attack and the pressure placed on North Vietnam's internal transportation system. In June the U.S. air forces operating in the panhandle claimed to have destroyed or damaged 565 vehicles, 877 watercraft, and 268 railroad cars. Attacks on the infrastructure yielded claims of 711 buildings, 166 bridges, and 149 road cuts, all along a 180-mile stretch of North Vietnam's panhandle.[32]

By this point in the war, air crews had recognized that no single raid was going to change things much, and had adopted tactics and rules of thumb designed to enable them to fight another day. The *Kitty Hawk's* Carrier Air Wing (CAW) 11, for example, flew throughout Freedom Train and Linebacker during a cruise that lasted from February 17 until November 28, 1972. During its seven rotations into operations, the wing experienced every aspect of the naval air operations against North Vietnam. These began with the defense-suppression strikes in early April and continued with the mining of Haiphong and the strikes and air battles of Linebacker. Upon its return to America, the wing summarized its lessons learned. First and foremost: "One strike planning factor . . . which is of vital importance is simplicity. Elaborate multi-pronged attacks which require intricate timing and precise positioning of attack elements are difficult to prosecute in [training] and virtually impossible in an environment with any SA-2 or MIG activity or one noted for its rapidly changing weather."[33] The wing put a premium on mutual support and on limiting exposure to North Vietnamese defenses: "Formation en route to the target must be a compact unit with no stragglers." There must be "only one run in the target area. Exit as a group, with no stragglers." The wing flew 79 Alpha strikes against fixed high-value targets in North Vietnam without a loss, but found the operations in theoretically lower-threat areas costly. It adopted the practice of constructing a "mini-Alpha" strike package for any strike into a SAM area, with defense suppression and escort fighters where necessary. The emphasis was on conducting strikes quickly, with no unnecessary exposure to defenses and no unnecessary risks. The wing considered communications critical: "Radio discipline is a direct reflection of the readiness of the Air Wing, and the simplest mission will become a confused and dangerous evolution without it."[34]

Losses mounted nonetheless. In the second half of May, CTF 77 lost seven aircraft.[35] Nine more went down between June 1 and June 20. The lost aircraft were serious enough, but they did not reflect the full extent of the attrition being imposed on the Navy air wings. As a general rule, for every aircraft lost in combat, three to four more suffered battle damage. Still others were damaged or destroyed in the always-dangerous task of operating a high-intensity air operation on a confined flight deck. The *Midway's* CAW 5, for example, lost thirteen aircraft in combat during its eleven-month Southeast Asia cruise. Another eight suffered serious battle damage and two more incurred moderate damage. Still others took damage that was repaired at the squadron level. During that period, "operational" losses, associated with combat but not directly caused by the enemy, cost the wing another six aircraft, with major damage to another eleven aircraft and moderate damage to three others.[36]

By early June the deputy CNO for air warfare, Admiral M. F. Weisner, was concerned enough to send Admiral Zumwalt a memorandum detailing the real costs of the air offensive on naval air forces. He characterized the situation as "grim": "We are short of A-7, A-6, and F-4 at the present time . . . If the conflict continues beyond 30 September we will very quickly be forced to reduce our fighter and attack force significantly."[37] Weisner also expressed concern over the decreasing stockpiles of the antiradiation missiles that had been indispensable weapons in the battle over North Vietnam. In May the services launched 382 AGM-45 Shrike antiradiation missiles and 57 of the deadlier AGM-78s, and in June they fired another 342 Shrikes and 96 AGM-78s.[38] Weisner pointed out: "Even though on April 1 we were 500 missiles above our inventory objective, expenditures during April and May and usage projections show inventory depletion in March of 1973."[39]

For Zumwalt, these material issues were a subset of a larger strategic dilemma. The operations in Southeast Asia were concentrating the Navy in a small corner of the world, far from more pressing strategic issues. Worse, they were bleeding Navy resources at a time when the Soviet navy was rapidly expanding its reach and capabilities. In mid-June he formally transmitted his concerns to the CJCS, Admiral Moorer. "I am concerned," he opened, "about the reduction in the Navy's capability to respond to other contingencies as a result of our SEAsia augmentation. Much of this reduction cannot be rigorously quantified, but in my judgment it is severe." Zumwalt recounted the threats to the Sixth Fleet in the Mediterranean, and to the U.S. ability to control the sea lines to Europe in case of a NATO war. Even in the absence of such a Soviet initiative, though, the war was imposing a formidable cost on America's military posture. If the war continued at a high tempo until September 30, he predicted, "worldwide ordnance inventories will be severely depleted." Further, losses of tactical aircraft would reach 90, with another hundred aircraft out of action for extended periods because of battle damage.[40]

Despite the mounting losses, Moorer considered the air offensive an opportunity that must be seized. On June 6 he sent a memorandum to Laird, proposing that the war should be viewed and prosecuted in a fundamentally new way, to take advantage of the confluence of overwhelming U.S. power in the western Pacific and an inevitably brief period of workable weather. Speaking for the Joint Chiefs of Staff, Moorer identified this as a brief window of opportunity, not just to cut off the flow of supplies, but also to strike at the resolve of the North Vietnamese and their leaders. He therefore proposed "a concentrated campaign against the enemy electrical power net, communications/command and control facilities, and warehousing." Moorer also identified other targets that should be attacked "both for their high impact on the NVN war-making capability, and for their high psychological impact."[41]

The JCS provided Laird with an intelligence study identifying six target systems and the targets that must be authorized to enable the scale of attack they envisioned. These included the rail and highway systems; equipment storage and repair centers; POL; command and control; electric power; and special categories, primarily the limited industrial base. They also recommended that armed reconnaissance missions be permitted within seven miles of the Chinese border. In all, the widened campaign would require the validation of 49 new targets by Laird, along with broadened operating areas for armed reconnaissance.[42]

Laird replied on June 12, approving 28 of the 49 targets for attack but refusing to grant the expanded authority to operate in the Chinese buffer zone.[43] The targets remaining off-limits were concentrated in Haiphong and along the Chinese border, indicating that he was influenced to a large extent by diplomatic constraints with respect to the Soviets and the Chinese. He also withheld approval of six communications/command and control targets, noting the need to coordinate these attacks with the overall psychological warfare plan for North Vietnam. Some of the targets, with little near-term relevance to the North Vietnamese war effort, he wished to withhold to use as hostages in case negotiations failed.[44] Finally, in approving these new targets, Laird specified: "I wish to emphasize that the air support requirements for support of the land battle in South Vietnam remain the highest priority."[45]

The request to conduct armed reconnaissance near the Chinese border suffered from unfortunate timing, arriving almost simultaneously with a PRC diplomatic protest against a U.S. incursion and air attack on Chinese buildings. This was the latest in a series of protests from Beijing that had arrived since early April. Earlier incidents had included overflights by American aircraft and splinter damage to Chinese ships from American combat operations. This latest and most serious allegation, however, included the warning: "The U.S. side should understand that the Chinese side has to date exercised restraint, but such restraint cannot possibly be unlimited. If the U.S. side does not take effective measures to stop such actions, efforts toward the normalization of relations between China and the United States will inevitably be affected."[46] The PRC had indeed acted with restraint, but with the strategic stakes so high, there was little prospect of narrowing the buffer along the border.

Despite the remaining restrictions, the newly approved target set largely met the JCS request. The air offensive would move another step closer to Nixon's ideal, a no-holds-barred, merciless assault. There would now ensue an all-out assault on the DRV's power network and its tiny industrial base, along with a number of storage and repair facilities in Hanoi.

Two other aspects of this exchange merit comment. First, the whole concept of this widened offensive rested on the precision weapons now being used and their ability to hold down collateral damage. The JCS memorandum requesting the target validations went so far as to specify that a number of the targets would be restricted to attack by precision weapons, and Laird's approval was contingent on their use. The list of targets can be seen as an attempt to move the air offensive back onto terms favoring the weapons and capabilities available in theater. Instead of working to stem the flow of goods through the DRV's supply system, the air offensive would focus on discrete high-value targets susceptible to precision attack. There was little doubt that the American air forces could destroy these targets; the question would be whether their destruction would yield any larger strategic benefits.

Second, the exchange marks an increasing use of campaign analysis in structuring the upcoming operations. A new conceptual sophistication now appeared. Through the years of Rolling Thunder, the political-military system in place had nominated and approved targets on an individual, incremental basis. There had been much more regard to the targets' political and psychological significance than to their relationships within an overall system. The air attacks in the first three years of the Nixon administration had been structured along geographic and chronological lines rather than with a view toward systemic effects. In this action, and subsequently throughout the campaign, Moorer and Laird addressed the target sets in terms of systems—transportation, power, industrial, air defense, and so on—instead of addressing individual targets in isolation. American conceptual and analytical capabilities had begun to catch up to the technology.

22

THE VIEW FROM HANOI

Great Britain continued to trade with North Vietnam through the entire course of the American war in Indochina. As a necessary by-product of that relationship, North Vietnam permitted the United Kingdom to maintain a consulate in Hanoi. It was never a comfortable or warm relationship; the British diplomats endured spartan living conditions and constant surveillance, as the North Vietnamese restricted them even more closely than they did most members of the diplomatic community. Sometimes these restrictions were relatively trivial, as when the government excluded the British from government briefings attended by other diplomats. At other times the limitations were more serious, as when the regime organized tours to the countryside but excluded the representative from the United Kingdom. During the air offensive in 1972, the strained relationship reached the point of being life threatening, as the DRV failed to provide an air raid shelter for the British consul, Joe Wright, and his wife.

These British diplomats could claim one of the few Western views of life in North Vietnam during the war. U.S. intelligence analysts sought to pull together some understanding of events in North Vietnam from aerial photography and news accounts. It was an external and distant view. The British diplomats, in contrast, had a first-hand view of life in the North. They could assess the mood of the population, the actions of the regime as it responded to the war, and the rumors rampant in the diplomatic corps. Their window into North Vietnam was small and sometimes quite cloudy, but it was still a far clearer and more balanced view than anything else available to the Americans.

Each week the British consuls filed "savings" with the foreign service back in London, reporting on events and rumors. These reached the U.S. state department, providing an important complement to the limited sources available to the United States through other means.[1] Joe Wright continued this practice through the spring of 1972, as preparations for the NVA offensive peaked, as rumors of its course reached the capital, and as Nixon's air offensive struck the city. Wright's reports create a running record of the measures taken by the DRV to counter the air offensive, and the effects of the bombing on the people of Hanoi. The accounts can be viewed as a gradual crescendo, as the bombing intensified, as the cost of the offensive mounted, and as the impact on the North Vietnamese people increased through the summer months.

By early 1972 Wright accepted the coming NVA offensive as a given; the only questions were its timing and its weight. The previous winter his predecessor had noted "preparations for a mass North Vietnamese offensive to coincide with the rundown of US troops in South Vietnam by about mid-1972," and had commented: "The busloads of new recruits leave with every sign of enthusiasm with cries of 'see you in 1972' to their families and relatives. When we leave the French compound after a film show we can again see trucks and, occasionally, guns hurtling past on their way south."[2]

As winter moved toward spring, Wright focused primarily on the routine activities of the diplomatic corps. That focus shifted dramatically in early April, as news arrived of the offensive striking into South Vietnam. Wright's attention turned to tracking its progress and its effects on the DRV regime and population. His report on April 4 emphasized the rather tentative opening of the civil defense effort in Hanoi, and the widespread attempts by the diplomats to ascertain the extent and aims of the offensive. In those first days of the attack, before the opening raids on the North, the DRV instituted a fairly desultory upgrade to its defenses. Early in the morning of April 2, "the central air-raid system in Hanoi let out its intimidating howl in what was clearly a practice, carried out without much sense of urgency." Hanoi's city government sent out direction to clean the small tubular concrete air raid shelters that lined the streets, "but as in January there were few signs that this was being done thoroughly and me-thodically."[3]

Wright spoke with a local informant, who described the NVA's attack on the South as merely "a warming-over of one originally designed to co-incide with President Nixon's visit to China, but deferred because of logis-tic difficulties." Wright's source suggested that this first attack was de-signed to throw the ARVN off balance before the real offensive, which would coincide with Nixon's trip to Moscow in late May. So in Hanoi, as in Washington and Saigon, observers studied the offensive but were slow to accept it as the "real thing" that had been so long expected.

The following week Wright turned to two subjects that would be of en-during interest through the remaining months of the offensive: the mood of the populace and the measures taken by the North Vietnamese to coun-ter the air attacks. He reported that during a "torch-light parade and mass rally outside the Municipal Theater on April 7, when news of endless vic-tories was trumpeted from the loud-speaker system, the population of Ha-noi was momentarily stirred out of its usual morose apathy."[4] With the first air attacks on the North having occurred that week, the city in-vigorated its defensive measures, conducting practice antiaircraft firing and issuing first-aid kits to schoolchildren. The Politburo and Hanoi's city administration had begun working their way through the menu of civil de-fense measures that would be required as the air assault intensified.

The creeping escalation of the air war over the North reached Hanoi the next week, with the raids on the rail yards and oil storage facilities on April 16. The people of Hanoi reacted calmly, according to Wright, though with "a mixture of anger and disappointment—disappointment that in the years since October 1968, there seems to have been no change in US attitudes." The regime stepped up its propaganda, with the govern-ment radio broadcasting special programs throughout the day, "in which Ho's 1966 broadcast to the nation, declaring that even if Hanoi and Haiphong were laid in ruins the DRV would still fight on, was frequently repeated." With the return of the bombing, the regime moved to exe-cute its civil defense plans. It established evacuation centers, from which women, children, and old people were sent in buses and trucks to recep-tion centers or villages in the country. Wright described Hanoi as "dead and silent, its population having been reduced nearly by half. All schools without exception are now closed." Government agencies had also begun their evacuation: "It is probable that the government and key ministries have made all preparations to evacuate Hanoi, if necessary, and that certain embassies would be asked to accompany them."⁵

The evacuation continued the following week, but as in any large-scale endeavor, there were false starts in this mass movement to the countryside. Further, the regime faced the same problem that it had during the First War of Destruction: the urban population being resettled in rural areas often met with a sour welcome.⁶ Wright's reports in early May commented on the halting start to the evacuation. Some evacuees returned to the city and were relocated away from the current areas of air attacks. Others came back permanently, complaining that they were "ill-housed and under-fed at their reception center."⁷ By that time it was evident that the regime planned this evacuation to last for some time, adjusting medical treatment and the food rationing system to ensure that the populace was protected wherever they might be through the summer. By May 9 about a third of the population had left Hanoi, though there had been no raids on the city since the strike in mid-April.

That changed dramatically the following week, with the opening of the Linebacker campaign. The air strikes of May 10 forced Wright and his wife to take shelter under a stairway in their residence, since the regime had not provided a shelter for them.⁸ After the all-clear signal, he took a brief ride out to the Paul Doumer Bridge to see its damage for himself. His next report included a full account of the massive raids that opened Linebacker, and of the regime's response. He described the heavy damage to the bridges in Hanoi and to the surrounding neighborhoods. In a prelude to later events, he noted: "The Red River embankment was breached . . . though, since the river is at the moment a mere trickle, there is no danger of flooding."⁹ Stray bombs had also struck the Russian-Vietnamese Friendship Hospital, the Chinese Economic Mission, and a few residential areas. The government sent "shock battalions" to work on repairing the damage to the transportation network.

The massive raids of May 10, and Nixon's speech outlining his decision to conduct a sustained bombing campaign, shocked the government into an abrupt upgrade in its civil defense measures. The government evacuated all citizens not involved in production or the war effort, and accelerated the production of bomb shelters. Wright observed wells being dug in many quarters of the city and described a prime ministerial decree calling on the population to consider themselves as in the front line and to report any suspicious persons or events immediately.

A sense of urgency had returned to the North Vietnamese capital. Nonetheless, the residents continued to enjoy the small pleasures left to them after decades of bitter war. Wright saw no sign that food supplies were any more erratic than before the evacuation. Ice cream and flowers remained available, and commodities like vegetables had actually come down in price, as peasants by now were bicycling daily into the city to sell their produce. In the emergency, authorities had loosened the normal state-run distribution arrangements.

This brief account offers powerful foreshadowing of the operations that would follow over the next months. First, the May 10 air strikes were directed at specific, well-defined targets, along routes well known to the American strike forces. Nevertheless, they inflicted significant collateral damage on homes and small businesses. More notably still, the strikes breached the Red River embankment. The dikes remained explicitly prohibited as targets by the raid's operational order, but this incident was the first of several that gave credence to North Vietnamese charges that American forces were deliberately targeting the dikes.

Wright's description of the DRV response to the raids identified several factors that would complicate the U.S. forces' efforts to close off the supply routes into the South. First, the North Vietnamese did not need to repair or replace the Paul Doumer Bridge linking Hanoi to the northeast railroad. Having anticipated the attacks, they had already placed three separate pontoon bridges as alternatives to the large, fixed bridge. Wright's account also points to the use of massed, mobilized manpower to respond to bomb damage and to ensure that supplies moved forward. The assault youth mobilized in the First War of Destruction would play an important part in this second war as well. At that point the DRV had already evacuated a full third of Hanoi's population, and had in motion plans to evacuate more if the situation demanded such measures. The Politburo had no intention of permitting the populace or the government to be held hostage.

With the air offensive finally under way, Wright's focus changed again, this time to the interaction of the attacks and the defense, while he continued to trace the effects of the bombing on the North Vietnamese population. On May 23 he noted: "A fairly common sight nowadays in the streets of Hanoi is of children playing with the tinfoil—some packages fall unopened—which is dropped with the aim of upsetting the accuracy of the city's radar." He followed this little sketch with a more in-depth account of the measures taken by the DRV regime to anticipate the air offensive. His local informant doubted that the air attacks could have any real effect on the flow of goods through North Vietnam, telling Wright that "over the past few years, the DRV authorities have constructed a number of roads, some of them passing through the High Frontier, linking Hanoi and the south with the frontier. These roads, which of course do not appear on any map, have been developed as alternative means of getting supplies from China." The informant also reported the construction of the pipeline extending to the China border, and emphasized that, in any case, the stocks held in Hanoi and Haiphong were supplemented by other concealed stores.[10]

Largely restricted to Hanoi, Wright was able nonetheless to report on local conditions, noting: "Dispersal, indeed, seems to be the order of the day: lorries drop off crates and machinery at the roadside, to be picked up later. On the way to the airport on 6 May, I noticed two complete lathes each under a tree." He was also able to describe the repairs being made at the Paul Doumer Bridge: "Repair work is going on night and day—floodlights are rigged up at night—and the big Russian helicopters based on Gia Lam airport maintain a shuttle service to bring in heavy stores."[11]

Wright entitled his next report "Hanoi a Month after the Evacuation." He aimed to provide a focused, though necessarily brief, view of life in the city as the North Vietnamese coped with the air attacks and the pressures of war. There was no curfew as yet, but patrols walked the streets, often young girls armed with automatic weapons. The evacuation had reached an extent far exceeding that of the earlier air campaign. "One hears complaints," Wright commented, "of evacuees being swindled by grasping peasants, and of children receiving little or no food or shelter at the evacuation centers, but there is no sign of any general discontent or mass disobedience of instructions." Food and kerosene rations remained at their pre-evacuation levels.[12]

In this report, Wright departed from his usual style to offer a deeper analysis of the North Vietnamese people and their staying power under the stress of this bombardment:

Of such a people, so controlled and directed, and battered daily by appeals to their patriotism (not to their devotion to the party, which at present is content to take a back seat in propaganda for home consumption), it is difficult to speak in terms of morale in its ordinary sense. No people I have ever encountered are less subject to changes of moral and direction: they have always been on the ground, from which it is impossible to fall. To me, it is clear that they will endure at the present level indefinitely, partly because they have been through experience as bad, if not worse (the famine of 1945, the resistance war of 1946/54, the land reform of 1953/6, the earlier bombings, the 1971 floods), partly because they have no other choice, and partly because of the rapidity with which the authorities try to repair the damage (with the help of Chinese labour, according to a local informant) mitigate the hardships and generally do everything possible to protect and care for them. It may not be much, but the effort is there, and the people know it.[13]

As the bombing campaign continued, observers in Hanoi "looked for signs of a change in the pattern of the US air offensive, possibly resulting from the summit meeting at Moscow . . . Most diplomatic observers thought there would be escalation, though the course of events since President Nixon's departure from Moscow has hardly supported this view." Wright was astonished at the mood of the population, finding "scenes reminiscent of pre-evacuation days: streams of cyclists, long beer queues, and crowds of pedestrians." His local informant told him that the Communist Party had relaxed its rules on the evacuation, permitting families to return to the city on weekends, especially cadres and others able to wield some influence.[14]

In the following report, a month after the onset of Linebacker, Wright for the first time noted real problems generated by the bombing campaign. The DRV had built redundancy and stockpiles into its logistical system, but the air attacks had begun to grind away at these and disrupt the movement of supplies. The nation had taken every step possible, within its resources, to sustain the flow of material from the north, establishing a system permitting road-to-rail transfers at almost any point along the route from China, and organizing trains to permit dispersal along the tracks. Nonetheless, the sustained air attacks had begun to take effect. There were shortages of electrical power and of fuel. Districts in Hanoi were without power for weeks at a time, despite the presence of emergency generators and electric cables snaking through the streets. Petrol rations had been cut, and half of the government's official vehicles had been parked to conserve fuel.

Further, the evacuation of the city had begun to impose serious hardships on families. A family of five with children in three different school grades might find everyone evacuated in different directions, to accommodate the children's school requirements. The financial needs on the evacuees were to be met by payments from the trade unions and from the villages to which the children were sent. In practice, these payments were not being made. Hanoi evolved a new economic structure, provisioned in part by the state, in part by a revitalized free market, and in part by private links with the evacuation centers.

The strains would build as the attacks mounted, with the city's electric power supply continuing to deteriorate. On June 17 Wright recorded that "all missions other than this one" had received a briefing from the ministry of foreign affairs, confirming that the bombing had affected the power supply. The ministry urged the diplomats to economize on the use of electricity and to acquire alternative sources of power. The ministry offered the embassies the use of backup generators. Most notably, the North Vietnamese advised the diplomats to acquire an inflatable boat, against the possibility of the dikes being breached during an attack.

This report also brought Wright's first comments on a North Vietnamese public diplomacy campaign designed to focus worldwide attention on the U.S. attacks on the dikes that shielded the heartland of North Vietnam from the Red River and its tributaries. The campaign opened on June 16 with the ministry of water conservancy accusing the Americans of deliberately trying to destroy the system of dikes. The ministry issued a statement charging the United States with conducting 68 attacks on dikes and waterworks thus far, dropping 665 bombs, and firing naval guns against the dikes as well.

The North Vietnamese followed this initial set of accusations by organizing a "dikes tour" for the diplomatic corps through the night of June 25–26. Wright was again excluded, but he gleaned information from the Swedish chargé d'affaires. The itinerary included stops to view dike repairs under way at Phu Ly and Nghia Hung. The latter effort included 1,000 workers, who would have to move 26,000 cubic meters of earth to complete their repairs. The work crews apparently had no mechanical equipment at all, and they were scheduled to finish the task in four days. The tour also included a stop in Nam Dinh, a textile center badly damaged by the bombing.

This tour was only one minor component of an aggressive propaganda offensive by the North Vietnamese. It would continue for about a month before gradually subsiding.[15] Wright reported through the next few weeks on the debates among the diplomats, first on whether the damage they saw had been caused by air attack, and then on whether the damage on the dikes had been intentionally inflicted by the Americans. The power of the North Vietnamese accusations waned as successive tours invariably returned to the same spots, and as the damage to the dikes remained controllable. In the end, the diplomats concluded that the damage from air attacks was an unintentional, though inevitable, consequence of the hundreds of attack sorties operating over North Vietnam, dropping tons of unguided ordnance every day.

The diplomats' assessment remains the most credible explanation of the damage inflicted on the waterway system. Nixon was unwilling to rule out attacks on the dikes, preferring to maintain pressure on the North Vietnamese through a posture of deliberate noncommittal.[16] However, at that point in the war, U.S. military planners saw little to be gained by attacking the dikes, preferring to spend attack sorties on the transportation infrastructure instead.

The dikes tours in late June gave the diplomats a rare glimpse of the countryside at the height of the air offensive, and a view of the efforts to sustain the lines of communication and transportation moving material to the fronts in the South. Wright relayed the diplomats' observation that "there was intense activity on all the roads they used: everywhere lorries were on the move, and road repair-gangs at work."[17] These efforts seemed to be succeeding at maintaining some movement through the road and rail systems; a French participant on the tour counted five trains moving between Hanoi and Nam Dinh during the four-hour trip.[18]

Wright continued to report on the steps taken by the DRV to sustain the movement of supplies, and on the preparations for the air attacks. He cited "hundreds of youths in 'shock battalions' up at the Chinese frontier forming an unconventional rail-head," and again emphasized the flexibility with which the DRV logistical system shifted cargo between road and rail in order to bypass destroyed lines of communication. His local informant told him that it had proven easier to repair rails than roads, so trains were still used. But the DRV was also making good use of the roads carved through the jungles of western Vietnam; Wright heard from the Swedish ambassador that as many as twelve such roads had been constructed in anticipation of the bombing. He noted the arrival of a consignment of paint as evidence that supplies were still moving, with even nonessential material arriving at the consulate. At the end of June, two months into the offensive, the city's food rations remained unaffected, but the ration for consumer goods, none too generous to begin with, had been cut as supplies were allocated to military forces.

Wright would keep sending his reports into the summer, but this initial series of messages established the pattern of events: a grinding series of attacks, slowly destroying the national infrastructure and eroding the limited quality of life of the North Vietnamese population. The DRV's response to these attacks called on every tool at the government's disposal, and was supported by construction and stockpiling efforts made well before the attacks. The air offensive was a far cry from the dramatic and rapid blows envisioned by air power theorists, but it had its own coercive power as its cumulative effects built.

For all the obstacles he faced, Wright's accounts offer a valuable perspective on events in Hanoi at the height of the bombing. Certainly they provide a clear view of the determination of the DRV regime to see things through, and the measures they took to keep transportation routes open to the South.

It is also striking just how rarely the city was disturbed by air attack in these first months of the air operation. Wright reported the first raid on April 16. On April 25 he noted: "Since the air-raid of 16 April, there has been only one 12-minute alert, during which no guns were fired, and no aircraft were heard overhead."[19] The next week "there was one full alert in Hanoi . . . There was no gunfire, and no aircraft were heard overhead."[20] Monday, May 8, brought a raid, apparently five miles north of the city, with antiaircraft guns being "heard in the distance."[21] The opening of the Linebacker campaign brought heavy raids on May 10 and 11, then a week passed before the next attacks on May 18 and 20. There followed another ten-day break, until June 1, when "two fighter-bombers flying very low, attracted some SAM fire, and are believed to have hit small workshops in the Gia Lam area."[22] That week did bring ten different alerts, probably for aircraft operating against the rail lines north of the city. The next week brought "8 alerts, but few over-flights. Some villages on the outskirts were bombed."[23] There then followed the pause directed by "higher authority" to allow Podgorny to meet with the Vietnamese leaders. Finally at the end of June, the pace increased. There was an alert on June 21, then five on the 24th and another eight on the 25th. On the 26th there were two alerts, "during the second of which US aircraft entered Hanoi airspace for the first time for some weeks." The following day brought "the heaviest barrage since 10/11 May with bombs being dropped in Hanoi."[24]

Through this period, the U.S. strike forces were fully occupied with attacks on the lines of communication north and south of the Hanoi-Haiphong complex, and were devoting hundreds of sorties per day to operations in the South. Weather resulted in many cancellations of strikes against Hanoi. All in all, at least in the North Vietnamese capital, through the end of June this air offensive fell far short of Nixon's intention to "bomb those bastards like they've never been bombed before."

23

"ONE OF THOSE DAYS"

"This was one of those days," opened General Vogt's daily wrap-up on June 27. That it was. Seventh Air Force had mounted a massive raid against Hanoi, and had lost an F-4 to SAMs over the city. On egress, a MiG-21 destroyed a Phantom on a hit-and-run attack. The strike forces set up for a rescue attempt, cycling flights of F-4s through the area to locate the survivors. Finally another flight of MiGs attacked, firing missiles into two more Phantoms; all four crew members ejected.[1]

It was a catastrophe, in some ways the worst day of the entire seven-year air war: four aircraft downed, three by MiGs, with no MiGs shot down in exchange. Numerically speaking, the losses were tolerable, especially given the Americans' successes against the SAM threat and their relative invulnerability to antiaircraft artillery. The overall loss rate remained lower than that of Rolling Thunder, and the damage inflicted by these attacks far exceeded anything achieved in that earlier campaign. There was little likelihood that the North Vietnamese fighters could seriously dislocate the air campaign. Nonetheless, this series of engagements triggered alarms all through the Air Force chain of command, and eventually led to significant revisions in the conduct of the air war.

The visceral reaction to this situation reflected several factors. Most immediately, kills and exchange ratios were at the heart of the Air Force's self-image. In a world of frustration and ambiguity, the air-to-air war offered a clear view of winners and losers, visible and precise. The service had compiled a 14:1 kill ratio in the Korean War—14 enemy aircraft destroyed for every U.S. aircraft lost—and even in the Rolling Thunder campaign had defeated the North Vietnamese at about a 2.5:1 ratio. Upon hearing of the June 27 losses, the Air Force chief of staff, General Ryan, sent a message to the PACAF commander, General Clay, noting: "Total loss to Migs is approaching a one for one ratio, something that has never before occurred in USAF/AAF history, and which I find unacceptable."[2]

The situation was even more dismaying given the wide disparity in numbers wielded by the opposing sides. During the engagements of June 27, the North Vietnamese air force apparently launched three flights of two MiG-21s each.[3] These operated in coordination with the missiles and warning network that protected the North Vietnamese heartland, but they were still a very small defense force to pit against the Americans. The U.S. strike package that day consisted of twelve F-4s, supported by another forty-five F-4s and eight F-105s. The sixty-five aircraft entering North Vietnam were, in turn, supported by the normal armada of tankers and intelligence assets—on this day, including a U-2 overhead, an RC-135 eavesdropping on North Vietnamese radios off the coast, and an EC-121 over Laos, in addition to the radar support offered by Navy picket ships offshore.[4] It was not even a case of the smaller force overcoming a numerical disadvantage by using superior technology; in terms of avionics and aircraft performance, the American aircraft were superior in most measures to the MiG-21s.

Interservice rivalries heightened the frustration of the Air Force leadership, as Navy fighters continued to dominate their North Vietnamese adversaries. To some extent this domination could be attributed to the difference in their adversaries; the Navy kills were almost all against the subsonic MiG-17s stationed in eastern North Vietnam, as opposed to the more advanced MiG-21s that normally faced the Air Force. The Navy also enjoyed a major advantage in their operating arena. Working along the coast, supported by the picket ships offshore, the Navy fighters benefited from the incomparably superior threat warnings provided by Red Crown. But it seems clear that the Navy also outdid the Air Force in the quality of its training infrastructure and focus. Much has been made of the Navy's high-end training programs, especially the "Top Gun" program instituted after Rolling Thunder. These were indeed highly effective, both in creating a cadre of extraordinarily well-trained air crews and in extending their expertise through the force. These programs could only reach their full potential, though, in unison with effective unit-training programs, and it was in this area that the Navy's mode of deployment and the carrier air wings' training cycles offered such powerful advantages.

The rivalry between the services had been a hallmark of the war since its inception. If anything, it intensified as the end of the war neared and the postwar world came more clearly into view, with modernization programs struggling for survival in the face of serious funding constraints. By 1972 the chief of naval operations, Admiral Zumwalt, had developed a strategic concept for the postwar U.S. military, focused on a "decisive force" characterized by its responsiveness and its combat effectiveness. He concluded that the Navy should form the core of this force, and should therefore receive funding priority in the impending budget decisions—ending the traditional even distribution of funding across the services. Zumwalt looked toward ongoing operations to provide data in support of his concept, directing his staff to gather information on the relative Air Force and Navy contributions to the campaign for use at the Pentagon and on Capitol Hill. As early as April 10, with the escalation still in progress, he asked the staff for information on the flow of reinforcements to Indochina "for use on hill."[5] The issue arose again in mid-June, with Zumwalt noting to his staff: "I have heard, unofficially, that USAF is initiating a campaign on how they responded to the current SEA crisis more rapidly than did USN. I would appreciate seeing any facts/figures to the contrary."[6] Late that summer Zumwalt prepared for future battles inside the Pentagon, asking his staff to compile a direct comparison of response times and combat effectiveness between the Navy and the Air Force. He planned to use the information in impending conversations with Deputy Secretary of Defense Rush.[7] Interservice rivalries thus went far beyond pride and bar talk. They carried the prospect of deciding the fate of future systems and the relative roles of the services.

From the perspective of Clay and Ryan, the worst aspect of the defeats on June 27 was that they were not an anomaly. They culminated trends that had been developing for weeks, and again exposed problems that had been evident since the opening of the campaign. In Clay and Ryan's view, these problems demanded hard decisions and rapid response that the Seventh Air Force leadership under Vogt's command was failing to provide. The losses were serious in themselves, and more so as an indicator of deeper problems in the command.

Right from the start of the air campaign, Clay and occasionally Ryan had dispatched messages to Vogt, offering suggestions on various aspects of ongoing operations. Most are unexceptional in themselves. They provide, however, clear evidence of Vogt's superiors' concerns over the conduct of the campaign, and their frustration over his evident unwillingness to adjust Seventh Air Force operations to correct obvious deficiencies. The messages are especially striking in view of the nearly inviolate military tradition that the theater commander has the clearest view of his mission and how to perform it with the forces on hand. They also offer a vivid exception to the normally anodyne style of military message traffic. Clay's frustration breaks through the conventions of civility, as does Vogt's resentment of the criticism to which he is subjected.

The series opened with the very first Linebacker missions, with Clay at PACAF offering advice on the use of the different models of F-4 now available in Seventh Air Force. The message noted that the newer F-4Es offered increased performance and an internal gun, and suggested that they be used for the combat air patrol and escort missions in the future.[8] This first salvo was followed on May 22, ten days into the air campaign, by a far more comprehensive critique by Clay of nearly every aspect of Seventh Air Force operations. He opened: "I have been concerned for some time that we are not doing our best in the air-to-air environment . . . we have been piecemealing the solution to this problem without coming to grips with the entire spectrum of associated items that, taken in their entirety, spell success or failure when contact with enemy aircraft occurs . . . There are in my opinion seven areas that call for attention if our air-to-air effort is going to achieve any kind of professionalism."[9] He went on to list and describe these areas for improvement, beginning with the same concern he had expressed earlier, that the air-to-air effort must feature the most advanced fighter available, the F-4E. He went so far as to forward a paper comparing the two models written by the Tactical Fighter Weapons Center, hoping that this would clarify Vogt's thinking on the subject.

Clay then worked through the other elements in the engagement chain, beginning with a proposal that the Air Force adopt the Navy's Tactical Data System as the primary control for all Air Force aircraft operating in North Vietnam. His next three suggestions focused on the air crews and tactics employed in the campaign. First, he emphasized: "We must specialize our air-to-air effort to the extent of assigning at least two squadrons to this mission." He next addressed a still more fundamental issue: air crew qualifications and flight discipline. He enumerated a long and painful litany of tactical errors that had been evident in the campaign, all building the case that a lack of flight discipline and training were destroying flight integrity in combat. Losses would be an inevitable result. Even worse, the basic tactical philosophy being used in combat was fundamentally flawed. Air Force fighters worked to achieve head-on intercepts ending in radar-guided missile kills. In principle, this was a sound tactic, given that the Soviet fighters equipping the North Vietnamese air force did not have any missiles capable of countering a head-on attack. The problems with this approach, however, were twofold. First, the radar missiles were so unreliable that they rarely worked even when fired in the heart of the envelope. More seriously, in working toward this intercept tactic, Air Force pilots had lost the ability to recognize and work toward other sorts of shot opportunities. Clay noted: "In ten IR missile [infrared-seeking AIM-9 Sidewinder] firings since Jan 72 not one has been within the parameters of the missile. Under those firing conditions improved hardware will be of minimum benefit."[10]

Ten days later, with no improvement yet apparent, Ryan weighed in from Washington. Omitting the normal pleasantries, he opened his message: "I am deeply concerned over the low success rate of air-to-air missiles in recent aerial engagements. Improvement in both maintenance and operational areas is imperative." Ryan directed PACAF to "advise what you plan to do to insure that air crews, fire control maintenance technicians, and weapons load crews are proficient."[11] Clearly Ryan perceived the problems as arising predominantly from training issues, and not from missile technology.

These exhortations and directives from higher headquarters accompanied a series of teams that were dispatched to observe the operation and offer suggestions. Ryan's message noted that Air Force and contractor assistance teams had been sent to the field. Clay emphasized the utility of the Tactical Fighter Weapons Center team already in theater, and sent his own team from PACAF as well. The chain of command also addressed the material problems that had become obvious, Ryan notifying Clay that the air staff had taken actions to expedite shipment of limited numbers of improved air-to-air missiles.

Vogt replied with a summary of the measures he had taken to cure the missile problems, but closed with a reminder that there was a limit to what could be achieved at that point: "In view of the long record of inadequacies in the missile systems now on our F-4 aircraft, however, I am certain we will not achieve perfection." He also reminded Clay and Ryan of the bright side of the picture. Since January 1 of that year, he noted, the Air Force and the Navy had each shot down 18 aircraft. The Air Force's kills had been largely MiG-21s, while the majority of the Navy kills were MiG-17s. He closed with an upbeat summary: "I am confident our pilots, with their vastly superior capability, need only a little experience in the combat area to get the job done."[12]

Clay did not share Vogt's confidence. He replied only three days later, again insisting that Vogt adjust Seventh Air Force's operations: "We have serious problems in three general areas all of which have a direct bearing on our success in the air-to-air war." As before, Clay emphasized pilot training and procedures and missile maintenance, this time adding the missiles themselves as a cause of the problem. His suggestions grew increasingly specific with repetition; this time he recommended that Seventh Air Force establish two or three squadrons dedicated to the air-to-air mission, and screen all the pilots in the command for those with the qualifications to serve in these squadrons. To solve the maintenance problems he suggested that Vogt reschedule visits by the teams that had visited previously, this time coordinating their efforts and adding visits by civilian technical representatives.[13]

Still the problems continued. On June 21 three MiG-21s executed a coordinated attack on the chaff flight and its escort; one aircraft on each side was destroyed. Three days later MiG-21s shot down two more F-4s, taking advantage of confusion occurring as the chaff flight, leaving the target area after dropping the chaff corridor, met the ingressing strike flight as it neared the target. The MiGs struck as the flights maneuvered to avoid a mid-air collision. The confusion was compounded by the fact that the two flights providing escort for the strikers had come from different bases, and had been briefed on their tactics during the prestrike air refueling. Further, their call signs—Lexington and Washington—were similar enough to cause still more confusion in the heat of battle.[14]

The trends were bad, and were soon to get worse. The disastrous mission on June 27 crystallized the perception of the problem in Washington and in Honolulu alike, and the more the chain of command learned about the day's engagements, the worse the situation seemed. The day's events provide a microcosm of the problems that Clay and Ryan had emphasized over the previous months. The Air Force analysis of these events pointed to communications problems, poor tactical decisionmaking, unreliable missiles, and poor lookout discipline.[15] The analysis also noted the predictability of the search and rescue effort, with F-4s cycling through the area regularly every twenty minutes, then running low on fuel and departing to the tankers. This predictability yielded almost complete initiative to the North Vietnamese air defense network, which was able to time its attacks at moments when the F-4s were low on fuel.

This series of engagements also illustrates the significant improvement in tactics and proficiency that the North Vietnamese had made since the opening of the campaign. In early May the North Vietnamese air defense system found itself inferior to its enemies in tactics, technology, and numbers. From that position of tactical and technical inferiority, the North Vietnamese carefully constructed tactics to exploit their adversaries' weaknesses. The Americans' stereotyped tactics, compounded by the F-4's limited endurance, created an opportunity which the North Vietnamese seized. The first MiG kill on June 27 resulted from a carefully orchestrated combined use of MiGs and SAMs. The air defense network then timed subsequent launches to hit the Phantoms as their fuel reached dangerously low levels. The MiGs executed effective decoy tactics, culminating in hit-and-run attacks that left their the U.S. aircraft burning on the ground as the MiGs egressed safely. It was all done with six MiG sorties, achieving three kills. There was no question that in the endless process of adjusting tactics in combat, the North Vietnamese were making the more rapid and appropriate changes.

Nor were their improvements only to be found among the air forces. The first Phantom lost that day, over Hanoi, had been destroyed by an optically guided SA-2. The crash program of modifications and training that had begun in mid-May had already borne fruit. Unable to counter the advanced U.S. jamming systems, the North Vietnamese and their Russian advisors had retrofitted their systems to enable optical tracking and engagement. It represented their best chance to neutralize the overpowering American advantage in electronics systems. Although only a partial solution, it certainly offered opportunities against the chaff bombers, flying in their parade formations over Hanoi.

Given their long-standing concerns over the air campaign, it was inevitable that Clay and Ryan would react strongly to such a vivid defeat. Ryan immediately dispatched General John J. Burns, the Air Staff's deputy director of requirements, to provide a first-hand assessment of the situation. He planned to follow Burns's report with a visit of his own. Clay dispatched General "Boots" Blesse, a Korean War ace and a highly respected fighter tactician, to Saigon for the same purpose. Finally, Ryan asked General William Momyer, who had been the Seventh Air Force commander during Rolling Thunder, to offer his ideas to Vogt from his current position as the commander of Tactical Air Command.[16]

Burns reported back within a week, on the Fourth of July. There were indeed fireworks, but none that anyone much enjoyed. Burns focused on tactical issues, rather than on the maintenance and logistical problems being worked on by others. In essence, he criticized the command for encouraging muddled counter-air tactics that left "no flight in a 12 to 20 aircraft formation which responds aggressively to an incoming MiG attack before he has closed to visual range." Burns then assessed the air crews themselves and their readiness for the air-to-air mission. He concluded: "Our crews are inadequately trained for air combat. In five of the six encounters analyzed adequate MiG warnings and information were available but the flight leaders did not utilize it effectively . . . our crews need more combat maneuvering training so that they can fly the aircraft more instinctively and free them to concentrate on the tactical situation . . . Actions to be taken by the element under offensive and defensive conditions are not well understood nor practiced by many of the pilots." Burns also found a continuing problem with communications: "Review of the tapes revealed a number of critical calls missed due to other transmissions on the mission frequency, on guard channel, or due to chatter within the aircraft itself between the front and back seater." He had administered a quiz to the combat air crews which had indicated that "although many had a general appreciation for the capabilities of the enemy aircraft, there were serious gaps in their knowledge."[17]

Finally, he commented on two fundamental features of the Linebacker attack packages as they had been constituted since May. First, the standardized package had become predictable, always a dangerous condition in combat: "There are indications that the enemy has observed the pattern of the Linebacker missions enough times now so that he is starting to pick on the more vulnerable elements with the appropriate weapon." Second, coordination remained poor: "Close coordination and understanding among the flights from separate wings making up the strike and chaff formations could have possibly saved three of the losses."[18] Seven weeks into the campaign, the multi-wing coordination was still a major factor in half the losses in a very bad week.

Burns offered a series of recommendations, going into detail in discussing ingress altitudes and the length of the chaff corridors. He placed his heaviest emphasis on air crew training, extending all the way to basic F-4 upgrade programs in the United States. He also proposed that, within Seventh Air Force, "monthly or bi-monthly tactics meetings among the wings and 7AF would be most beneficial," and suggested that Seventh Air Force consider scheduling the major force elements for any given strike out of a single wing.[19]

General Ryan visited Seventh Air Force the week after Burns's return. The Seventh Air Force account of his visit describes the normal staff visit, including the standard comprehensive briefings on theater operations and logistics issues. The discussion started with the basics of sortie rates and requirements, and covered everything from the conduct of the in-country air war to press relations and various logistical issues.[20] Ryan listened, looked around, and went back to Washington.

Things moved quickly on his return. Ryan called in General George Eade, the Air Staff director of plans and operations, and told him that he wanted the Air Staff's director for operations, Major General Carlos M. Talbott, to get out to Saigon and replace Major General Alton Slay as Seventh Air Force's director of operations. Talbott arrived in Saigon to find a situation far worse than he had imagined possible:

Slay wouldn't talk to me when I got there. He left a few hours later, and that suited me just fine. That place was a shambles. All the systems that we had established, even [in the early 1960s], had been cast aside. Things were in utter chaos. There were no planning meetings. Sometime in the afternoon the DI [director of intelligence] would be running wildly down the hall headed for Vogt's office with some pictures. He and Vogt would plan what they were going to do up north tomorrow. The DO [director of operations] wasn't even consulted. There was no morning meeting to review what transpired yesterday; no evening planning meeting where the whole staff was brought in to discuss these things. The frag order was getting out about 2:00 or 3:00 in the morning, much later than it should have been. The DO was calling up and making verbal changes in bomb loads and fusing up until takeoff. The wings were ready to revolt! They were tasking them at a rate that they couldn't sustain. We were losing airplanes to the North Vietnamese—not that many but the kill ratio was pretty bad. I can't believe how bad things were.[21]

Talbott went out to Vietnam with specific orders from Ryan, whom Talbott described as "beside himself on air losses; couldn't get any information out of Southeast Asia. There was no feedback as to what happened, how it went . . . there was never any critique or feedback."[22] Ryan directed Talbott to establish a critique of every mission, attended by representatives from every wing that had participated, and report back to Washington. The first step in solving the myriad long-standing operational issues would be to create a standard management structure to control operations.

Talbott took two officers with him to help establish control of the air operation: Major General Jack Bellamy and Colonel Bill Kirk. These two worked to organize the staff and began to develop the improved intelligence and warning systems to support operations. As Talbott settled in to his new responsibilities, Slay moved on to his new assignment, taking command of the Lowry Technical Training Center in Colorado.[23]

Meanwhile Vogt did little to earn Talbott's regard; Talbott commented that Vogt "was on the phone to Kissinger all the time, circumvented everyone and talked to Henry. Henry called him daily, I think."[24] From the tenor of his messages and his actions during this period, it seems clear that Ryan shared Talbott's view of Vogt's operational skills. Vogt, who had the most powerful possible sponsor in Kissinger, was well beyond Ryan's ability to remove from command; and so Ryan did the next best thing, replacing Slay.

The Air Force operation had struck rock bottom and would only improve in the future. A situation that had been years in the making, though, could not be repaired overnight. Issues of air crew training and proficiency continued to emerge. Clay and Vogt engaged in another testy exchange of messages in late July, after another disastrous mission had resulted in another F-4 destroyed by a MiG-21. Clay opened by charging that the mission had "revealed a lack of operational professionalism." After recounting the tactical errors committed, Clay summarized:

> The inability of the operational commanders to correct deficiencies that have been pointed out in the past is of concern. Flight discipline, tactics knowledge, specialization of the air-to-air effort, flight leadership, improvement of flight tracking and vectoring in the combat area, techniques involving the use of the gun have all been made subjects of special attention since as early as 20 May 1972 yet we continue to repeat these

same errors time after time. I cannot continue to accept a degree of professionalism that fails to meet standards.[25]

This was more than Vogt could tolerate, and he replied the same day, defending his command and his achievements. He disputed Clay's charge of unprofessional performance, pointing to the sophisticated defenses facing his crews and the crews' success in their primary attack mission. Vogt then reviewed the actions that were under way to strengthen the operation, emphasizing the technical programs designed to improve air crew warning. It would take some time to bring the new warning system on line, and then more time to work out the inevitable problems of a new and complicated system. The Linebacker review conferences directed by Ryan took effect more quickly and had an immediate impact on the orchestration of these complex missions. Finally, the bare fact that American pilots lost in action could be quickly replaced, while trained North Vietnamese pilots were few in number, shaped this battle of attrition. In the coming months, these factors would again tip the balance in this hotly contested air campaign.

24

TOWARD THE PEACE PATH

The South Vietnamese counteroffensive toward Quang Tri in late June visibly marked a turn in the campaign. Less visibly, it forced a major diplomatic and military reassessment of the situation by the Politburo in a week-long series of deliberations in late June and early July. By that point it had become clear that the DRV's great offensive had crested. The NVA had recovered enough of a position on the battlefield to strengthen North Vietnam's diplomatic posture—though falling well short of the hopes at the outset of the offensive. Moreover, Nixon's campaign to isolate the DRV from its allies had achieved a measure of success. Both Russia and China had made it clear to the Politburo that they wanted to see the war settled, above all the military issues—though both continued the flow of supplies to North Vietnam. The Politburo decided to move "toward the peace path," finally seriously pursuing negotiations to end the war.[1] For the first time since 1968, the negotiations would involve two partners both seeking an end to the conflict.

At just that moment the American war effort reached a congruent turning point, as General Abrams returned to Washington to replace Westmoreland as chief of staff of the Army. He was succeeded as commander of MACV by his deputy, General Fred Weyand. Abrams's departure marked another milestone in the war. Weyand was clearly there to end America's involvement in the war, a transitional figure who would never be as formidable as Abrams or Westmoreland, or as influential in shaping events. But none of these changes, either in Saigon or Hanoi, moved immediately to end the conflict. The succeeding months were to bring intense combat—in the air, on the ground, and at the negotiating table.

The Air Force's losses in late June finally galvanized a series of changes in Linebacker—technical, tactical, and procedural. These initiatives coincided with an inevitable growth in air crew proficiency, as crews refined their operations, mission by mission. The inexperience that had cost the air operation much efficiency in its early days slowly faded, as air crews attended the school of hard knocks over North Vietnam. Perhaps most important, the simple grinding pressure of attrition slowly eroded the North Vietnamese Air Force, widening the gap between these opponents and forcing the North Vietnamese into a desperate battle for survival.

General Talbott moved quickly on his arrival at Seventh Air Force, installing an orderly mission-planning process and focusing on improving the coordination of the Linebacker strike package. The command instituted debriefing sessions after every Linebacker mission, where the crews could discuss tactics and coordination and take the lessons back to their units for following missions. In the beginning these conferences were limited to air crews; they quickly expanded to include coordinating agencies as well. These gatherings were a logistical headache, given the need to assemble officers from bases scattered all across Indochina. But they quickly paid benefits in package coordination, as fighter units, refueling wings, radar warning operators, and mission planners could work out problems that had developed in operations. During this period the command also brought the computer to the aid of the mission-planning process, simplifying and speeding up the routine yet critical process of generating daily mission orders, or "frags."[2]

Meanwhile Vogt pushed for the creation of a fusion center, a place where all the intelligence platforms operating during a strike could send their data for relay to the fighters doing battle over the North. Codenamed "Teaball" and located at Nakhon Phanom RTAFB, this center quickly demonstrated its worth, improving warning for fighters over the North and cutting into the loss rate. Given the technology of the day, however, this system fell well short of a panacea. The center received feeds from all sorts of sensors—radio and signals intercepts, along with radar tracking data from Red Crown and the EC-121s—but these were then manually plotted in grease pencil, roughly as had been done in the Battle of Britain, and warnings went out by the same radio system that was a serious problem for the F-4s. Still, the system did improve the warning available to crews, and through the remainder of the summer it contributed to the improvement in the exchange ratio between the U.S. and the North Vietnamese fliers.

Two other factors propelled changes to the air campaign as summer turned to fall. First was the unceasing pressure from the White House to exert more force against the North Vietnamese heartland. Admiral McCain retired in late August, with Nixon selecting Admiral Noel Gayler, the director of the National Security Agency, to succeed him as CINCPAC. Kissinger attended the change-of-command ceremony, and took the opportunity to belabor Moorer about the insufficient weight of effort being applied in Route Pack 6. Moorer directed Gayler to develop a planning system for strikes against North Vietnam, to move away from the day-to-day decisions on targeting that had been used to that point. By mid-October Gayler settled on a twelve-day planning cycle, with Pacific Command establishing targeting objectives and the weight of effort to be applied in Linebacker attacks. This planning process would rationalize planning for the air campaign, but would necessitate a far greater degree of PACOM control over operations by Seventh Air Force, MACV, and CTF 77 than the command had ever before attempted.

The second factor was the weather, the monsoonal patterns that shaped every aspect of this war. Anticipating the arrival of the northeast monsoon, Vogt directed the development of an instrument-bombing capability over North Vietnam which would permit operations to continue once the weather deteriorated. The only system available was the LORAN, a long-range navigation system developed by the Coast Guard. It would never be a precision bombing system, and it imposed grave limitations on tactics, requiring extended straight and level flight over the target for the system to maintain lock-on. It was unreliable and inaccurate, suitable only for use against area targets like rail yards. But it permitted the bombing to continue, and it met the White House's demands for sustained pressure on North Vietnam.[3]

North Vietnamese air defenses struggled to maintain a presence on the battlefield in the face of constantly increasing pressure from the Americans. The victories of late June soon became a distant memory, as U.S. fighter forces reversed the trends that had developed in the early summer.

Already by July, airfield attacks had forced a crash program to disperse fuel and aircraft from the NVAF fields, and fuel shortages stemming from the closure of Haiphong were affecting operations.[4] North Vietnamese pilots trained in the new hit-and-run tactics prepared at any moment to transition to combat operations should U.S. fighters appear. Losses mounted nonetheless. Both the 923rd Regiment, with its MiG-17s, and the 925th with its MiG-19s were forced out of action for extended periods, and the two regiments flying MiG-21s suffered severe losses as well. By the end of July the Air Force Party Committee felt it necessary to institute a round of political activities, aimed at combating "rightist deviationism and wavering"—or in Western terms, pessimism and fear.[5]

North Vietnamese antiaircraft forces conducted their own search for tactics and technical innovations that would enable them to fulfill their mission. In late June the Air Defense Service worked to strengthen the local forces, providing equipment and training as the nation mobilized new air defense units to counter Nixon's air campaign. SAM radar operators worked out tactics to counter American jamming and the Shrike anti-radiation missiles fired freely by U.S. defense-suppression forces—though this remained a deadly cat-and-mouse game. SAM operators adopted the tactic of firing at long range to force an early Shrike launch—then guiding their SA-2 until impact, shutting down the radar before the Shrike arrived. This was a delicate and dangerous sequence, but it allowed the SAMs to continue to play a role on the battlefield.

In late July the Air Defense Service adopted a new tactic, massing antiaircraft and missile forces in clusters, and shifting these clusters as needed to counter American attacks. Through the summer the command moved these concentrations into different areas through the North Vietnamese panhandle, seeking a combination of mass and surprise to counter the predominantly Navy air strikes in this region.[6] Nonetheless, the American air offensive continued its relentless crescendo. During the first three months of attacks over the North, from April through June, U.S. forces sent 14,155 attack sorties against the DRV. The next three months saw that number grow to 19,737, nearly a 40 percent increase in an already intense tempo.

Meanwhile the South Vietnamese generated counteroffensives in all three sectors of combat—in each case learning, at great cost, that while the NVA had lost its offensive capability during the savage battles of the spring, it remained a tenacious and formidable foe when fighting on the defensive. Moreover, under constant prodding by the Politburo, NVA and

Viet Cong forces continued to seek opportunities to expand their control over lines of communication, terrain, and population, in preparation for the battles they knew would follow. In the central highlands, ARVN forces managed to reopen Route 14 between Pleiku and Kontum, but never managed to push the NVA from the terrain it had gained north of Kontum. This would remain in NVA hands and provide a logistical base for operations over the next two years. Similarly, the NVA held on to the area north of An Loc, only grudgingly yielding its grip on Route 13 in the summer of 1972.

But the most sustained, bloody, and consequential counteroffensive took place in MR I, after Thieu demanded that General Truong recapture Quang Tri—regardless of the cost. The counteroffensive that opened in late June made fairly rapid progress until reaching the area of Quang Tri City, where it stagnated as the South Vietnamese waited for American air power to destroy the NVA defenses. The Politburo recognized the value of Quang Tri as clearly as Thieu did, and directed the NVA to hold the city at whatever price. The offensive stalled and became a bloody battle of attrition, as the rains came and flooded the trenches occupied by both sides. The deluge of firepower, from fighters, offshore bombardment, and B-52 strikes, exacted a daily toll on the defenders; each night they sent another company of soldiers forward into the fight to replace those who had died that day. Over time, the battle of attrition destroyed four NVA divisions, but at a prohibitive price for Thieu: the fight for Quang Tri eliminated South Vietnam's strategic reserve, leaving the Airborne and the Marines decimated and deprived of their strategic mobility. Finally the city fell to the South Vietnamese on September 16.

The RVNAF's military success at Quang Tri, Pyrrhic though it was, again forced the Politburo to reassess its negotiating strategy and its strategic objectives. This final adjustment again illustrated the inseparable tie between the battlefields and the negotiations in Paris. More significantly, this reassessment marked a final turn in the convoluted story of the search for a negotiated settlement to the war. At long last, with the Politburo's decision, both sides could meet their minimum objectives: for the North Vietnamese, the withdrawal of U.S. forces and the preservation of the dearly bought NVA presence in South Vietnam, and for the Americans, the return of prisoners of war and the preservation of the Thieu regime. Although much agony and drama remained before the final settlement, the end had finally come into view.

The Politburo maintained a staff section designated CP-50, under Deputy Foreign Minister Nguyen Co Thach, responsible for monitoring the battlefield and the negotiations and advising the Politburo on negotiating strategies. Comprising both civilian and military members, the section watched closely as the South Vietnamese counteroffensive neared success at Quang Tri. Finally on the day following the loss of the city, CP-50 recommended a review of the DRV's negotiating strategies, in order to set priorities among their objectives given the new situation.[7]

Recognizing the new weakness in their negotiating position, the staff recommended that the Politburo direct the negotiators to lower their demands on the South Vietnamese political issue—at least to the extent of moving away from their demand that the United States remove Thieu from power. After the Politburo had met, Thach reported back to the section. Le Duan had directed that it was necessary to reach an agreement before the U.S. elections, and that the two most important aspects of an agreement would be the withdrawal of U.S. forces and the maintenance of NVA forces in the South. These provisions would establish, in a practical sense, the existence of two armies, two zones of control, and two governments in the South. With these achievements, the DRV could anticipate total victory in the end. It would be the task of the negotiators to nail the Americans' agreement on the DRV's primary objectives, trading off lesser objectives to gain the greater.

On October 4 the Politburo cabled the new guidance to the negotiating teams in Paris. The Politburo's guidance swept away the last major obstacle to an agreement, and from that point events moved quickly, with both negotiating teams working to beat the deadline that hung over every aspect of the war: the American presidential election on November 7. On October 12, having reached agreement with Le Duc Tho on the basic framework of an agreement, Kissinger joined Nixon in his hideaway office to congratulate the president on going "3 for 3"—achieving the opening with China, détente with Russia, and peace in Vietnam, all in a single year.[8] There remained, however, a welter of details demanding further negotiation with the DRV, and beyond that lay the task of gaining Thieu's concurrence with the agreement. Kissinger and Tho agreed on a timeline that would take Kissinger to Saigon from October 19 to October 23, then directly to Hanoi for two days before his return to Washington. The agreement would be announced on October 26, and signed on October 31.

With this breakthrough the wheel turned once again. Having used military action over the preceding months to shape the negotiations, both sides now adjusted their military strategies to accommodate the demands and results of diplomacy. As Kissinger and Le Duc Tho neared agreement in Paris, the Politburo sent direction to its forces in the South, outlining the details of the agreement and directing military action to be taken prior to and after the cease-fire. The NVA also conducted a transportation offensive, rushing troops and supplies to the South to rebuild its forces before the cease-fire took effect. In a sad commentary on the state of U.S.–South Vietnamese relations at this point, Thieu learned of the terms of settlement through a copy captured in an NVA bunker near Quang Tri.

Like the North Vietnamese, the Americans adjusted their military operations in response to the movement on the diplomatic front. As in the turning points in April and May, the U.S. civil-military structure found it difficult to adjust to a new set of strategic requirements, and there followed yet another period of fractious confusion in the chain of command. In a broad sense, the difficulties this time were the inverse of the problem in April and May. Instead of the civil authorities exhorting the military to maximum aggressiveness, now the White House attempted to orchestrate innumerable minor adjustments to the bombing, working to balance the diplomatic and military goals of the air action, while the military chain of command tried to accommodate these subtle shifts.

The sequence began as Kissinger approached the climactic negotiations with Le Duc Tho in early October. In preparation, he directed the Pentagon to conduct B-52 strikes up to 20 degrees north to signal his intent to negotiate from strength. This widened authority would extend for ten days, to cover the negotiating sessions in Paris. In a now-familiar sequence, Laird reduced the bombers' operating area to the 19 degree line, and the White House then complained to the CJCS about the strikes hitting too far to the south.[9] As the negotiations in Paris neared agreement, Kissinger directed Haig to orchestrate a gradual reduction in air operations over North Vietnam—a combination of incentive and signal, both directed at the Politburo. The adjustment was fairly simple, just imposing a limit of 150 attack sorties per day over North Vietnam, divided about equally between the Navy and the Air Force. The direction reached the Pentagon on October 14, and Laird signed out guidance to reduce the daily sorties from the current rate of about 250 to 150 over the next three days.

On October 16 Gayler flew to Saigon and introduced Weyand to his new scheme for allocating attack sorties in North Vietnam. In order to ensure that the Air Force and Navy could meet the White House's tasking for Linebacker attacks, Gayler proposed a set allocation of sorties for MACV's use in the South, using the sortie levels flown in September to establish an allocation of 225–275 sorties per day. That limitation on attacks in the South would provide a predictable flow of sorties to be turned against North Vietnam, achieving the weight of effort demanded by Kissinger. Weyand was uncomfortable with the sortie level, and even more unwilling to accept a set allocation of sorties, even though Gayler assured him that any ceiling on sorties would be dropped in an emergency.

The whole process might have remained simply another source of quiet tension between Weyand and Gayler, had Kissinger not come to Saigon shortly thereafter. On October 19 Kissinger arrived in Saigon on his mission to persuade Thieu to accept the terms negotiated in Paris earlier that month. While there he joined Weyand at a cocktail party. Over drinks he took the opportunity to impress the MACV commander with the importance of the South Vietnamese extending their control over every possible village and hamlet before the impending cease-fire. Weyand replied that he would be hamstrung by the recently imposed limits on air support, since no unit in the South Vietnamese military would take offensive action without ample air cover. The freedom to use all available sorties in an emergency missed the point, in his view; the real problem was that he needed full freedom to offer support all over South Vietnam on a daily basis. He added that the Air Force was planning a partial standdown, to repair its aircraft and prepare for redeployment.

Kissinger had heard nothing about Gayler's new system or about any limitations on sorties over the South. Already under tremendous pressure from his diplomatic role, he responded furiously to Weyand's remarks, vowing to take every aircraft in Thailand, and every sortie from the carriers offshore, and send them into South Vietnam. The conversation also rekindled his mistrust of the military in general and the Air Force in particular.

For Moorer, who heard about these events very quickly, the sequence threatened to open several Pandora's boxes all at once. He was irritated with Weyand for taking the issue to Kissinger, fuming to Haig: "This jumps the track."[10] Nor did he understand Weyand's complaint, noting that MACV had very rarely needed even 200 sorties a day over the previous months, and had regularly turned back sorties scheduled by Seventh

Air Force. The CJCS telephoned Weyand to resolve the issue, and found him to be firmly against the whole concept of sortie allocation. In the end, more than any specific restriction, Weyand's concern was over his status as commander. As he told Moorer: "I don't know why, all of a sudden, I should start to be put in some sort of straight-jacket. Not only that, I feel I took over this Command and I don't have the prestige and experience that Abe had and I get the feeling that I got a bunch of rug merchants who are moving in on me. It is just a lot of things."[11]

The next day Weyand sent two messages up the chain of command to the CJCS, both very reminiscent of the battles the CJCS had fought through the spring with Abrams. The first cited the increases to the North Vietnamese infiltration efforts that were becoming evident and identified ongoing NVA "land grab" operations, and the second outlined his conclusions and recommendations. Weyand complained that air support for operations in South Vietnam was inadequate, argued against any reduction in sorties, and asked that any redeployments back to the United States be put on hold. Emphasizing the importance of B-52 strikes against the NVA logistics networks, he asked for authority to send the heavy bombers back up north, and even more significantly, to assign the entire area of the DRV panhandle south of 19.15 degrees north to MACV. The Navy, which had operated in that sector to this point, could simply shift its operations farther north.[12] The issue of tasking authority over B-52s was back on the table again. Moorer's frustration increased when Laird received Weyand's messages and sent a memo asking Moorer to "personally reassure me again" that all of MACV's requirements, along with those in Laos, would be fully met over the next fourteen days.[13]

Moorer spoke with Vogt a few days later, still trying to make sense of Weyand's arguments. He elicited a salvo of complaints by Vogt, all centering on Gayler, whom Vogt described as a "disaster." Vogt complained of Gayler's muzzle rule restricting Vogt and Weyand from communicating directly with the CJCS. More seriously, the PACOM staff had clamped down on target validations, refusing Seventh Air Force permission to attack new, high-value targets. Vogt also noted his frustration with South Vietnamese operations and tactics; the ARVN had grown completely dependent on massive air support: "That's the way they fight and they just aren't going to fight without that air support . . . this is the way Westmoreland taught them to fight and you can't change that overnight." Between the demands created by this dependence and the unceasing pressure to take Linebacker sorties up north, Vogt reported, "we can't surge because we are flat on our ass and have been surging since 1 April, Admiral, my airplanes are broken."[14] The sequence culminated on October 23, when Kissinger issued direction to restrict strikes in the North to the 20 degree line, leaving Moorer to complain to his staff: "They seem to turn it on and turn it off like a water faucet . . . It looks like we are right back to 1968 again with the bombing halt. None of us could figure out exactly what the rationale behind this was."[15]

The tension across the civil-military divide was all the more serious because the case of General Lavelle, largely dormant since his removal from command of Seventh Air Force in March, had lurched back into the headlines. Senate confirmation hearings to confirm Abrams's appointment as the Army chief of staff had provided a platform for investigation of the unauthorized attacks conducted under Lavelle. While Abrams had been confirmed without further damage, the hearings gave the Senate an opportunity to put the military on notice with respect to issues of civilian control.[16] As Moorer commented to Vogt: "Lavelle has left us in a position back here where neither the Congress, the President nor anybody else has got any faith in the military structure."[17] It was no time to be calling attention to new problems with military command and control.

Still more trauma would follow in the weeks to come. Kissinger's discussions with Thieu on October 19–23 completely failed to gain the South Vietnamese president's agreement with the terms reached in Paris. Thieu rejected the central provision that the NVA would be permitted to remain in his nation, along with provision for a role of the communists in South Vietnam's political structure. Kissinger had been warned by his staff: "The emerging settlement package will constitute a large mouthful for Thieu to swallow—in fact, several large mouthfuls."[18] He nonetheless arrived in Saigon expecting to gain Thieu's agreement on a compressed timeline, then committed the incredible gaffe of arriving without a Vietnamese-language text of the agreement—which then had to be couriered from Paris. His mishandling of the situation, compounding Thieu's long-standing mistrust of Kissinger, made a difficult situation impossible. If Nixon was to gain Thieu's agreement with the settlement—a political and strategic imperative—then Kissinger would have to reopen the negotiations with the North Vietnamese, reneging on the agreement reached in October.[19]

An extended drama ensued as Nixon and Kissinger sought the combination of negotiating terms, coercion, and blandishments that would induce the North and South Vietnamese to agree to a single document. It would entail another complex series of adjustments to air operations, as Kissinger returned to the long-standing practice of using air attacks to coerce the Politburo. This round of diplomacy would extend the war by nearly three months, finally culminating in a massive spasm of violence that became known as the Christmas bombing, with B-52 attacks throughout North Vietnam from December 18 to December 28. In the end, though, the terms agreed in January would mark no fundamental change from those defined in October. As both sides had anticipated, the Easter Offensive had set this conflict on a path toward decision.

As is normally the case in war, neither side fully anticipated the course or the outcome of the campaign. Nor did either side fully reach its objectives. But peace of a sort returned to Indochina, at least to the extent of permitting the Americans to withdraw from the conflict. The Vietnamese on both sides prepared for the war they knew would continue.

CONCLUSION

On November 30, 1972, Nixon and Kissinger finally met with the Joint Chiefs of Staff, for the first time since the opening of the Easter Offensive. They had multiple purposes in doing so. The first was to ensure the Chiefs' support for the settlement Kissinger had negotiated in Paris. Already the recently retired Westmoreland had expressed his disagreement with the terms reached by Kissinger, arguing that the United States should hold out for the NVA's withdrawal from South Vietnam.[1] Were the JCS to take that position publicly, the fragile negotiating structure built by Kissinger might collapse. Moreover, Nixon needed the JCS to develop military options for two scenarios: for a North Vietnamese refusal to accept the agreement; and for possible violations following its signing. For the latter contingency, the president directed the JCS to develop a range of options, to respond to a variety of possible violations by the DRV. These would include both direct actions to stop the violations and massive punitive attacks on North Vietnam.

In selling the agreement to the Chiefs, Nixon emphasized: "For the past two years the Administration has been one step ahead of the sheriff insofar as obtaining Congressional approval for funding the SVN war."[2] But he argued that the agreement was not just the best available; it was a victory, and met America's stated objectives as defined in his speech of May

8. The president depicted Thieu as "hung up on the language cosmetics" of the treaty, failing to see the larger strategic realities that would work to preserve South Vietnam. It would not be the various control mechanisms operating after the cease-fire that would keep the peace. In Nixon's terms: "The settlement we are speaking about is not just the specific treaty itself. It is a series of interlocking understandings with other powers and reflects the strategic realities related to the conflict. It is these realities of power that count."[3]

That may all have been true, but it left much room for uncertainty about the future of South Vietnam. Certainly at that moment both North and South were preparing feverishly for a continued conflict. In early 1973 a CIA analysis observed: "During the last half of 1972—and possibly through January 1973—the Communists maintained one of the highest monthly rates of military imports of the war." Pulling together information from communications intercepts, observations of North Vietnamese expenditures, and sightings of weapons moving into the DRV, the CIA estimated that imports into North Vietnam reached a rate three times the already high figure achieved in 1971.[4]

Those supplies fed a rapid reconstitution of the North Vietnamese forces after the devastation they suffered during their 1972 offensive. Soviet and Chinese equipment continued to flow into the NVA logistical system, replenishing the matériel destroyed in the offensive and, in some cases, upgrading North Vietnam's air and coastal defenses.[5] Much of the matériel flowed on to the forces rebuilding in the South. Beginning in October, the North Vietnamese fed 50,000 tons of supplies through their system into Laos, more than half of this tonnage in ordnance, both artillery and small arms. NVA troops marched southward at nearly the rate observed during the frenetic buildup for the Easter Offensive, with 79,000 soldiers moving south between September 1972 and February 1973.[6] Most of these reinforcements were moving into the area controlled by COSVN and into the forces along the DMZ, rebuilding the units that had borne the brunt of the fighting the previous summer. It would take more time to rebuild the armored units destroyed in the offensive, but the NVA infantry units were largely reconstituted—at least numerically—by early 1973. While feeding forces forward, the NVA rapidly constructed new logistical networks through the areas occupied during the Easter Offensive—extending into Quang Tri Province and then southward along the east side of the Truong Son Mountains into the central highlands. Meanwhile, the United States conducted a parallel rearmament in South Vietnam with Operations Enhance and Enhance Plus, stripping matériel from units and allies around the world to equip the South Vietnamese and upgrade their air force before the cease-fire.[7]

Thieu finally accepted the settlement only days before Rogers and Le Duc Tho signed the "peace" accord in Paris on January 27. He held out to the last possible moment in the face of Nixon's threat of a bilateral U.S.-DRV peace settlement and the cutoff of all U.S. support for South Vietnam—military, economic, and diplomatic. Nixon supplemented these threats with a promise of open-ended U.S. military support for South Vietnam, promising the return of the B-52s should the DRV violate the peace agreement.

Thieu's capitulation meant that Nixon had won his bigger game. His combination of military force and diplomatic maneuver had enabled Nixon to pull off the extremely delicate process of extricating the United States from an unpopular war, while maintaining America's credibility as a great power and an ally. The summits in Moscow and Beijing had reshaped the landscape of the Cold War, culminating a diplomatic strategy that had seemed a remote dream only a few years before. The presidential campaign had already yielded a historic margin of victory, Nixon defeating the Democratic candidate, George McGovern, with 60.7 percent of the popular vote.

The question still to be answered was whether this win would stand the test of time. There could be little doubt that combat would continue between the Vietnamese parties after America's withdrawal, with the ambiguous results of the Easter Offensive having shaped such an ambiguous peace settlement.[8] The military provisions of the Paris agreement left the NVA in place in South Vietnam, in a "leopard spot" arrangement, with the zones of control undefined—making combat after the notional cease-fire almost inevitable. American forces and technical support would withdraw within sixty days and their bases would be dismantled. The NVA would not be demobilized or regrouped, though the agreement restricted North Vietnam's right to reinforce its forces and established a four-party control mechanism, the International Commission of Control and Supervision (ICCS), to supervise the cease-fire. This would operate on the principle of unanimity, as would the two- and four-party military commissions that would address military issues that might arise after the cease-fire took effect. The prospect of the four nations of the ICCS—Poland, Hungary,

Zones of Control in South Vietnam, January 1973

Canada, and Indonesia—agreeing on any aspect of enforcement was slim, as was the likelihood of their having a real cease-fire to supervise. These elaborate structures were convenient artifices that helped bring the Paris negotiations to an end by deferring impossible decisions until later; but given the mistrust between the Vietnamese parties, the terms of the agreement, and its broad areas of ambiguity, the chances of a stable peace were thin.[9]

The political aspects of the agreement were more complex, but no more favorable to the GVN. The agreement legitimized the communist Provisional Revolutionary Government as one of three parties—along with the Thieu government and a neutral party—in the National Council of National Reconciliation and Concord (NCNRC), which was to organize elections to settle Vietnam's political future. The agreement left even the basic question of this body's authority undefined: the English version defined its role as "promoting" elections, the Vietnamese text as "supervising" them. Once the NCNRC had begun working, the two Vietnamese parties were to consult about forming councils at lower levels—formalizing a rival to the GVN at all levels of government. Like the other mechanisms established in the agreement, the NCNRC was to operate on the basis of unanimity, which under the circumstances was a formula for paralysis.

The United States committed to "healing the wounds of war and to postwar reconstruction," a provision that the DRV considered a form of reparations. Nixon viewed this provision as an important means of pressuring the North Vietnamese to abide by the terms of the agreement, and was enthusiastic about the principle of a communist nation accepting support from the West. However, the funds would have to provided by Congress, and its enthusiasm for this provision was conjectural at best.

So if there was to be a stable peace, it would have to rest, as Nixon put it, on the "interlocking understandings with other powers and . . . the strategic realities related to the conflict." Nixon and Kissinger had high expectations that Russia and China would impose restraint on the North Vietnamese, both through their influence and more directly, by restricting the flow of arms that might enable another NVA offensive.[10] But both of the communist superpowers had already proved their reluctance to cut off arms to the DRV during the Easter Offensive, under all the pressure that Nixon and Kissinger could exert and with American lives at stake. Their willingness to do so in the future remained speculative.

Nixon's ability to commit the United States to renewed military action in the case of the DRV's violation of the treaty was equally speculative. The Watergate scandal, at that point a growing threat to Nixon's presidency, would eventually eliminate any prospect of an American return to the war. But well before those developments the North Vietnamese showed complete willingness to violate the accords, with little reaction from the White House. The nation's divisions and war weariness had been exacerbated by the Christmas bombing, which had been executed in large part in an effort to bring the war to an end before the new Congress could cut off its funding. Nixon might have summoned the will to recommit U.S. forces to combat, but the decision would have come at a very high price even if Congress had gone along. Nor is it certain that even a re-commitment of U.S. air forces to the war would have been decisive. The withdrawal of the U.S. advisors who had directed targeting during the Easter Offensive would have undermined the effectiveness of U.S. air attacks. So would the dismantling of the theater command and control system accompanying America's withdrawal from South Vietnam. Furthermore, the North Vietnamese had long experience with U.S. air power, and would plan their operations to stay below a threshold triggering American reentry. They would also undoubtedly shape their plans to succeed quickly, before an American redeployment could take effect.

So the most reliable guarantor of South Vietnam's existence would be its own military forces. At the outset of the Vietnamization program, American policymakers expected it to take eight to ten years. Instead, propelled by the demands of the U.S. electoral cycle, the RVNAF had undergone a hothouse growth both in size and quality. With the withdrawal of U.S. forces in March 1973, the South Vietnamese stood on their own. Their performance during the intensive fighting of the past eight months had left grounds for hope, but none for certainty, that they could stand up to the NVA. Some of their units had fought as bravely and well as any fighting force in the war. Territorial and regional forces fought better than anyone had expected, in some cases better than the ARVN. General Truong proved a master in command, as fine a leader as any in the war.

But the fighting had also confirmed crippling weaknesses in South Vietnam's military. There were damaging recurrences of the command issues, tactical shortcomings, and security lapses that had plagued RVNAF operations for years, along with a heavy reliance on the elite forces for offensive action. The deployment of the Marines and the Airborne in the counteroffensive against Quang Tri had bled both of those units, and left them de-

ployed in the far northern section of the country, unable to play their former role as a strategic reserve. By taking these units "off the board" for
further use, the offensive met one of the NVA's primary objectives for the
attack.

The unwillingness to risk failure, which emanated all the way from the
White House to the theater of conflict, had driven "re-Americanization"
of critical and complex functions such as fire support and air control,
leaving the South Vietnamese on the margins. Such reversions to American control did little to build the institutional self-confidence that would
be essential to the RVNAF's success once it stood on its own. All observers
acknowledged the critical role of American advisors, both in solidifying
South Vietnamese forces and as conduits to U.S. air and naval power; it
was unclear whether the South Vietnamese could perform these functions
effectively once the advisors were withdrawn. American air power inflicted
the vast majority of North Vietnamese casualties during the Easter Offensive, while disrupting and limiting the DRV's supply routes. The seemingly endless availability of U.S. air power accustomed South Vietnamese
units to rely on air forces to play a primary role in all engagements, large
or small, defensive or offensive. Outgrowing this reliance would be very
difficult, yet essential to their future effectiveness.

But in January 1973 these elements of risk lay in the future. Nixon's
massive commitment of forces to Indochina had saved South Vietnam for
the present. The military power Nixon sent into Indochina in April and
May had proved to be a multipurpose instrument, serving a range of strategic and military requirements. From the beginning of the air operations
to the end, for example, the White House used them as a signal—sometimes to the North Vietnamese, sometimes to the Soviets, sometimes to
the South Vietnamese. The Linebacker campaigns, from a strategic perspective, were designed to coerce North Vietnam into serious negotiations, meanwhile providing a bargaining chip for later use. From a domestic political perspective, the all-out offensive against the DRV protected
Nixon from the prospect of a South Vietnamese collapse; he calculated
that he could survive a GVN defeat so long as he was seen to have done
everything possible to prevent it. Through most of the Linebacker campaign these strategic ends matched more conventional military objectives.
The intermittent mismatches between the White House's purposes and
MACV's, however, contributed to the acrimonious relationship between
Abrams and Nixon.

The air and naval forces Nixon sent into battle met a wide range of traditional military objectives as well. The campaign against the North opened as an interdiction operation, focusing on the lines of communication and the supplies moving southward through the DRV. The United States quickly added an element of strategic bombardment, targeting North Vietnam's power infrastructure and its minuscule industrial base—which had a disproportionate value to the Politburo as the seed of a socialist economy. These attacks had direct effects, quickly wiping out North Vietnam's industry and eliminating 70 percent of its electrical capacity in the first two months of bombing. Meanwhile the campaign to isolate the DRV from its sources of supply in China reduced imports to about 60 percent of their level before the harbor mining—unsatisfying to the White House, but enough to place a heavy strain on the North Vietnamese economy. Military imports were prioritized over bulk imports of fertilizer and food, placing further strain on the economy and the populace.[11] Attacks on cities forced their evacuation, disrupting the nation's economy and its social fabric. All in all, the bombing acted as a major depressant to the population, but this was a price the Politburo was willing to pay.

The Linebacker campaign never managed to eliminate military imports from China, but it levied a heavy toll on equipment and supplies moving south to the battle area. By early July U.S. forces had conducted nearly 7,600 air attacks in the DRV panhandle, plus another 223 naval gunfire missions. Attacks throughout the DRV had struck 125 rail bridges and another 270 highway bridges, in time creating an almost ritualistic process of destruction and repair, and seriously disrupting the movement of supplies.

The air assets had their most powerful effect, however, in blunting the NVA offensive in the South. The cascade of firepower that Nixon ordered into battle accounted for most NVA casualties, crippling the North's offensive capability both through direct attrition and by restricting the NVA's mobility and resupply. It also generated considerable psychological distress in the NVA troops, who were never free of worry about a crushing attack by B-52s.

Yet despite all these effects, the North Vietnamese managed somehow to maintain their position on the battlefield, to keep the supplies moving to the front, and ultimately to achieve their minimum strategic objectives. In doing so, they created the conditions for their eventual victory in 1975. Their seemingly improbable success stemmed from several factors. First and most important was their total national commitment to the conflict, in terms of the price they would pay, the resources they would invest, and the time they would devote to gaining victory.

But without other qualities, this commitment would only have raised the price of failure. This was probably the most thoroughly mobilized society in humankind's long and violent history. The government was able to turn every element of national power toward its ends, and to organize forces at the operational level to take full advantage of the power it mobilized. The organization and function of the Ho Chi Minh Trail, for example, gave the logistical structure a resilience and flexibility that made it possible to move forces and supplies in the face of the most intensive, high-technology air campaign the Americans could create.

It is remarkable how well the North Vietnamese managed to counter the technology and firepower wielded by the U.S. forces—by patiently studying American systems and tactics, defining, testing, and then employing counters, seeking always to shape the battles to their advantage. Their ability to turn search and rescue operations to their favor, and the care with which they studied these operations, is a striking example. Their ability to study their own operations and make necessary adjustments was equally important, and equally remarkable.

North Vietnam's Easter Offensive shaped the end game of the entire thirty-year struggle for independence and unity in Vietnam, and in that sense it was a decisive campaign. Its results certainly never matched the normal vision of decisive combat. There was no dramatic culminating point. There were no vivid scenes of heroism that turned the tide of battle—no equivalent of Pickett's Charge at Gettysburg or the advance of the Old Guard at Waterloo. Instead there was a sequence of battles, each leaving the NVA a little weaker than before, each gaining terrain, but also failing to meet the Politburo's hopes for dramatic successes and battles of annihilation. In the end, however, the campaign did transform the situation in South Vietnam enough for the North Vietnamese to achieve their minimum essential outcome in the negotiations, and to position themselves for the war that would follow the war with the Americans. The offensive was thus a strategic success, despite its ambiguous, or even failed, military outcome. One could find no finer example than this campaign of the Prussian theorist Karl von Clausewitz's dictum: "War is merely an extension of politics through other means." This was no abstraction or theoretical construct; both sides expected the results on the battlefield to translate directly into results at the negotiating table, and they were exactly correct in that expectation.

As they reconstituted their forces in the South, the North Vietnamese conducted a clear-eyed analysis of the reasons for the disappointing results of their massive assault. They attributed their problems to "deficiencies in our command organization, in our preparation of the battlefield, and in our rear service preparations." They then took decisive steps to correct those deficiencies. Over a seven-month period beginning in October 1973, the NVA organized four army corps for operations in South Vietnam, creating command structures capable of coordinating multidivisional combined-arms operations. The Central Military Party Committee established a general technical department in April 1974 to coordinate the provision of technical and logistical support to the entire army.[12] Beginning in 1973, the NVA developed a road network on the east side of the Truong Son Mountains, paralleling the already established logistical network through Laos, across terrain taken in the 1972 offensive. The sum of these initiatives enabled the NVA to integrate its forces effectively and avoid the stop-and-start flow of its 1972 operations.

The North Vietnamese brought great analytic care to their operations, but they were far from infallible. Their forces often fell into stereotypical patterns of operations, which could be read and defeated by an alert adversary. They badly underestimated the progress in American technology during the years of the bombing pause, and the effect that this technology could exert on the battlefield. On occasion they had the same problems with political-military coordination as did the Americans, with the leadership losing a feel for conditions at the front and ordering costly attacks that had no chance of success. This insistence on continued attack cost the NVA dearly in all three theaters of the offensive. From scattered accounts, it appears that the insistence reflected, in part, a triumph of ideology over military realism, fed by the political officers assigned to all North Vietnamese forces.

But the Politburo's most serious error was to misread the dynamics of American strategic decisionmaking, and most especially to misread Richard Nixon. Nixon viewed this conflict as the keystone of his new strategic architecture. He cared little for South Vietnam as a democratic ally, or for Thieu as the leader of a sovereign state. He cared a great deal, however, for the maintenance of America's credibility as an ally and as leader of the Free World. In his judgment a failure of the United States to meet its commitments would lead to a storm of recriminations, poisoning the domestic atmosphere and making it impossible to govern the nation. It would turn the USSR and China away from the new strategic alignments he had so carefully constructed. Nations around the world would feel free to test U.S. resolve, creating instability everywhere. To avoid these outcomes he would marshal every instrument of power at his disposal.

His decisions through this period exemplify Nixon's mode of governing. Nixon governed through a strange parody of the statutorily defined system for strategic decisionmaking in the United States. The secretaries of state and defense had no effective role in shaping American actions, except sometimes to goad Nixon into decisions more dramatic than he might otherwise have taken. The president consulted the National Security Council only once during this offensive, on May 8, and then only to present the outward form of deliberations and avoid a one-on-one discussion with his secretary of state. Kissinger's scorched-earth bureaucratic tactics, designed to secure his influence with the president, reinforced Nixon's own powerful tendencies toward isolation.

Operations across the civil-military divide, similarly, reflected the symbiosis between Nixon and Kissinger much more than they did the formal apparatus of American government. This mode of governance fit Nixon's personality, but it was also shaped by the sort of policy he wished to implement: forceful and dramatic, with a careful integration of military and political elements. The centralization of policymaking within the White House created the basis for those characteristics, though the exclusion of major elements of the government from decisionmaking processes raised the risk of miscalculation and errors in execution. In earlier actions, most vividly the Lam Son 719 incursion into Laos, the results were catastrophic. However, that experience led the Nixon White House to pay more attention to military activity during the Easter Offensive, reducing the risk of serious misalignment of political and military measures. Moorer's role as CJCS was also pivotal in that regard, as he worked to smooth out the wild swings in emotion and direction coming out of the White House, and to translate policy guidance into executable military plans.

The way the government worked during this period brightly illustrates the incredible power of the American presidency. Operating from the seclusion of his hideaway office, working with a tightly confined group of advisors, Nixon dispatched the might of the U.S. military into a campaign half a world away, against the advice of his cabinet and without any consultation with Congress. His latitude in responding to the NVA invasion is especially remarkable in contrast to the collective decisionmaking process in North Vietnam. In that state, as totalitarian and fully mobilized as any in history, no single leader possessed anything like the authority in strategic decisionmaking exercised by Nixon within a democratic system.

In the end, the decisions shaping America's response to the NVA offensive reflected Nixon's philosophy of power. He believed in power's utility and was comfortable wielding it. He was fascinated by its potential and spent endless hours with his advisors working through military and diplomatic combinations, their branches and sequels.

The massive mobilization of power orchestrated by Nixon and Kissinger met their near-term goals, enabling them to end America's role in the war while leaving Thieu in power. But the costs and limitations of their power, even when skillfully wielded, should not be overlooked. Nixon could force Thieu to agree to the settlement. He could pummel the North Vietnamese, as Kissinger's aide John Negroponte is reported to have said, into accepting America's surrender. But he could not compel an agreement that would be stable over the long term, nor could he offer the DRV's communist sponsors the blend of incentives and threats that would induce them to deny North Vietnam the materials it would need to rebuild its capabilities. Meanwhile, the escalation of the conflict, through Linebacker and then in the Christmas bombing, levied an enormous price on the United States. Militarily, the nation would not recover for a decade or more. The economic impact of the war lasted at least that long, and the social and political wounds have not yet begun to heal. In wielding the apparently overwhelming power of the U.S. military, Nixon was working against time and local dynamics to achieve his ends. But in the long run, time and local dynamics proved to have power of their own, power that was beyond his ability to overcome.

WEAPONS AND TACTICS

A-1	Propeller-driven attack aircraft flown by USAF and VNAF
A-6	Two-seat, all-weather Navy attack aircraft
A-7	Single-seat, all-weather Navy attack aircraft
A-37	Light attack aircraft developed from T-37 trainer
AC-130	Gunship developed from C-130 transport aircraft
AIM-7	Radar-guided air-to-air missile carried on F-4 Phantom
AIM-9	Heat-seeking air-to-air missile carried on all U.S. fighters
AT-3	Soviet-built "Sagger" wire-guided antitank missile
B-52	Eight-engine heavy bomber
C-123	Twin-engine transport aircraft flown by VNAF
C-130	Four-engine USAF transport aircraft
CH-53	"Jolly Green" rescue helicopter
Chaff	Strips of tinfoil used to mask aircraft from enemy radar
EB-66	USAF jamming aircraft developed from twin-engine B-66 bomber
EC-121	Early warning aircraft based on Lockheed Constellation
F-4	Two-seat multipurpose fighter flown by USN, USAF, and USMC
F-105G	Two-seat development of F-105 designed to suppress SAMs
Huey	Utility helicopter, workhorse for U.S. Army and RVNAF forces
KC-135	USAF air-refueling aircraft

MiG-17   Soviet-built fighter, single-engine, swept wing

MiG-19   Soviet-built fighter, twin-engine, swept wing

MiG-21   Soviet supersonic fighter, single-engine, delta wing

O-1   Forward air controller aircraft

OV-10   Forward air controller aircraft flown by USAF and USMC

PT-76   Light Soviet-built amphibious tank used by NVA

PT-85   Chinese version of PT-76

Red Crown   Call sign for Navy picket ships in the Gulf of Tonkin

SA-2   Soviet-built "Guideline" radar-guided SAM

SA-7   Heat-seeking shoulder-fired SAM

T-54   Soviet medium tank used by NVA

T-55   Chinese-built version of T-54 medium tank

NOTES

Abbreviations

AFHRA	Air Force Historical Research Agency, Maxwell AFB, AL
AFHSO	Air Force Historical Studies Office, Bolling AFB, Washington, DC
CDEC	Combined Document Exploitation Center
CHECO	Contemporary Historical Evaluation of Combat Operations
CMH	U.S. Army Center of Military History, Washington, DC
CORDS/SRAG	Civil Operations and Rural Development Support/Second Regional Assistance Group
CREST	CIA Records Search Tool
JPRS	Joint Publications Research Service
NARA	National Archives and Records Administration, College Park, MD
NPMP	Nixon Presidential Materials Project
USAMHI	U.S. Army Military History Institute, Carlisle Barracks, PA
WHSF	White House Special Files

1. Nixon's War

1. Military History Institute, *Victory in Vietnam: The Official History of the People's Army of Vietnam, 1954–1975*, trans. Merle Pribbenow (Lawrence: University Press of Kansas, 2002), 540–544.

2. H. R. Haldeman, *The Haldeman Diaries: Inside the Nixon White House* (New York: G. P. Putnam's Sons, 1994), provides the clearest view of the skirmishing among Kissinger, Laird, and Rogers.

3. On this restructuring and its effects, see Alexis Johnson with Jef Olivarius McAllister, *The Right Hand of Power: Memoirs of an American Diplomat* (Englewood Cliffs, NJ: Prentice-Hall, 1984), 512–525.

4. For broader accounts of Nixon's handling of the war, see Jeffrey Kimball, *Nixon's Vietnam War* (Lawrence: University Press of Kansas, 1998), and *The Vietnam War Files: Uncovering the Secret History of Nixon-Era Strategy* (Lawrence: University Press of Kansas, 2004); Larry Berman, *No Peace, No Honor: Nixon, Kissinger, and Betrayal in Vietnam* (New York: Simon and Schuster, 2001); Pierre Asselin, *A Bitter Peace: Washington, Hanoi, and the Making of the Paris Agreement* (Chapel Hill: University of North Carolina Press, 2002).

5. Luu Van Loi and Nguyen Anh Vu, *Le Duc Tho–Kissinger Negotiations in Paris* (Hanoi: The Gioi, 1996), 236.

6. On Abrams's command of MACV see Lewis Sorley, *A Better War: The Unexamined Victories and Final Tragedy of America's Last Years in Vietnam* (New York: Harvest, 1999), and *Vietnam Chronicles: The Abrams Tapes, 1968–1972* (Lubbock: Texas Tech University Press, 2004).

7. Quoted in Phillip B. Davidson, *Vietnam at War: The History 1946–1975* (Oxford: Oxford University Press, 1988), 657.

8. COMUSMACV 091232 Mar 1971, 2. USAMHI/Abrams Messages.

9. XXIV Corps, "An Assessment of the Performance of South Vietnamese Forces during Operation Lamson 719 (30 January–6 April 1971)," 13 (undated staff study, 1971). NARA/RG 471/MACV J-3 Records/Lam Son 719 Lessons Learned.

10. Memorandum, Lt. Col. Loeffke to Gen. Haig, "Vietnamization," 26 March 1971, 5. NARA/NPMP/NSC Files/Haig Chronological Files.

11. Military History Institute, *Victory in Vietnam*, 272–273.

12. Official Voice of Vietnam website, article celebrating the "Glorious History" of the Vietnamese Communist Party, accessed 21 July 2005 at *www.vov.org.vn/chuyenmuc/75DangCongSanVietNam/lichsuvevang/lichsu4.html*; Phan Huu Dai, "Memoir of the Route 9—Southern Laos Campaign," People's Army newspaper, 20 February 2006, accessed 20 February 2006 at *www.quandoinhandan.org.vn/news.php?id_new=57214&subject=2*. Translation by Merle Pribbenow.

13. XXIV Corps, "Assessment of the Performance of South Vietnamese Forces During Operation Lamson 719," 13, 13–14.

14. Davidson, *Vietnam at War*, 655.

15. Message text, Kissinger to Bunker, untitled, 18 March 1971, 1. NARA/NPMP/NSC Files/Haig Special Files.

16. Memorandum, Loeffke to Haig, "Vietnamization," 26 March 1971, 5.

17. Henry A. Kissinger, *The White House Years* (Boston: Little, Brown, 1979), 1002.

18. Military History Institute, *Victory in Vietnam*, 271–278, 653.

19. Oval Office Conversation 472-13, Nixon, Kissinger, Haldeman, 12:16–1:07 P.M., 23 March 1971. NARA/NPMP/White House Tapes. The quotation is from Kissinger.

20. Alexander M. Haig, *Inner Circles: How America Changed the World: A Memoir* (New York: Warner, 1992), 272–275.

21. Louis Harris poll, 3 May 1971, 1. NARA/NPMP/WHSF/Haldeman Files.

22. Seymour Hersh, *The Price of Power: Kissinger in the Nixon White House* (New York: Summit, 1983), 454–479.

23. Quoted ibid., 476.

2. The Politburo's Strategic Calculus

1. Douglas Pike, "North Vietnam in the Year 1972" (manuscript), 32–35, 32. Texas Tech University/Vietnam Archive/Douglas Pike Collection/Unit 6.

2. Ibid., 11, 2.

3. CIA Intelligence Memorandum, "Factors Influencing the Decision-Making Process in Hanoi" (draft), 3 August 1972, 2. NARA/CREST CIA-RDP80T01719R000400060006-9.

4. Douglas Pike, *PAVN: The People's Army of North Vietnam* (Novato, CA: Presidio, 1986), 213–253.

5. AF/IN 242137Z May 72, "Comments of Le Duc Tho." Corona Harvest 0579052, Maxwell AFB/AFHRA. All quotations from Tho in this section are from this document.

6. Seymour Hersh, *The Price of Power: Kissinger in the Nixon White House* (New York: Summit, 1983), 442.

7. Stephen J. Morris, "The Soviet-Chinese-Vietnamese Triangle in the 1970s: The View from Moscow," Working Paper no. 25, Cold War International History Project, Washington, April 1999, 14–15.

8. Luu Van Loi and Nguyen Anh Vu, *Le Duc Tho–Kissinger Negotiations in Paris* (Hanoi: The Gioi, 1996), 218–219.

9. PRP Central Committee (COSVN), Directive Six, September 1972, 4, 6, 8. Texas Tech University/Vietnam Archive/Pike Collection/Unit 6.

10. *Collected Party Documents*, ed. Nguyen Thi Nhan, vol. 33, 1972, cable 119, 27 March 1972, "On the Politburo Decision to Launch a General Offensive on Three Fronts—Military, Political, and Diplomatic—in Order to Defeat the Enemy's 'Vietnamization' Policy" (Hanoi: National Political Publishing House, 2004), 211. Translation by Merle Pribbenow.

11. Ibid.

12. Loi and Vu, *Le Duc Tho–Kissinger Negotiations*, 215.

13. Truong Nhu Tang, with David Chanoff and Doan Van Toai, *A Viet Cong Memoir: An Inside Account of the Vietnam War and Its Aftermath* (New York: Vintage, 1986), 198–214.

14. *Collected Party Documents*, Party Secretariat cable 70, "On Strengthening Combat Readiness and People's Air Defense Activities," 25 March 1972.

15. *Collected Party Documents*, Politburo cable 182/B, 29 March 1972.

16. *Collected Party Documents*, Politburo Guidance Cable 119, 27 March 1972, 221. Translation by Merle Pribbenow.

17. Cecil B. Currey, *Victory at Any Cost: The Genius of Viet Nam's Gen. Vo Nguyen Giap* (London: Brassey's, 1997), 283–284.

18. Military Art Faculty of the Military Science Institute, "The 1972 Quang Tri Offensive Campaign" (Hanoi, 1976), 16. Partial translation by Merle Pribbenow.

19. Military Science Institute, *Victory in Vietnam*, 283.

20. Military Art Faculty, "Quang Tri Offensive Campaign," 21.

3.   The NVA Prepares

1. Military History Institute, *Victory in Vietnam: The Official History of the People's Army of Vietnam, 1954–1975*, trans. Merle Pribbenow (Lawrence: University Press of Kansas, 2002), 259.

2. MACV, "The Nguyen Hue Campaign," undated staff study, A-4. Alfred M. Gray Marine Corps Research Center/Gerald C. Turley Collection.

3. CIA Memorandum, "Patterns and Trends in Soviet Military Assistance to North Vietnam," 17 April 1972, 7–13 and appendix B. NARA/CREST CIA-RDP80T0179R000300120001-8.

4. Phillip B. Davidson, *Vietnam at War: The History 1946–1975* (Oxford: Oxford University Press, 1988), 675.

5. CIA Memorandum, "Patterns and Trends in Soviet Military Assistance to North Vietnam," 7.

6. Ibid., 2, 8.

7. Ibid., 12.

8. Ibid., 10–13.

9. CIA Memorandum, "Answers to NSC Staff Queries on Topics Treated in 8 June Memorandum—The Effect of the Past Month's Events on North Vietnamese Military Capabilities," 27 June 1972, 6. NARA/CREST CIA-RDP80T01719R000300230002-5.

10. Qiang Zhai, *China and the Vietnam Wars, 1950–1975* (Chapel Hill: University of North Carolina Press, 2000), 137. Figures for artillery and shells include mortars above 60 mm, accounting for the very large numbers.

11. Military History Institute, *Victory in Vietnam*, 269.

12. Ibid., 267.

13. Hoang Dinh Lien et al., *History of Vietnam's Ordnance: Calendar of Events (1954–1975)* (Hanoi: People's Army Publishing House, 1997), 353, 381. Translation by Merle Pribbenow.

14. CDEC, "Study of Military Information on the 5th Battalion, 203d Armored Regiment, NVA Armor Command on the An Loc Battlefield." CDEC report 6 028 0335 72, 21 July 1972. Texas Tech University/Vietnam Archive/Pike Collection/Unit 6.

15. DOD Intelligence Information Report (IIR) 6-029-0288-72, "OB of the 202d Armored Regiment," 18 August 1972. NARA/RG 472/MACV J213/CDEC Bulletins.

16. Ibid., 25.

17. Ibid., 26.

18. Military History Institute, *Victory in Vietnam*, 272, 281.

19. Ibid., 285.

20. See, for example, CDEC Bulletin 48,923, "COSVN Directive 001-8 and the Mission of the 209th Regiments, 7th NVA Division, Headquarters, SVNLA during the Nguyen Hue Campaign," 1–2, CDEC log no. 05-1077-72, 7 May 1972, NARA/RG 472/MACV J213/CDEC Bulletins; and CDEC Bulletin 49,666, "Resolution Adopted by the 320th NVA Division on Forthcoming Missions in the B3 Front," 1, CDEC log no. 07-1207, 19 July 1972, ibid.

21. Military History Institute, *Victory in Vietnam*, 284.

22. Lewis Sorley, *Vietnam Chronicles: The Abrams Tapes, 1968–1972* (Lubbock: Texas Tech University Press, 2004), 820, 819–821.

23. CDEC Bulletin 48,427, "Study of Resolution 2 Adopted by the VC Quang Da Special Zone Party Committee and Missions of the Forward Supply Council, VC Quang Nam-Da Nang Province People's Revolutionary Committee," 3. CDEC log no. 04-1213, 8 April 1972. NARA/RG 472/MACV/J213/CDEC Bulletins.

24. CDEC Bulletin 49,974, "Resolution 19 from the VN Lao Dong Party Central Executive Committee; and the Forward Supply Council, VC Quang Da Special Zone Party Committee, VC Region 5," 9. CDEC log no. 09-1009-72, 1 Sept. 1972. NARA/RG 472/MACV/J213/CDEC Bulletins.

25. Military History Institute, *Victory in Vietnam*, 267.

4. Commando Hunt VII

1. Khanh Van, "We Followed the Convoys to the Front," *Quan Doi Nhan Dan*, 3, 4, 5, 7 March 1971, in "Principal Reports from Communist Press Sources," 3 March 1971. Texas Tech University/Vietnam Archive/Douglas Pike Collection/Unit 6.

2. Military History Institute, *Victory in Vietnam: The Official History of the People's Army of Vietnam, 1954–1975,* trans. Merle Pribbenow (Lawrence: University Press of Kansas, 2002), 262–263.

3. The missile was command-guided by the Fansong radar system and had a maximum operating range of 19 miles. Its boost-sustainer propulsion system gave it a maximum Mach number of 2.2. First deployed in the late 1950s, the missile, which remains in use, is 27 feet long at launch and was nicknamed the "flying telephone pole" for its appearance in flight. American jamming techniques evolved through the war, at different times working on the radar acquisition, target tracking, and missile guidance signals.

4. *A Number of Air Defense Battles during the Resistance War against the Americans to Save the Nation,* vol. II, "Mobile Ambush of AC-130 Aircraft Conducted by 67th Battalion/275th Missile Regiment at the Entrance to Corridor 559 on 29 March 1972," 124. Translation by Merle Pribbenow.

5. Seventh Air Force, *Commando Hunt VII,* June 1972, 14–16. Maxwell AFB/AFHRA.

6. Truong Nhu Tang, with David Chanoff and Doan Van Toai, *A Viet Cong Memoir: An Inside Account of the Vietnam War and Its Aftermath* (New York: Vintage, 1986), 177.

7. Ibid., 168.

8. Bill Gunston, *The F-4 Phantom* (London: Ian Allan, 1977), 8–13. Richard Wood, *Call Sign Rustic: The Secret Air War over Cambodia, 1970–1973* (Washington: Smithsonian, 2002), 83–85.

9. Jack S. Ballard, *Development and Employment of Fixed-Wing Gunships, 1962–1972* (Washington: Office of Air Force History, 1982).

10. Military History Institute, *Victory in Vietnam,* 261–263.

11. Nghiem Dinh Tich and Thy Ky, *377th Air Defense Division* (Hanoi: People's Army Publishing House, 1998), 119–146. Translation by Merle Pribbenow.

12. Henry S. Shields, "IGLOO WHITE, January 1970–September 1971—Continuing Report" (PACAF: CHECO, 1 November 1971), 32.

13. Ibid., 1.

14. Ibid., 10.

15. COMUSMACV 011028Z Dec 71, "Arclight," 1–2. CMH/Abrams Messages.

16. Seventh Air Force, *Commando Hunt VII,* 50.

17. Ibid., 48–49.

18. Ibid.

19. Tich and Ky, *377th Air Defense Division,* 119–146.

20. Lewis Sorley, *Vietnam Chronicles: The Abrams Tapes, 1968–1972* (Lubbock: Texas Tech University Press, 2004), 792, 753.

21. Moorer Diary, 10 December 1971. NARA/RG 218/Moorer Diary.

22. Seventh Air Force, *Commando Hunt VII,* 144–145.

23. Military History Institute, *Victory in Vietnam*, 289.

24. Ibid.

25. COMUSMACV 081155Z Mar 72, "COMUSMACV Personal Appraisal of the Enemy/Friendly Situation." National Security Archive/Prados Collection.

26. Memorandum, Moorer to Laird, "Urgent Request for Air Authorities," 9 March 1972. Prados Collection.

27. Memorandum, Laird to Kissinger, "Situation in Southeast Asia," 10 March 1972. Prados Collection. The attack zone would be an L-shaped area along the northern edge of the DMZ and then north along the Laotian border. The area would be 24 miles deep, corresponding with the maximum tactical range of the SA-2 missile.

28. Memorandum, Kissinger to Nixon, "Request for Operating Authorities to Counter the North Vietnamese Threat," 14 March 1972. Prados Collection.

29. Tich and Ky, *377th Air Defense Division*, 169–182.

30. Interview, Lt. Col. Stephen J. Opitz with Lt. Col. Robert G. Zimmerman, 18 July 1972, 6, 11. Bolling AFB/AFHSO/K239.0512-846.

31. Ibid., 21–23.

32. Seventh Air Force, *Commando Hunt VII*, 69.

33. Tich and Ky, *377th Air Defense Division*, 169–182.

34. Seventh Air Force, *Commando Hunt VII*, 135, 141, 134.

35. Ibid., 61.

36. Nguyen Viet Phuong, "Strategic Military Transportation on the Ho Chi Minh Trail during the Resistance War against the Americans" (Hanoi: General Department of Rear Services, 1988), appendix 6, 428–429, 424. Translation by Merle Pribbenow.

37. Ibid., 424, 437. The NVA figures list a 13.44 percent loss rate in 1968–1969, 12.33 percent in 1969–1970, and 13.70 percent in 1970–1971. The history also summarizes overall loss rates for the ten-year war: 34,289 cadres and soldiers, 83,832 tons of supplies, and 14,540 vehicles of all types.

38. Seventh Air Force, *Commando Hunt VII*, 133.

39. D. L. Evans, "Personal Observations on the Air War in SEA, 1 August 1971 to 1 June 1972," 6 July 1972, 63. Bolling AFB/AFHSO/TS-HOA-72-82.

40. Ibid., 133.

41. Duong Duy Ngu, "Fire Zone," *Van Bghe Quan Doi*, no. 10, October 1971 (JPRS 54845 3 January 1972, "Translations from North Vietnam," no. 1070), 32–34.

42. Practical Military Matters by HV, "Small Caliber Magnetic Bombs," *Quan Doi Nhan Dan*, 10 December 1972, 2; Phuc Tho, "The Fragmentation, Ball-Form Demolition Bomb and How to Guard against and Destroy It," *Quan Doi Nhan Dan*, 18 November 1927, 2. Both in Texas Tech University/Vietnam Archive/Douglas Pike Collection/Unit 3.

43. Ibid.
44. COMUSMACV 010940Z Aug 71, quoted in Wayne Thompson, *To Hanoi and Back: The United States Air Force and North Vietnam, 1966–1973* (Washington: Air Force History and Museums Program, 2000), 204–205.
45. Thompson, *To Hanoi and Back*, 199–210.
46. Lt. Gen. Carlos M. Talbott, oral history interview, 10–11 June 1985, 208–212. Maxwell AFB/AFHRA/K239.0512-1652.

5. The Initial Surges

1. Gerald Turley, *The Easter Offensive, Vietnam, 1972* (Novato, CA: Presidio, 1985), 56.
2. Ngo Quang Truong, *The Easter Offensive* (Washington: CMH, 1979), 21.
3. XXIV Corps, "An Assessment of the Performance of South Vietnamese Forces during Operation Lamson 719 (30 January–6 April 1971)" (undated staff study, 1971). NARA/RG 471/MACV J-3 Records/Lam Son 719 Lessons Learned. Memorandum, Lt. Col. Loeffke to Gen. Haig, "Vietnamization," 26 March 1971, 5. NARA/NPMP/NSC Files/Haig Chronological Files.
4. FRAC 311215Z Mar 72, "Quang Tri Situation," 1. CMH/Abrams Messages.
5. Ibid., 2.
6. COMUSMACV 011400Z Apr 72, "COMUSMACV Personal Appraisal of the Enemy and Friendly Situation," 2. Alfred M. Gray Marine Corps Research Center/Gerald C. Turley Collection.
7. "Commanding Officer, 56th Regiment, 3d ARVN Division, Message of Surrender," translated text of Lt. Col. Dinh's radio address, 3 April 1972. Turley Collection.
8. Capt. Donald E. Morse, SAR report, 3 April 1972. 56th Special Operations Wing History, April–June 1972, vol. II. Maxwell AFB/AFHRA.
9. Turley, *The Easter Offensive*, 201–203.
10. See Darrell Whitcomb, *The Rescue of Bat 21* (Annapolis: Naval Institute Press, 1998), for an outstanding account of this incident.
11. Truong, *Easter Offensive*, 106–108.
12. "Biographical Sketches Selected ARVN Commanders," biography of Minh. Turley Collection.
13. Truong, *Easter Offensive*, 108.
14. Phillip B. Davidson, *Vietnam at War: The History, 1946–1975* (Oxford: Oxford University Press, 1988), 699–701.
15. James F. Hollingsworth, "Communist Invasion in Military Region 3," June 1972, 6 (draft manuscript). USAMHI/MACV Collection.
16. Ibid, 6–7.

17. Paul T. Ringenbach and Peter J. Melly, "The Battle for An Loc 5 April–26 June 1972" (PACAF: CHECO, 31 January 1973), 7.

18. Memorandum for the Chief of Naval Operations, "Command and Control of TACAIR in SEA," 24 May 1972, M. F. Weisner, Deputy Chief of Naval Operations (Air Warfare). Naval Historical Center/Operational Archives/M-0038-05W.

19. Truong, *Easter Offensive*, 117.

20. "The Attacks on An Loc City by 20th Tank Battalion + one Armored company of 21st Tank Battalion of the COSVN's 26th Armored Group, Operating Under the Operational Control of the 5th and 9th Infantry Divisions, from 13 April to 11 May 1972," in *A Number of Battles Fought by Our Armor Troops*, vol. IV (Hanoi: Armor Command, 1983), 39–40. Translation by Merle Pribbenow.

21. Ibid., 40.

22. James H. Willbanks, *The Battle of An Loc*, Twentieth-Century Battles Series (Bloomington: Indiana University Press, 2005), 32.

23. Truong, *Easter Offensive*, 118.

24. *Collected Party Documents*, Politburo cable 149, 15 April 1972, 242.

25. "The Attacks on An Loc City by 20th Tank Battalion + one armored company of 21st Tank Battalion of the COSVN's 26th Armored Group, operating under the operational control of the 5th and 9th Infantry Divisions, from 13 April to 11 May 1972," in *A Number of Battles Fought by Our Armor Troops*, vol. IV (Hanoi: Armor Command, 1983), 47. Translation by Merle Pribbenow.

26. Advisory Team 70 ops log. 15 April 1972, item 79. NARA/RG 472.

6. Nixon Takes Charge

1. Memorandum, Haig to Kissinger, "Situation in I Corps Area," 30 March 1972. NARA/NPMP/NSC Files/Haig Chronological Files.

2. Oval Office Conversation 697-2, Nixon, Haldeman, Kissinger, 9:38–11:10 A.M., 30 March 1972. NARA/NPMP/White House Tapes. All quotations of this conversation, unless otherwise noted, are from that source.

3. The opposing views on the appropriate degree of civilian management of military operations are best laid out in Eliot Cohen, *Supreme Command: Soldiers, Statesmen, and Leadership in Wartime* (New York: Free Press, 2002), and in Samuel P. Huntington, *The Soldier and the State: The Theory and Politics of Civil-Military Relations* (New York: Vintage, 1957).

4. Quoted in Theodore H. White, *The Making of the President 1972* (New York: Atheneum, 1973), 302.

5. Kissinger-Moorer telcon, 6:30 P.M., 3 April 1972, 1. NARA/NPMP/Kissinger Telcons.

6. Oval Office Conversation 698-2, Nixon, Kissinger, et al., 3:13–4:40 P.M., 30 March 1972. NARA/NPMP/White House Tapes.

7. Oval Office Conversation 697-2.

8. Oval Office Conversation 699-1, Nixon, Kissinger, 10:13–11:14 A.M., 31 March 1972. NARA/NPMP/White House Tapes.

9. CINCPAC memorandum, "Authorities for Operations in North Vietnam," 13 June 1972. Corona Harvest 0579403, Bolling AFB/AFHSO/Vogt Papers.

10. Oval Office Conversation 700-2, Nixon and Kissinger, unknown time between 8:40 A.M. and 9:09 A.M., 3 April 1972. NARA/NPMP/White House Tapes.

11. Rush had known Nixon while a law professor at Duke, and later served as Ambassador to Germany from 1969 to 1972. Nixon and Kissinger brought him to the department of defense to provide a reliable alternative to Laird in DOD's senior leadership.

12. Oval Office Conversation 700-3, Nixon, Kissinger, Haldeman, 9:18–9:59 A.M., 3 April 1972. NARA/NPMP/White House Tapes.

13. Oval Office Conversation 700-5, Nixon, Kissinger, Moorer, Rush, 10:06–10:20 A.M., 3 April 1972. NARA/NPMP/White House Tapes. Moorer's summary is available in CJCS Memo M-18-72, 3 April 1972, "Meeting with President NIXON, Monday, 3 April 1972, White House." NARA/RG 218/Moorer Diary.

14. Secretary of Defense Memorandum for the President, "Army General Officer Actions," 29 March 1972. NARA/NPMP/NSC Files/Haig Chronological Files.

15. Oval Office Conversation 700-6, Nixon and Kissinger, unknown time between 10:20 and 10:23 A.M., 3 April 1972. NARA/NPMP/White House Tapes.

16. Executive Office Building Conversation 328-25, Nixon, Kissinger, and Haig, 12:55 to 1:28 P.M., 3 April 1972. NARA/NPMP/White House Tapes.

17. U. Alexis Johnson with Jef Olivarius McAllister, *The Right Hand of Power: The Memoirs of an American Diplomat* (Englewood Cliffs, NJ: Prentice-Hall, 1984), 536–537.

18. Memorandum, Haig to Kissinger, untitled, 3 April 1972, 1. NARA/NPMP/NSC Files/Haig Chronological Files.

19. Kissinger-Laird telcon, 4:50 P.M., 3 April 1972, 1. NARA/NPMP/Kissinger Telcons.

20. CINCPAC memorandum, "Authorities for Operations in North Vietnam," 13 June 1972. Corona Harvest 0579403, Bolling AFB/AFHSO/Vogt Papers.

21. JCS 040355Z Apr 72, untitled, 1, 2, 3. Corona Harvest 0561477, Bolling AFB/AFHSO/Vogt Papers.

22. Oval Office Conversation 701-2, Nixon and Kissinger, 4 April 1972. NARA/NPMP/White House Tapes.

23. Oval Office telcon 22-73, Nixon and Moorer, 9:24 to 9:28 A.M., 4 April 1972. NARA/NPMP/White House Tapes.

24. Oval Office Conversation 698-2, Nixon, Kissinger, et al., 3:13 to 4:40 P.M., 30 March 1972. NARA/NPMP/White House Tapes.

25. Haldeman Diaries, 6 April 1972. CD Edition, Sony Imagesoft, 1994.

26. Executive Office Building Conversation 22-80, Nixon, Kissinger, and Moorer, 9:27 to 9:32 A.M., 5 April 1972. NARA/NPMP/White House Tapes.

27. Ho Si Huu et al., *History of the Air Defense Service*, vol. III (Hanoi: People's Army Publishing House, 1994), 88–89. Translation by Merle Pribbenow.

28. History of 17th Wild Weasel Squadron, January–March 1972, 21 August 1972, 4. 388 TFW History, 1972, vol. II. Corona Harvest 0581325, Maxwell AFB/ AFHRA.

29. Huu, *Air Defense Service*, vol. III, 89.

30. Ibid., 90.

31. Ibid., 37.

32. Ibid., 92.

33. Executive Office Building Conversation 329-13, Nixon, Kissinger, Vogt, Haldeman, 9:26 to 10:10 A.M., 6 April 1972. NARA/NPMP/White House Tapes. Emphasis added where indicated by voices.

34. Haldeman Diaries, 6 April 1972.

35. Oval Office telephone conversation 22-80, Nixon, Kissinger, and Moorer, 9:26 to 9:32 A.M., 5 April 1972. NARA/NPMP/White House Tapes.

36. Elmo R. Zumwalt Jr., *On Watch: A Memoir* (New York: Quadrangle, 1976), 395–433, provides a critical assessment of Kissinger by the chief of naval operations.

37. Kissinger-Vogt telcon, 1:55 P.M., 5 April 1972. NARA/NPMP/Kissinger Telcons.

38. Vogt worked for Abrams in his direction of the air war in South Vietnam, Laos, and Route Pack 1 in southern North Vietnam. Clay was his supervisor in the air offensive against Route Packs 5 and 6 in the North Vietnamese heartland. Vogt answered through the Air Force chain of command to Ryan for administrative, logistical, and personnel matters.

39. *CINCPAC Command History 1972*, vol. II (31 August 1973), 152.

40. Memorandum, Laird to Kissinger, "Contingency Plans for Operations against North Vietnam," 6 April 1972. NARA/NPMP/NSC Files/Haig Chronological Files.

41. Haig to Kissinger, "SEA Contingency Planning," 6 April 1972. NARA/ NPMP/NSC Files/Haig Chronological Files.

42. Haig-Moorer telcon, 8:10 P.M., 5 April 1972. NARA/NPMP/NSC Files/Haig Chronological Files.

43. In his diary entry that night, Moorer noted his suspicion that Abrams had been "partying" before the phone call. NARA/RG 218/Moorer Diary.

44. Haig-Moorer telcon, 8:30 P.M., 5 April 1972. NARA/NPMP/NSC Files/Haig Chronological Files.

7. The Forces Flow Forward

1. National Security Council Decision Memorandum 149, "Additional Authorities for Southeast Asia," 4 February 1972. National Security Archive/Prados Collection.
2. Charles K. Hopkins, *SAC Bomber Operations in the Southeast Asia War,* vol. III, 667. SAC Historical Monograph #204, 1983.
3. "Attack Carrier Air Wing Eleven Cruise Report, February-November 1972," iii. Naval Historical Center/Naval Aviation Branch.
4. Charles A. Nicholson, "The USAF Response to the Spring 1972 NVN Offensive: Situation and Redeployment," CHECO, 1972, 34.
5. Charles D. Melson and Curtis G. Arnold, *U.S. Marines in Vietnam: The War That Would Not End, 1971–1973* (Washington: Headquarters USMC, 1991), 153, 157.
6. Ibid., 157, 676.
7. "Attack Carrier Air Wing Eleven Cruise Report, February-November 1972," I-1. Naval Historical Center/Naval Aviation Branch.
8. CNO Briefing, "Seventh Fleet Disposition," 7 April 1972. Naval Historical Center/Operational Archives.
9. CNO Briefing, "NGFS Augmentation," 6 April 1972. Naval Historical Center/Operational Archives.
10. Memorandum for the CNO, "TACAIR SURGE," 22 June 1972, M. F. Weisner, Deputy Chief of Naval Operations (Air Warfare). Naval Historical Center.
11. Ibid.
12. Nicholson, "Situation and Redeployment," 46.
13. Ibid., 51.
14. Ibid., 61–63.
15. Melson and Arnold, *U.S. Marines in Vietnam,* 165–168.
16. Memorandum, Nixon to Kissinger and Haig, untitled, 19 May 1972. NARA/NPMP/NSC Files.
17. Hopkins, *SAC Bomber Operations,* 684.
18. Nicholson, "Situation and Redeployment," 44–45.
19. Elmo R. Zumwalt Jr., *On Watch: A Memoir* (New York: Quadrangle, 1976), 380.
20. Kissinger-Laird telcon, 12:55 P.M., 8 April 1972. NARA/NPMP/Kissinger Telcons.
21. Zumwalt, *On Watch,* 381.
22. Memorandum, Haig to Kissinger, "U.S. Force Augmentations in Southeast

Asia," 21 April 1972. NARA/NPMP/NSC Files/Haig Chronological Files. The points presented in the text represent Haig's summary of Laird's arguments.

23. Kissinger-Laird, "U.S. Force Augmentation in South East Asia," 24 April 1972. NARA/NPMP/NSC Files/Haig Chronological Files.

24. Hopkins, *SAC Bomber Operations*, 669, 681–682. See Henry C. Eccles, *Logistics in the National Defense* (Harrisburg: Stackpole, 1987), 102–108, for a general description of the "logistics snowball."

25. Harry H. Elmendorf, "Project CORONA HARVEST End-of-Tour Report," 16 April 1973, 8–9. Bolling AFB/AFHSO/K717.131.

26. Oral history, David Howard Emory, interviewed by Monte Alan Hostetler, 8 February 1990. Texas Tech University/Vietnam Archive.

27. Zumwalt, *On Watch*, 381.

28. Memorandum, Zumwalt to Moorer, "Impact of SEAsia Buildup on Risks in Other Areas," 17 June 1972, 1. Naval Historical Center.

29. Zumwalt, *On Watch*, 216, 214.

30. Ibid., 205–210, 214.

31. Ibid., 219.

32. Ibid., 222.

33. Adm. Thomas H. Moorer, CJCS diary, 9 November 1972. NARA/RG 218/ Moorer Diary.

8.   B-52s over the North

1. Abrams quoted in Bernard Nalty, *Air War over South Vietnam, 1968–1975* (Washington: Air Force History and Museums Program, 2000), 141. Oral history interviews, Robert C. Seamans Jr., with Lt. Col. Lyn R. Officer and Mr. Hugh N. Ahmann, conducted September 1973, November 1973, March 1974, 87. Maxwell AFB/AFHRA/K239.0512-687.

2. U.S. Naval Institute, *The Reminiscences of Admiral Thomas Hinman Moorer, USN (ret)* (Annapolis: U.S. Naval Institute, 1984), 1268.

3. Charles K. Hopkins, *SAC Bomber Operations in the Southeast Asia War*, vol. III (Offutt AFB: SAC, 1983), 724.

4. COMUSMACV message 051120Z April 72, quoted in CNO briefing for 8 April. Naval Historical Center/Operational Archives.

5. Hopkins, *SAC Bomber Operations*, 732–734.

6. Ibid., 734.

7. Kissinger-Laird telcon, 9:40 A.M., 12 April 1972. NARA/NPMP/Kissinger Telcons.

8. Ho Si Huu et al., *History of the Air Defense Service*, vol. III (Hanoi: People's Army Publishing House, 1994), 93. Translation by Merle Pribbenow.

9. Hopkins, *SAC Bomber Operations*, 734–735.

10. Oval Office Conversation 710-4, Nixon, Kissinger, Haig, Laird, Moorer, 5:01 to 5:50 P.M., 17 April 1972. NARA/NPMP/White House Tapes.

11. The negotiations between Washington and Saigon can be traced in the JCS and MACV messages included in Haig's trip book for his visit to Saigon that April. NARA/NPMP/NSC Files/Haig Trip Files.

12. Moorer, *Reminiscences*, 1244.

13. Kissinger-Laird telcon, 11:50 A.M., 12:45 P.M., 15 April 1972.

14. Moorer, *Reminiscences*, 1244–1245.

15. Huu, *Air Defense Service*, 94.

16. Nguyen Xuan Mau with The Ky, *Defending the Skies: A Memoir* (Hanoi: People's Army Publishing House, 1982), 291–293. Translation by Merle Pribbenow.

17. Ibid.

18. Bill Angus, quoted in John Darrell Sherwood, *Fast Movers: Jet Pilots and the Vietnam Experience* (New York: Free Press, 1999), 72–73.

19. Hopkins, *SAC Bomber Operations*, 736–737.

20. Anthony Lewis, "Communists Report Mines at Haiphong Swept, Ships Sailing," *New York Times*, 18 May 1972, 1.

21. Ibid.

22. CINCPAC 192241Z May 72, "French Representative Hanoi Report on North Vietnam as of May 16," 5–6. Bolling AFB/AFHSO/Vogt Papers.

23. Craig R. Whitney, "B-52 Is Relied on More Than Troops to Blunt Foe's Offensive in Vietnam," *New York Times*, 19 May 1972, 9.

24. Oval Office conversation 334-44, Nixon, Kissinger, Haig, Connally, Moorer, 3:04 to approx. 5:35 P.M., 4 May 1972. NARA/NPMP/White House Tapes.

25. Headquarters PACAF, "Air Operations in Southeast Asia, April 1972," 4-5 to 4-8. Maxwell AFB/AFHRA/K717-7063 April 1972.

26. 7AF 161115Z April 72, "Daily Wrap-Up," 4–5. Bolling AFB/AFHSO/Vogt Papers.

27. Kissinger message text, 4 May 1972, 1. NARA/NPMP/NSC Files/Haig Chronological Files.

28. Hopkins, *SAC Bomber Operations*, 737–738.

29. CNO Daily Briefing, 7 April 1972, "Seventh Fleet Disposition."

30. Seventh Fleet, "Command History 1972," 14. Naval Historical Center/Operational Archives/Post 1946 Command File.

31. U.S. Naval Institute, *Reminiscences of VADM William Paden Mack, USN (ret)* (Annapolis: U.S. Naval Institute), 612.

32. Seventh Fleet, "Command History 1972," 18.

33. Ibid.

34. Ta Hong, Vu Ngoc, and Nguyen Quoc Dung, *History of the People's Air Force*

(1955–1977) (Hanoi: People's Army Publishing House, 1993), 99. Translation by Merle Pribbenow.

35. Ibid., 236.
36. OCNO Memorandum, "Lessons Learned during the Battle of Dong Hoi Gulf," 12 May 1972, 2.
37. Hong et al., *History of the People's Air Force*, 240.
38. Huu et al., *Air Defense Service*, 92, 98.
39. Ibid., 96.
40. Ibid.
41. Ibid., 99.
42. Ibid., 101.
43. Ibid.

9. Attack in the Highlands

1. Neil Sheehan, *A Bright Shining Lie: John Paul Vann and America in Vietnam* (New York: Random House, 1988).
2. CIA Intelligence Memorandum, "Communist Military Build-up in the Central Highlands of South Vietnam," 5 January 1972, 3. CREST CIA-RDP85100875R001100140001-8. CIA Memorandum, "The Communist Winter-Spring Offensive in South Vietnam," 7 February 1972, 4. CIA-RDP85T00875R001100140005-6.
3. Lewis Sorley, *Vietnam Chronicles: The Abrams Tapes, 1968–1972* (Lubbock: Texas Tech University Press, 2004), 730, 731.
4. CIA, "Communist Winter-Spring Offensive," 4.
5. Pham Cuong, "The Former Saigon General Who Did Not Know How to Shoot," 25 April 2005. Vietnam Net, accessed 23 July 2005 at *http://www.vnn.vn.chinhtri/doinoi/2005/04/414031*. Translation by Merle Pribbenow.
6. CIA, "Communist Winter-Spring Offensive," 3.
7. Ngo Quang Truong, *The Easter Offensive* (Washington: CMH, 1979), 81.
8. SRAG 070225Z Feb 72, "Daily Commander's Evaluation." USAMHI/MACV Collection.
9. SRAG 130156Z Mar 72, "Daily Commander's Evaluation for 24 Hours from 1000H, 13 March." CMH/Abrams Messages.
10. SRAG 280534Z Mar 72, "Battlefield Situation in the Kontum Area," 2. CMH/Abrams Messages.
11. Luc Luong Vu Trang et al., *History of the Central Highlands People's Armed Forces in the Anti-U.S. War of Resistance for National Salvation* (Hanoi: People's Army Publishing House, 1980), ch. 7. Translation by Merle Pribbenow.
12. Military History Institute, *Victory in Vietnam: The Official History of the People's*

Army of Vietnam, 1954–1975, trans. Merle Pribbenow (Lawrence: University Press of Kansas, 2002), 285, 286.

13. Trang, *Central Highlands People's Armed Forces*, ch. 7.

14. Dale Andrade, *America's Last Vietnam Battle: Halting Hanoi's 1972 Easter Offensive* (Lawrence: University Press of Kansas, 2001), 220–227, 228–231.

15. Peter A. Leibchen, "Kontum: The Battle for the Central Highlands, 30 March–10 June 1972" (PACAF: CHECO, 27 October 1972), 25.

16. CORDS/SRAG Military Region Overview for the Month Ending 30 April 1972, 12 May 1972, 1–2. Texas Tech University/Vietnam Archive/Glenn Helm Collection.

17. Ibid., 3.

18. Ibid., 2.

19. Ibid., 7.

20. SRAG 080456Z May 72, "Evacuation of Refugees from Kontum," 1. USAMHI/MACV Collection.

10.   The Fall of Quang Tri

1. FRAC 050349Z Apr 72, "Commander's Daily Evaluation," 1, 3–4. CMH/Abrams Messages.

2. FRAC 080248Z Apr 72, "Commander's Daily Evaluation," 1–2. CMH/Abrams Messages.

3. Ngo Quang Truong, *The Easter Offensive* (Washington: CMH, 1979), 36.

4. Ibid.

5. Ibid., 32–33, 38.

6. FRAC 130225Z Apr 72, "Daily Commander's Evaluation," 2. CMH/Abrams Messages.

7. Truong, *Easter Offensive*, 37.

8. Annex F, Combat Operations After Action Report, MACV Advisory Team 155, 7–8. NARA/RG 472.

9. Appendix 6 to Annex D, Artillery After Action Report, MACV Advisory Team 155, 1.

10. Appendix 7 to Annex D, Artillery After Action Report, MACV Advisory Team 155, 2.

11. Appendix 1 to Annex D, Artillery After Action Report, MACV Advisory Team 155, 1.

12. Appendix 7 to Annex D, Artillery After Action Report, MACV Advisory Team 155, 2.

13. David A. Brookbank, "VNAF TACS and the Fall of Quang Tri," 31 July 1972, 11. Alfred M. Gray Marine Corps Research Center/Gerald C. Turley Collection.

14. Ibid., 8, 9.

15. Ho Si Huu et al., *History of the Air Defense Service*, vol. II (Hanoi: People's Army Publishing House, 1994), 41.

16. Truong, *Easter Offensive*, 41.

17. Interview, Col. Donald Metcalf with Maj. Robert G. Flowers Jr., September 15, 1972, 12. Draft transcript. USAMHI/MACV Collection.

18. Truong, *Easter Offensive*, 44.

19. Ibid., 44–45.

20. MACV 241111Z Apr 72, "Personal Assessment of the Situation in RVN as of 24 April 1972," 2, 6, 9. CMH/Abrams Messages.

21. MACV 011601 May 72, "Personal Assessment of the Situation in RVN as of 1 May 1972," 6, 12. CMH/Abrams Messages.

22. Ibid.

23. Chris Hobson, *Vietnam Air Losses: United States Air Force, Navy and Marine Corps Fixed-Wing Aircraft Losses in Southeast Asia, 1961–1973* (Hinckley, U.K.: Midland, 2001), 223.

24. Alton Slay, "Personal Observations on the Air War in SEA, 1 August 1971 to 1 June 1972," 68. Maxwell AFB/AFHRA/TS-HOA-72-82.

25. Ibid.

11.   The Path to Linebacker

1. Kissinger-Nixon telcons, 8–10 April 1972. NARA/NPMP/Kissinger Telcons.

2. Haig-Kissinger memorandum, "Southeast Asia Trip Report," 19 April 1972, 1, 3. NARA/NPMP/NSC Files/Haig Chronological Files.

3. Nixon to Kissinger, 24 April 72, 1–2. NARA/NPMP/Kissinger Trip Files.

4. Ibid., 4, 5, 6, 7.

5. Kissinger-Nixon memorandum, "My Trip to Moscow," April 24, 1972, 1. NARA/NPMP/NSC Files/Haig Chronological Files.

6. Luu Van Loi and Nguyen Anh Vu, *Le Duc Tho–Kissinger Negotiations in Paris* (Hanoi: The Gioi Publishers, 1996), 222–223.

7. Haldeman diary, 22 April 1972.

8. Abrams-Laird message, "U.S. Force Posture in the RVN," 21 April 1972, 6. NARA/NPMP/NSC Files/Haig Chronological Files.

9. Laird-Nixon memorandum, "US Force Redeployments from SVN," 21 April 1972, 12. NARA/NPMP/NSC Files/Haig Chronological Files.

10. Kissinger-Nixon memorandum, "Force Reduction in Vietnam," 24 April 1972, 2. NARA/NPMP/NSC Files/Haig Chronological Files.

11. Nixon-Kissinger message text, untitled, 27 April 1972, 1. NARA/NPMP/NSC Files/Haig Chronological Files.

12. Nixon-Kissinger memorandum, untitled, 30 April 1972, 1–2. NARA/NPMP/NSC Files.

13. Ibid., 3.

14. Haig to Kissinger memorandum, "Short Term Actions," 1 May 1972, 2. NARA/NPMP/NSC Files/Haig Chronological files.

15. Oval Office Conversation 716-2, unknown time after 4:11 P.M. to 5:29 P.M., 1 May 1972, Nixon, Kissinger, Haig, Ziegler, Rogers, Butterfield. NARA/NPMP/White House Tapes.

16. Oval Office Conversation 716-4, 5:57–6:47 P.M., 1 May 1972, Nixon, Kissinger, Haldeman. NARA/NPMP/White House Tapes.

17. Kissinger-Nixon memorandum, "My May 2 Meeting with the North Vietnamese," 2 May 1972, 1. NARA/NPMP/NSC Files.

18. Kissinger-Nixon telcon, 9:55 A.M., 1 May 1972. NARA/NPMP/Kissinger Telcons.

19. Alexander M. Haig Jr. with Charles McCarry, *Inner Circles: How America Changed the World: A Memoir* (New York: Warner Books, 1992), 287.

20. Kissinger-Haig message text, untitled, 2 May 1972. NARA/NPMP/NSC Files/Haig Chronological Files.

21. Laird-Nixon memorandum, untitled, 2 May 1972. NARA/NPMP/NSC Files/ Haig Chronological Files.

22. Kissinger-Moorer telcon, 9:15 P.M., 2 May 1972. NARA/NPMP/Kissinger Telcons.

23. Kissinger-Laird telcon, 9:45 P.M., 2 May 1972. NARA/NPMP/Kissinger Telcons.

24. EOB Conversation 334-44, 3:04 to unknown time before 5:35 P.M., 4 May 1972, Nixon, Haldeman, Connally, Haig, Moorer. Continues on to EOB Conversation 338-1, unknown time after 5:25 until 5:55. All quotations from this conversation are taken from this tape.

25. Kissinger-Bunker message text, untitled, 4 May 1972, 1, 2. NARA/NPMP/ NSC Files/Haig Chronological Files.

26. EOB Conversation 335-33, 2:10 to 3:15 P.M., 5 May 1972, Nixon, Haig. NARA/NPMP/White House Tapes. All quotations from this conversation are taken from this tape.

27. Haig-Kissinger memorandum, "Talking Points for Your Breakfast Meeting with Secretary Laird, 8:00 A.M., Saturday, May 6, 1972," May 5, 1972, 1–2. NARA/NPMP/NSC Files/Haig Chronological Files.

28. Kissinger-Nixon telcon, 10:27 A.M., 6 May 1972, 2. NARA/NPMP/Kissinger Telcons.

29. Ibid.

30. Kissinger-Nixon telcon, 1:45 P.M., 6 May 1972, 3. NARA/NPMP/Kissinger Telcons.

31. Haig-Kissinger memorandum, "Items to Discuss with Secretary Laird at Breakfast, Sunday, May 7," 7 May 1972. NARA/NPMP/NSC Files/Haig Chronological Files.

32. Oval Office Conversation 721-6, 8:59 A.M. to 9:06 A.M., 8 May 1972, Nixon, Kissinger. NARA/NPMP/White House Tapes.

33. Memorandum for the President's Files, "National Security Council Meeting, 8 May 1972," undated, 2. NARA/NPMP/NSC Files/Haig Chronological files.

34. Ibid., 18, 15, 20–21.

35. Ibid., 6–8.

36. Ibid., 11.

37. Jeffrey Kimball, *The Vietnam War Files: Uncovering the Secret History of Nixon-Era Strategy* (Lawrence: University Press of Kansas, 2004), 221–228.

38. Moorer-Kissinger telcon (secure phone), 6:18 P.M., 8 May 1972. NARA/NPMP/Kissinger Telcons.

39. Kissinger-Laird telcon, 6:37 P.M., 8 May 1972, 1. NARA/NPMP/Kissinger Telcons.

40. Kissinger-Rush telcon, 6:58 P.M., 8 May 1972; Kissinger-Sullivan telcon, 7:09 P.M., 8 May 1972, 1. Both in NARA/NPMP/Kissinger Telcons.

41. Kissinger-Nixon telcon, 6:55 P.M., 8 May 1972, 1. NARA/NPMP/Kissinger Telcons.

12. Closing the Ports

1. Command History Branch, Headquarters Pacific Command, "Commander in Chief Pacific Command History," (Pacific Command: Camp H. M. Smith, 1973), vol. I, 188.

2. Mine Warfare Project Office, "The Mining of North Vietnam, 8 May 1972 to 14 January 1973," 30 June 1975, 2-4 to 2-5. Naval Historical Center/Naval Operational Archives.

3. Ibid., 2-11, 2-12.

4. Ibid., 2-12.

5. Elmo R. Zumwalt Jr., *On Watch: A Memoir* (New York: Quadrangle, 1976), 385.

6. William P. Mack, oral history, vol. II, 617. Naval Historical Center/Naval Operational Archives.

7. "Mining of North Vietnam," 2–18.

8. Quoted in John Darrell Sherwood, *Fast Movers: Jet Pilots and the Vietnam Experience* (New York: Free Press, 1999), 85.

9. "Mining of North Vietnam," 3–6.

10. Ibid., 3–7.

11. Mack, oral history, 618.

12. The full text of Nixon's speech can be found at "Nixon: Choose Path to Peace," *Washington Post*, 9 May 1972, A15.

13. "Harris Poll Finds 59% Backed Harbor Mining," *New York Times*, 14 May 1972, 28.

14. Spencer Rich and Richard L. Lyons, "President Rebuffed by Democrats," *Washington Post*, 10 May 1972, A1.

15. Haldeman diaries, 9 May 1972. CD Version, Sony Microsoft, 1994.

16. Rich and Lyons, "President Rebuffed by Democrats," A1.

17. Luu Van Loi and Nguyen Anh Vu, *Le Duc Tho–Kissinger Negotiations in Paris* (Hanoi: The Gioi, 1996), 234.

18. Stanley Karnow, "Hanoi Appears to Ask Allies to React Strongly to Moves," *Washington Post*, 10 May 1972, A11.

19. Lewis Sorley, *Thunderbolt: Creighton Abrams and the Army of His Times* (New York: Simon and Schuster, 1992), 322–326.

20. Sorley attributes the late notification to Laird having been kept in the dark until very late in the planning process, and then simply forgetting to inform Abrams. That is unlikely on several counts. Kissinger notified Laird of Nixon's close interest in mining on 5 May, and Laird had approved the JCS message alerting CINCPAC that was transmitted around noon on 6 May, Washington time. It is more likely that Laird, caught between Nixon's determination to proceed and Abrams's steady opposition to the use of air assets in the North, chose to present the theater commander with a fait accompli and then apologize as necessary to move past the incident. Nixon and Kissinger's use of the back channel to inform Abrams of their decision, evidently without telling Laird they had done so, only increased the level of confusion.

21. "Mining of North Vietnam," 3–41.

22. "Mining of North Vietnam," 3–24.

23. CINCPAC 100723Z May 72, "Employment of Aerial Munitions," authorized use of the Destructor mines as part of the Linebacker campaign. Summarized in Corona Harvest K717.291-2, Maxwell AFB, AFHRA.

24. "Mining of North Vietnam," 3–41.

13.   Linebacker Planning and Direction

1. EOB Conversation 334-44.

2. Laird-Kissinger Memorandum, "'Indicator' Actions against North Vietnam," 8 May 1969, 1. NARA/WHSF/NSC Files/Haig Special Files.

3. Ibid.

4. Jeffrey Kimball, *The Vietnam War Files: Uncovering the Secret History of Nixon-Era Strategy* (Lawrence: University Press of Kansas , 2004), 99–110.

5. JCSM-712-69, "Pruning Knife Alpha," 13 November 1969, 1. NARA/RG 218/JCS Central Files.

6. Ibid., 13.

7. Ibid., 10.

8. Ibid., 19.

9. Richard M. Nixon, *RN: The Memoirs of Richard Nixon* (New York: Grosset and Dunlap, 1978), 393–414.

10. JCS Fact Sheet, "Current Plans for Air Strikes Against NVN." Undated, from December 1971. NARA/ RG 218/ JCS Central File.

11. Command History Branch, Headquarters Pacific Command, "Commander in Chief Pacific Command History," (Pacific Command: Camp H. M. Smith, 1973), vol. II, 144.

12. Kissinger-Moorer telcon, 6:18 P.M., 8 May 1972. NARA/NPMP/Kissinger Telcons.

13. Ibid.

14. AF SSO PACAF 120355Z May 72, "NVN Interdiction Plan," 3. Maxwell AFB/AFHRA/K717.291-2.

15. AF SSO 7AF 090820Z May 72, "NVN Interdiction Campaign." Maxwell AFB/AFHRA/K717.291-2.

16. JCS 2307Z May 72, "NVN Interdiction Plan Public Affairs Guidance." Maxwell AFB/AFHRA/K717.291-2.

17. These included JCS 09247Z May 72, "NVN Interdiction Program"; JCS 092307Z May 72, "NVN Interdiction Plan Public Affairs Guidance"; and JCS 092356Z May 72, "NVN Interdiction Plan." Maxwell AFB/AFHRA/K717.291-2.

18. AF SSO PACAF 120355Z May 72, "NVN Interdiction Plan," 6, 7.

19. Ibid.

20. Marshall L. Michel III, *Clashes: Air Combat over North Vietnam, 1965–1973* (Annapolis: Naval Institute Press, 1997), 31–32.

21. PACAF 120355Z May 72, "NVN Interdiction Plan," 5.

22. Frank M. Machovec, "Southeast Asia Tactical Data Systems Interface" (CHECO, 1 January 1975), 5–18.

23. These included JCS 092356Z May 72, "NVN Interdiction Plan;" CINCPAC 100427Z May 72, "NVN Interdiction Plan," which forwarded a list of 166 targets for validation; JCS 112336Z May 72, "Linebacker," directing naval forces to avoid a hospital/POW camp while striking in Thanh Hoa and a hospital when striking Nam Dinh; CINCPAC 120448Z May 72, "CINCPAC Master Target List," providing the current authorized targets; and a series of messages among Seventh Air Force, PACAF, and PACOM addressing the Vu Chua railroad bridges. See Corona Harvest Microfilm K717.291-2, 1 May–31 July 1972, Maxwell AFB/AFHRA.

24. Air Force Intelligence working group, "Authorized Linebacker Targets," 21 June 72. Bolling AFB/AFHSO/Vogt Papers.

25. "Photographic Interpretation Report, KH-4 Mission 1116-2, 29 April–8 May 1972," May 1972. CIA-RDP78T04562A004300010001-0.

26. Paul W. Elder, "Buffalo Hunter" (CHECO, 24 July 1973), 32.

27. Haig-Murphy telcon, 15 June 1972. NARA/NPMP/NSC Files/Haig Chrono-logical Files.

28. JCS 152340Z May 72, "Linebacker." Summarized in Corona Harvest Mi-crofilm K717.291-2, Maxwell AFB/AFHRA.

29. JCS 161617Z May 72, "Strike Request." Summarized ibid.

30. JCS 132000Z Jun 72, "Linebacker." Summarized ibid.

31. JCS memorandum, "Pertinent Air/NGFS Authorities Granted, 30 March–14 December 1972," 31 December 1972. NARA/RG 218/Moorer Diary.

32. By the end of the campaign in December, the Joint Staff calculated that the 10-mile circle prohibiting attacks around Hanoi had been imposed 57 percent of the time since the opening of Linebacker. See 31 Dec 72 CJCS Memo for Record, "Air and NGFS Authorities Requested and Approved/Ignored, 30 March-14 December 1972," 2. NARA/RG 218/Moorer Diary.

33. CINCPAC 240403Z May 72, quoted in "Commander in Chief Pacific Com-mand History," vol. II, 539–540.

34. JCS 062018Z Aug 72, quoted ibid., 541.

35. 7AF 251055Z Feb 73, "Preparations for a JCS Review of Follow-on Southeast Asian Command Arrangements," 2–3, 5. Bolling AFB/AFHSO/Vogt Papers/Feb 1973 Read File.

14.   The Initial Strikes

1. Nixon-Kissinger memorandum, untitled, 9 May 1972. NARA/NPMP/NSC Files.

2. Jeffrey Ethell and Alfred Price, *One Day in a Very Long War: May 10, 1972* (New York: Random House, 1989), provides a comprehensive look at the day's events, largely from the pilots' perspectives. Except where otherwise indicated, my account here is based on this work.

3. Ethell and Price, *One Day in a Long War*, 32–34.

4. North Vietnamese MiG interceptors relied heavily on their ground-controlled radar support, which in turn meant that the ground controllers needed to be able to find and identify the MiGs. The fighters' Identification Friend or Foe (IFF) system transmitted electronic signals to meet that requirement. In late 1971 the United States fielded the Combat Tree system, enabling U.S. fighters to trigger and read the North Vietnamese fighters' IFF system. This multiplied the effectiveness of the Phantoms that were equipped with Combat Tree, since they no longer needed to rely on the basic F-4 radar for target acquisition.

5. Ethell and Price, *One Day in a Long War*, 20–26. The full strike force is listed on 50–51.

6. Ibid., 90.

7. Ibid., 94–95.

8. The MiG-17 Fresco was a direct development of the Korean War–vintage

MiG-15. Very maneuverable, the aircraft was armed only with guns and suffered from a slow roll rate and limited acceleration. North Vietnamese histories recount the low-altitude engagement near Hai Phuong, but list only two MiG-17s lost of four launched to intercept the Navy strike. See Ta Hong et al., *History of the People's Air Force* (Hanoi: People's Army Publishing House, 1993), 253–255. Translation by Merle Pribbenow.

9. Ho Si Huu et al. *History of the Air Defense Service*, vol. III (Hanoi: People's Army Publishing House, 1994), 117. Translation by Merle Pribbenow.

10. 7AF, "Daily Wrap Up," 111200Z May 1972, 7. Bolling AFB/AFHSO/Vogt Papers.

11. Ibid., 8–9.

12. 7AF, "Daily Wrap Up," 121140Z May 1972, 3. Vogt Papers.

13. Ibid., 8, 9.

14. Karen Gottschalk Turner with Phan Thanh Hao, *Even the Women Must Fight: Memories of War from North Vietnam* (New York: Wiley, 1998).

15. 7AF, 121140Z May, "Daily Wrap Up," 9. Vogt Papers.

16. In this discussion the targets are taken from PACAF's "Air Operations Southeast Asia, May 1972," pp. 4-B-7 to 4-B-14. The sortie counts come from Vogt's daily reports to PACAF and CSAF on 14–16 May.

17. PACAF, "Air Operations Southeast Asia, May 1972," 4-B-11.

18. Patrick J. Breitling, "Guided Bomb Operations in SEA: The Weather Dimension, 1 Feb–31 Dec 1972" (CHECO, October 1, 1973).

19. The best-known example of this was in Operation Bolo, in 1967, when a force led by Robin Olds engaged PAVNAF MiG-21s and destroyed seven without a loss. Olds "borrowed" call signs usually used by F-105s for his force of F-4s, and the MiGs intercepted them expecting to find bombers. See Wayne Thompson, *To Hanoi and Back: The United States Air Force and North Vietnam, 1966–1973* (Washington: Air Force History and Museums Program, 2000), 52–55.

20. "History of 7/13th Air Force, 1 January–31 December 1972," vol. I. Maxwell AFB/AFHRA/K744.01 1972.

15. The DRV Responds

1. *Collected Party Documents*, "Report on Recommendation to Shift the Direction of Activities and Urgent Operational Duties to be Completed in Response to the Current New Situation," 18 May 1972, 272.

2. Ibid., 274.

3. Ibid., 283.

4. Anatoly Dobrynin, *In Confidence: Moscow's Ambassador to America's Six Cold War Presidents (1962–1986)* (New York: Times Books, 1995), 101.

5. *Collected Party Documents*, 289–318.

6. For the gradual and mild Chinese reaction to the mining, see "Peking Says U.S. Jets Hit Its Ships," *Washington Post*, 10 May 1972, A17; "Peking Newspaper Hits 'Escalation,'" ibid., 11 May 1972, A30; Stanley Karnow, "Peking Reaction Regarded as Moderate," ibid., 12 May 1972, A15.

7. Chen Jian, *Mao's China and the Cold War* (Chapel Hill: University of North Carolina Press, 2001), 252–253.

8. Qiang Zhai, *China and the Vietnam Wars, 1950–1975* (Chapel Hill: University of North Carolina Press, 2000), 203.

9. Alexander M. Haig Jr. with Charles McCarry, *Inner Circles: How America Changed the World: A Memoir* (New York: Warner, 1992), 259–262; Richard M. Nixon, *RN: The Memoirs of Richard Nixon* (New York: Grosset and Dunlap, 1978), 613–615.

10. Chen Jian, *Mao's China and the Cold War*, 221–229.

11. Qiang Zhai, *China and the Vietnam Wars*, 203.

12. Hoang Van Hoan, *Another Drop in the Ocean: Hoang Van Hoan's Revolutionary Reminiscences* (Beijing: Foreign Language Press, 1986), 291.

13. Ho Si Huu et al., *History of the Air Defense Service*, vol. III (Hanoi: People's Army Publishing House, 1994), 144. Translation by Merle Pribbenow.

14. Ibid., 110.

15. DIA Fact Sheet, "Soviet Bloc Aid to Vietnam." Undated, from late 1971. NARA/RG 218/JCS Central File, 1972.

16. "Soviet Is Reportedly Moving Aid for Hanoi across China by Rail," *New York Times*, 19 May 1972, 8.

17. Jack Anderson, "U.S. Moves May Reunite Russia, China," *Washington Post*, 19 May 1972, B23.

18. Ibid., 107.

19. Ibid., 108.

20. Ibid., 102.

21. Ibid., 117.

22. Ibid., 106.

23. Ibid., 115.

24. "Hanoi Week—Ending 16 May 1972," FCO 15/1674, 1, 2. National Archives, Kew, U.K.

16. Nixon Triumphant

1. Haldeman Diaries, 6 April 1972. CD Edition, Sony Imagesoft, 1994.

2. Henry A. Kissinger, *White House Years* (Boston: Little, Brown, 1979), 1126–1135; Elmo R. Zumwalt Jr., *On Watch: A Memoir* (New York: Quadrangle, 1976), 400–411.

3. Nixon-Kissinger memorandum, untitled, 10 May 1972. NARA/NPMP/NSC Files.

4. Ibid.

5. Haig-Kissinger memorandum, untitled, 10 May 1972. NARA/NPMP/NSC Files. Haig's reference was to Ambassador William Sullivan, previously ambassador to Laos during the first portion of the war and now an assistant secretary of state.

6. Nixon–Kissinger and Haig memorandum, untitled, 15 May 1972, 1. NARA/NPMP/NSC Files.

7. Nixon-Haldeman memorandum, untitled, 15 May 1972, 1, 2. NARA/NPMP/WHSF/Haldeman Files.

8. Nixon-Kissinger memorandum, untitled, 18 May 1972, 1. NARA/NPMP/WHSF/Haldeman Files.

9. Nixon-Haldeman memorandum, copy for Fred Malek, untitled, 18 May 1972, 1. NARA/NPMP/WHSF/Haldeman Files.

10. Haldeman Diaries, CD edition, 19 May 1972.

11. Oval Office Conversation 726-1, Nixon, Kissinger, Agnew, Moorer, Haldeman, Ziegler, 10:30–11:42 A.M., 19 May 1972. NARA/NPMP/White House Tapes. The proximate issue was a four-day clearance for the Air Force to attack four targets in the Chinese buffer zone, with the time limits established to coincide with Nixon's trip to Moscow. The Air Force had been unable to attack all four targets in the time allotted.

12. Haig-Pursley telcon, 5:15 P.M., 19 May 1972. NARA/NPMP/NSC Files/Haig Chronological Files.

13. Moorer diary, 19 May 1972. NARA/RG 218/Moorer Diary.

14. Nixon–Kissinger and Haig memorandum, untitled, 19 May 1972, 1. NARA/NPMP/NSC Files.

15. Ibid., 1, 2.

16. Ibid., 2.

17. Nixon-Haig memorandum, untitled, 20 May 1972, 1. NARA/NPMP/NSC Files.

18. Nixon-Kissinger memorandum, untitled, 19 May 1972. NARA/NPMP/NSC Files. Haig complied by conducting a background interview on 23 May, pointedly excluding the *New York Times*.

19. Nixon-Haig memorandum, untitled, 20 May 1972, 3, 4. NARA/NPMP/NSC Files.

20. JCS 212319 May 72, "Linebacker," summarized in index to Corona Harvest Microfilm K717.291-2, 8. Maxwell AFB/AFHRA.

17.   The Siege of An Loc

1. "The Attacks on An Loc City by 20th Tank Battalion + One Armored Company of 21st Tank Battalion of the COSVN's 26th Armored Group, Operating under the Operational Control of the 5th and 9th Infantry Divisions, from 13

April to 11 May 1972," in *A Number of Battles Fought by Our Armor Troops*, vol. 4 (Hanoi: Armor Command, 1983), 47. Translation by Merle Pribbenow.

2. Ngo Quang Truong, *The Easter Offensive* (Washington: Center for Military History, 1979), 123.

3. General Staff, "A Number of Battles Fought by Our Armor Troops," vol. IV, 49–52.

4. Ibid., 52.

5. Paul Ringenbach, "Airlift to Besieged Areas" (CHECO, 7 December 1973), 13.

6. Ibid., 2.

7. Truong Nhu Tang with David Chanoff and Doan Van Toai, *A Viet Cong Memoir: An Inside Account of the Vietnam War and Its Aftermath* (New York: Vintage, 1986), 119.

8. "Interview with MAJ Ingram and CPT Moffett with TRAC HQS Staff and HQ TRAC 011700 June 1972—MAJ Cash," 1 June 1972. Typewritten notes from interview. USAMHI/MACV Collection.

9. Col. William E. Miller, senior advisor, 5th ARVN Division, interview notes, undated from May 1972, 2. USAMHI/MACV Collection.

10. "Interview w/MAJ Ingram, Kenneth A. Sr Arty Advisor the 5th DCAT at AN LOC from 1-31 May 72, interviewed by MAJ Cash at HQ TRAC 011400 June 72," 1 June 1972, 4. Typewritten notes from interview. USAMHI/MACV Collection.

11. Miller interview, 2.

12. Hollingsworth, "Communist Invasion in Military Region 3," June 1972, 16. Draft manuscript, USAMHI/MACV Collection.

13. Maj. Allen R. Borstorff, interview by Maj. Dave Cash, 25 May 1972, 1. USAMHI/MACV Collection.

14. Paul T. Ringenbach and Peter J. Melly, "The Battle for An Loc 5 April–26 June 1972" (CHECO, 31 January 1973), 13.

15. Miller interview, 3, 7.

16. "A Number of Battles Fought by Our Armor Troops," 53.

17. Hollingsworth, "Communist Invasion in Military Region 3," 18.

18. Ibid.

19. "A Number of Battles Fought by Our Armor Troops," vol. IV, 55.

20. Ingram interview, 4.

21. "A Number of Battles Fought by Our Armor Troops," 53.

22. Ibid.

23. Dale Andrade, *America's Last Vietnam Battle: Halting Hanoi's 1972 Easter Offensive* (Lawrence: University Press of Kansas, 2001), 414–427. A post-campaign assessment by MACV noted that Hung's performance during the battle was "poor," and that he believed ARVN was being "duped" into defending An Loc

so the NVA could make an end run on Saigon. The assessment emphasized that he "spent most of the time in An Loc complaining of his plight." This report very probably came from Miller, reflecting the degree and the basis of his frustration in An Loc. "Biographical Sketches Selected ARVN Commanders," biography of Hung. Undated briefing cards, apparently drafted in 1973 and updated as late as 1974, for use of American staff officers and commanders. Alfred M. Gray Marine Corps Research Center/Gerald C. Turley Collection.

24. Advisory Team 70 Daily Journal, 11 May 72, 1–2, 3, 4. NARA/RG 472.

25. Ibid., 5.

26. Ingram interview, 4.

27. 5th Division Daily Journal, 11 May 1972, 20.

28. Interview, Lt. Col. Stephen J. Opitz with Lt. Col. Robert G. Zimmerman, 18 July 1972, 43. K239.0512-846. Bolling AFB/AFHSO..

29. Ringenbach and Melly, "Battle for An Loc," 47.

30. 7AF 131110Z May 72, "Daily Wrap-Up," 10. Bolling AFB/AFHSO/Vogt Papers.

31. Military History Institute, *Victory in Vietnam: The Official History of the People's Army of Vietnam, 1954–1975*, trans. Merle Pribbenow (Lawrence: University Press of Kansas, 2002), 296.

32. Ibid., 307.

33. Hollingsworth, "Communist Invasion in Military Region 3," 30.

34. MACV, "The Nguyen Hue Offensive," 6. Turley Collection.

35. "Biographical Sketches Selected ARVN Commanders," biography of Minh. Turley Collection.

36. "A Number of Battles Fought by Our Armor Troops," 61.

37. Ibid., 61, 62, 60.

38. *Collected Party Documents*, Cable no. 453, 16 June 1972, 330.

39. "Central Office for South Vietnam Directive 06, Including a Statement on Ceasefire Conditions and Military Intentions during October 1972," acq. Vietnam, Bien Hoa (30 September 1972), 2.

18.   The Defense of Hue

1. John A. Graham, "Anatomy of a Crisis—Hue City (Phase One—April 30–May 10 1972)," 11 May 1972, 2; 3 June 1972, 2. Advisory Team 18, Civil Operations and Rural Development Support, First Regional Assistance Command. Texas Tech University/Vietnam Archive/John Graham Collection.

2. Ngo Quang Truong, *The Easter Offensive* (Washington: U.S. Army Center of Military History, 1979), 50.

3. Ibid., 54.

4. Graham, "Anatomy of a Crisis," 11 May 1972, 3.

5. Ibid., 5.

6. Seventh Air Force 051100Z May 72, "Daily Wrap Up," 3. Bolling AFB/ AFHSO/Vogt Papers.

7. Ibid., 5.

8. Ho Si Huu et al., *History of the Air Defense Service*, vol. III (Hanoi: People's Army Publishing House, 1994), 49. Translation by Merle Pribbenow.

9. Ibid., 50.

10. Seventh Air Force 061110Z May 72, "Daily Wrap Up," 3. Vogt Papers.

11. Nguyen Huu An took command of the 308th Division in July 1972, and commanded the unit through the remainder of the summer. His memoirs provide fascinating insight into the relationships among the General Staff, campaign headquarters, and operational units. By this time the General Staff and the Central Military Party Committee had lost touch with the situation of the units along the My Chanh front. Their unremitting commitment to the counteroffensive was completely unrealistic under the circumstances facing the 308th. Subordinate commanders were reluctant to question the counteroffensive strategy being followed, fearing that they would be accused of "wavering and not thinking offensively." General An considered the strategy responsible for the eventual loss of Quang Tri City and for the prohibitively high casualties taken by his unit through the summer. See Colonel General Nguyen Huu An (as told to Nguyen Tu Duong), *New Battlefield* (Hanoi: People's Army Publishing House, 2002). Translation by Merle Pribbenow.

12. Seventh Air Force 071130Z May 72, "Daily Wrap Up," 4–5. Vogt Papers.

13. Seventh Air Force 051100Z May 72, "Daily Wrap Up," 5. Vogt Papers.

14. Seventh Air Force 061110Z May 72, "Daily Wrap Up," 2. Vogt Papers.

15. Graham, "Anatomy of a Crisis," 20 May 1972, 4.

16. *History of the Air Defense Service*, vol. III, 54.

17. Ibid., 51.

18. Ibid., 54.

19. The Center Holds

1. CORDS/SRAG Military Region II Overview for April 1972, 12 May 1972, 4. Texas Tech University/Vietnam Archive/Glenn Helm Collection.

2. COMUSMACV 011601Z May 1972, "Personal Assessment of the Situation in RVN as of 1 May 1972," 3. CMH/Abrams Messages.

3. Gary R. Swingle, "Battle of Kontum," Part I (Second Draft), undated, late 1972. USAMHI/MACV Collection.

4. SRAG 290309Z Apr 72, "Daily Commanders Evaluation for 24 Hours from 1000H, 28 April," 3. USAMHI/Abrams Messages.

5. Ibid.

6. SRAG 260213Z April 72, "Daily Commander's Evaluation for 24 Hours from 1000H, 25 April," 1. USAMHI/Abrams Messages.

7. "The Advance and Attack conducted by 297th Tank Battalion, Assigned to Support 28th Regiment/10th Infantry Division, 320th Infantry Division, and 2nd Infantry Division, from 14 to 27 May 1972," in *A Number of Battles Fought by Our Armored Troops,* vol. IV (Hanoi: Armored Command, 1983), 103. Partial translation by Merle Pribbenow.

8. MACV 271334Z April 72, "AT Weapons Systems," 2. USAMHI/Abrams Messages.

9. SRAG 040411Z May 72, "Daily Commander's Evaluation for 24 Hours from 1000H 3 May," p. 3. USAMHI/Abrams Messages.

10. SRAG 021551Z May 72, "Presidential Called Meeting with the Four Corps Commanders and Key Staff—2 May 72," 1–2. USAMHI/Abrams Messages.

11. SRAG 0903 40Z May 72, "Daily Commander's Evaluation for 24 Hours from 1000H, 8 May." USAMHI/Abrams Messages.

12. SRAG 260213 Apr 72, "Daily Commander's Evaluation for 24 Hours from 1000H, 25 April," 1. USAMHI/Abrams Messages.

13. SRAG 07028Z May 72, untitled, 2–3. USAMHI/Abrams Papers.

14. Ngo Quang Truong, *The Easter Offensive of 1972* (Washington: Center for Military History, 1979), 92.

15. SRAG 130134Z May 72, "Daily Commanders Evaluation for 24 Hours from 1000H 12 May," 2. USAMHI/Abrams Messages.

16. Truong, *The Easter Offensive,* 98.

17. Ibid., 99.

18. Peter A. Leibchen, "Kontum: The Battle for the Central Highlands, 30 March–10 June 1972" (PACAF: CHECO, 27 October 1972), 57.

19. MACV 171034Z May 72, "Memcon of Meeting at TSN Air Base VIP Lounge," 2. USAMHI/Abrams Messages. Later in this trip Agnew stopped at Guam, where the chance remark on target limitations set off the verbal explosions by Nixon and Kissinger discussed in Chapter 16.

20. Ibid.

21. Leibchen, "Kontum," 52.

22. Truong, *Easter Offensive,* 103.

23. SRAC 292220 Z May 72, "Daily Commander's Evaluation for 24 Hours from 1000H 28 May," 3. USAMHI/Abrams Messages.

24. "The Advance and Attack conducted by 297th Tank Battalion," 109, 110.

20.   Stalemate at the My Chanh River

1. End of Tour Report, Lt. Col. James H. Grady, Assistant Director, I-DASC, 15 March–20 June 1972, 5. NARA/RG 472/FRAC Senior Officer Debriefs.

2. Ngo Quang Truong, *The Easter Offensive* (Washington: CMH, 1979), 55–56.

3. Ibid., 61.

4. John Graham, "Thua Thien Province Report—June 1972," 2 June 1972, 3. Texas Tech University/Vietnam Archive/John Graham Collection.

5. CINCPAC 110238Z May 72, summarized in COMUSMACV 181140Z May 72, "Linebacker Operations," 1. Corona Harvest Microfilm K717.291-2, Maxwell AFB/AFHRA.

6. COMUSMACV 181140Z, "Linebacker Operations," 2. Corona Harvest Microfilm K717.291-2, Maxwell AFB/AFHRA.

7. 7AF 211240Z May 72, "Counter-Logistics OPORD," 2. Corona Harvest Microfilm K717.291-2, Maxwell AFB/AFHRA.

8. COMUSMACV 101500Z Jun 72, "Linebacker," 2. Corona Harvest Microfilm K717.291-2, Maxwell AFB/AFHRA.

9. COMUSMACV 150522Z Jun 72, "Linebacker Strike Effort," 1. Corona Harvest Microfilm K717.291-2, Maxwell AFB/AFHRA.

10. 7AF 270210Z Jun 72, "Linebacker," 2. Corona Harvest Microfilm K717.291-2, Maxwell AFB/AFHRA.

11. 7/13AF History, 1 January–31 December 1972, vol. I, 134. Corona Harvest Microfilm K717.291-2, Maxwell AFB/AFHRA.

12. Ibid.

13. Truong, *Easter Offensive*, 56–57.

14. Military Science Institute, *Victory in Vietnam: The Official History of the People's Army of Vietnam, 1954–1975*, trans. Merle Pribbenow (Lawrence: University Press of Kansas, 2002), 293.

15. Truong, *Easter Offensive*, 66.

16. *History of the Air Defense Service*, vol. III (Hanoi: People's Army Publishing House, 1994), 57. Translation by Merle Pribbenow.

17. Ibid., 51.

18. Ibid.

19. 7AF 231140Z Jun 72, "Daily Wrap Up," 6. Bolling AFB/AFHSO/Vogt Papers.

20. Military Science Institute, *Victory in Vietnam*, 293.

21. *History of the Air Defense Service*, vol. III, 59.

22. Nguyen Huu An, *New Battlefield* (Hanoi: People's Army Publishing House, 2002). Partial translation by Merle Pribbenow.

21. Reactive Adversaries

1. PACAF Air Operations Summary, May 1972, 4-B-8 to 4-B-9. Maxwell AFB/AFHRC/K717-063 May 1972.

2. Ibid., 4-C-1.

3. Ho Si Huu et al., *History of the Air Defense Service*, vol. III (Hanoi: People's Army Publishing House, 1994), 115. Translation by Merle Pribbenow.

4. Ibid., 119.

5. Ibid., 119, 121.

6. Ibid., 123.

7. Ibid., 124.

8. Ibid.

9. Joe Wright, "Hanoi Week—Ending 30 May," 1. FCO 15/1674, "Reviews of Political Events in North Vietnam, 1972 Jan 01–1972 Dec 31," National Archives, Kew, U.K.

10. *Quan Doi Nhan Dan*, "Common Sense in Air Defense—Organize Defensive Measures Well at Evacuation Sites," 30 September 1972, 3.

11. P.V., "Thai Nguyen, Nam Ha, Ha Tinh, and Quang Binh Organize Passive Defense, Guarantee Good Productivity, Prepare for Battle and Effective Resistance," *Quan Doi Nhan Dan*, 25 November 1972.

12. Ibid.

13. DJSM 983-72, "Interdiction in North Vietnam," 15 May 1972, 2, 3. NARA/RG 218/JCS Central File 1972.

14. Ibid.

15. Nghiem Dinh Tich, *The 375th Air Defense Division* (Hanoi: People's Army Publishing House, 1998), 105–106. Partial translation by Merle Pribbenow.

16. DIA Intelligence Appraisals, 26 May 1972, 10 June 1972. Quoted in notes taken by Lt. Col. Gregory, AF/IN, to respond to a 19 June request by Gen. Keegan. Bolling AFB/AFHSO/Vogt Papers/Linebacker Targeting Folder.

17. CIA Memorandum, "The Overall Impact of the US Bombing and Mining Program on North Vietnam," August 1972, 8, i.

18. Wright, "Hanoi Week—Ending 30 May," 1.

19. CIA Memorandum, "The Overall Impact of the US Bombing and Mining Program on North Vietnam," 10.

20. Melvin F. Porter, "Interdiction of Waterways & POL Pipelines, SEA: Continuing Report" 21, 11. CHECO, 1 October 1973.

21. AF/IN draft memorandum, "Logistics flow in NVN," 21 June 1972, 1. Vogt Papers/Linebacker Targeting Folder. The memo summarizes the few reported attacks on water-borne logistics craft by blockading USN ships and aircraft. On June 10 the *Stoddert* boarded and towed a WBLC damaged earlier in an air strike. The vessel was powered by a Soviet-made diesel engine, and carried 141 bags of rice totaling approximately seven tons. On June 14 aircraft from the *Kitty Hawk* attacked WBLCs near Hon Gai, sinking 21 and damaging another 17.

22. Charles D. Melson and Curtis G. Arnold, *U.S. Marines in Vietnam: The War That Would Not End, 1971–1973* (Washington: Headquarters USMC, 1991), 145–152.

23. Quoted ibid., 146.

24. Military History Institute, *Victory in Vietnam: The Official History of the People's*

Army of Vietnam, 1954–1975, trans. Merle Pribbenow (Lawrence: University Press of Kansas, 2002), 299–300.

25. PACAF Air Operations Summary, June 1972, 4-A-1, 4-A-4. These figures represent the total of strike, flak suppression, and armed reconnaissance missions.

26. Seventh Air Force "Daily Wrap Up," 131110Z May 72, 2; 201130Z May 72, 2; 251100Z May 1972, 8. Vogt Papers.

27. PACAF Air Operations Summary, June 1972, 4-B-3 to 4-B-5.

28. 7AF Commander's Conference (18–19 July 1972), 2. K168.06-228. Maxwell AFB/AFHRA.

29. Untitled JCS working paper, May 1972. Vogt Papers.

30. PACAF/INT Ltr to DOX, DTG 13 Jun 72, "Reply to CINCPAC Msg." Summarized in index to Corona Harvest Microfilm K717.291-2, 11. Maxwell AFB/AFHRA.

31. PACAF Air Operations Summary, June 1972, 4-A-6.

32. Ibid., 4-A-8 to 4-A-10.

33. Memorandum of transmittal, "Attack Carrier Air Wing Eleven Cruise Report of February to November 1972," 1 December 1972, 2.

34. "Attack Carrier Air Wing Eleven Cruise Report of February to November 1972," 1 December 1972, I-2.

35. PACAF Air Operations Summary, May 1972, 5-A-11 to 5-A-14.

36. "Attack Carrier Air Wing Five Cruise Report for Westpac Deployment during Period April 1972-March 1973," 20 March 1973, A-XIII-2 to A-XIII-3.

37. Op-508C memo 0066-72, "Impacts of the Southeast Asia Air Operations," 2 June 1972, 1.

38. PACAF Air Operations Summary, May 1972, 4-A-6; June, 4-A-6.

39. Op-508C memo 0066-72, "Impacts of the Southeast Asia Air Operations," 2.

40. Memorandum for the CJCS, "Impact of SEAsia Buildup on Risks in Other Crises," 17 June 1972, [s] E. R. Zumwalt, 1, 3. Naval Historical Center/Naval Operational Archives.

41. Ibid., 2–3.

42. JCS Enclosure to JCSM 265-72, "Campaign Against NVN and Capability to Wage War," 1, 5.

43. SecDef memorandum, "Linebacker Target Validations," 12 June 1972, 1. NARA/NPMP/NSC Files/Haig Chronological Files.

44. Kissinger-Laird telcon, June 1972. NARA/NPMP/Kissinger Telcons.

45. SecDef memorandum, "Linebacker Target Validations," 12 June 1972, 1.

46. Text of PRC protest, 11 June 1972. NARA/NPMP/NSC Files/HAK Office Files.

22. The View from Hanoi

1. Although the reports routinely went to the state department, I have not seen any reference to them in military archives.

2. J. M. Liudzius, "Some Reflections on a Year in Hanoi," January 1972. FCO 15/1474, National Archives, Kew, U.K.

3. Joe Wright, "Hanoi Week—Ending 4 April," 2. FCO 15/1674, National Archives, Kew, U.K.

4. "Hanoi Week—Ending 11 April," 1.

5. "Hanoi Week—Ending 18 April," 2.

6. Charles N. Spinks, John C. Durr, and Stephen Peters, *The North Vietnamese Regime: Institutions and Problems* (Washington: American University Center for Research in Social Systems, April 1969), 70–76.

7. "Hanoi Week—Ending 2 May," 1.

8. Jeffrey Ethell and Alfred Price, *One Day in a Very Long War: May 10, 1972* (New York: Random House, 1989), 64.

9. "Hanoi Week—Ending 16 May," 1.

10. "Hanoi Week—Ending 23 May," 1.

11. Ibid.

12. "Hanoi Week—Ending 30 May: Hanoi a Month after the Evacuation," 1–2.

13. Ibid., 2.

14. "Hanoi Week—Ending 6 June, 1.

15. John Gliedman, *Terror from the Sky: North Viet-Nam's Dikes and the U.S. Bombing* (Cambridge, MA: Vietnam Resource Center, 1972) provides a comprehensive guide to the system of dikes and the North Vietnamese allegations of deliberate U.S. attacks.

16. Ibid., 88–89. At a press conference on 30 April, Nixon characterized dikes as "a strategic target and indirectly a military target," but emphasized that attacks on them would result in "an enormous number of civilian casualties. That is something that we want to avoid. It is also something that we believe is not needed."

17. "Hanoi Week—Ending 27 June," 2.

18. "Hanoi Week—Ending 11 July," 3.

19. "Hanoi Week—Ending 25 April," 1.

20. "Hanoi Week—Ending 2 May," 1.

21. "Hanoi Week—Ending 8 May," 1.

22. "Hanoi Week—Ending 6 June," 2.

23. "Hanoi Week—Ending 13 June," 1.

24. "Hanoi Week—Ending 27 June," 1.

23. "One of Those Days"

1. 7AF, 271215Z Jun 1972, "Daily Wrap Up," 7. Bolling AFB/AFHSO/Vogt Papers.

2. AFSSO 271955Z Jun 72. Untitled. Vogt Papers.

3. Project Red Baron III, "Air to Air Encounters in Southeast Asia," vol. II: Event Reconstruction, Part 1, 281–289. Vogt Papers.

4. Charles K. Hopkins, *SAC Bomber Operations in the Southeast Asia War,* vol. III. SAC Historical Monograph #204 (1983), 697.

5. Memorandum for the CNO, "Air and Surface Support for Southeast Asia," 10 April 1972, George C. Talley Jr., Assistant Deputy Chief of Naval Operations (Plans and Policy). BM#00001081-72. Naval Historical Center/Operational Archives.

6. Memorandum for the CNO, "TACAIR SURGE," 22 June 1972, [s] M. F. Weisner, Deputy Chief of Naval Operations (Air Warfare). M-0060-05W. Naval Historical Center/Operational Archives.

7. Memorandum for the CNO, "SEAsia Air War Statistics, 1 April-1 August 1972," 5 September 1972, W. D. Houser, Deputy Chief of Naval Operations (Air Warfare). M-0086-05W. Naval Historical Center/Operational Archives.

8. AFSSO PACAF 120345Z May 72, "Utilization of F-4D/F-4E Assets for Counter Air Role." Vogt Papers.

9. AFSSO PACAF, 222040 May 72, "Air-to-Air War North Vietnam," 1–2. Vogt Papers.

10. Ibid.

11. AFSSO USAF 012100Z Jun 72, "Air-to-Air Missile Effectiveness." Vogt Papers.

12. AFSSO 7AF 030820Z Jun 72, "Air-to-Air Missile Effectiveness," 2, 3. Vogt Papers.

13. AFSSO PACAF 060250Z Jun 72, "Air-to-Air War NVN." Vogt Papers.

14. Project Red Baron III, "Air to Air Encounters in Southeast Asia," vol. II: Event Reconstruction, Part 1, 258–265, 270–275. Bolling AFB/AFHSO.

15. Ibid., 281–290.

16. AFSSO TAC 301930Z Jun 72, "Tactics for SEA." Vogt Papers.

17. AFSSO 7AF 040600Z Jul 72, 2, 5–7. Untitled message to Gen. Ryan from Gen. Burns, info Gen. Clay. Vogt Papers.

18. Ibid., 7.

19. Ibid., 11.

20. AFSSO 7AF 101345Z Jul 72, "Visit of CSAF." Vogt Papers.

21. Carlos M. Talbott, oral history interview with Hugh N. Ahmann, 10–11 June 1985, 211. Maxwell AFB/AFHRA/K239.0512-1652.

22. Ibid., 212.

23. AFSSO USAF 142200Z Jul 72, untitled message from Lt. Gen. Dixon to Gen. Clay and Gen. Vogt. Vogt Papers.

24. Talbott interview, 214.

25. AFSSO PACAF 300318Z Jul 72, "Linebacker Victor III Mission 24 July 72." Vogt Papers.

24. Toward the Peace Path

1. Luu Van Loi and Nguyen Anh Vu, *Le Duc Tho–Kissinger Negotiations in Paris* (Hanoi: The Gioi, 1996), 239.

2. HQ Seventh Air Force, "History of Linebacker I Operations, 10 May 1972–23 October 1972," 24.

3. Ibid., 27–29.

4. Ta Hong, Vu Ngoc, and Nguyen Quoc Dung, *History of the People's Air Force, 1955–1977* (Hanoi: People's Army Publishing House, 1993), 268–269. Translation by Merle Pribbenow.

5. Ibid., 270–271.

6. Ho Si Huu et al., *History of the Air Defense Service*, vol. III (Hanoi: People's Army Publishing House, 1994), 140–142. Translation by Merle Pribbenow.

7. Dang Van Thu, "Defeating the Americans: Fighting and Talking," in *The Diplomatic Front during the Paris Peace Talks on Vietnam* (Hanoi: National Political Publishing House, 2004). Translation by Merle Pribbenow.

8. Henry A. Kissinger, *White House Years* (Boston: Little, Brown, 1979), 1360.

9. 2300 Secure Telcon/In-ADM Gayler-10/05/72. NARA/RG 218/Moorer Diary/5 October 1972. See also the Joint Staff summary of operating authorities for September–December 1972 in Moorer's diary. NARA/RG 218/Moorer Diary.

10. Moorer-Haig telcon, 1355 20 October 1972. Moorer Diary.

11. Moorer-Weyand telcon, 1206 19 October 1972. Moorer Diary.

12. MACV 20 1253Z Oct 72, untitled. Moorer Diary.

13. Laird to Moorer, "Enemy Activity in South Vietnam and Laos," 20 October 1972. Moorer Diary.

14. Ibid.

15. Moorer Diary, 23 October 1972.

16. George C. Wilson, "Senate Confirms Gen. Abrams, 84–2," *Washington Post*, 13 October 1972, A4.

17. Moorer-Vogt telcon, 0811 24 October 1972. Moorer Diary.

18. George A. Carver Jr., "President Thieu's Probable Reaction to the Emerging Package," 16 October 1972. NARA/NPMP/NSC Files/Haig Chronological Files.

19. Nguyen Phu Duc, *The Viet-Nam Peace Negotiations: Saigon's Side of the Story*, ed. Arthur J. Dommen (Christiansburg, VA: Dalley Book Service, 2005), 283–336. Duc was Kissinger's South Vietnamese equivalent, Thieu's national security advisor. Kissinger has contended that the proposal for a "stand in place" settlement, leaving the NVA in South Vietnam, had been a position held by the United States since 1970. Duc argues that the South Vietnamese leadership never conceived that this could have been meant as a permanent condition, but only as a way to bring the fighting to a quick close.

Conclusion

1. CJCS Memo M-68-72, "Meeting with the President, Thursday, 30 November 1972, The White House." NARA/RG 218/Moorer Diary. Moorer commented, "This is typical Westy. He always had a solution after the fact."

2. Ibid.

3. NSC Memorandum, "The President's Meeting with the Joint Chiefs of Staff, Thursday, November 30, 1972, 10:15 A.M.," 4. NARA/NPMP/NSC Files/ Haig Chronological Files.

4. CIA Intelligence Memorandum, "Trends in Military Imports to North Vietnam," 8 March 1973, 4, 3. CREST CIA-RDP80T01719R000400160001-3.

5. CIA Intelligence Memorandum, "Recent Communist Military and Economic Assistance to North Vietnam," 13 July 1973, 3. CREST CIA-RDP80T01719R000400300001-7.

6. CIA Intelligence Memorandum, "Recent Communist Logistical and Manpower Developments in Indochina," 6 March 1973, 10. CREST CIA-RDP80T01719R000400150001-4.

7. William E. LeGro, "Vietnam: Cease Fire to Capitulation" (Washington: Center for Military History, 1985), 18.

8. See Pierre Asselin, *A Bitter Peace: Washington, Hanoi, and the Making of the Paris Agreement* (Chapel Hill: University of North Carolina Press, 2002), for a full account of the negotiations, with the full text of the agreement. Nguyen Phu Duc provides the South Vietnamese perspective in *The Viet-Nam Peace Negotiations: Saigon's Side of the Story*, ed. Arthur J. Dommen (Christiansburg, VA: Dalley Book Service, 2005), assessing the final terms on pages 375–380.

9. For an account of MACV's dedicated but futile attempt to implement the Paris terms, see Walter Scott Dillard, *Sixty Days to Peace: Implementing the Paris Peace Accords, Vietnam 1973* (Washington, DC: National Defense University Press, 1982).

10. NSC Memorandum, "The President's Meeting with the Joint Chiefs of Staff, Thursday, November 30, 1972, 10:15 A.M.," 4.

11. SecDef Memo, "Assessment of the Air and Naval Campaign Against North Vietnam," 15 July 1972. NARA/NPMP/NSC/H-089, 2 November 1972 WSAG.

12. Military History Institute, *Victory in Vietnam: The Official History of the People's Army of Vietnam, 1954–1975*, trans. Merle Pribbenow (Lawrence: University Press of Kansas, 2002), 298, 342–351.

ACKNOWLEDGMENTS

This book represents a collective achievement. At the outset I planned to write about air operations during the Easter Offensive, focusing on operational and technical issues. The scope broadened as opportunities presented themselves—first to encompass strategic decisionmaking in the Nixon White House, and then to include the North Vietnamese perspective on these events.

Wayne Thompson provided the initial encouragement to take on this study, along with masses of material on Air Force operations that would otherwise have remained inaccessible. The extraordinary generosity and skill of Merle Pribbenow, in his translation and provision of North Vietnamese histories and source material, created a cornerstone of the final product. John Sherwood added invaluable sources on Navy operations and on high-level concerns about the course of air operations.

Many people commented on various versions of this work, most notably Ron Spector, Hope Harrison, Wayne Thompson, Dale Andrade, Mark Clodfelter, Debra Avant, Bill Becker, Shaun McHale, Ken Moss, Alan Gropman, and Amy Frisk. All contributed important guidance and suggestions; any remaining errors are my own responsibility.

Archivists around the world have invariably proven both capable and diligent in assisting my research. I owe special thanks to Jeannine Swift and Herb Rawlings-Milton at the National Archives and Records Administration, Joe Caver and Archie DiFante at the Air Force Historical Research Agency, Kathy Lloyd at the Naval Historical Center, and Dave Keough at the U.S. Army Military History Institute.

Joyce Seltzer's blend of advice, guuidance, and direction propelled this book through the publication process, improving it every step of the way. Camille Smith and Elizabeth Gilbert's patience, helpfulness, and professionalism through the editing cycle were invaluable in shaping the final product. Phil Schwartzberg's maps reflected his unique balance of creativity, technical proficiency, and passion for accuracy. It was a privilege to work with this group, and I hope to do so again.

My family continued their pattern of decades, sacrificing to support my work. I have had the great good fortune to spend my life surrounded by the finest people I know—my parents Clint and Jane, and then my wife Donna and children Will and Nina. This book is dedicated to them.

Index